649229

THE LEGACY OF MUSLIM RULE IN INDIA

K.S. LAL

ADITYA PRAKASHAN
NEW DELHI

First published: 1992
© K.S. Lal

ISBN. 81-85689-03-2
Rs. 350

Published by Pradeep Kumar Goel for Aditya Prakashan,
F-14/65, Model Town II, Delhi - 110 009.
and Printed at Crescent Printing Works (Pvt.) Ltd.,
P-14, Connaught Circus, New Delhi - 110 001.

Contents

Preface

Had India been completely converted to Muhamma-danism during the thousand years of Muslim conquest and rule, its people would have taken pride in the victories and achievements of Islam and even organised pan-Islamic movements and Islamic revolutions. Conversely, had India possessed the determination of countries like France and Spain to repulse the Muslims for good, its people would have forgotten about Islam and its rule. But while India could not be completely conquered or Islamized, the Hindus did not lose their ancient religious and cultural moorings. In short, while Muslims with all their armed might proved to be great conquerors, rulers and proselytizers, Indians or Hindus, with all their weaknesses, proved to be great survivors. India never became an Islamic country. Its ethos remained Hindu while Muslims also continued to live here retaining their distinctive religious and social system. It is against this background that an assessment of the legacy of Muslim rule in India has been attempted.

Source-materials on such a vast area of study are varied and scattered. What we possess is a series of glimpses furnished by Persian chroniclers, foreign visitors and indigenous writers who noted what appeared to them of interest. It is not an easy task, on the basis of these sources, to reconstruct an integrated picture of the medieval scenario spanning almost a millennium, beginning with the establishment of Muslim rule. The task becomes more difficult when the scenario converges on the modern age with its pre- and post-Partition politics and slogans of the two-nation theory, secularism, national integration and minority rights. Consequently, some generalisations, repe-

titions and reiterations have inevitably crept into what is
otherwise a work of historical research. For this the author
craves the indulgence of the reader.

10 January 1992   K.S. Lal

Abbreviations used in references.

For complete titles of works see Bibliography.

Afif   : *Tarikh-i-Firoz Shahi* by Shama Siraj Afif
Ain   : *Ain-i-Akbari* by Abul Fazl, trans. by H. Blochmann
Akbar Nama   : *Akbar Nama* by Abul Fazl, trans. by H. Beveridge
Babur Nama   : *Memoirs of Babur*,trans. by Ms. A. Beveridge
Badaoni   : *Muntakhab-ut-Tawarikh* by Abdul Qadir Badaoni
Barani   : *Tarikh-i-Firoz Shahi* by Ziyauddin Barani
Bernier   : *Travels in the Mogul Empire* by Francois Bernier
C.H.I.   : *Cambridge History of India*
E and D   : *History of India as told by its own Historians* by Henry Elliot and John Dowson.
Farishtah   : *Gulshan-i-Ibrahimi* or *Tarikh-i-Farishtah* by Muhammad Qasim Hindu Shah Farishtah
Foster   : *Early Travels in India*, edited by William Foster
Ibn Battuta   : *Rehla of Ibn Battuta*, trans. by Mahdi Husain
Khafi Khan   : *Mutakhab-ul-Lubab* by Khafi Khan
Lahori   : *Badshah Nama* by Abdul Hamid Lahori
Manucci   : *Storia do Mogor* by Niccolao Manucci
Pelsaert   : *Jahangir's India* by Francisco Pelsaert
P.I.H.C.   : *Proceedings of the Indian History Congress*
J.A.S.B.   : *Journal of the (Royal) Asiatic Society of Bengal*
J.R.A.S.   : *Journal of the Royal Asiatic Society of Great Britain*

Chapter 1

The Medieval Age

"If royalty did not exist, the storm of strife would never subside, nor selfish ambition disappear."

Abul Fazl

Muslim rule in India coincides with what is known as the Middle Ages in Europe. The term Middle Ages or the Medieval Age is applied loosely to that period in history which lies between the ancient and modern civilizations. In Europe the period is supposed to have begun in the fifth century when the Western Roman Empire fell and ended in the fifteenth century with the emanation of Renaissance in Italy, Reformation in Germany, the discovery of America by Columbus, the invention of Printing Press by Guttenberg, and the taking of Constantinople by the Turks from the Byzantine (or the Eastern Roman) Empire. In brief the period of Middle Ages extends from C.E. 600 to 1500.

Curiously enough the Middle Age in Europe synchronises exactly with what we call the medieval period in Indian history. The seventh century saw the end of the last great Hindu kingdom of Harshvardhana, the rise of Islam in Arabia and its introduction into India. In C. 1500 the Mughal conqueror Babur started mounting his campaigns. And since these foreign Muslim invaders and rulers had come not only to acquire dominions and extend territories, but also to spread the religion of Islam, war and religion became the two main currents of medieval Indian Muslim history.

Kingship

War is the work of kings turned conquerors or conquerors turned kings. Therefore it was necessary for the medieval monarch to be autocratic, religious minded and one who could conquer, rule and subserve the interest of religion. Such was the idea about the king in medieval times, both in the West and the East.

The beginnings of the institution of kingship are obscure. Anatole France attempts to trace it in his *Penguin Island*, a readable satire on (British) history and society. That is more or less what he writes: Early in the beginning of civilization, the people's primary concern was provision of security against depradations of robbers and ravages of wild animals. So they assembled at a place to find a remedy to this problem. They put their heads together and arrived at a consensus. They will raise a team of security guards who will work under the command of a superior. These will be paid from contributions made by the people. As the assembled were still deliberating on the issue, a strong, well-built young man stood up. He declared he would collect the said contributions (later called taxes), and in return provide security. Noticing his physical prowess and threatening demeanour they all nodded their assent. Nobody dared protest. And so the king was born.

In whatever manner and at whatever time the king was born, he was, in the Middle Ages, personally a strong warrior, adept at horsemanship, often without a peer in strength. He gathered a strong army, collected taxes and contributions and was surrounded by fawning counsellors. They bestowed upon him attributes of divinity, upon his subjects those of devilry, thus making his presence in the world a sort of a benediction necessary for the good of mankind. Once man was declared to be bad and the king full of virtues, there was hardly any difficulty for political philosophy and religion to recommend strict control of the people by the king.

There were thus monarchs both in the West and the East and in both autocracy reigned supreme. Still in the West they could wrest a Magna Carta from the king as early as in 1215 C.E. and produce thinkers like Hobbes, Locke, Rousseau, Montesqueue and Bentham who helped change the concept of kingship in course of time. But in the East, especially in Islam, a rigid, narrow and limited scriptural education could, parrot-like, repeat only one political theory—Man was nasty, brutish and short and must be kept suppressed.

In the *Siyasat Nama*, Nizm-ul-Mulk Tusi stressed that since the kings were divinely appointed, "they must always keep the subjects in such a position that they know their stations and never remove the ring of servitude from their ears."[1] Alberuni, Fakhr-i-Mudabbir, Amir Khusrau, Ziyauddin Barani and Shams Siraj Afif repeat the same idea.[2] As Fakhr-i-Mudabbir puts it, "if there were no kings, men would devour one another."[3] Even the liberal Allama Abul Fazl could not think beyond this: "If royalty did not exist, the storm of strife would never subside, nor selfish ambition disappear. Mankind (is) under the burden of lawlessness and lust...."[4] "The glitter of gems and gold in the Taj Mahal or the Peacock Throne," writes Jadunath Sarkar, "ought not to blind us to the fact that in Mughal India, man was considered vile;—the mass of the people had no economic liberty, no indefeasible right to justice or personal freedom, when their oppressor was a noble or high official or landowner; political rights were not dreamt of.... The Government was in effect despotism tempered by revolution or fear of revolution."[5] Consequently, medieval Muslim political opinion could recommend only repression of man and glorification of king.

1. Cited in Bosworth, *The Ghaznavids*, p. 49.
2. Alberuni II, p. 161. Also Barani, *Fatawa-i-Jahandari*.
3. Fakhr-i-Mudabbir, *Tarikh-i-Fakhruddin Mubarak Shah*,p. 13.
4. *Ain*, I, p. 2.
5. Sarkar, *A Short History of Aurangzeb* , p.464.

The king was divinely ordained. Abul Fazl says that "No dignity is higher in the eyes of God than royalty...Royalty is a light emanating from God, and a ray from the sun, the illuminator of the universe."[6]

Kingship thus became the most general and permanent of institutions of medieval Muslim world. In theory Islam claims to stand for equality of men, in practice it encourages slavery among Muslims and imposes an inferior status on non-Muslim. In theory Islam does not recognize Kingship; in practice Muslims have been the greatest empire builders. Muhammadans themselves were impressed with the concept of power and glamour associated with monarchy. The idea of despotism, of concentration of power, penetrated medieval mind with facility. Obedience to the ruler was advocated as a religious duty. The ruler was to live and also enable people to live according to the Qur'anic laws.[7] In public life, the Muslim monarch was enjoined to discharge a host of civil, military and religious duties. The Sultan was enjoined to do justice, to levy taxes according to the Islamic law, and to appoint honest and efficient officers "so that the laws of the *Shariat* might be enforced through them."[8] At times, he was to enact *Zawabits* (regulations) to suit particular situations, but while doing so, he could not transgress the *Shariat* nor "alter the Qur'anic law!"[9] His military duties were to defend Muslim territories, and to keep his army well equipped for conquest and extension of the territories of Islam.[10] The religious duty of a Muslim monarch consisted in helping the indigent and those learned in the Islamic law. He was to prohibit what was not permitted by the *Shara*. The duty of propagating Islam and carrying

6. *Ain*, I, pp. 2-3, 6.
7. Barani, pp. 293-94.
8. Barani, p. 64.
9. Barani, *Fatawa-i-Jahandari*, p. 73. Also Tripathi, *Some Aspects of Muslim Administration*, p. 5.
10. *Adab-ul-Harb*, fols.132b-133a.

on *Jihad* mainly devolved on him.[11] *Jihad* was at once an individual and a general religious duty.[12] According to a contemporary *Alim*, if the Sultan was unable to extirpate infidelity, "he must at least keep the enemies of God and His Prophet dishonoured and humiliated."[13] It must be said to his credit that the Muslim Sultan, by and large, worked according to these injunctions, and sometimes achieved commendable success in his exertions in all these spheres.

As said earlier, there were autocratic monarchs both in the West and the East. Still in the West there appeared a number of liberal political philosophers who helped to change the concept of kingship in course of time. But Muslims could not think on such lines, so that when in England they executed their king after a long Civil War (1641-49), in India Shahjahan, a contemporary of Charles I ruled as an autocrat in a 'golden age'. Even so autocracy took time to go even in Europe and there was no check on the powers of the king in the Middle Ages, except for the institution of feudalism.

Feudalism

Feudalism was a very prominent institution of the Middle Ages. It was prevalent both in Europe as well as in India, although there were many differences between the two systems. In Europe feudalism gathered strength on the decline of the Western Roman Empire. After Charlemagne (800-814) in particular, there was rapid decline in the monarchical power throughout Europe, and governments failed to perform their primary duty of protecting their peoples. The class of people who needed protection the most was the petty landowner. In the earliest times

11. *Ibid,* fols.56b; Barani,p. 73; *Adab-ul-Harb,*fols.8b-10c.

12. Hasan Nizami, *Tajul Maasir,* trs.by S.H. Askari, Patna University Journal (Arts), Vol.18,No.3 (1963),p. 58. Also Ruben Levy, *Social Structure of Islam,* p. 252.

13. Barani, p. 72. See also *Fatawa-i-Jahandari,* p. 40.

the lands were free whether these were held by ordinary freeman or a noble. In the absence of strong monarchy, the possessor of the free land, threatened or oppressed by powerful neighbours, sought refuge in submitting to some lord, and in the case of a lord to some more powerful lord. In the bargain he surrendered his land. For, when he begged for protection, the lord said: 'I can protect (only) my own land.' The poor man was thus forced to surrender the ownership of his land to his powerful and rich neighbour, receiving it back in fief as a vassal. (The word feudalism itself is derived from the French *feodalite* meaning faithfulness). His children were left without any claim on that land. He was also obliged to render service to his superior lord. In return he was promised protection in his lifetime by his lord. The origins of feudalism are thus to be traced to the necessity of the people seeking protection, and exploitation by those who provided it.

Conditions were not the same everywhere, but the system was based on contract or compact between lord and tenant, determining all rights and obligations between the two. The vassal was obliged to render military service, take his cases only to his own lord and submit to the decisions of the lord's court, and pay certain aids to the lord in times of need, like free gifts or 'benevolences', aids at the marriage of the chief's daughter, some tax when the chief was in trouble or as ransom to redeem his person from prison. These aids varied according to local customs and were often extorted unreasonably.

On the other hand, for providing security to the vassal, it became common for a chief or lord to have a retinue of bodyguards composed of valiant youths who were furnished by the chief with arms and provisions and who in turn devoted themselves to his service. These 'companions' received no pay except their arms, horses and provisions. With these companions or troops the lords also conquered lands, and gave certain portions of it to their attendants to enjoy for life. These estates were called *bene-ficia* or fiefs, because they were only lent to their possess-ors, to revert after death to their grantor, who immediately gave them to another of his servants on the same terms. As the son commonly esteemed it his duty, or was forced by necessity, to devote his arms to the lord in whose serv-ice his father had lived, he usually received his father's fief, or rather he was invested with it anew. By the usage of centuries this custom became hereditary. A fief ren-dered vacant by the death of the holder was taken posses-sion of by his son, on the sole condition of paying homage to the feudal superior.

In the feudal system, therefore, the vassal and the lord benefited from one another, although the latter much more, at the cost of the king. Junior vassals could become powerful and rise in hierarchy to become sub-lords or even great lords. They could have their own subordinate vassals in sub-infeudation. Kingly power, as always, continued to exist, but under feudalism it was widely diffused. The privileges the lords enjoyed often comprised the right of coining money, raising armies and waging private wars, exemption from public tributes and freedom from legislative control.[14] Sometimes the kings had to make virtue of necessity even to the extent of granting titles and administrative fiefs to Counts etc. to be admini-stered by them. But the struggle between royalty and no-bility (as in England under William the Norman), contin-ued. Of course, and ultimately, it ended in the power of the lords sinking before that of the king.

In India feudalism did not usher in that spirit of civil liberty which characterised the constitutional history of medieval England. Here the king remained supreme whether among the Turks or the Mughals, and the assign-ments of conquered lands were granted by him to lords, soldiers or commoners or his own relatives as salary or

14. Hallam, *The Middle Ages*, I, pp.227-28.

reward in consideration of distinguished military service in the form of *iqtas* or *jagirs*[15], sometimes even on a hereditary basis, but they were not wrested from him. This system was bureaucratic. There was also a parallel feudalistic organisation but the possessor of land remained subservient to the king. It was based on personal relationship. The vassals were given *jagirs* and assignments primarily because of blood and kinship. On the other hand, the practice of permitting vanquished princes to retain their kingdoms as vassals, or making allotment of territories to brothers and relatives of the king, or giving assignments to particular families of nobles, learned men and theologions as reward or pension were feudalistic in nature. Some feudatories would raise their own army, collect taxes and customary dues, pay tributes, and rally round the standard of their overlord or king with their military contingents when called upon to do so. But the assignee had no right of coining money. (In fact, coining of money was considered as a signal of rebellion.) He maintained his own troops but he had no right of waging private war.[16] He could only increase his influence by entering into matrimonial alliances with powerful neighbours or the royal family. In the Sultanate and the Mughal empire the feudal system was more bureaucratic than feudalistic, in fact it was bureaucratic throughout.[17] Here the feudal nobility was a military aristocracy which incidentally owned land, rather than a landed aristocracy which occasionally had to defend Royal lands and property by military means but at other times lived quietly.

But there were also many points of similarity between Indian and European feudalism. In India *Nazrana* was offered to the lord or king when an estate or *jagir* was bestowed upon the heir of the deceased lord (*Tika*), like

---

15. Barani, p.62

16. P.Saran, *Studies in Medieval Indian History*, p. 10.

17. Moreland, W.H., *The Agrarian System of Muslim India*, p.221; Also Easton, Stewart C., *The Heritage of the Past*, pp. 285, 290, 297.

the feudal relief in Europe. As in Europe, here too the practice of escheat was widely prevalent. Aids, gifts or benevolences were common to both. These consisted of offerings at the ascension of the king to the throne, his weighment ceremony, on important festivals, cash and gifts at the marriage of the chief's daughter or son, gifts or a tax when the chief was in trouble. In India the king always stood at the top of the regime. Feudal institutions are apt to flourish in a state which lacks centralised administration. The vastness of India makes it a veritable subcontinent, and the ruler's position was naturally different in each kingdom or region according to local condition found there. But there was a central authority too. The idea of a strong monarch was inseparable from Muslim psyche and Turco-Mongol political theory. In India, under Muslim rule, great importance was attached to the sacrosanct nature of the king's person. The Indian system arose from certain social and moral forces rather than from sheer political necessity as in Europe, and that is why it survived throughout the medieval period.

Whatever its merits and demerits, Indian feudalism recognised division of society into people great and small, strong and weak, haves and have-nots. Nobles were not equal to nobles; there were great Khans and petty Amïrs. Men were not equal to men; some were masters, others their slaves. Women were not equal to men; they were subservient to men and considered to be their property. Perhaps the most prominent characteristic of the Medieval Age was the belief and acceptance of the 'fact' that men are not born equal, or at least they could not be recognised as such.

Feudalism in Europe gradually disappeared with the coming of Renaissance and Reformation, and formation of nation-states. In India phenomena such as these did not occur. There was nothing like a Renaissance in medieval India. There could be no reformation either, because "innovation" in religious matters is taboo in Islam. Some Muslim monarchs were disillusioned with the state of religion and the power of the Ulama (religious scholars).[18] That is why, probably, Alauddin Khalji (C.E. 1296-1316) contemplated 'founding' a new religion,[19] Muhammad Tughlaq (1325-51) was credited with similar intentions; and Akbar (1556-1605) actually established the *Din-i-Ilahi*. Muslims feared that Alauddin's "new religion must be quite different from the Muhammadan faith, and that its enforcement would entail slaughter of a large number of Musalmans".[20] He was dissuaded by his loyal counsellors from pursuing his project. All the same it is significant that Alauddin Khalji and Jalaluddin Muhammad Akbar did think of some sort of 'Reformation' in Islam, but the former was scared into abandoning the idea and the latter contented himself by just organising a sort of brotherhood of like-minded thinkers.[21] Such endeavours, strictly prohibited in Islam, could hardly affect India's Muslim feudalistic society.

Europe in the middle ages too lived under a Roman Catholic imperium. Its unity was theological, while its divisions were feudal. After Renaissance the unity of the theological imperium was shattered and so were the old divisions. European societies, after centuries of theological and territorial wars, learnt to aggregate around a new category of the nation-state. In India Muslim theological imperium never came to an end, nor persistent resistance to it. Hence, the idea of a secular nation-state never found a ground here.

Among other chief agencies that overthrew the feudal system were the rise of cities, scouring of the oceans for Commercial Revolution and the spread of knowledge,

18. *Ain*, I, pp.xxxii-xxxiii.
19. Barani, pp.262-66.
20. Lal, *History of the Khaljis*, p.74 n.3; Barani, pp. 262-64.
21. "Akbar's *Din-i-Ilahi*" in Lal, K.S., *Studies in Medieval Indian History*, pp.233-47.

scientific knowledge in particular. In India there was urbanisation under Muslim rule, but it has been grossly exaggerated.[22] India had large urban centres before the arrival of Muslims. Arab geographers become rapturous when describing the greatness of India's cities—both in extent and in demography—on the eve of Muslim conquest and immigration.[23] During his sojourn in India Ibn Battuta visited seventy-five cities, towns and ports.[24] Under Muslim rule many old cities were given Muslim names. Thus Akbarabad (Agra), Islamabad (Mathura), Shahjahanabad (Delhi) and Hyderabad (Golkunda) were not entirely new built cities, but old populated places that were given new Islamic names, mostly after the ruling kings. Giving new names to old cities was not an extension of urbanisation as such, although it must be conceded that Muslims loved city life and encouraged *qasba* like settlements. Urbanisation in Europe gave impetus to industry and personal property and founded a new set of power cluster—the middle class. The rise of this new class, with its wealth and industrial importance, contributed more than anything else to social and political development in Europe before which the feudal relations of society almost gradually crumbled. The rise and spread of this class in India and its impact on society remained minimal and rather imperceptible. Edward Terry noted that it was not safe for merchants and tradesmen in towns and cities, "so to appear, lest they should be used as filled sponges."[25] Moreland on the testimony of Bernier and

22. Naqvi, Hamida Khatoon, *Urbanisation and Urban Centres under the Great Mughals*, Simla, 1971.

23. Alberuni, Introduction, p.xxiii, I, pp. 199, 202; Al Idrisi, *Nuzhat-ul-Mushtaq,* E and D, I, p.77. Also R.C.Majumdar, H.C.Raychaudhuri and K.K. Datta, *An Advanced History of India*, Macmillan & Co. (London,1958). pp.186.

24. S.A.A.Rizvi, Hindi trs. of *Rehla* in*Tughlaq Kalin Bharat* (Aligarh, 1956) pp. jklm. For detailed references see Lal, K.S., *Growth of Muslim Population*, pp. 36, 46, 55-63.

25. Terry, Edward, *A Voyage to East India* (London, 1655), p.112.

others, arrives at the conclusion that in India the number
of middle class people was small and they found it safe to
wear "the garb of indigence."[26] Europe broke the shackles
of feudalism by embarking upon Commercial Revolution
and took to the seas for the same. The Mughals in India
fared miserably on water. Even the great emperor Akbar
had to purchase permission of the Portuguese for his relatives to visit places of Islamic pilgrimage. Throughout
medieval India there was little change in the field of scientific learning and thought.

Religious Wars

Like feudalism, inter- and intra- religious wars too
were a very prominent feature of the medieval age. There
were two great Semetic religions, Judaism and Christianity, already in existence when Islam was born. Most of the
world religions like Vedic Hinduism (C. 2000-1500 B.C.),
Judaism (C. 1500 B.C.), Zoroastrianism (C. 1000 B.C.), Jainism and Buddhism (C. 600 B.C.), Confucianism (C. 500
B.C.) and Christianity had already come into being before
Islam appeared on the scene in the seventh century. All
these religions, especially Hinduism, had evolved through
its various schools a very highly developed philosophy.
Jainism and Buddhism had said almost the last word on
ethics. So that not much was left for later religions to
contribute to religious philosophy and thought. So far as
rituals and mythology are concerned, these abounded in
all religions and the mythology of neighbouring Judaic
and Christian creeds was freely incorporated by Islam in
its religion, so that Moses became Musa; Jesus, Isa; Solo-
man, Sulaiman; Joseph, Yusuf; Jacob, Yaqub; Abraham,
Ibrahim; Mary, Mariam; and so on. But to assert its own
identity, rules were made suiting the requirements of
Muslims imitating or forbidding Jewish and Christian
practices.[27]

---

26. Moreland, *India at the Death of Akbar*, p.264.
27. Margoliouth, D.S., *Mohammed and the Rise of Islam*, pp. 107, 125-26,
145-46, 250.

Muhammad was born in Arabia in 569 and died in 632. In 622 he had to migrate from Mecca to Medina (called *hijrat*) and this year forms the first year of the Muslim calendar (*Hijri*). Islam got much of its mythology and rituals from Judaism and Christianity, but instead of coming closer to them it confronted them. From the very beginning Islam believed in aggression as an instrument of expansion, and so "spreading with the rapidity of an electric current from its power-house in Mecca, it flashed into Syria, it traversed the whole breadth of north Africa; and then, leaping the Straits of Gibraltar it ran to the Gates of the Pyrenees".[28] Such unparalleled feats of success were one day bound to be challenged by the vanquished. As a result Christians and Muslims entered into a long-drawn struggle. The immediate cause of the conflict was the capture of Jerusalem by the Seljuq Turks in 1070 and the defeat of the Byzantine forces at Manzikart in Asia Minor in 1071. For the next two centuries (1093-1291) the Christian nations fought wars of religion or Crusades against Muslims for whom too these wars meant the holy *Jihad*.

Christianity thus found a powerful rival in Islam because the aim of both has been to convert the world to their systems. In competition, Islam had certain advantages. If because of its late arrival, there was any problem about obtaining followers, it was solved by the simple method of just forcing the people to accept it. Starting from Arabia, Islam pushed its religious and political frontiers through armed might. The chain of its early military successes helped establish its credentials and authority. It was also made more attractive than Christianity by polygamy, licence of concubinage and frenzied bigotry.[29] It sought outward expansion but developed no true theory of peaceful co-existence. For example, it framed unlimited

28. Arnold, *The Legacy of Islam*, p. 42.
29. William Muir, *Calcutta Review*, 1845.

rules about the treatment to be accorded to non-Muslims
in an Islamic state, but nowhere are there norms laid
down about the behaviour of Muslims if they happen to
live as a minority in a non-Muslim majority state. Its tactic
of violence also proved to be its greatest weakness. In the
course of Islamic history, Muslims have been found to be
as eager to fight among themselves as against others.

The Crusades (so called because Christian warriors
wore the sign of cross), were carried on by European
nations from the end of the eleventh century till the latter
half of the thirteenth century for the conquest of Palestine.
The antagonism of the Christian and Muhammadan
nations had been intensified by the possession of Holy
Land by the Turks and their treatment of the Christian
pilgrims to Jerusalem. In these wars, the pious, the adventurous, and the greedy flocked under the standards of
both sides. The first crusade was inspired by Peter the
Hermit in 1093, and no less than eight bloody wars were
fought with great feats of adventure, heroism and killings.
In the last crusade the Sultan of Egypt captured Acre in
1291 and put an end to the kingdom founded by the
Crusaders. Despite their want of success, the European
nations by their joint enterprises became more connected
with each other and ultimately stamped out any Muslim
influence in Western Europe. But the most fruitful element
in the crusades was the entry of the West into the East.
There was a constant conflict and permanent contact
between Christianity and Islam.

In this contact both sides lost and gained by turns,
both culturally and demographically, for both strove for
expansion through arms and proselytization. The successors of Saladin, who defeated the Christians in the last
crusade, were divided by dissensions. By the grace of
those disenssions the Latins survived. A new militant
Muhammadanism arose with the Mameluke Sultans of
Egypt who seized the throne of Cairo in 1250. However,

shortly afterwards there was a setback to Muslim power when the Caliph of Baghdad was killed by the Mongols in 1258. On the other hand, the prospect of a great mass conversion of the Mongols, which would have linked a Christian Asia to a Christian Europe and reduced Islam to a small faith, also dwindled and disappeared. "The (Mongol) Khanates of Persia turned to Muhammadanism in 1316; by the middle of the fourteenth century Central Asia had gone the same way; in 1368-70 the native dynasty of Mings was on the throne and closing China to foreigners; and the end was a recession of Christianity and an extension of Islam which assumed all the greater dimensions with the growth of the power of the Ottoman Turks.... But a new hope dawned for the undefeated West; and this new hope was to bring one of the greatest revolutions of history. If the land was shut, why should Christianity not take to the sea? Why should it not navigate to the East, take Muhammadanism in the rear, and as it were, win Jerusalem a *tergo*? This was the thought of the great navigators, who wore the cross on their breasts and believed in all sincerity that they were labouring in the cause of the recovery of the Holy Land, and if Columbus found the Caribbean Islands instead of Cathay, at any rate we may say that the Spaniards who entered into his labours won a continent for Christianity, and that the West, in ways in which it had never dreamed, at last established the balance in its favour."[30]

Crusades saved Western civilization in the Middle Ages. "They saved it from any self-centred localism; they gave it breadth—and a vision." On the other hand, Muslim victories made Muslim vision narrow and myopic. So that today Christians are larger in numbers and technologically and militarily more advanced than Muhammadans. As these lines are being written (August 1990), their armies and ships are spreading all over the West Asian region beginning with Saudi Arabia.

30. Arnold, *The Legacy of Islam*, pp. 76-77.

To return to the medieval period. Religious wars between Christians and Muhammadans alone did not account for killings on a large scale. The Christians also fought bloody and long-drawn wars among themselves. The Thirty Years War (1618-1648), for instance, decimated one-fifth population of the region affected by it. Then there was the Inquisition. Inquisition was a court or tribunal established by the Roman Catholic Church in the twelfth century for the examination and punishment of heretics. England never introduced it, Italy and France had only a taste of it. But in Spain it became firmly established towards the end of the fifteenth century. It is computed that there were in Spain above 20,000 officers of the Inquisition, called *familiars*, who served as spies and informers. Imprisonment, often for life, scourging, and the loss of property, were the punishments to which the penitent was subjected. When sentence of death was pronounced against the accused, burning the heretic in public was ordered as "the church never polluted herself with blood". The number of victims of the Spanish Inquisition from 1481 to 1808 amounted to 341,021. Of these nearly 32,000 were burned at the stake.[31]

Islam outstripped Christianity in contributing to large-scale killings in wars waged for religion or persecution of heretics. Each human being has an idea or image of God in his mind. Consequently, there can be as many Gods as there are human beings. Even "according to one outstanding Sufi, the paths by which its followers seek God are in number as the souls of men."[32] In view of this it is presumptuous to claim that there is only one God or there are many Gods or there is no God at all. And yet in the name of One God, and at that "Merciful and Compassionate", what cruelties have not been committed in the history of Islam? Arabia was converted during the life-time

---

31. *The Modern Cyclopaedia*, under Inquisition.
32. Rizvi, *History of Sufism*, I, p. 20.

of Muhammad. Immediately after the death of Muhammad, to borrow the rhetoric of Edward Gibbon, "in the ten
years of the administration of (Caliph) Omar (634-644) the
Saracens reduced to his obedience thirty-six thousand cities or castles, destroyed four thousand churches or
temples of the unbelievers, and edified fourteen hundred
moschs (mosques) for the exercise of the religion of Muhammad."[33] In these unparalleled feats the number of the
killed cannot be computed. Since many pages in this book
will be devoted to Muslim exertions in their endeavour to
spread Islam in India we may feel contented here to state
that in this scenario religion and religious wars became
the very soul of thought, action and oppression in the
Middle Ages.

Censorship

Middle Ages is also known as Dark Ages. It is so
called because there were restrictions placed on the freedom of thought and any aberrations were punished as
'heresy'. Any idea away from the traditional was looked
upon with suspicion. New conceptions or knowledge
gathered on the basis of new experiments was taboo if it
came into conflict with the Church or contravened the
Christian scriptures. This restriction on any new notions
made the period a dark age. But it required constant monitoring of people's thoughts and actions. The invention of
printing and the rapid diffusion of opinion by means of
books, induced the governments in all western countries
to assume certain powers of supervision and regulation
with regard to printed matter. The popes were the first to
institute a regular censorship (1515) and inquisitors were
required to examine all works before they were printed.
Only one example would suffice to illustrate the position.
Nicholas Copernicus was born in Poland in 1473: he
taught mathematics at Rome in 1500 and died in Germany

---

33. Gibbon, *Decline and Fall of The Roman Empire*, II, p. 713.

in 1543. He researched on the shape of the Earth, and concluded that the Sun was the centre round which Earth and other planets revolved. In his *De Orbium Celestium Revolutionibus* (On the Revolutions of the Celestial Orbs) he even measured the diameter and circumference of the Earth fairly accurately. But the Church believed the Earth to be flat, and the fear of Inquisition discouraged Copernicus from publishing his 'outrageous' researches till about the close of his life, for the Church could do little harm to a man about to die. Even so, his book was forbidden to the Roman Catholics for long. The Inquisition freely used torture to extort confession; 'heretics' were broken on the wheel, or burnt at stake on cross-roads on Sundays for punishment as well as an example for others.

In the medieval India under Muslim rule there was no printing press and no research of the type done by Copernicus. The need for censorship arose because Islam forbade any innovation in the thought and personal behaviour of Muslims. "Beware of novel affairs," said Muhammad, "for surely all innovation is error." What was not contained in the Quran or Hadis was considered as innovation and discouraged. That is why Muslim learning in India remained orthodox, repetitive and stereotyped. Free thought and research in science and technology were ruled out. Fundamentalist writers like Khwaja Baqi Billah (1563-1603), Shaikh Ahmad Sarhindi (1564-1624) and Shah Waliullah (1702-1763) were considered as champion thinkers.

As Muslims must live in accordance with a set of rules and a code of conduct, there was an official Censor of Public Morals and Religion called *Muhtasib*. It was his duty to see that Muslims did not absent themselves from public prayers, that no one was found drunk in public places, that liquors or drugs were not sold openly. He possessed arbitrary power of intervention and could enter the houses of wrong-doers to bring them to book. Sir Alexander Burnes relates that he saw persons publicly scourged because they had slept during prayer-time and smoked on Friday.[34] I.H. Qureshi writes, "It was soon discovered that people situated as the Muslims were in India could not be allowed to grow lax in their ethical and spiritual conduct without endangering the very existence of the Sultanate."[35] Hurriedly converted, half-trained, Indian Muslims were prone to reverting to their original faith which was full of freedom. Therefore, all the sultans were very strict about enforcing Islamic behaviour on Muslims through the agency of Muhtasibs. Balban, Alauddin Khalji and Muhammad bin Tughlaq were known for their severity in this regard. Muhammad bin Tughlaq regarded wilful neglect of prayers a heinous crime and inflicted severe chastisement on transgressors.[36] Women too were not spared; Firoz Shah and Sikandar Lodi in particular forbade women from going on pilgrimage to the tombs of saints.[37] The Department of Censor of Public Morals was known as *hisbah*.[38]

Non-Muslims suffered even more because of censorial regulations. Tradition divided them into seven kinds

34. Burnes, Sir Alexander, *Travels in Bokhara*, I, p.313; Hughes, *Dictionary of Islam*, p.418.
35. Qureshi, Ishtiaq Husain, *Administration of the Sultanate of Delhi*, p.166.
36. Barani, pp.35, 41, 72, 285; Ibn Battuta, Def. and Sang., II, 34, 52.
37. Lal, *Twilight of the Sultanate*, p.269.
38. It has its modern counterparts in Saudi Arabia and Iran. In Iran it is known as *Komiteh*, or Committee, in Saudi Arabia *Mutawar*. The Saudi religious police is called the Committee for commendation of virtue and prevention of vice. They enforce strict adherence to Islamic code of conduct. In Iran, while the regular police are charged with enforcement of laws dealing with common crimes such as burglary or assault, the armed officers of the *Komiteh* walk the streets in their olive green fatigues, making sure that the strict moral standards of Islam are upheld. It is their job to make certain that unmarried men and women do not hold hands or walk together on the sidewalk, that storekeepers display large, glossy photographs of the nation's senior Islamic clerics in their shops, that liquor is not served at private parties, and that women keep their hair, arms, and feet covered, preferably in the black robes called *chadors*.

of offenders like unbelievers, infidels, hypocrites, polytheists etc. who are destined to go to seven kinds of hell from the mild *Jahannum* to the hottest region of hell called *Hawiyah*, 'a bottomless pit of scorching fire.' A strict watch was kept on their thought and expression. They were to dress differently from the Muslims, they could not worship their gods in public and they could not claim that their religion was as good as Islam. A case which culminated in the execution of a Brahmin may be quoted in some detail as an example.

"A report was brought to the Sultan (Firoz Tughlaq 1351-88) that there was in Delhi an old Brahman (*Zunar dar*) who persisted in publicly performing the worship of idols in his house; and that the people of the city, both Musalmans and Hindus, used to resort to his house to worship the idol. This Brahman had constructed a wooden tablet (*muhrak*), which was covered within and without with paintings of demons and other objects. On days appointed, the infidels went to his house and worshipped the idol, without the fact becoming known to the public officers. The Sultan was informed that this Brahman had perverted Muhammadan women, and had led them to become infidels. (These women were surely newly converted and had not been able to completely cut themselves off from their original faith). An order was accordingly given that the Brahman, with his tablet, should be brought in the presence of the Sultan at Firozabad. The judges, doctors, and elders and lawyers were summoned, and the case of the Brahman was submitted for their opinion. Their reply was that the provisions of the Law were clear: the Brahman must either become a Musalman or be burned. The true faith was declared to the Brahman, and the right course pointed out, but he refused to accept it. Orders were given for raising a pile of faggots before the door of the *darbar*. The Brahman was tied hand and foot and cast into it; the tablet was thrown on the top and the pile was lighted. The writer of this book (Shams Siraj Afif) was present at the *darbar* and witnessed the execution.... the wood was dry, and the fire first reached his feet, and drew from him a cry, but the flames quickly enveloped his head and consumed him. Behold the Sultan's strict adherence to law and rectitude, how he would not deviate in the least from its decrees."[39]

The above detailed description gives the idea of burning at stake under Muslim rule. Else similar cases of executions are many. During the reign of Firoz himself the Hindu governor of Uchch was killed. He was falsely accused of expressing affirmation in Islam and then recanting.[40] In the time of Sikandar Lodi (1489-1517) a Brahman of Kaner in Sambhal was similarly punished with death for committing the crime of declaring as much as that "Islam was true, but his own religion was also true."[41]

Astrology and Astronomy

Most medieval people of all creeds and countries believed in astrology. Astrology literally means the science of the stars. The name was formerly used as equivalent to astronomy, but later on became restricted in meaning to the science or psuedo-science which claims to enable people to judge of the effects and influences of the heavenly bodies on human and other mundane affairs. Astrology was not to the medievals an unscientific aberration. It was based on the understanding that the relationship of man to the Universe is as the microcosm (the little world) is to the macrocosm (the great world). Thus a knowledge of the heavens is essential for a true understanding of man himself. "A knowledge of the movements

39. Afif, p.388; trs. in E and D, III, p.365.

40. Farishtah, II, pp.417-18.

41. Nizamuddin Ahmad *Tabqat-i-Akbari*, I, p.323; Farishtah, I,p.182; Niamatullah trs. by Dorn, *Makhzan-i-Afghana*, pp.65-66. Also Lal, *Twilight of the Sultanate*, p.191.

of the planets and their position in the heavens, would therefore be of the utmost importance for man since, in the medieval phrase, superiors (in the heavens) ruled inferiors (on earth): and not only man but.... all were subject to the decrees of heavens, which themselves... expressed the will of God."[42] Roger Bacon (1214-1292?) considered astrology as the most practical of sciences.[43]

Astrology was practised by Muslims as by all other medieval people. Muhammad bin Qasim, the first invader of India, was despatched on his mission only after astrologers had pronounced that the conquest of Sind could be effected only by his hand.[44] Mahmud of Ghazni too believed in the predictions of astrologers.[45] Timur the invader writes in his *Malfuzat*: "About this time there arose in my heart a desire to lead an expedition against the infidels and become a ghazi", and felt encouraged when he opened a *fal* (omen) in the Quran which said: "O Prophet, make war upon infidels and unbelievers and treat them with severity"—and he launched his attack on Hindustan.[46] The practice of consulting the Quran for *fal* was common among medieval Muslims.[47] The savant Alberuni gives details of Hindu literature on astrology and astronomy seen by him.[48] By and large Muslim kings and commoners in India decided their actions on the advice of the astrologers, sooth-sayers and omen mongers.

People's faith in astrology was reinforced for seeking solution to their immediate problems and their curiosity to know their future. The first was done by astrologers and

---

42. Easton, Stewart C., *The Heritage of the Past*, p.399.
43. *Ibid.*, p.403.
44. Elliot's Appendix, E and D, I, p.432. He cites *Chachnama* and *Tuhfutul Kiram* for source; *Chachnama*, trs. Kalichbeg, pp. 44-45, 190.
45. Farishtah, I, pp 32, 33, 37. Also M.Habib, *Sultan Mahmud of Ghaznin*, p.56.
46. Timur, *Mulfuzat-i-Timuri*, E and D, III, pp.394-95.
47. Amir Khurd, *Siyar-ul-Auliya*, trs. Quddusi, p.657; Sijzi, *Favaid-ul-Fvad* trs. Ghulam Ahmad, pp.157-58.
48. Alberuni, I, pp.152-159.

palm-readers by "examining the hand and face of the applicant, turning over the leaves of the large book, and pretending to make certain calculations" and then "decide upon the *Sahet* (saiet) or propitious moment of commencing the business he may have in hand."[49] Amulets and charms were also prescribed for warding off distress, removing fear, obtaining success in an undertaking or victory in battle and a hundred other similar problems.[50] The second was done by preparing a horoscope. As usually practised, the whole heavens, visible and invisible, was divided by great circles into twelve equal parts, called *houses*. The houses had different names and different powers, the first being called the house of life, the second the house of riches, the third of brethren, the sixth of marriage, the eighth of death, and so on. To draw a person's horoscope, or cast his *nativity*, was to find the position of the heavens at the instant of his birth. The temperament of the individual was ascribed to the planet under which he was born, as *saturnine* from Saturn, *jovial* from Jupiter, *mercurial* from Mercury and so on. The virtues of herbs, gems, and medicines were also supposed to be due to their ruling planets.

Kings and nobles gave large salaries to astrologers. The astrologers prepared horoscopes of princes and the elite. Muslim kings got horoscopes of all princes like Salim, Murad and Daniyal cast by Hindu Pandits.[51] Jotik Ray, the court astrologer of emperor Jahangir used to make correct predictions after reading the king's horoscope. He was once weighed against gold and silver for reward.[52] There were men and women *Rammals* (soothsayers) and clairvoyants at the court.[53] In short, the prac-

49. Bernier, p.244.

50. Jafar Sharif, *Islam in India*, trs. by G.A. Herklots, pp.247-63.

51. Abul Fazl, *Akbar Nama*, trs. Beveridge, II, pp.346-47, 354-55 and 543 respectively.

52. *Tuzuk-i-Jahangiri*, II, pp. 160, 203, 215, 235.

53. *Ibid.*, p.235.

tice of consulting astrologers was common with high and low. The people never engaged even in the most trifling transaction without consulting them. "They read whatever is written in heaven; fix upon the *Sahet*, and solve every doubt by opening the Koran."[54] "No commanding officer is nominated, no marriage takes place, and no journey is undertaken without consulting Monsieur the Astrologer."[55] Naturally, the astrologers "who frequented the court of the grandees are considered by them eminent doctors, and become wealthy."[56]

But there were charlatans also. They duped and exploited the poor and the credulous. Besides some people then as now had no faith in astrology. The French doctor Bernier was such an one. Describing the bazar held in Delhi near the Red Fort, Francois Bernier (seventeenth century) says that "Hither, likewise, the astrologers resort, both Mahometan and Gentile. These wise doctors remain seated in the sun, on a dusty piece of carpet, handling some old mathematical instruments, and having open before them a large book which represents the sign of the Zodiac. In this way they attract the attention of the passenger....by whom they are considered as so many infallible oracles. They tell a poor person his fortune for a *payssa* ... Silly women, wrapping themselves in a white cloth from head to foot, flock to the astrologers, whisper to them all the transaction of their lives, and disclose every secret with no more reserve than is practised by a penitent in the presence of her confessor. The ignorant and infatuated people really believe that the stars have an influence (on their lives) which the astrologers can control."[57]

Astrology and astronomy are closely interlinked. In medieval times astronomy was also considered a branch

54. Bernier, p.245, also pp. 161-163.
55. *Ibid.*, p.161.
56. *Ibid.*, p.245.
57. Bernier, pp.243-44.

of psychology and medicine. Astronomy has an undoubtedly high antiquity in India. The Arabs began to make
scientific astronomical observations about the middle of
the eighth century, and for 400 years they prosecuted the
science of *najum* with assiduity. The Muslims looked upon
astronomy as the noblest and most exalted of sciences, for
the study of stars was an indispensable aid to religious
observances, determining for instance the month of
Ramzan and the hours of prayers. Halaku Khan (Buddhist) founded the great Margha observatory at Azer-
baijain. One at Jundishapur existed in Iran. In the fifteenth
century Ulugh Beg, grandson of Amir Timur (Tamerlane),
built an observatory at Samarqand. In Europe Copernicus
in the fifteenth and Galileo and Newton in the seventeenth
century did valuable work in the field of astronomy. In
medieval India many Muslim chroniclers wrote about the
movements of planets and stars,[58] but the name of Sawai
Jai Singh II of Jaipur has become famous for his contribution to the science of astronomy. He built observatories or
Jantar-Mantars at many places in the country for the study
of the movements of stars and planets. A reputed geome-
ter and scholar, Sawai Jai Singh II built the Delhi Jantar-
Mantar in C.E. 1710 at the request of Mughal emperor
Muhammad Shah. The observatory was used for naked-
eye sighting, continuously monitoring the position of the
sun, moon and planets in relation to background stars in
the belt of the Zodiac. His aim was basically to make
accurate predictions of eclipses and position of planets. He
devised instruments of his own invention — the Samrat
Yantra, the Jai Prakash, and the Ram Yantra. The Misr
Yantra was added later by Jai Singh's son Madho Singh.
The Samrat Yantra is an equinoctial dial. The Yantra
measures the time of the day, correct to half a second; and
the declination of the sun and other heavenly bodies.

---

58. e.g. Barani, p.167; *Ain*, I,p.50.

Other Jantar-Mantars of Jai Singh were built at Ujjain, Mathura, Banaras and Jaipur.[59]

Alchemy, Magic, Miracles and Superstitions

Alchemy flourished chiefly in the medieval period, although how old it might be is difficult to say. It paved the way for the modern science of chemistry, as astrology did for astronomy. In the medieval age alchemy was believed to be an exact science. But its aims were not scientific. It concerned itself solely with indefinitely prolonging human life, and of transmuting baser metals into gold and silver. It was cultivated among the Arabians, and by them the pursuit was introduced into Europe. "Raymond Lully, or Lullius, a famous alchemist of the thirteenth and fourteenth centuries, is said to have changed for king Edward I mass of 50,000 lbs. of quicksilver into gold."[60] No such specific case is found in medieval India, although there was firm belief in the magic or science of alchemy. A Sufi politician of the thirteenth century, Sidi Maula by name, developed lot of political clout in the time of Sultan Jalaluddin Khalji (1290-1296). He built a large *khanqah* (hospice) where hundreds of people were fed by him every day. "He used to pay for what he bought by the queer way of telling the man to take such and such amount from under such and such brick or coverlet, and the *tankahs* (gold/silver coins) found there looked so bright as if they had been brought from the mint that very moment."[61] He did not accept anything from the people but spent so lavishly that they suspected him of possessing the knowledge of *Kimya va Simya* (alchemy and natural magic).[62]

---

59. In Ujjain (Ozene of Ptolemy's geography) there was an astronomical laboratory in ancient times "on the meridian of which town the 'world summit'—originally an Indian conception—was supposed to lie" (Arnold, *The Legacy of Islam*, p.93).
60. *The Modern Cyclopaedia* under Alchemy.
61. Barani, p.209. Also Badaoni, Ranking, I, p.233.
62. Amir Khurd, *Siyar-ul-Auliya*, trs. Quddusi, pp.246-47.

The general solvent which at the same time was supposed to possess the power of removing all the seeds of
disease out of the human body and renewing life, was
called the *philosopher's stone*. Naturally, there was a keen
desire to get hold of one. India was known for possessing
knowledge of herbs which prolonged life. Alberuni writes
about the science of alchemy *(Rasayan)* about which he so
learnt in India: "Its *(Rasayan's)* principles (certain operations, drugs and compound medicines, most of which are
taken from plants) restore the health... and give back
youth to fading old age... white hair becomes black again,
the keenness of the senses is restored as well as the capacity for juvenile agility, and even for co-habitation, and the
life of the people in this world is even extended to a long
period."[63] In *Jami'ul Hikayat* Muhammad Ufi narrates that
certain chiefs of Turkistan sent ambassadors with letters to
the kings of India on the following mission. The chiefs
said that they "had been informed that in India drugs
were procurable which possessed the property of prolonging human life, by the use of which the kings of India
attained to a very great age. The Rais were careful in the
preservation of their health, and the chiefs of Turkistan
begged that some of this medicine might be sent to them,
and also information as to the method by which the Rais
preserved their health so long. The ambassadors having
reached Hindustan, delivered the letters entrusted to
them. The Rai of Hind having read them, ordered the
ambassadors to be taken to the top of an excessively lofty
mountain" (Himalayas?) to obtain it. In the same book a
story refers to a chief of Jalandhar, who had attained to the
age of 250 years. In a note Elliot comments that "this was
a favourite persuasion of the Orientals".[64] But Alberuni's

---

63. Alberuni, I, pp.188-89. Also Khusrau, *Nuh Sipehr*, E and D, III,
p.563.
64. E and D, II, pp. 173-74 and note. Muhammad Ufi had occasion to
live in India during the reign of Sultan Iltutmish (1210-1236 C.E.). He is
"something better than a mere story-teller" (E and D, II, p.156).

conclusion is crisp and correct. He writes: "The Hindus do not pay particular attention to alchemy, but no nation is entirely free from it, and one nation has more bias for it than another, which must not be construed as proving intelligence or ignorance; for we find that many intelligent people are entirely given to alchemy, whilst ignorant people ridicule the art and its adepts."[65]

Belief in magic too was a universal weakness of the middle ages. "The invocation of spirits is an important part of Musalman magic, and this (dawat) is used for the following purposes: to command the presence of the *Jinn* and demons who, when it is required of them, cause anything to take place; to establish friendship or enmity between two persons; to cause the death of an enemy; to increase wealth or salary; to gain income gratuitously or mysteriously; to secure the accomplishment of wishes, temporal or spiritual."[66] So, magic was practised both for good purposes and evil intentions, for finding lucky days for travelling, catching thieves and removing diseases as well as inflicting diseases on others. The first was called spiritual (*Ilm-i-Ruhani*) and the latter *Shaitani Jadu*. Although Islam directs Musalmans to "believe not in magic",[67] yet the belief was universal.[68] It involved visit to tombs, use of collyrium or *pan* (betel), and all kinds of antics and ceremonials for desiring death for others and success for self. There were trained magicians (*Sayana*).[69] They fleeced the fools, both rich and poor, to their hearts' content. A highly popular book on magic among the Muslims in the medieval period was *Jawahir-i-Khamsa* by Muhammad Ghaus Gauleri.[70]

65. Alberuni, I, p.187.
66. Jafar Sharif, *Islam in India*, p.218.
67. Quran, II,96.
68. Amir Khusrau, *Nuh Sipehr*, E and D,III, p.563; Amir Khurd, *Siyar-ul-Auliya*, trs.Quddusi, pp.338, 650; Sijzi, *Favaid-ul-Fvad*, trs. Ghulam Ahmad, p.292.
69. Jafar Sharif, *op.cit.*, pp.218-246, 274-77.
70. *Ibid.*, p.219.

Belief in magic and sorcery and worship of saints living and dead was linked with belief in miracles and superstition. The argument was that the elders and saints helped when they were alive, they could still help when dead and so their graves were worshipped. There was belief in miracles for the same reason. An evil eye could inflict disease and there was fear of witchcraft. A blessing could cure it and so there was faith in the miraculous powers of saints. In medieval times physicians were few, charlatans many, and even witch doctors flourished. Amir Khusrau mentions some of the powers "of sorcery and enchantment possessed by the inhabitants of India. First of all they can bring a dead man to life. If a man has been bitten by a snake and is rendered speechless, they can resuscitate him even after six months."[71]

There is nothing surprising about the belief in miracles by medieval Muslims, in particular about their Sufi Mashaikh. In theory Islam disapproved of miracles. In practice it became a criterion by which Sufi Shaikhs were judged and the common reason why people reposed faith in them. Many Sufi Shaikhs and *Faqirs* were considered to be *Wali* who could perform *karamat* or miracles and even *istidraj* or magic and hypnotism.[72] Shaikh Nizamuddin Auliya held that it was improper for a Sufi to show his *karamat* even if he possessed supernatural powers.[73] But belief in alchemy and miracles was common even among Sufi Mashaikh[74] and there are dozens of hagiological works and biographies of Sufi saints containing stories of such miracles including *Favaid-al-Fuad, Siyar-ul-Auliya* and *Khair-ul-Majalis* which are considered by many Muslims to be pretty authentic. There are unbelievable stories, hardly

---

71. Amir Khusrau, *Nuh Sipehr*, E and D, III, p.563.

72. Amir Khurd, *Siyar-ul-Auliya*, Muhibb-i-Hind Press (Delhi 1309 H., C.E. 1891) pp.351-52.

73. *Ibid.*, p.354.

74. Amir Khusrau, *Afzal-ul-Favaid*, Urdu trs. in Silsila-i-Tasawwuf No. 81, Kashmiri Bazar Lahore, p.95; Ibn Battuta, pp.164-66.

worth reproducing. It is difficult to say when the stories of
the *karamat* of the Sufi saints began to be told. But they
helped the Sufis take Islam to the masses. It is believed
that impressed by these stories or actual performance of
miracles, many Hindus became their disciples and uti-
mately converted to Islam.

Belief in ghosts of both sexes was widespread. Nights
were frightfully dark. Right upto the time of Babur there
were "no candles, no torches, not a candle-stick".[75] Even
in the Mughal palace utmost economy was practised in
the use of oil for lighting purposes.[76] The common man
lived in utter darkness after nighfall. And ghosts, goblins
and imaginary figures used to haunt him. Sorcerers and
witch doctors tried to help men and particularly women
who were supposed to have been possessed by ghosts.

Education

Belief in astrology and alchemy, magic and witchcraft,
miracles and superstition was there both in the West and
the East in the middle ages. Europe released itself from
mental darkness sooner because of spread of education
and early establishment of a number of universities. Oxford was set up in the twelfth century, Cambridge in 1209.
Paris University came into being in the twelfth, Angers in
the thirteenth and Orleans in 1231. In Italy, Salerno was
founded in the tenth century, Arezzo in 1215, Padua 1222,
Naples 1224, Siena 1246, Piacenza 1248, Rome 1303, and
Pisa 1343. Such was the situation throughout Europe.[77]
The emergence of universities in such large numbers, with
still larger number of schools whose selected pupils went
to the universities, led to a spurt in learning which may
explain the birth and flowering of Renaissance in Italy and

---

75. *Babur Nama*, II, p.518.
76. *Ain*, I, p.50; Lal, K.S. *The Mughal Harem*, pp.182-84.
77. Stewart C.Easton, *The Heritage of the Past* (New York, 1957), map on
the end leaf showing University Centres and dates of their establishment.

Reformation in Germany. Martin Luther, who created a revolution in religion, was a student at the University of Erfurt founded in 1343.

In the early years of Islam the Muslims concentrated mainly on translating and adopting Greek scholarship. Aristotle was their favourite philosopher. Scientific and mathematical knowledge they adopted from the Greeks and Hindus. This was the period when the Arabs imbibed as much knowledge from the West and the East as possible. In the West they learnt from Plato and Aristotle and in India "Arab scholars sat at the feet of Buddhist monks and Brahman Pandits to learn philosophy, astronomy, mathematics, medicine, chemistry and other subjects." Caliph Mansur's (754-76) zeal for learning attracted many Hindu scholars to the Abbasid court. A deputation of Sindhi representatives in 771 C.E. presented many treatises to the Caliph and the *Brahma Siddhanta* of Brahmagupta and his *Khanda-Khadyaka*, works on the science of astronomy, were translated by Ibrahim al-Fazari into Arabic with the help of Indian scholars in Baghdad. The Barmak (originally Buddhist Pramukh) family of ministers who had been converted to Islam and served under the Khilafat of Harun-ur-Rashid (786-808 C.E.) sent Muslim scholars to India and welcomed Hindu scholars to Baghdad. Once when Caliph Harun-ur-Rashid suffered from a serious disease which baffled his physicians, he called for an Indian physician, Manka (Manikya), who cured him. Manka settled at Baghdad, was attached to the hospital of the Barmaks, and translated several books from Sanskrit into Persian and Arabic. Many Indian physicians like Ibn Dhan and Salih, reputed to be descendants of Dhanapti and Bhola respectively, were superintendants of hospitals at Baghdad. Indian medical works of Charak, Sushruta, the *Ashtangahrdaya*, the *Nidana*, the *Siddhayoga*, and other works on diseases of women, poisons and their antidotes, drugs, intoxicants, nervous diseases etc. were translated into Pahlavi and Arabic during the Abbasid Caliphate. Such works helped the Muslims in extending their knowledge about numerals and medicine.[78] Havell goes even as far as to say that "it was India, not Greece, that taught Islam in the impressionable years of its youth, formed its philosophy and esoteric religious ideals, and inspired its most characteristic expression in literature, art and architecture."[79] Avicenna (Ibn Sina) was a Persian Muslim who lived in the early eleventh century and is known for his great canon of medicine. Averroes (Ibn Rushd), the jurist, physician and philosopher was a Spanish Muslim who lived in the twelfth century. Al Khwarizmi (ninth century) developed the Hindu nine numbers and the zero (*hindisa*). Al Kindi (ninth century) wrote on physics, meteorology and optics. Al Hazen (Al Hatim C. 965-1039) wrote extensively on optics and the manner in which the human eye is able to perceive objects. Their best known geographers were Al Masudi, a globe-trotter who finished his works in 956 and the renowned Al Idrisi (1101-1154). Although "there is little that is peculiarly Islamic in the contributions which Occidental and Oriental Muslims have made to European culture",[80] even this endeavour had ceased by the time Muslim rule was established in India. In the words of Easton, "when the barbarous Turks entered into the Muslim heritage, after it had been in decay for centuries, did Islam.... destroy more than it created or preserved".[81] For instance, Ibn Sina had died in Hamadan in 1037 and in 1150 the Caliph at Baghdad was committing to the flames a philosophical library, and among its contents the writings of Ibn Sina himself. "In days such as these the Latins of the East were hardly likely to become scholars of the Muhammadans nor were they

---

78. Alberuni, Introduction, p.xxxi; Singhal, *India and World Civilization*, I, p.149.
79. Havell, E.B., *History of Aryan Rule in India*, p.256.
80. Arnold, *The Legacy of Islam*, Preface, p. v.
81. Easton, *The Heritage of the Past*, p.242.

stimulated by the novelty of their surroundings to any original production."[82]

Similar was the record of the Turks in India. No universities were established by Muslims in medieval India. They only destroyed the existing ones at Sarnath, Vaishali, Odantapuri, Nalanda, Vikramshila etc. to which thousands of scholars from all over India and Asia used to seek admission. Thus, with the coming of Muslims, India ceased to be a centre of higher Hindu and Buddhist learning for Asians. The Muslims did not set up even Muslim institutions of higher learning. Their *maktabs* and *madrasas* catered just for repetitive, conservative and orthodox schooling. There was little original thinking, little growth of knowledge as such. Education in Muslim India remained a private affair. Writers and scholars, teachers and artists generally remained under the direct employment of kings and nobles. There is little that can be called popular literature, folk-literature, epic etc. in contemporary Muslim writings. "The life of the vast majority of common people was stereotyped and unrefined and represented a very low state of mental culture."[83]

Tenor of Life

The chief amusement of the nobles of the ruling class was warfare. In this they took delight that was never altogether assuaged. If they could not indulge in this, then, in later ages, they made mock fights called jousts or tournaments. If they could not always fight men, they hunted animals. Every noble learned to hunt, not for food—though this was important too—but for pleasure. They developed the art of hunting birds as well as taming and flying birds.[84] Some nobles were "learned, humble, polite

---

82. Arnold, *The Legacy of Islam*, pp. 55-56.
83. Ashraf, K.M., *Life and Conditions of the People of Hindustan*, p.329.
84. Al Qalqashindi, *Subh-ul-Asha*, trs. Otto Spies, p. 68; Barani, p. 318.

and courteous",[85] but such were exceptions rather than the rule. Since there was little academic activity, most of the elite passed their time in field sports, swordsmanship and military exercises. Their coat of mail was heavy and cumbersome; a fall from horse was very painful and sometimes even fatal. Such a situation was common both in Europe and India. But in Europe the medieval age was an age of chivalry. It tended to raise the ideal of woman-hood if not the status of women. Chivalrous duels and combats were generally not to be seen among Muslims in India. "Such artificial sentimentality has nothing in com-mon with (their) warrior creed."[86]

The medieval age, by and large, conjures up vision of times in which everything was backward. Life was nasty, brutish and short. The ruler and the ruling classes were unduly cruel. Take the case of hunting animals and birds. In the process fields with standing crops were crushed and destroyed, often wantonly. The common man suff-ered. Man wallowed in ignorance. Man was dirty, there was no soap, no safety razor. Potable water was provided by rivers, else it was well-water or rainwater collected in tanks, ponds and ditches. Political and religious tyranny, the institution of slavery, polygamy and 'inquisition' or 'hisbah' rendered life unpalatable. Men had few rights, women fewer. Wife was a possession; *parda* was a denial of the dignity of woman as woman. Medicine was limited, treatment a private affair, medicare was no concern of the state. Police was nowhere to be seen for seeming redressal of grievances while sorcery and magic, and ghosts and goblins were ever present to frighten and harm. Means of transport and communication were primitive. Most people hardly ever moved out of their villages or towns. Society was closed as was the mind.

---

85. Ibn Battuta, p.13; Ahmad Yadgar, *Tarikh-i-Salatin-i-Afghana*, Per-sian text, p.42.
86. Arnold, *The Legacy of Islam*, p.185.

But there was no scarcity of daily necessities of life.
True, in medieval India there was no tea, no bed-tea. Coff-
ee came late. It is mentioned by Jahangir in his memoirs.[87]
Tomato or potato did not arrive before the sixteenth century. Still, there was no dearth of palatable dishes for the
medieval people to eat. Wheat and rice were common
staples.[88] Rice is said to be of as many kinds as twenty-
one.[89] *Paratha, halwa* and *harisa*, were commonly eaten by
the rich,[90] *Khichri* and *Sattu* by the poor.[91] Muslims were
generally meat-eaters and mostly ate "the flesh of cow and
goat though they have many sheep, because they have
become accustomed to it."[92] Fowls, pigeons and other
birds were sold very cheap.[93] Vegetables mentioned in
medieval works are pumpkin, brinjal, cucumber, jackfruit
(*kathal*), bitter gourd (*karela*), turnip, carrot, asparagus,
various kinds of leafy vegetables, ginger, garden beet,
onion, garlic, fennal and thyme.[94] Dal and vegetables were
cooked in ghee, tamarind was commonly used, and pick-
les prepared from green mangoes as well as ginger and
chillies were favourites.[95] There were fresh fruits, dry
fruits and sweets. Apples, grapes, pears and pomegran-
ates[96] were for important people. Melons, green and yellow (*kharbuza* and *tarbuz*), were grown in abundance.[97]
Orange, citron (*utrurj*), lemon (*limun*), lime (*lim*), jamun,

---

87. *Tuzuk-i-Jahangiri*, p.155.

88. Ahmad Yadgar, *op. cit.*, p.52; Amir Hasan Sijzi, *Favaid-ul-Fvad*,
Nawal Kishore Press, Lucknow, Urdu trs. p. 174.

89. Al Qalqashindi, *Subh-ul-Asha*, pp. 48, 49. Also *Ain*, I, pp.65, 66.

90. Barani, pp.316-19.

91. Ibn Battuta, pp.38,49; *Babur Nama*, II, pp.517-18.

92. Al Qalqashindi, *op.cit.*, p.56. For various kinds of meat preparations see Jafar Sharif, *Islam in India*, pp.315-324.

93. Barani, p. 315. Also *Masalik-ul-Absar*, E and D, III, p.583.

94. Ahmad Yadgar, *op.cit.*, p.59; Ibn Battuta, p.17.

95. Ibn Battuta, p.16; Al Qalqashindi, p.50. Also K.M.Ashraf, *Life and
Conditions of the People of Hindustan*, pp.282-83.

96. Ahmad Yadgar, *op. cit.*, pp.50-52; Barani, p.569; Afif, pp.295-96.

97. Afif, pp.295-96; Ibn Battuta, p.17. In the time of Balban one *man* of
kharbuza was sold for 2 *jitals* (*Siyar-ul-Auliya*, Urdu trs. Quddusi, p.205).

khirni, dates and figs were in common use as also the plan-
tains.[98] Sugar-cane was grown in abundance and Ziyauddin Barani, writing in Persian, gives its Hindustani name
ponda. Mango, then as now, was the most favourite fruit of
India.[99] Sweet-meats were of many kinds, as many as sixty
five.[100] Some names like *reori*, sugar-candy, *halwa* and
samosa are familiar to this day. Ibn Battuta's description of
the preparation of *samosa* would make one's mouth water
even today: "Minced meat cooked with almond, walnut,
pistachios, onion and spices placed inside a thin bread and
fried in ghee."[101] Wine and other intoxicants like hemp
and opium, though prohibited in Islam, were freely taken
by those who had a liking for it.[102] Betel (then known by
its Sanskrit name *tambul*) was an after dinner delicacy.[103]

Muslim elite were very fond of eating rich and fatty
food, both in quality and quantity. Their gluttony was
whipped up as much by the love of sumptous dishes as by
their habit of hospitality. It also received stimulus from the
use of drinks and drugs and was best exhibited during
excursions, picnics and arranged dinners. According to Sir
Thomas Roe, twenty dishes at a time were served at the
tables of the nobles, but sometimes the number went even
beyond fifty. But for the extremely poor, people in general
enjoyed magnificent meals with sweetmeats and dry and
fresh fruit added.[104] All this was possible because food
grains were extremely cheap throughout the medieval
period as vouched by Barani for the thirteenth, Afif for the
fourteenth, Abdullah for the fifteenth and Abul Fazl for

---

98. Barani, pp.568-70; J.R.A.S., 1895, p.531.
99. Ahmad Yadgar, *op. cit.*, pp.51, 90.
100. Al Qalqashindi, p.50; Barani, p.318.
101. Ibn Battuta, p.15.
102. Jafar Sharif, *Islam in India*, pp.325-30.
103. Barani, p.182; Amir Khusrau, *Deval Rani*, p.60; Abdur Razzaq in
Major, *India in the Fifteenth Century*, p.32. Also Ibn Battuta.
104. *Ain.*, I, pp. 59-78; Ashraf,*op. cit.*, pp. 282-84; Lal,*Mughal Harem*, pp.
125, 189.

the sixteenth centuries.[105] The poor benefited by the situation but the benefit was probably offset by the force and coercion used in keeping prices low as asserted by Barani and Abdullah, the author of *Tarikh-i-Daudi*.

In matters of clothing also, India was better placed than many other countries in the middle ages. The textile industry of India was world-famous. The Sultan, the nobles and all the rich dressed exceedingly well.[106] The costly royal robes, the gilded and studded swords and daggers, the parasols (*chhatra*) of various colours were all typically Indian paraphernalia of royal pomp and splendour. The use of rings, necklaces, ear-rings and other ornaments by men was also due to Indian wealth and opulence. The dress of the Sultan and the elite consisted of *kulah* or head-dress, a tunic worked in brocade and long drawers. The habit of dyeing the beard was common. It added in the old a zest for life as did the slanting of cap in the young. The Hindu aristocracy dressed like the Muslim aristocracy,[107] except that in place of *kulah* they used a turban, and in place of long drawers they wore *dhoti* trimmed with gold lace. The Muslims dressed heavily but the Hindus were scantily dressed. "They cannot wear more clothing on account of the great heat," says Nicolo Conti.[108] "The orthodox Muslims wore clothes made of simple material like linen. The dress worn by scholars at the Firoz Shahi Madrasa consisted of the Syrian *jubbah* and the Egyptian *dastar*.[109] But there was no special uniform for any one, not even for soldiers. In the villages the poor put on only a loin-cloth (*langota*) which Babur takes pains to describe in detail.[110]

105. Barani, p.305; Afif 293-98; Abdullah, *Tarikh-i-Daudi*, Bankipore Ms., pp.223-24; Abul Fazl, *Ain*, I, pp.65-78.

106. Jafar Sharif, *Qanun-i-Islami*, p.304.

107. J.R.A.S., 1895, p.88.

108. Nicolo Conti in Major, *India in the Fifteenth Century*, p.33.

109. *Diwan-i-Mutahhar* quoted in K.A.Nizami, *Studies in Medieval Indian History*, Aligarh, 1956, p.90.

110. *Babur Nama*, II, p.519.

Muslim women dressed elaborately and elegantly. The inmates of the harems of the kings and nobles, indeed even their maids and servants dressed in good quality clothes.[111] *Lehanga, angia* and *dupatta* were the common set for women as seen in medieval miniatures. They wore shoes made of leather and silk, often ornamented with gold thread and studded with precious stones. Besides women all over the country wore all kinds of ornaments, the rich of gold and silver, pearls and precious stones, the poor of silver and beads. Care of the teeth, painting the eyes, use of antimony, lampblack, *henna*, perfumed powders, sandal-wood, aloes-wood, otto of roses and wearing of flowers added elegance to personality and beauty to life.[112]

Cities in medieval India were few, but they were large and impressive. Foreign visitors like Athnasius Nikitin and Barbosa give a favourable comparison of Indian cities with those of Europe. Cities and towns generally were built on the pattern of the metropolis of Delhi. Shihabuddin Ahmad, the author of *Masalik-ul-Absar* (fourteenth century), writes: "The houses of Delhi are built of stone and brick... The houses are not built more than two storeys high, and often are made of only one."[113] Besides, there must have been hut-like houses of the poor huddled together in congested localities. In the Delhi of the medieval period there was the fort and palace of the Sultan, cantonment area of the troops, quarters for the ministers, the secretaries, the Qazis, Shaikhs and *faqirs*. "In every quarter there were to be found public baths, flour mills, ovens and workmen of all professions."[114] In the villages, the peasants lived in penury. But if there was little to spare, there was enough to live by.[115] There were indoor and outdoor

---

111. Lal, K.S., *The Mughal Harem*, pp.120-123,169.
112. Jafar Sharif, *Islam in India*, pp.301-313.
113. *Masalik-ul-Absar*, trs. E and D, III, p.576.
114. *loc. cit.*
115. Lal, K.S., *Twilight of the Sultanate*, pp.259-60.

games for all to play—chess,[116] backgammon, *pachisi*, *chausar*, dice, cards, kite-flying, pigeon-flying, polo, athletics; cock, quail and partridge fighting; and children's games.[117] Public entertainments, as on the occasion of marriage in the royal family, comprised "triumphal arches, dancing, singing, music, illuminations, rope-dancing and jugglery. The juggler swallowed a sword like water, drinking it as a thirsty man would *sherbet*. He also thrust a knife up his nostril. He mounted little wooden horses and rode upon the air... Those who changed their own appearance practised all kinds of deceit. Sometimes they transformed themselves into angels, sometimes into demons.[118]

Conclusion

There were certain characteristics of the medieval age which have survived to this day among the Muslims. These give an impression that Muslims are still living in medieval times. Therefore, the legacy of the medieval age is medievalism, especially among the Muslims. The days of autocracy, feudalism and religious wars are over, but not so in many Islamic countries. While Christians in the West are becoming modern and secular, the same cannot be said about Muhammadans. In the field of education, the Printing Press in Europe became a potential medium of developing and spreading knowledge. Medieval Indian Muslims were not interested in this development, but even now the teaching in *maktabs* and *madrasas* is no different from what it used to be in the medieval period. In

---

116. "Chess is so characteristic a product of the legacy of Islam that it deserves more than a passing mention. Modern European chess is the direct descendant of an ancient Indian game, adopted by the Persians, handed on by them to the Muslim world, and finally borrowed from Islam by Christian Europe" (Arnold, *Legacy of Islam*, p.32, citing H.J.R. Murray, *A History of Chess*, Oxford, 1913).

117. Jafar Sharif, *Islam in India*, pp.331-338.

118. Amir Khusrau, *Ashiqa*, trs. E and D, III, p. 553.

religious matters freedom of expression and critical analysis is still suppressed as was done in the medieval age. As for example, the translator of the the Japanese edition of Salman Rushdie's controversial novel, *The Satanic Verses*, Professor Hitoshi Igarashi, was found murdered in his University Campus on 12 July 1991. Mr. Gianni Palma, the Italian publisher of its translation, was attacked by an angry Muslim during a news conference in February1990. And Salman Rushdie himself lives in hiding in perpetual scare of assassination because of the *Fatwa*. "The Islamic Government of Pakistan has decided to make death by hanging mandatory for anyone who defames Prophet Muhammad. Previously, a person convicted of blasphemy had a choice of hanging or life imprisonment.[119] No wonder a Muslim like Rafiq Zakaria could write about Muhammad in the only way he did though many chapters of this book "fail to carry conviction... because they are too defensive and apologetic."[120] On the other hand many innocuous books concerning medieval studies or Islam have been banned in India in deference to the wishes of Muslim fundamentalists. Even now Muslim festivals and auspicious days are declared so, as was done in medieval times, after actually sighting the new moon, despite the strides made in the field of Astronomy which tell years in advance when the new moon would appear. In the social sphere, Muslim women are still made to live in *parda*, and polygamy is practised as a matter of personal law if not as a matter of religious duty. In the political field, Muslim rule in medieval India was based on the doctrines of Islam in which discrimination against non-Muslims was central to the faith. Even today Hindu shrines are broken not only in Pakistan and Bangladesh but even in Kashmir as a routine matter.

---

119. Reported in *The Statesman*, New Delhi, 4 August, 1991.
120. Review by G.H. Jansen of Rafiq Zakaria's *Muhammed and the Quran*, Penguin Books, U.K., in *The Times of India*, 11 August, 1991.

It would normally be expected that historical writing on Muslim rule in medieval India would tell the tale of this discrimination and the sufferings of the people, their forced conversions, destruction of their temples, enslavement of their women and children, candidly and repeatedly mentioned by medieval Muslim chroniclers themselves. But curiously enough, in place of bringing such facts to light there is a tendency to gloss over them or even suppress them. Countries which in the middle ages completely converted to Islam and lost links with their original religion and culture, write with a sense of pride about their history as viewed by their Islamic conquerors. But India's is a different story. India could not be Islamized and it did not lose its past cultural anchorage. Naturally, it does not share the sense of glory felt by medieval Muslim chroniclers. But some modern "secularist" writers do praise Muslim rule in glowing terms. All historians are not so brazen or such distortionists. Hence the history of Muslim rule in India is seen through many coloured glasses. It is necessary, therefore, to take a look at the "schools" or "groups" of modern historians writing on the history of medieval India so that a balanced appraisal of the legacy of Muslim rule in India may be made.

Chapter 2

Historiography of Medieval India

"History to be above evasion or dispute, must stand on documents, not opinions."

Lord Acton

There is no dearth of Muslim historical works on medieval India. Muslims have been prolific writers of history. Pre-Islamic traditions of writings were in the form of *Qasidas* or odes and geneologies. When Islam appeared on the scene, historical consciousness became inherent in the faith. The interpretation of the Quran rendered historical knowledge indispensable. The military achievements of the new creed needed to be maintained in chronological order. The retaining of records of treaties between early Islamic states and conquered people implied composition of historical works. Thus, instructive and glorious events and facts beneficial to the community were collected and history writing became a passionate pursuit with the Muslims. The historical literature produced under Arabic inspiration or Persian tradition was replete with religious fervour, and Islamic historiography has remained clerical in nature. The life and teachings of Muhammad, the expansion of Islam under the Caliphs and later achievements of Islam remained the principal contents of *Sirah* (biographies), *Ansab* (geneologies), *Tabaqat* (sketches), *Malfuzat* (memoirs), *Maktubats* (letters) and *Maghazi* (narratives of war and conquest). A secular turn was tried to be given to Islamic history by Ibn Khaldun. But books written by Muslims on world history, Islamic history, general history, dynastic history, or histories of countries and regions, aimed only at delineating the achievements of Islam. History of Islamic conquests is an unfoldment of the divine plan according to Muslim historian Barani.

Contemporary Chronicles

No wonder, a continuous chronological record of the major events of Islamic history in India is available in a series of works ranging from the seventh to the nineteenth century, and covering both dynasties and regions. There are a number of authentic historical works on the conquest of Sind by Muhammad bin Qasim and on the invasions of Mahmud of Ghazni and Muhammad Ghauri. With the establishment of Muslim rule in India official and non-official chroniclers produced works covering all the dynasties of the Central Sultanate of Delhi (C. 1200-1526) as well as the dynasties of the various Muslim kingdoms that arose on the ashes of the Sultanate. Some of the writers, though religious bigots like Ziyauddin Barani and Abdul Qadir Badaoni, were geniuses in their own way. Barani's contemporary Amir Khusrau too wrote historical works doing credit to his versatility. Zahiruddin Muhammad Babur, the founder of the Mughal empire in India (1526), wrote his own memoirs. His daughter Gulbadan Begum followed in his footsteps and produced an autobiographical sketch entitled *Humayun Nama*. Before them Amir Timur wrote his *Malfuzat-i-Timuri* and after them emperor Jahangir (1605-1627) wrote his memoirs under the title of *Tuzuk-i-Jahangiri*. Nowhere else in the history of the world can a ruling dynasty boast of having four royal autobiographers as the Mughals of India. Of regular historical works, of course, there is no dearth. Scholars like Abul Fazl, Abdul Hamid Lahori and Khafi Khan wrote in a style and with the comprehension of Edward Gibbon,

Thomas Babington Macaulay, Theodore Mommsen and Thomas Carlýle. Abdul Hamid Lahori's *Badshah Nama* and Khafi Khan's *Muntakhab-ul-Lubab* were followed by works of Sujan Rai Bhandari, Ishwar Das Nagar, Bhim Sen, Ghulam Husain Salim and Ghulam Husain Tabatabai. These later writers, instead of merely chronicling events also sometimes showed concern for their causation. These are just a few names. There are scores and scores of contemporary Muslim chroniclers of medieval Muslim history. The information provided by them is supplemented by inscriptions carved on the Muslim monuments, both original or converted from Hindu shrines.

This historical material has certain peculiarities. Firstly, medieval Muslim chroniclers wrote with a strong religious bias. To some belief in the *superiority* of the Islamic faith was an obsession, to others it appeared as a patent fact. Therefore, whenever they referred to non-Muslims, they did not fail to use the most uncomplimentary epithets against them. It is sometimes argued that their's was just a style of writing and no serious notice should be taken of their choice of words. But the manner of their writing surely reflects their psyche.

Secondly, Persian chroniclers, by and large, wrote at the command of kings and nobles. As panegyrists, they naturally extolled their patrons and the burden of their theme was that medieval monarchs left no stone unturned to destroy infidelity and establish the power of the people of the Islamic faith. Thus, almost all Persian writers have exaggerated the achievements of their contemporary rulers, especially in the spheres of conquest and crushing of infidelity. Even their acts of cruelty and atrocity have been painted as virtuous deeds.

Thirdly, even those who wrote independently suffered from racial pride and prejudice. While they write little about the life of the common people, their economic problems and social behaviour, they do not tire of portraying their rulers as champions of Islam and destroyers of disbelief. Their words of hate have left a trail of bitter memories which it is difficult to erase. As an example, the language of some contemporary chroniclers may be quoted as samples. Nawasa Shah was a scion of the Hindu Shahiya dynasty and was converted to Islam by Mahmud of Ghazni. Such conversions were common. But return to one's original religion was considered apostasy punishable with death. Al Utbi, the author of *Tarikh-i-Yamini*, writes how Sultan Mahmud punished Nawasa Shah:

"Satan had got the better of Nawasa Shah, for he was again apostatizing towards the pit of plural worship, and had thrown off the slough of Islam, and held conversation with the chiefs of idolatry respecting the casting off the firm rope of religion from his neck. So the Sultan went swifter than the wind in that direction, and made the sword reek with the blood of his enemies. He turned Nawasa Shah out of his government, took possession of all the treasures which he had accumulated, re-assumed the government, and then cut down the harvest of idolatry with the sickle of his sword and spear. After God had granted him this and the previous victory, which were tried witnesses as to his exalted state and proselytism, he returned without difficulty to Ghazna."[1]

Hasan Nizami, author of *Taj-ul-Maasir*, thus wrote about the conquest of Ajmer by Muhammad Ghauri in 1192:

"The victorious army on the right and on the left departed towards Ajmer....When the crow-faced Hindus began to sound their white shells on the backs of the elephants, you would have said that a river of pitch was flowing impetuously down the face of a mountain of blue...The army of Islam was completely victorious, and a hundred thousand grovelling Hindus swiftly departed to the fire of hell... He destroyed (at Ajmer) the pillars and

---

1. E and D, II, p.33.

foundations of the idol temples, and built in their stead mosques and colleges, and the precepts of Islam, and the customs of the law were divulged and established."[2]

And here is Maulana Ziyauddin Barani. He writes: "What is our defence of the faith," cried Sultan Jalaluddin Khalji, "that we suffer these Hindus, who are the greatest enemies of God and of the religion of Mustafa, to live in comfort and do not flow streams of their blood."[3]

And again, Qazi Mughisuddin explained the legal status of the *Zimmis* (non-Muslims) in an Islamic state to Sultan Alauddin:

"The Hindu should pay the taxes with meekness and humility coupled with the utmost respect and free from all reluctance. Should the collector choose to spit in his mouth, he should open the same without hesitation, so that the official may spit into it... The purport of this extreme meekness and humility on his part... is to show the extreme submissiveness incumbent upon the *Zimmis*. God Almighty Himself (in the Quran) commands their complete degradation[4] in as much as these Hindus are the deadliest foes of the true prophet: Mustafa has given orders regarding the slaying, plundering and imprisoning of them, ordaining that they must either follow the true faith, or else be slain or imprisoned, and have all their wealth and property confiscated."[5]

Even after his conversion to Islam, the Hindu remained an object of abhorrence. In his *Fatawa-i-Jahandari*, Barani writes: "Teachers are to be sternly ordered not to thrust precious stones (scriptures) down the throats of dogs (converts). To shopkeepers and the low born they are to teach nothing more than the rules about prayer, fasting,

---

2. E and D, II, pp.214-15.
3. Barani, pp.216-17.
4. The Qazi quoted from the Quran, *Yan yad vaham saghrun*, Sale's trs. p. 152. See also *Ain*, I, p.237, n.1.
5. Barani, pp.290-291.

religious charity and the Hajj pilgrimage along with some
chapters of the Quran...They are to be instructed in nothing more...The low born are capable of only vices..."[6]
Barani is so maliciously vituperative against Hindus that
even many modern Muslim scholars feel embarrassed at
his language and find it difficult to defend him.[7] It must,
however, be remembered that Barani belonged to the
common run of Muslim theologians and chroniclers. He
was a personal friend of men like Amir Khusrau and Ala
Hasan Sijzi and was a disciple of no less a Sufi than Shaikh
Nizamuddin Auliya. He possessed charming manners and
was known for his wit and humour.[8] But in the case of
Hindus, his wit turned into rage. He is copiously quoted
by future chroniclers like Nizamuddin Ahmad, Badaoni
and Farishtah, who all praise him highly. Most of medieval Muslim chroniclers wrote in the idiom of Barani; only
he excelled them all. All medieval chroniclers were scholars of Islamic scriptures and law. They often quote from
these to defend or justify the actions of their kings in relation to their non-Muslim subjects.

It is sometimes argued that in the early years of
Muslim rule Muslim chroniclers did not know much
about the Hindus. Unlike the later historians like Abul
Fazl, Badaoni and Khafi Khan, who tried to understand
the social and cultural milieu of the country, chroniclers
like Hasan Nizami and Ziyauddin Barani do not refer to
the vast majority of the Hindus at all. Only rarely do they
speak about them but then only in derogatory terms,
which also shows their ignorance. But that is not always
true. Even when times had changed in the sixteenth-seventeenth century, the attitude and language of the chroniclers did not change. For instance, Badaoni writes that

---

6. Barani, *Fatawa-i-Jahandari*, pp.49, 98.
7. Nizami, K.A.; *Religion and Politics in India during the Thirteenth Century*, p.317; M. Habib, Introduction to *Fatawa-i-Jahandari*, p. v.
8. Amir Khurd, *Siyar-ul-Auliya*, Urdu trs. Quddusi, pp.472-73.

"His Majesty (Akbar), on hearing...how much the people of the country prized their institutions, commenced to look upon them with affection."[9] Similarly, he respected Brahmans who "surpass other learned men in their treatises on morals".[10] Then, "The Hindus are, of course, indispensable; to them belongs half the army and half the land. Neither the Hindustanis (Indian Muslims) nor the Mughals can point to such grand lords as the Hindus have among themselves."[11] So also said Abul Fazl when he wrote that "the king, in his wisdom, understood the spirit of the age, and shaped his plans accordingly".[12] And yet this very Badaoni sought an interview with Akbar, when the King's troops started marching against Rana Pratap, begging "the privilege of joining the campaign to soak his Islamic beard in Hindu, infidel blood". Akbar was so pleased at this expression of allegiance to his person and to the Islamic idea of *Jihad* that he bestowed a handful of gold coins on Badaoni as a token of his pleasure.[13] This was in 1576. Akbar became more and more rational and tolerant as years passed by. His so-called infallibility decree was passed in 1579, his *Din-i-Ilahi* promulgated in 1582. And yet the language of the chroniclers about the non-Muslims did not change. For, in 1589, Badaoni thus wrote about the two greatest personalities of the Mughal Empire: "In the year 998 (H./1589 C.E.) Raja Todarmal and Raja Bhagwandas who had remained behind at Lahore hastened to the abode of hell and torment (that is, died) and in the lowest pit became food of serpents and scorpions. May Allah scorch them both."[14]

Abdul Qadir Badaoni is not an exception. This style of writing, born out of the ingrained prejudice against non-

9. Badaoni, II, p.258.

10. *Ibid.*, p.257.

11. *Ibid.*, p.258.

12. *Ain*, I, p.2.

13. Smith, *Akbar the Great Mogul*, p.108; Badaoni, II, p.383; C.H.I., IV, p.115.

14. Badaoni, II, p.383.

Muslims, is found in all medieval chronicles in various shades of intensity. They denounce non-Muslims. They write with jubilation about the destruction of their temples, massacre of men, raising towers of skulls and such other "achievements". They also write about the enslavement of women and children, and the licentious life of their captors, their polygamy and concubinage. There is a saying that no man is condemned save by his own mouth. By painting their heroes as cruel and atrocious destroyers of infidelity, Muslim chroniclers themselves have brought odium on the kings and conquerors of their own race and religion, all the while thinking that they were bringing a good name to them.

Contribution of Western scholars

Working on the writings of these chroniclers for almost his whole life-time, Sir Henry Elliot rightly arrived at the conclusion that medieval histories were "recorded by writers who seem to sympathise with no virtues and to abhor no vices", and that medieval rulers were "sunk in sloth and debauchery" and "parasites and eunuchs" revelled in the spoil of plundered provinces.[15] And with the white man's burden on his shoulders he even felt encouraged to hope that these chronicles "will make our native subjects more sensible to the immense advantages accruing to them under the mildness and equity of our rule".[16]

Any other writer's denunciation of the medieval chroniclers or Muslim rulers would have gone unnoticed, for similar statements appear in the writings of many British historians on medieval Indian history but are not taken quite seriously. But no research worker on medieval Indian history could help reading and rereading Elliot's works, so that whether one liked it or not, one could not do without Elliot. Indeed Lanepoole opined: "To realize

---

15. Elliot and Dowson, Vol.I, Preface, pp.xx-xxi.
16. *Ibid.*, p.xii.

Medieval India there is no better way than to dive into the eight volumes of the priceless History of India as Told by its Own Historians... a revelation of Indian life as seen through the eyes of the Persian court annalists."[17] Lanepoole, Pringle Kennedy,[18] and Ishwari Prasad depended primarily on Elliot and Dowson's eight volumes. Dr. Ishwari Prasad went to the extent of saying: "In preparing this volume (*Medieval India*).....I am not so presumptuous as to think that I have improved upon Elphinstone and Lanepoole, to whom I must gratefully acknowledge my indebtedness."[19]

Now, it is a recognised fact that the contribution of European scholars in general and of British historians in particular to the study of Muslim literature and history is invaluable. In the early phase, their main task was to translate medieval historical works from Arabic and Persian into English and other European languages. For example, Majors H.R. Raverty and George S.A. Ranking, two army officers, translated from Persian into English the *Tabqat-i-Nasiri* of Minhaj Siraj (1881) and *Muntakhab-ut-Tawarikh* of Abdul Qadir Badaoni (1889), respectively. Their painstaking diligence and honesty compel our admiration. Similarly, Blochmann, Jarret, Lowe and the Beveridge couple are but a few names from among those who have done stupendous work in this sphere. Elliot and Dowson's great work, in spite of a chorus of disparagement by some modern Indian historians, still holds the field even now for more than a hundred years, against any translations in Urdu or Hindi. Scholars are still learning from and working on Elliot's meritorious volumes. S.H. Hodivala wrote a critical commentary on this work entitled *Studies in Indo-Muslim History* (Bombay, 1939) and

---

17. *Medieval India under Muhammadan Rule* (London,1903), Preface, p.v-vi.
18. *A History of the Great Mughals* (Calcutta,1905,1911).
19. *History of Medieval India* (Allahabad,1925),p.ii.

added a supplement to it in 1957. K.A. Nizami has added some fresh information on the first two volumes of Elliot in addition to Hodivala's commentary in his *On History and Historians of Medieval India* (Delhi,1983). Elliot's original work is still going through repeated reprints. This in itself is indicative of its importance.

Assisted by the translations of Muslim chroniclers by the first generation scholars, foreign and Indian historians embarked on writing on medieval Indian history. Some Indian scholars worked under British historians in England. Many others worked in India utilizing research techniques provided by the West. Indian historians owe a lot to the pioneering researches of British historians, whatever may be said about their merits and shortcomings. The first comprehensive history of India entitled *History of British India* (1818), was attempted by James Mill. He believed in the superiority of the British people over the Indians. But there were other scholars thinking on different lines. The work of Sir William Jones and other European scholars unearthed a volume of evidence on India's glorious past. However, despite the European discovery of India's past greatness and well-developed civilization, the British, having become the paramount power in India, remained generally convinced of their own superiority over Indians, and continued to feed themselves on Mill and Macaulay. They held Indians and their literature in low esteem, insisting on accepting the degenerate conditions of the eighteenth century Muslim India as its normal condition. Seeley declared that nothing as great was ever done by Englishmen as the conquest of India, which was "not in the ordinary sense a conquest at all", and which he put on par "with the Greek conquest of the East", pointing out that the British who had a "higher and more vigorous civilization than the native races" founded the Indian Empire "partly out of a philanthropic desire to put an end to enormous evils" of the "robber-states of India". There is no need to get ruffled about such assertions. Most of the conclusions of British historians about Muslim history do find confirmation in the description of cruelties perpetrated by the Muslims in their own chronicles as well as their reiteration in indigenous source materials in Hindi, Sanskrit, Rajasthani and Marathi. Hindu source materials are few. They are also not as informative as the Muslim chronicles. But curiously enough the meagre Hindu and the voluminous Muslim source-materials corroborate and supplement rather than contradict each other about the behaviour of the Muslim regime.

Paucity of Hindu Source-materials

Professor D.P.Singhal asserts that, contrary to the general belief, Indians in ancient times did not neglect the important discipline of historiography. On the contrary, they were good writers of history. He states: "Ancient India did not produce a Thucydides, but there is considerable evidence to suggest that every important Hindu court maintained archives and geneologies of its rulers. And Kalhana's *Rajatarangini*, written in twelfth century Kashmir, is a remarkable piece of historical literature. Despite his lapses into myths and legends, Kalhana had an unbiased approach to historical facts and history writing. He held that a true historian, while recounting the events of the past, must discard love (*raga*) and hatred (*dvesha*). Indeed, his well-developed concept of history and the technique of historical investigation have given rise to some speculation that there existed at the time a powerful tradition of historiography in which Kalhana must have received his training."[20]

If that was so, why is there hopeless deficiency of Hindu historical writings during the medieval period? In

---

20. Singhal, D.P. 'Battle for the Past' in *Problems of Indian Historiography*, Proceedings of the Indian History and Culture Society, Ed. Devahuti, D.K. Publishers, Delhi, 1979.

this regard, James Tod, the famous author of the monumental classic *Annals and Antiquities of Rajasthan*, has this
to say: 1. that ancient Hindus were good historiographers;
2. that medieval times were not propitious for them for
writing history; and 3. that much of the Hindu, Jain and
Buddhist literature was destroyed by Muslim invaders
and rulers. He needs to be quoted at length. "Those who
expect," writes he, "from a people like the Hindus a spe-
cies of composition of precisely the same character as the
historical works of Greece and Rome commit the very
gregarious error of overlooking the peculiarities which
distinguish the natives of India from all other races, and
which strongly discriminate their intellectual productions
of every kind from those of the West. Their philosophy,
their poetry, their architecture, are marked with traits of
originality; and the same may be expected to pervade their
history, which, like the arts enumerated, took a character
from its intimate association with the religion of the
people. It must be recollected, moreover,...that the chronicles of all the polished nations of Europe, were, at a much
more recent date, as crude, as wild, and as barren, as those
of the early Rajputs." He adds, "My own animadversions
upon the defective condition of the annals of Rajwarra
have more than once been checked by a very just remark:
'When our princes were in exile, driven from hold to hold,
and compelled to dwell in the clefts of the mountains,
often doubtful whether they would not be forced to abandon the very meal preparing for them, was that a time to
think of historical records?' "[21] "If we consider the political
changes and convulsions which have happened in Hindustan since Mahmood's invasion, and the intolerant
bigotry of many of his successors, we shall be able to
account for the paucity of its national works on history,
without being driven to the improbable conclusion, that

21. James Tod, *Annals and Antiquities of Rajasthan*, Routledge and
Kegan Paul (London,1829,1957), 2 vols., I, Introduction, pp. xiv-xv.

the Hindus were ignorant of an art which has been cultivated in other countries from almost the earliest ages. Is it
to be imagined that a nation so highly civilized as the
Hindus, amongst whom the exact sciences flourished in
perfection, by whom the fine arts, architecture, sculpture,
poetry, music, were not only cultivated, but taught and
defined by the nicest and most elaborate rules, were totally unacquainted with the simple art of recording the
events of their history, the character of their princes and
the acts of their reigns?" The fact appears to be that "After
eight centuries of galling subjection to conquerors totally
ignorant of the classical language of the Hindus; after
every capital city had been repatedly stormed and sacked
by barbarous, bigoted, and exasperated foes; it is too much
to expect that the literature of the country should not have
sustained, in common with other interests, irretrievable
losses."[22]

Indians as a whole today exhibit keen interest in history. This interest has not sprung all of a sudden. It has
always been there. To the uneducated common man it has
come down in legends, stories, mythologies and anecdotes. There is no dearth of professional historians. The
works produced by Jadunath Sarkar, G.S. Sardesai, G.H.
Ojha, Tara Chand, Mohammad Habib and R.C. Majumdar
apart, the sustained assiduity shown by hundreds of other
writers of history in modern times is proof enough of the
fact that the Indian mind is not devoid but indeed keenly
concerned with its history and culture. If it did not produce historical works in medieval times to the extent
expected, the reasons are obvious; it is not necessary to
repeat what has been said above. But a few words from

---

22. *Ibid.*, p.xiv. For stray references to works destroyed and Hindus
forgetting how to read their ancient scripts, see Minhaj, *Tabqat-i-Nasiri*, I,
p.552; Afif, p.333; Thomas, Edward, *Chronicles of the Pathan Kings of Delhi*,
pp.292-93 and Carr Stephen, *Archaeology and Monumental Remains of Delhi*,
pp. 130, 137-38.

Jadunath Sarkar may be reproduced. He says that "when a class of men is publicly depressed and harassed (as under Muslim rule)... it merely contents itself with dragging on an animal existence. The Hindus could not be expected to produce the utmost of what they were capable... Amidst such social conditions, the human hand and the human mind cannot achieve their best; the human soul cannot soar to its highest pitch."[23] The "barrenness of the Hindu intellect" is just one more bestowal of inheritance of Muslim rule in India.

There is no doubt that whatever Hindu historical literature was extant, was systematically destroyed by Muslim invaders and rulers. It is well known that pre-Islamic literature was destroyed by the Arabs in their homeland as they considered it belonging to the *Jahiliya*. It is not surprising therefore that many Muslim heroes in their hour of victory just set libraries to flames. They razed shrines to the ground, burnt books housed in them and killed Brahman, Jain and Buddhist monks who could read them. The narrative of Ikhtiyaruddin Bakhtiyar Khalji's campaigns in Bihar is full of such exploits. Only one instance may be cited on the destruction of the works of the 'enemy'. Kabiruddin was the court historian of Sultan Alauddin Khalji (1296-1316) and wrote a history of the latter's reign in several volumes. But his work entitled the *Fatehnama* is not traceable now and a very important source of Alauddin's reign has been lost. It is believed that the *Fatehnama* contained many critical and uncomplimentary comments on the Mongol invaders whom the Sultan repeatedly defeated, so that when the Mughal dynasty was established in India, this work was destroyed.[24] Similarly, only one instance may be given to show how the Indians tried to protect their books from marauding armies. In the Jinabhadra-Sureshwar temple located in the

23. Sarkar, *A Short History of Aurangzeb*, p.153.
24. Lal, *History of the Khaljis*, p.355.

Jaisalmer Fort in Rajasthan, I saw a library of Jain manuscripts called Jain Gyan Bhandar located in a basement, 5
storeys deep down, each storey negotiated with the help
of a staircase, and in each floor manuscripts are stacked.
The top of the cell is covered with a large stone slab
indistinguishable from other slabs of the flooring to delude the invader. Such basement libraries set up for security against vandalism are also found in other places in
Rajasthan.

Bards and Charans were the historians of the Rajputs.
They indulged in gross exaggeration while praising their
patrons. But the beauty of their work lies in the fact that
these chroniclers also dared utter truths, sometimes most
unpalatable to their masters. Only a few of their works
have survived and have been rescued from princely states
which were generally friendly to the Mughals and therefore escaped repeated sackings. From Chand Bardai's
Prithviraj Raso to the accounts by the Brahmans of the
endowments of the temples, from the disputations of the
Jains to *Kalpadruma*, a diary kept by Raja Jai Singh of Datia
"in which he noted every event," Tod was able to get lot
of historical material. Padmanabh's *Kanhadde-Prabandh*,
Bhandu Vyas' *Hammirayan*, Nainsi's *Khyat*, Vidyapati's
Purush Pariksha and *Kirtilata* and Kaviraj Shymaldas'*Vir
Vinod*, are regular and not so regular historical works of
Hindus through the centuries.[25] When the Marathas
mounted national resistance agaalts the Mughal empire
there was so much to write about, and they wrote excellent histories. And all these works corroborate Muslim
chronicles. Persian writers boast of the achievements of
their conquerers secured through brute force. The Indians
confirm the facts and denounce their atrocities.[26]

---

25. See Bibliography, Sanskrit and Hindi Works, in K.S. Lal, *History of
the Khaljis*, pp.374-75.

26. For example, see the comparable account of terror-tactics of the
Muslim army as described by Persian chroniclers and Vidyapati in *Kirtilata*
in K.S.Lal, "Striking power of the Army of the Sultanate" in the *Journal of
Indian History*, Trivandrum. Vol.LV, Pt.III, December 1977, pp.85-110.

Modern Indian Historiography

On the basis of chronicles available in Persian, Arabic and Hindi, but mainly in Persian, European and Indian writers set about reconstructing the history of medieval India. The study of medieval Indian history in modern times may be said to have begun about a century ago when, in the eighteen-sixties, and under the patronage of the Asiatic Society of Bengal, the Indo-Persian chronicles of the medieval period began to be printed in the Bibliotheca Indica Series, and in 1867-77 appeared Elliot and Dowson's *History of India as Told by its Own Historians*. Elliot's work contained in eight fairly bulky volumes translations of extracts from most of the then known Persian chronicles, and soon became indispensable for the researcher on medieval history. The original Persian works were so eulogistic of the cruelties of Muslim conquerors and rulers that the great painstaking scholar Elliot and his followers were perforce constrained to be critical of medieval Indian rulers, and this school held the ground for quite some time.

Soon other writers, who would not agree with this criticism, or who were determined to refute it, appeared on the scene, and the situation so created divided the modern Indian writers on medieval history into "objective" and pro-Muslim or "apologist" historians.

In the beginning, medieval historiography remained confined to political history or biography writing. Then, gradually, the non-political features of medieval India like the cultural influence of Muslim rule, Islam as a civilisation, literature and art, social and economic life, began to attract the attention of scholars. That history is not to be merely a narrative of kings and wars, but has to be a story of the people as well, has now become well recognized. But this concept has taken time to grow. There is now the conviction that history is a form of critical inquiry into the past and not merely a repetition of testimony and author-

ity. The modern historiographer of Medieval History tries
to probe into the ideas behind human actions performed
in the past. These motives they find, unlike the medieval
historiographer, not only in religious, but in political,
economic, social and other causes and try to discover a
relationship between them. And lastly, modern historiography applies the critical apparatus of footnotes, appendi-
ces, bibliography, and sometimes maps also.

However, when medieval Indian historiography was
making good headway, India was partitioned into two.
Partition of the country has been tragic in many ways, but
no branch of study has been perhaps so much directly and
vitally affected by it as the historiography on medieval
India. Many distinguished scholars conversant with classical Persian went over to Pakistan and history has suffered
from their migration. This can be easily seen in the number of students offering Medieval History in colleges and
universities and in articles published in the historical jour-
nals of the country or papers read at various conferences
— as compared with the Ancient or the Modern periods of
Indian history. At the Trivandrum session of the Indian
History Congress (1958) a seminar was held to probe into
the causes of this decline and suggest means of checking
it, but nothing much seems to have been done to improve
the position. On the other hand, once in a while one even
comes across the puerile argument: Where is the necessity
of continuing with medieval historical studies in India
after the creation of Pakistan?

But the worst effect of partition has been that 1947 has
tended to produce two historiographies based on territorial differentiation. Comparing the works of Ahmad Ali
entitled *Culture of Pakistan* with Richard Symond's *The
Making of Pakistan* (London, 1950) on the one hand and
Humayun Kabir's *Indian Heritage* and Abid Hussain's
National Culture of India on the other, W. Cantwell Smith
says that the Pakistani historian "flees from Indian-ness,

and would extra-territorialize even Mohenjodaro (linking the Indus-valley civilisation with Sumer and Elam) as well as the Taj (yet though left in India, the monuments and buildings of Agra and Delhi are entirely outside the Indian tradition and are an essential heritage and part of Pakistani culture, — p.205), and omits from consideration altogether quite major matters less easily disposed of (such as Asoka's reign, and the whole of East Pakistan)....." The Indians "on the other hand seek for the meaning of Muslim culture within the complex of Indian 'unity in diversity' as an integral component."[27] So, after 1947, besides the 'objective' and 'apologist', 'Secular' and 'Communal' versions, there are the Pakistani and Indian versions of medieval Indian history.[28]

Today, besides individual workers in many places, some universities in particular, like the Aligarh Muslim University, are specially devoted to medieval Indian historiography. Aligarh has funds, facilities and professoriate for medieval history, and all these have given her advantage over other universities in devoting itself mainly to medieval Indian historical studies. The *Medieval India Quarterly*, the various texts and books edited and published under Aligarh Historical Series and the studies on Sufi saints may be recounted with a feeling of satisfaction.

However, the revised edition of the second volume of Elliot and Dowson's *History of India as Told by its Own Historians* published from Aligarh contains a long introduction on dialectical materialism and the materialistic interpretation of history by Mohammed Habib. The idea has caught on and there is a clear Marxist influence on the Aligarh school which has prompted Peter Hardy to say

27. Philips, *Historians of India, Pakistan and Ceylon*, pp.322-23.
28. As an illustration see Arvind Sharma, 'The Arab invasion of Sind: a study in divergent perspectives' in *Historical and Political Perspectives (India and Pakistan)* ed. Devahuti, Indian History and Culture Society, Books & Books, New Delhi, 1982, pp.193-200.

that "the significant feature of Professor Habib's Marxist interpretation of medieval Indian history is not that Marxism has absorbed Islam but that Islam has absorbed Marxism."[29]

Marxist History

Today, Marxist historians and writers are well entrenched in academic and media sectors. Their rise has been encouraged by the Indian government. After Partition, Pakistan declared itself a theocratic state as is natural with Muslim nations. India opted to remain a secular country. This situation was very convenient to the special brand of Indian secularists; they could not become nationalist, so they turned Marxist.

What are the salient features of Marxist history in India? To understand this we have to consult Marx himself. Between 1853 and 1857, Marx wrote twenty-three articles on India, and Engels eight, bearing on British rule in India. Marx took the "Europe-centred" view of India's past. He shared all his assumptions on India with British rulers. Britain was to lay the foundations of the material progress in India on the annihilation of the traditional Indian society. He wrote in 1853:

"Indian society has no history at all, at least no known history. What we call its history, is but the history of the successive intruders who founded their empires on the passive basis of that unresisting and unchanging society. The question, therefore, is not whether the English had a right to conquer India, but whether we are to prefer India conquered by the Turk, by the Persian, by the Russian, to India conquered by the Briton." England had to fulfil a double mission in India: One destructive, and the other regenerating — the annihilation of old Asiatic society, and the laying of the material foundations of Western

---

29. Peter Hardy in Philips, *Historians of India, Pakistan and Ceylon*, p.309.

society in Asia. Arabs, Turks, Tartars, Moguls, who had successively overrun India, soon became Hinduised, the barbarian conquerors being, by an eternal law of history, themselves conquered by the superior civilization of their subjects. According to him the British were the first conquerors who were superior, and therefore inaccessible to Hindu civilization. They destroyed it by breaking up the native communities, by uprooting the native industry, and by levelling all that was great and elevated in the native society. The historic pages of their rule in India, report hardly anything beyond that destruction. "The work of regeneration hardly transpires through a heap of ruins. Nevertheless, it has begun."[30] Indian Marxists accept this thesis and fully subscribe to it.

Harold Laski could write in 1927 that "the effort to read the problem of India in the set terms of Marxism is rather an exercise in ingenuity than a serious intellectual contribution to socialist advance."[31] In the early stages there was no concerted effort by Indian historians to interpret Indian history in Marxist terms. M.N. Roy attempted to give a Marxist interpretation of the Indian National Movement,[32] but it was not until 1940 that a serious Marxist history was produced by R.Palme Dutt entitled *India Today.* D.D. Kosambi's *An Introduction to the Study of Indian History* (1956), is regarded as a substantial Marxist interpretation of Indian history from the earliest times to the rise of British power in India. During the post-independence period, there has been a tremendous proliferation of Marxism in Indian universities. It appeared to be a fashionable creed, as compared with Gandhism which appeared to be traditional and somewhat unmodern.

30. Karl Marx, "The Future Results of British Rule in India", vide *The Newyork Daily Tribune*, 22 July 1853, cited by D.P. Singhal in his Presidential Address to the Indian History and Culture Society, 1981, Proceedings, p.155.
31. H. Laski, *Communism* (London, 1927), p.194.
32. In his *India in Transition*, 1922.

Where the Marxist, Imperialist, 'Secularist' and Muslim communalist historians concur is in their attitude towards Hindu culture. Marxists, as did Marx himself, regard culture as bourgeois and anti-revolutionary. Culture, therefore, had to be denounced, including religion, God and morals, as an obstacle to proletarian change. Culture in the Indian context meant mainly Hindu religion and heritage. Hindu culture had, therefore, to be derided and held as the cáuse of India's predicament. The Muslim communalists, who openly believed in religious distinctions and were naturally convinced of their own cultural superiority over that of the others, looked upon Hindu culture with disfavour. While the Marxists denounce in unmistakable terms imperial rule and imperialist historians, they join hands with them to demolish nationalist historians whose nationalism carried with it pride in their cultural past. They also denounce objective historians who, unlike the Marxists, do not seek to employ history as an instrument of change. Marxist attacks on culture also aim at hitting at the roots and source of inspiration of nationalism.

Marxist history also lays claim to be counted as objective history. The phrase 'objective history' is very attractive, but sometimes under this appellation, all shadows are removed and medieval times are painted in such bright colours by Marxist historians as to shame even the modern age. At others, modern ideas of class-conflict, labour-exploitation and all that goes with it, and many other modern phenomena and problems are projected backwards to fit in the medieval social structure. The word 'religion' is tried to be eschewed because it is thought to be associated with bitter memories. If the medieval chronicler cries out 'Jihad', it is just not heard: but if he cries aloud persistently, it is claimed that he never meant it. The Marxists or leftists read into history what they think history should be. All this makes the content of Marxist history dubious, needing it to be buttressed by brochures, statements and booklets under a number of signatures. Often, Marxist writers work in groups, mutually admiring each other's discoveries. The need for this also arises from the fact that Muslim rule in India remained Islamic basically, with firm belief in the superiority and propagation of Islam as an article of faith.[33] Atrocities committed by its followers in the name of Islam are often very graphically described by Muslim chroniclers as acts of piety and grace. This aspect has produced an unfortunate character in the Muslim civilization as a whole. It is in the combination of the spiritual and temporal powers, in the confusion of moral and physical authority, that the tyranny which seems inherent in this civilization originated. Its history is soaked in blood of the supposed enemies of Islam. But all this is denied by Marxists who always try to cover up the black spots of Muslim rule with thick coats of whitewash. Sometimes, this tryanny is sought to be condoned by fundamentalists on the plea that the ruler was only performing his duty, or denied by declaring that Muslim polity was not religion-oriented. But condonation or denial has not saved the Muslim regime from the harm its nature has brought to bear upon the reputation of the community and the history of the country.[34]

With regard to medieval Indian history the Marxist historians unwillingly tow the line of British writers of whom they are otherwise critical. The main interest of the British was to write a history which justified their conquest of India. They claimed that their rule in India was nothing new and that they were legitimate successors of former conquerors like Arabs, Turks and Mughals. The Mughals were represented as empire builders, who united India and gave it law and order, peace and stability.

33. T.W. Arnold, *The Legacy of Islam*, p.viii.
34. Cf K.S. Lal., *Early Muslims in India* (New Delhi,1984), pp.92-93.

Similar was the mission of the British, they said. Facts, sometimes, compelled the British historians to speak of the atrocities and vandalism of Muslim rule but this did not deter them from upholding its authority. Thus British historians, while trying to legitimise their own rule, also gave legitimacy to their Muslim predecessors. But in the larger national conciousness both were considered as foreign impositions and constantly resisted. This resistance the British historians presented as "revolts" and "rebellions" against the "legitimate" Imperial authority. Marxist and communal historians apply these epithets in the case of Muslim rule, as also did the medieval chroniclers. Like the latter, the protestations of Marxist historians about Muslim rule in India are lofty, but their conclusions are grotesque. Such dichotomy is not new. Even a fourteenth century medieval historian Ziyauddin Barani suffered from such contradiction. He becomes lyrical when describing the benefits derived from the study of history,[35] but turns a die-hard fundamentalist when he actually writes it.[36]

On the basis of the study of medieval chronicles, scholars like Ishwari Prasad and A.L. Srivastava arrived at the conclusion that the medieval age was a period of unmitigated suffering for the Hindus; to others like I.H. Qureshi and S.M. Jaffar it was an age of all-round progress and prosperity. Writing about the Sultanate period, Ishwari Prasad says: "There was persecution, partly religious and partly political, and a stubborn resistance was offered by the Hindus... The state imposed great disabilities upon the non-Muslims... Instances are not rare in which the non-Muslims were treated with great severity... The practice of their religious rites even with the slightest publicity was not allowed, and cases are on record of men who lost their lives for doing so."[37] According to A.L. Srivastava the

35. Barani, *Tarikh*, pp.10-13.
36. *Ibid.*, eg. pp.216, 290-91.
37. *History of Medieval India* (Allahabad, 1940 Edition), pp.509-513.

Sultanate of Delhi "was an Islamic State, pure and simple, and gave no religious toleration to the Hindus... and indulged in stifling persecution."[38] About the Mughal times his conclusion is that "barring the one short generation under Akbar when the moral and material condition of the people was on the whole good, the vast majority of our population during 1526-1803 led a miserable life."[39] On the other hand, I.H. Qureshi had the mendacity to declare that "The Hindu population was better off under the Muslims than under the Hindu tributaries or independent rulers. Their financial burden was lighter than it had been for some centuries in pre-Muslim days... Nor was the Hindu despised socially. The Muslims, generally speaking, have always been remarkably free from religious prejudice."[40]

Manipulated History

"History, to be above evasion or dispute," says Lord Acton, "must stand on documents, not opinions."[41] But history written by people like Qureshi and Jaffar suited the Nehruvian establishment for achieving what it described as national integration. Towards that end many pseudo-secularist and Marxist historians joined the cadre of such writers.

And funny though it may sound it was decided to falsify history to please the Muslims and draw them into the national mainstream. Guidelines for rewriting history were prepared by the National Council of Educational Research and Training (NCERT), and a summary of the same appeared in *Indian Express* datelined New Delhi, 17 January 1982. The idea was "to weed out undesirable textbooks (in History and languages) and remove matter which is prejudicial to national integration and unity and

---

38. *The Mughal Empire* (Agra, 1964), p.568.
39. *Ibid.*, p.571.
40. *The Administration of the Sultanate of Delhi*, pp.207-13.
41. Acton, *The Study of History*, Macmillan & Co. (London, 1905), p.45.

which does not promote social cohesion... Twenty states and three Union Territories have started the work of evaluation according to guidelines, prepared by NCERT."

The West Bengal Board of Secondary Education issued a notification dated 28 April 1989 addressed to schools and publishers suggesting some 'corrections' in the teaching and writing of 'Muslim rule in India' — like the real objective of Mahmud Ghaznavi's attack on Somnath, Aurangzeb's policy towards the Hindus, and so on. These guidelines specifically say: "Muslim rule should not attract any criticism. Destruction of temples by Muslim invaders and rulers should not be mentioned." One instruction in the West Bengal circular is that "schools and publishers have been asked to ignore and delete mention of forcible conversions to Islam." The notification, says the *Statesman* of 21 May 1989, was objected to in many quarters. "A row has been kicked up by some academicians who feel that the 'corrections' are unjustified and politically motivated..." Another group feels that the corrections are "justified".

This experiment with untruth was being attempted since the 30's-40's by Muslim and Communist historians. After Independence, they gradually gained strength in university departments. By its policy the Nehruvian state just permitted itself to be hijacked by the so-called progressive, secular and Marxist historians. Communism never struck roots in India, a land of great and deep philosophy. But some Communists, always suspect in the eyes of the majority of the Indian people, did help in the division of the country. After partition they were joined by those communal elements which could never be nationalist, but they also did not want to be dubbed as communalist, and so became communist. The impressive slogan of secularism came handy to them and in place of educating the divisionists, they read repeated lectures to Hindus on secularism. Armed with money and instructions from the

Ministry of Education, the National Council of Educational Research, University Grants Commission, Indian Council of Historical Research, secular and Stalinist historians began to produce manipulated and often manifestly false school and college text-books of history and social studies in the Union Territories and States of India. This has gone on for years.

But the exercise has proved counter-productive. In place of encouraging national integration, distorted history has only helped increase communalism. For one thing, it has provided a welcome opportunity to the vested interests to assert that no temples were broken, no mosques raised on their sites and no forcible conversions to Islam were made. If people are truthfully educated about the circumstances of their conversion,[42] they would not behave as they are prone to at present. On the one hand, the government through the Department of Archaeology preserves monuments the originals of which were destroyed by Islamic vandalism, and on the other, history text-books are directed to say that no shrines were destroyed. Students are taught one thing in the class rooms through their text-books, while they see something else when they go on excursions to historical monuments. At places like Qutb Minar and Quwwat-ul-Islam mosque they see that "the construction is all Hindu and destruction all Muslim". History books are not written only in India; these are written in neighbouring countries also, and what is tried to be concealed here for the sake of national integration, is mentioned with pride in the neighbouring Muslim countries. Scholars in Europe are also working on Indian history and untruths uttered by India's secular and progressive historians are easily countered.

One thing that arouses unneccesary controversy is about the destruction and desecration of temples and

---

42. For example, see Lal, K.S., *Indian Muslims : Who Are They* (New Delhi, 1990).

construction of mosques in their stead. Muslim chroniclers repeatedly make mention of success of conquerors and rulers in this sphere. The chroniclers with first hand knowledge wrote that their patrons did so with the avowed object of spreading Islam and degrading infidelity in Hindustan. So Hajjaj instructed Muhammd bin Qasim. So Mahmud of Ghazni promised the Khalifa. Amir Timur (Tamerlane) also proclaimed the same intention. Still it is asserted by some writers that temples were attacked for obtaining their wealth and not because of religious fervour. The declaration of Mahmud of Ghazni in this regard is conclusive. It is related that when Mahmud was breaking the idol of Somnath, the Brahmans offered him immense wealth if he spared the idol which was revered by millions; but the champion of Islam replied with disdain that he did not want his name to go down to posterity as Mahmud the idol-seller (*but farosh*) instead of Mahmud the breaker-of-idols (*but shikan*).[43] All appeals for pity, all offers of wealth, fell on deaf ears. He smashed the sacred *lingam* into pieces and as an act of piety sent two of its pieces to be thrown at the steps of the Jama Masjid at Ghazni and two others to Mecca and Medina to be trampled upon on their main streets.[44] Alberuni, the contemporary witness writes: "The image was destroyed by Prince Mahmud in 416 H. (1026 C.E.). He ordered the upper part to be broken and the remainder to be transported to his residence, Ghaznin, with all its coverings and trappings of gold, jewels and embroidered garments. Part of it has been thrown into the hippodrome of the town, together with the *Cakraswamin*, an idol of bronze that had been brought from Thaneshar. Another part of the idol from Somnath lies before the door of the mosque of Ghaznin, on which people rub their feet to clean them from dirt and wet."[45]

43. Farishtah, I, p.33.
44. *loc. cit.*
45. Alberuni, II, p.103. Also I, p.117 for *Cakraswamin*.

So, the consideration was desecration, primarily. Mahmud had come to spread Islam and for this undertaking was bestowed the title of Yamin-ud-daula (Right hand of the Caliph) and Amir-ul-Millat (Chief of the Muslim Community) by the Khalifa al Qadir Billah.[46] No wonder, in the estimation of his Muslim contemporaries — historians, poets, and writers — the exploits of Mahmud as a hero of Islam in India were simply marvellous and their encomiums endless.[47] Of course, invaders like Mahmud also collected lot of loot from wherever they could get, including the precious metals of which idols were made or the jewellery with which they were adorned. The *Rasmala* narrates that after the destruction of Somnath, Mahmud acquired possession of diamonds, rubies and pearls of incalculable value.[48] But spoliation of temple was not the sole or principal aim. If acquisition of wealth was the motive for attacking a temple, where was the need to raze it to the ground, dig its very foundations, desecrate and break the idols, carry the idols hundreds of miles on carts or camels, and to throw them at the stairs of the mosques for the faithful to trample upon, or to distribute their pieces to butchers as meat-weights. For this is exactly what was done not only by invaders but even by rulers, not only during wars but also in times of peace, throughout the medieval period from Mahmud of Ghazni to Aurangzeb.[49] We have seen what Mahmud of Ghazni did to the idols of *Chakraswamin* and Somnath. Let us see what Aurangzeb did to the temple of Keshav Rai at Mathura

---

46. Aziz Ahmad, *Studies in Islamic Culture*, p.5.

47. For detailed references see Bosworth, *The Ghaznavids*, p.50. For praise of Mahmud by modern writers, M. Nazim, *The Life and Times of Sultan Mahmud of Ghazna* and M. Habib, *Sultan Mahmud of Ghaznin*.

48. Forbes, *Rasmala*, I, p.77.

49. Hasan Nizami, *Taj-ul-Maasir*, E and D, II, p.219; Abdulla, *Tarikh-i-Daudi*, p.39; Ahmad Yadgar, *Tarikh-i-Salatin-i-Afghana*, p.47; Rizqullah, *Waqiat-i-Mushtaqi*, fol. 31b; *Tuzuk-i-Jahangiri*, II, pp.185-86, 223; Lahori, I, p.452, II, p. 58; Kamboh, *Amal-i-Salih*, I, p.522, II, p.41; Khafi Khan, I, p. 472.

built at a cost of rupees thirty-three lakhs by Raja Bir Singh Bundela. The author of *Maasir-i-Alamgiri* writes : "In this month of Ramzan (January 1670), the religious-minded Emperor ordered the demolition of the temple at Mathura. In a short time by the great exertions of his officers the destruction of this great centre of infidelity was accomplished... A grand mosque was built on its site at a vast expenditure... The idols, large and small, set with costly jewels which had been set up in the temple were brought to Agra and buried under the steps of the mosque of Begum Sahib (Jahanara's mosque) in order to be continually trodden upon. The name of Mathura was changed to Islamabad..."[50]

In brief, temples were destroyed not for their "hoarded wealth" as some historians propagate, but for humiliating and persecuting the non-Muslims. Destruction of religious shrines of the vanquished formed part of a larger policy of persecution practised in lands under Muslim occupation in and outside India. This policy of oppression was meant to keep down the people, disarm them culturally and spiritually, destroy their self-respect and remind them that they were *Zimmis*, an inferior breed. Thousands of pilgrims who visit Mathura or walk past the site of Vishvanath temple and Gyanvapi Masjid in Varanasi everyday, are reminded of Mughal vandalism and disregard for Hindu sensivities by Muslim rulers.

And yet some writers delude themselves with the mistaken belief that they can change their country's history by distorting it, or brain-wash generations of young students, or humour fundamentalist politicians through such unethical exercise. To judge what happened in the past in the context of today's cultural milieu and consciously hide the truth, is playing politics with history. Let history be ac-

---

50. Saqi Mustaad Khan, *Maasir-i-Alamgiri*, pp.95-96; p.175 for idols from temples of Jodhpur. Also Manucci, II, p.116. *Mirat-i-Ahmadi* gives detailed account of temple destruction by Aurangzeb.

cepted as a matter of fact without putting it to any subjective interpretations. Yesterday's villains cannot be made today's heroes, or, inversely, yesterday's Islamic heroes cannot be made into robbers ransacking temples just for treasures. Nor can the medieval monuments be declared as national monuments as suggested in some naive 'secularist' quarters. They represent vandalism. No true Indian can be proud of such desecrated and indecorous evidence of 'composite culture'. "History," says Froude, "does teach that right and wrong are real distinctions. Opinions alter, manners change, creeds rise and fall, but the moral law is written on the tablets of humanity."[51] It is nobody's business to change this moral law and prove the wrongs of the medieval period to be right today by having recourse to misrepresentation of history. Manipulation in the writing of medieval Indian history by some modern writers is the worst legacy of Muslim rule in India.

Islamic Scriptures as Source-materials

The best way to understand the content and spirit of Muslim rule in India and to assess the hollowness of manipulated history is by going through Muslim scriptures besides of course faithfully perusing Muslim historical literature in Arabic and Persian. All medieval chroniclers and historians were scholars of Islamic literature and law. Many of these Ulama were even advisers of kings in matters religious and political. In their writings they often quote from the Quran and Hadis to vindicate the actions of their conquerors and kings. Very often they quote from or use the very idiom of Islamic religious texts in their chronicles. Muslim invaders, conquerors and rulers also repeatedly assert that they worked according to the dictates of the Shara and Sunna to suberve the interests of Islam. Therefore to understand the true nature of Muslim

---

51. Inaugural lecture at St. Andrews, 1869, cited in Acton, *The Study of History*, p.45.

rule and history it is necessary to have at least an elemen-
tary knowldege of the religion and scriptures of Islam.

The religion and theology of Islam are based on four
great works — (1) The Quran, (2) the Hadis, (3) the *Sirat-
un-Nabi* or the Biography of Muhammad, and (4) the *Shariat* or Islamic law as elaborated in the *Hidaya*. The word
'Quran' literally means recitation, lecture or discourse.
Muslims consider it to be the word of God conveyed to his
prophet Muhammad through the angel Gabriel. "The first,
final and only canonized version of the Koran was collected nineteen years after the death of Muhammad ('from
ribs of palm-leaves and tablets of white stone and from the
breasts of men')when it was seen that the memorizers of
the Koran were becoming extinct through the battles that
were decimating the ranks of the believers..."[52] The religion of Quran comes nearer to Judaism of the Old Testament as well as the Christianity of the New Testament.[53]
The Quran, the Book of Allah, is treated with unbound
reverence by the Muslims. "Its 6,239 verses, its 77,934
words, even its 323,621 letters have since been painstak-
ingly counted."[54] The book is not only heart of a religion,
but it is still "considered by one-eighth of mankind as the
embodiment of all science, wisdom and theology".[55] Because of the dearth of efficacious writing material, written
copies of Quran would have taken time to make, but it
does seem to have been available by the middle of the
eighth century.[56]

Every Muslim chronicler of medieval India had mas-
tered the Quran. For an *Alim* and a *Maulana* it was the first
must among the works he studied. It is not surprising

---

52. P.K. Hitti, *The Arabs* (London, 1948), pp.32-33.

53. *Ibid.*, pp.24, 33.

54. *Ibid.*, p.33.

55. *Ibid.*, p.31.

56. Patricia Crone and Michael Cook, *Hagarism: The Making of the
Islamic World,* Cambridge University Press, 1977, paperback, 1980, p.3, also
p.159.

therefore that its *surahs* (chapters) and *ayats* (verses) are sometimes quoted in historical works and its phraseology freely used. A study of the Quran by a scholar of medieval Indian history will be helpful to him in appraising the achievements and spirit of Muslim rule in India. There are many good translations of the Quran in English; a summary translation is also available in T.P. Hughes's *Dictonary of Islam.*[57]

The study of Quran and the necessity of expounding it gave rise to that most characteristically Muslim literary activity, the books of tradition or Hadis, literally meaning "narrative". It is a compendium of doings, sayings, revelations and judgements of Muhammad. Muslim theologians make no distinction between Quran and Hadis. To them both are works of revelation or inspiration. "In the Quran, Allah speaks through Muhammad; in the *Sunnah* He acts through him... No wonder that the Muslim theologians regard the Quran and the Hadis as being supplementary or even interchangeable."[58] Within three hundred years of the death of Muhammad, the Hadis acquired substantially the form in which it is known today. Imam Bukhari (d. C.E. 870) compiled 'authentic' traditions from a plethora of voluminous traditions. Next in importance are the collections of Imam Muslim (d. 875) and Imam Tirmizi (d. 892).

Equally important guide for the Muslims in the performance of their duties is the life-story of Muhammad. Apart from several *maghazi* books dealing with the prophet's campaigns, his first authentic biography too was ready in the eighth century. Its author Ibn Ishaq was born at Medina in 85 H. and died in Baghdad in 151 H. (704-768 C.E.). He wrote the *Sirat Rasul Allah.*[59] Other biographers

---

57. pp.483-531.
58. Ram Swarup, *Understanding Islam through Hadis*, New Delhi, Reprint, 1983, pp.vii, xi.
59. Trs. by A. Guillaume under the title *The Life of Muhammad* (Oxford, 1958).

of note who succeeded him were al-Waqidi, Ibn Hisham, and At-Tabari. Muslims try to mould their lives after the model of Muhammad. "No one regarded by any section of human race as perfect man has been imitated so minutely."[60]

The Quran and the Hadis provided the foundation upon which theology and law of Islam were raised. "Law in Islam is more intimately related to religion than to jurisprudence as modern lawyers understand it."[61] Named after their founders Abu Hanifa (C. 699-767), Abu Abdullah Muhammad bin Idris (C. 767-820), Ahmad bin Hanbal (C. 780-855) and Malik bin Anas (C. 715-795) — the four *mazahib* or schools of Islamic law named Hanafi, Sha'fai, Hanbali and Malaki respectively, too had come into being in the eighth-ninth century. Their compilation is called *Hidaya*. If at all anything was wanting with regard to Muslim law, it was provided by *Hidaya* or Guidance.[62] The *Hidaya* is a voluminous treatise based on Sunni law composed by Shaikh Burhanuddin Ali who was born at Marghinan in Transoxiana about 530 H. and died in 593 H. (1135-1196).[63]

Muslim law in its ultimate form was thus available to the conquerors and Sultans who established their rule in India in the thirteenth century. True, there were no printed editions of these works. But beautiful hand written copies were always available at least to distinguished conquerors and kings and their counsellors. Muslim law is definite, clear and universal. This law was the actual sovereign in Muslim lands: no one was above it and all were ruled by it.[64] Such is the reverence paid to these religio-legal treatises that they have remained the model

---

60. Hitti, *op. cit.*, p.29.
61. *Ibid.*, p.78.
62. Trs. by Charles Hamilton, 4 vols. (London, 1791).
63. Hughes, *Dictionary of Islam*, p.174; D.S. Margoliouth, *Mohammed and the Rise of Islam*, pp. xix-xx.
64. A. Khuda Bakhsh, *Essays, Indian and Islamic* (London 1927), p.51.

of prose in literary works. The rhymed prose of the Quran has set the standard which almost every conservative Arabic writer consciously strives to imitate. The diction, the idiom, the very phrases of these religio-legal works were adopted by Muslim chroniclers in writing the history of Islamic achievements in India.[65] There are two sorts of Muslim historians, the dry annalist, and the pompous and flowery orator. But both use the language of their scriptures — a style more natural to their ideas and sentiments. It is necessary therefore to read these scriptures. It is necessary to know Islam in order to understand the ethos and legacy of Muslim rule in India.

65. An impressive Bibliography has been provided by Hughes, *op. cit.*, pp.405, 406.

Chapter 3

Muslims Invade India

"My principal object in coming to Hindustan... has been to accomplish two things. The first was to war with the infidels, the enemies of the Mohammadan religion; and by this religious warfare to acquire some claim to reward in the life to come. The other was... that the army of Islam might gain something by plundering the wealth and valuables of the infidels: plunder in war is as lawful as their mothers' milk to Musalmans who war for their faith."

Amir Timur

While studying the legacy of Muslim rule in India, it has to be constantly borne in mind that the objectives of all Muslim invaders and rulers were the same as those mentioned above. Timur or Tamerlane himself defines them candidly and bluntly while others do so through their chroniclers.

After its birth in Arabia, Islam spread as a conquering creed both in west and east with amazing rapidity. In the north and west of Arabia Muslim conquest was swift. The Byzantine provinces of Palestine and Syria were conquered by the newly converted Arabs after a campaign of six months in C.E. 636-37. Next came the turn of the Sassanid empire of Persia which included Iraq, Iran and Khurasan. The Persians were defeated decisively in 637 and their empire was so overrun in the next few years that by 643 the boundaries of the Caliphate touched the frontiers of India. In the west the Byzantine province of Egypt had fallen in 640-641, and territories of Inner Mongolia, Bukhara, Tashkand and Samarqand were annexed by 650. The Arab armies marched over North Africa and crossed into Spain in C.E. 709. Thus within a span of about seventy years (637-709) the Arabs achieved astounding success in their conquests. Still more astounding was the fact that the people of these conquered lands were quickly converted to Islam and their language and culture Arabicised.

Naturally India, known to early Arabs as Hind va Sind, too could not escape Muslim expansionist designs, and they sent their armies into India both by land and sea. They proceeded along the then known (trade) routes — 1. from Kufa and Baghadad, via Basra and Hormuz to Chaul on India's west coast; 2. from West Persian towns, via Hormuzz to Debal in Sind; and 3. through the land route of northern Khurasan to Kabul via Bamian. But progress of Muslim arms and religion in India was slow, very slow. For, the declarations of objectives of Muslim invaders had not taken into account the potentialities of Indians' stiff and latent resistance. Caliph Umar (634-44 C.E.) had sent an expedition in 636-37 to pillage Thana on the coast of Maharashtra during the reign of the great Hindu monarch Pulakesin II. This was followed by expeditions to Bharuch (Broach) in Gujarat and the gulf of Debal in Sind. These were repulsed and Mughairah, the leader of the latter expedition, was defeated and killed. Umar thought of sending another army by land against Makran which at that time was part of the kingdom of Sind but was dissuaded by the governor of Iraq from doing so. The next Caliph Usman (644-656) too followed the same advice and refrained from embarking on any venture on Sind. The fourth Caliph, Ali, sent an expedition by land in 660 but the leader of the expedition and most of his troops were slain in the hilly terrain of Kikanan (42 H./662 C.E.). Thus the four 'pious' Caliphs of Islam died without hearing of the conquest of Sind and Hind.

The reason why the Arabs were keen on penetrating into Sind and always bracketed it with Hind, was that Sind was then a big 'country' — as big as Hind in their eyes. According to the authors of *Chachnama* and *Tuhfatul Kiram*, the dominion of Sind extended on the east to the boundary of Kashmir and Kanauj, on the west to Makran, on the south to the coast of the sea and Debal, and on the north to Kandhar, Seistan and the mountains of Kuzdan and Kikanan.[1] It thus included Punjab and Baluchistan, parts of North-West Frontier Province and parts of Rajasthan. Muawiyah, the succeeding Caliph (661-80), sent as many as six expeditions by land to Sind. All of them were repulsed with great slaughter except the last one which succeeded in occupying Makran in 680. Thereafter, for twenty-eight years, the Arabs did not dare to send another army against Sind. Even Makran remained independent with varying degrees of freedom commensurate with the intensity of resistance so that as late as 1290 Marco Polo speaks of the eastern part of Makran as part of Hind, and as "the last Kingdom of India as you go towards the west and northwest".[2] The stubborn and successful opposition of Makran to the invaders was simply remarkable.

Meanwhile the Arabs had started attacking Hind from the north-west. Emboldened by their success in annexing Khurasan in 643 C.E., the first Arab army penetrated deep into Zabul by way of Seistan which at that time was part of India, territorially as well as culturally. After a prolonged and grim struggle the invader was defeated and driven out. But in a subsequent attack, the Arab general Abdul Rahman was able to conquer Zabul and levy tribute from Kabul (653 C.E.). Kabul paid the tribute but reluctantly and irregularly. To ensure its regular payment another Arab general Yazid bin Ziyad attempted retribu-

---

1. *Chachnama*, trs. Kalichbeg, p.11 and n.
2. Yule, *Ser Marco Polo*, II, pp.334-36, 359; Alberuni, I, p.208; Biladuri, E and D, I, p.456.

tion in 683. But he was killed and his army put to flight with great slaughter. The war against Kabul was renewed in 695, but as it became prolonged it bore no fruitful results. Some attempts to force the Hindu king of Kabul into submission were made in the reign of Caliph Al-Mansur (745-775 C.E.), but they met only with partial success and the Ghaznavid Turks found the Hindus ruling over Kabul in 986 C.E.

The First Invasion

In the south, attempts to subjugate Sind continued through land and sea. And in 712 a full-fledged invasion was launched after prolonged negotiations. The genesis of war was this. The king of Ceylon had sent to Hajjaj bin Yusuf Sakifi, the governor of the eastern provinces of the Caliphate, eight vessels filled with presents, Abyssinian slaves, pilgrims, and the orphan daughters of some Muslim merchants who had died in his dominions. These ships were attacked and plundered by pirates off the coast of Sind. Hajjaj demanded reparations from Dahir, the king of Sind, but the latter expressed his inability to control the pirates or punish them. At this Hajjaj sent two expeditions against Debal (708 C.E.), the first under Ubaidulla and the other under Budail. Both were repulsed, their armies were routed and commanders killed. Deeply affected by these failures, Hajjaj fitted out a third and grandiose expedition. Astrological prediction and close relationship prompted him to confer the command of the campaign on his seventeen year old nephew and son-in-law Imaduddin Muhammad bin Qasim.

It was the heyday of Arab power. Wherever Muslim armies went they earned success and collected spoils. "The conquest of Sind took place at the very time in which, at the opposite extremes of the known world, the Muhammadan armies were subjugating Spain, and pressing on the southern frontier of France, while they were adding Khwarizm to their already mighty empire."[3]

Under the auspices of Hajjaj, who, though nominally governor only of Iraq, was in fact ruler over all the countries which constituted the former Persian empire, the spirit of more extended conquest arose. By his orders, one army under "Kutaiba penetrated... to Kashgar, at which place Chinese ambassadors entered into a compact with the invaders. Another army... operated against the king of Kabul, and a third (under Muhammad bin Qasim) advanced towards the lower course of the Indus through Mekran."[4] The reigning Ummayad Caliph Walid I (86-96 H./705-715 C.E.) was a powerful prince under whom the Khilafat attained the greatest extent of dominion to which it ever reached. But because of earlier failures of Ubaidulla and Budail, he was skeptical about the outcome of the venture. He dreaded the distance, the cost, and the loss of Muhammadan lives.[5] But when Hajjaj, an imperialist to the core, promised to repay the Caliph the expenses of the enterprise, he obtained permission for the campaign. That is how Muhammad bin Qasim came to invade Sind. The aims of the campaign were three: 1. Spreading the religion of Islam in Sind, 2. Conquest of Sind and extension of the territory of Islam, and 3. Acquisition of maximum wealth for use by Hajjaj and payment to the Caliph.[6]

The knowledge of Hajjaj and Muhammad bin Qasim about Sind and Hind was naturally not extensive. It was

---

3. Muhammad Qasim Hindu Shah Farishtah, a seventeenth century historian, basing his researches (*Khama-i-Tahqiq*) on the works of *Khulasat-ul-Hikayat*, *Hajjaj Nama* and the history of Haji Muhammad Qandhari says that before the advent of Islam Indian Brahmans used to travel to and fro by sea to the temples of Ka'aba to administer worship of the idols there, and there was constant movement of people between Ceylon, India and the countries of what is now called West Asia (Farishtah, II, p.311); Biladuri, *Futuh-ul-Buldan*, E and D, I, pp. 118-119; Elliot's Appendix, E and D, I, pp.414-484, citing *Chachnama*, p.432.

4. Elliot's Appendix, pp.428-29.

5. *Ibid.*, p.431 citing Abul Fida, *Chachnama* and *Tuhfat-ul-Kiram*.

6. Al Biladuri, p.123; *Chachnama*, p.206.

confined to what the sea-and-land traders had told about the people and wealth of what was known to them as Kabul va Zabul and Hind va Sind. About India's history, its hoary civilisation, its high philosophy, its deep and abiding faith in spiritualism and non-violence, they knew but little. One thing they knew was that it was inhabited by infidels and idol-worshippers. And they knew their religious duty towards such unbelievers. Instruction and inspiration about this duty came to them from three sources — The Quran, the Hadis and the personal exploits of the Prophet. Every Muslim, whether educated or illiterate knew something about the Quran and the Hadis. The learned or the Ulama amongst them usually learnt the Quran by heart and informed their conquerors and kings about its teachings and injunctions. The Prophet's deeds, even the most trivial ones, too were constantly narrated with reverence. The one supreme duty the Quran taught them was to fight the infidels with all their strength, convert them to Islam and spread the faith by destroying their idols and shrines.

In *Surah* (Chapter) 2, *ayat* (injunction) 193, the Quran says, "Fight against them (the *mushriks*) until idolatry is no more, and Allah's religion reigns supreme." The command is repeated in *Surah* 8, *ayat* 39. In *Surah* 69, *ayats* 30-37 it is ordained: "Lay hold of him and bind him. Burn him in the fire of hell." And again: "When you meet the unbelievers in the battlefield strike off their heads and, when you have laid them low, bind your captives firmly" (47.14-15). "Cast terror into the hearts of the infidels. Strike off their heads, maim them in every limb" (8:12). Such commands, exhortations and injunctions are repeatedly mentioned in Islamic scriptures. The main medium through which these injunctions were to be carried out was the holy *Jihad*. The *Jihad* or holy war is a multi-dimensional concept. It means fighting for the sake of Allah, for the cause of Islam, for converting people to the 'true faith'

and for destroying their temples. Iconoclasm and razing
other people's temples is central to Islam; it derives its
justification from the Quranic revelations and the
Prophet's *Sunnah* or practice. Muhammad had himself
destroyed temples in Arabia and so set an example for his
followers. In return the *mujahid* (or fighter of *Jihad*) is
promised handsome reward in this world as well as in the
world to come. Without *Jihad* there is no Islam. *Jihad* is a
religious duty of every Muslim. It inspired Muslim invaders and rulers to do deeds of valour, of horror and of
terror. Their chroniclers wrote about the achievements of
the heroes of Islam with zeal and glee, often in the very
language they had learnt from their scriptures.

Inspired by such belligerent injunctions, Muhammad
bin Qasim (and later on other invaders) started on the Indian expedition with a large force. On the way the
governor of Makran, Muhammad Harun, supplied rein-
forcements and five catapults. His artillery which included
a great ballista known as 'the Bride', and was worked by
five hundred men, had been sent by sea to meet him at
Debal.[7] Situated on the sea-coast the city of Debal was so
called because of its Deval or temple. It contained a citadel-temple with stone walls as high as forty yards and a
dome of equal height. Qasim arrived at Debal in late 711
or early 712 C.E. with an army of at least twenty thousand
horse and footmen.[8] Add to this the Jat and Med mercenaries he enlisted under his banner in India.[9]

A glance at the demographic composition of Sind at
this time would help in appraising the response of the
Sindhians to Muhammad's invasion. At the lower rung
of the social order were Jats and Meds. Physically strong
and thoroughly uneducated they flocked under the standard of the foreigner in large numbers in the hope of

---

7. Al Biladuri, *Futuh-ul-Buldan* trs. E and D, I, pp.119-120.
8. For details see Lal, K.S., *Early Muslims in India*, p.14.
9. Al Biladuri, p.119. Also E and D, I, Appendix, p.434.

material gain. They also supplied Muhammad with information of the countryside he had come to invade.[10] The majority of the Sindhi population was Buddhist (Samanis of chronicles), totally averse to fighting. Their religion taught them to avoid bloodshed and they were inclined to make submission to the invader even without a show of resistance. Then there were tribal people, like Sammas, to whom any king was as good as any other. They welcomed Muhammad Qasim "with frolicks and merriment".[11] Thus the bulk of population was more or less indifferent to the invasion. In such a situation it were only Raja Dahir of Sind, his Kshatriya soldiers and Brahman priests of the temples who were called upon to defend their cities and shrines, citadels and the countryside. This is the Muslim version and has to be accepted with caution.

When Muhammad began the invasion of Debal, Raja Dahir was staying in his capital Alor about 500 kms. away. Dabal was in the charge of a governor with a garrison of four to six thousand Rajput soldiers and a few thousand Brahmans, and therefore Raja Dahir did not march to its defence immediately. All this while, the young invader was keeping in close contact with Hajjaj, soliciting the latter's advice even on the smallest matters. So efficient was the communication system that "letters were written every three days and replies were recieved in seven days,"[12] so that the campaign was virtually directed by the veteran Hajjaj himself.[13] When the siege of Debal had continued for some time a defector informed Muhammad about how the temple could be captured. Thereupon the Arabs, planting their ladders stormed the citadel-temple and swarmed over the walls. As per Islamic injunctions, the inhabitants were invited to accept Islam, and on their

---

10. Elliot, Appendix, E and D, I, p.435.

11. *Chachnama*, p.191.

12. Al Biladuri, p.119; Elliot's Appendix, p.436.

13. *Chachnama*, E & D, I, pp.188, 189.

refusal all adult males were put to the sword and their wives and children were enslaved. The carnage lasted for three days. The temple was razed and a mosque built. Muhammad laid out a Muslim quarter, and placed a garrison of 4,000 in the town. The legal fifth of the spoil including seventy-five damsels was sent to Hajjaj, and the rest of the plunder was divided among the soldiers.[14] As this was the pattern of all future sieges and victories of Muhammad bin Qasim — as indeed of all future Muslim invaders of Hindustan — it may be repeated. Inhabitants of a captured fort or town were invited to accept Islam. Those who converted were spared. Those who refused were massacred. Their women and children were enslaved and converted. Temples were broken and on their sites and with their materials were constructed mosques, khanqahs, sarais and tombs.

Muhammad bin Qasim next advanced towards Nirun, situated near modern Hyderabad. The people of Nirun purchased their peace. Notwithstanding its voluntary surrender, Muhammad destroyed the "temple of Budh" at Nirun. He built a mosque at its site and appointed an Imam.[15] After placing a garrison at the disposal of the Muslim governor, he marched to Sehwan (Siwistan), about 130 kilometres to the north-west. This town too was populated chiefly by Buddhists and traders. They too surrendered to the invader on condition of their remaining loyal and paying *jiziyah*.

Nirun's surrender alarmed Raja Dahir and he and his men decided to meet the invader at Aror or Rawar. Qasim was bound for Brahmanabad but stopped short to engage

---

14. W. Haig, C.H.I., III, p.3.

15. Al Biladuri, p.121; *Chachnama*, pp.157-58; Elliot's Appendix, E and D, I, p.432. See *Chachnama*, trs. Kalichbeg, pp.85, 113, 128 for forcible conversions; pp.83, 87, 155, 161, 173-74 for massacres; pp.190, 196 for enslavement; pp.92, 99, 100, 190 for destruction of temples and construction of mosques at their sites.

Dahir first. In the vast plain of Rawar the Arabs encountered an imposing array of war elephants and a large army under the command of Dahir and his Rajput chiefs ready to give battle to the Muslims. Al Biladuri writes that after the battle lines were drawn, a dreadful conflict ensued such as had never been seen before, and the author of the *Chachnama* gives details of the valiant fight which Raja Dahir gave "mounted on his white elephant". A naptha arrow struck Dahir's *howdah* and set it ablaze. Dahir dismounted and fought desperately, but was killed towards the evening, "when the idolaters fled, and the Musulmans glutted themselves with massacre". Raja Dahir's queen Rani Bai and her son betook themselves into the fortress of Rawar, which had a garrison of 15 thousand. The soldiers fought valiantly, but the Arabs proved stronger. When the Rani saw her doom inevitable, she assembled all the women in the fort and addressed them thus: "God forbid that we should owe our liberty to those outcaste cow-eaters. Our honour would be lost. Our respite is at an end, and there is nowhere any hope of escape; let us collect wood, cotton and oil, for I think we should burn ourselves and go to meet our husbands. If any wish to save herself, she may."[16] They entered into a house where they burnt themselves in the fire of *jauhar* thereby vindicating the honour of their race. Muhammad occupied the fort, massacred the 6,000 men he found there and seized all the wealth and treasures that belonged to Dahir.

Muhammad now marched to Brahmanabad.[17] On the way a number of garrisons in forts challenged his army, delaying his arrival in Brahmanabad. The civil population, as usual, longed for peace and let the Muslims enter the city. Consequently, it was spared, but Qasim "sat on the

---

16. *Chachnama*, pp.122, 172.
17. Elliot's note on Brahmanabad is worthy of perusal (Appendix, E and D, I, pp.369-74).

seat of cruelty and put all those who had fought to the sword. It is said that about six thousand fighting men were slain, but according to others sixteen thousand were killed".[18] Continuing his ravaging march northward, he proceeded to Multan, the chief city of the upper Indus with its famous Temple of Sun. Multan was ravaged and its treasures rifled. During his campaigns Muhammad bin Qasim concentrated on collecting the maximum wealth possible as he had to honour the promise he and his patron Hajjaj had made to the Caliph to reimburse to the latter the expenses incurred on the expedition. Besides the treasure collected from the various forts of the Sindhi King, freedom of worship to the Hindus could bring wealth in the form of pilgrim tax, *jiziyah* and other similar cesses. Hence, the temple of Brahmanabad was permitted to be rebuilt and old customs of worship allowed.[19] In Multan also temple worship more or less went on as before. The expenses of the campaign had come to 60 thousand silver *dirhams*. Hajjaj paid to the Caliph double the amount — 120 thousand *dirhams*.[20]

Muhammad bin Qasim set about organising the administration of the conquered lands like this. The principal sources of revenue were the *jiziyah* and the land-tax. The *Chachnama* speaks of other taxes levied upon the cultivators such as the *baj* and *ushari*. The collection of *jiziyah* was considered a political as well as a religious duty, and was always exacted "with vigour and punctuality, and frequently with insult". "The native population had to feed every Muslim traveller for three days and nights and had

---

18. Mohammad Habib, "The Arab Conquest of Sind" in *Politics and Society During the Early Medieval Period* being the collected works of M.Habib, Ed. K.A. Nizami, II, pp.1-35. Al Biladuri, p.122 has 8,000 or 26,000.

19. *Chachnama*, pp.185-86.

20. *Chachnama*, p.206. Al Biladuri, however, has 60 million and 120 million respectively (E and D, I, p.123). See also Elliot's Appendix, I, p. 470 and n.

to submit to many other humiliations which are mentioned by Muslim historians."[21]

Muhammad bin Qasim remained in Sind for a little
over three years.[22] Then he was suddenly recalled and
summarily executed, probably by being sewn in an animal's hide, on the charge of violating two Sindhi princesses meant for the harem of the Caliph. Such barbaric
punishments to successful commanders by their jealous
masters were not uncommon in Islamic history.[23]
However, the recall of Qasim was a God-sent relief to the
Sindhis. After his departure the Arab power in Sind declined rapidly. Most of the neo-converts returned to their
former faith. The Hindus had bowed before the onrush of
the Muslim invasion; but they re-asserted their position
once the storm had blown over.[24] Denison Ross also says
that after the recall of Muhammad bin Qasim, the Muslims
retained some foothold on the west bank of the river
Indus, but they were in such small number that they

---

21. Ishwari Prasad, *Medieval India* (1940 ed.), p.63.
22. *Chachnama*, pp.185-86.
23. Exactly at this very point of time a similar story of success and punishment was being enacted at the other end of the then known world.
Musa, the governor of North Africa, sent his commander Tariq with 7,000
men to march into the Iberian peninsula. Tariq landed at Gibraltar and
utterly routed the armies of Visigothic King Roderick in July 711. He then
headed towards Toledo, the capital, and attacked Cordova. Jealous of the
unexpected success of his lieutenant, Musa himself with 10,000 troops
rushed to Spain in June 712. It was in or near Toledo that Musa met Tariq.
Here he whipped his subordinate and put him in chains for refusing to
obey orders to halt in the early stage of the campaign. Musa nevertheless
continued with the conquest himself. Ironically enough, in the autumn of
the same year the Caliph Al-Walid in distant Damuscus recalled Musa.
Musa entered Damuscus in February 715. Al-Walid was dead by then, and
his brother and successor Sulaiman humiliated Musa, made him stand in
the sun until exhausted, and confiscated his property. The last we hear of
the aged conqueror of Africa and Spain ("he affected to disguise his age by
colouring with a red powder the whiteness of his beard"), is as a beggar in
a remote village near Mecca (Hitti, *op. cit.*, pp.62-67; Gibbon, *op. cit.*, II,
pp.769-779).
24. Al Biladuri, p. 126. Also cf. Idrisi, p.89.

gradually merged into Hindu population. In Mansura (the Muslim capital of Sind) they actually adopted Hinduism.[25]

But Muslims or Islam did not disappear from Sind. A dent had been made in India's social fabric, and its wealth looted. Muslims who continued to retain the new faith remained confined mostly to cities, particularly Multan,[26] and Multan according to Al Masudi (writing about C.E. 942) remained one of the strongest frontier places of the Musulmans.[27] Ibn Hauqal, who finished his work in C.E. 976, also calls Multan a city with a strong fort, "but Mansura is more fertile and prosperous". He also says that Debal "is a large mart and a port not only of this but neighbouring regions". It would thus appear that by the tenth century the Muslim population had stabilized and integrated with the people of Sind. Ibn Hauqal writes: "The Muslims and infidels of this tract wear the same dresses, and let their beards grow in the same fashion. They use fine muslin garments on account of the extreme heat. The men of Multan dress in the same way. The language of Mansura, Multan and those parts is Arabic and Sindian..."[28] This, in brief, was the social change brought about in Sind after the introduction of Islam there.

Before closing the discussion on the Arab invasion of Sind, a few aspects of the campaign may be evaluated. As Andre Wink points out, "In contrast to Persia...there is no indication that Buddhists converted more eagerly than brahmans. The theory that Muslim Arabs were 'invited' to Sind by Buddhist 'traitors' who aimed to undercut the brahmans' power has nothing to recommend itself with. If Buddhists collaborated with the invaders, the brahmans did so no less...There was in short, no clear-cut religious

25. Denison Ross, *Islam*, p.18. Also Lal, K.S., *Indian Muslims: Who are They* (New Delhi, 1990), pp.3-4.
26. Lal, K.S., *Growth of Muslim Population in Medieval India* (Delhi 1973), p.99.
27. *Muruj-ul-Zuhab*, p.20. Also Idrisi, *Nuzhat-ul-Mushtaq*, p.82.
28. *Ashkalal-ul Bilad*, pp.36, 37.

antagonism that the Arabs could exploit." At the same time, points out Gidumal, "It is extremely doubtful if Sind could have been conquered at all, had these (Sindhi) chiefs remained true to their king, and, curious as it may seem, it was ostensibly astrology that made traitors of them. For they said: 'Our wise men have predicted that Sind will come under the sway of Islam. Why then should we battle against fate?' " And lastly, the misleading belief in the tolerance and kindness of Muhmamad bin Qasim stands cancelled on a study of the campaign in depth. The statement of Mohammad Habib that "Alone among the Muslim invaders of India Muhammad Qasim is a character of whom a concentious Musalman need not be ashamed", and similar conclusions do not hold ground if his massacres, conversions and iconoclasm detailed in the *Chachnama* alone are any indicator.[29]

Second Invasion

A more terrifying wave of Islamic invasion came with Mahmud of Ghazni, three hundred years after the Arab invasion of Sind. During this period Islam was spreading in various regions outside India with varying degrees of success. Furthermore, the newly converted Turks, the slave protectors of the pious Caliphs, had carved out their own kingdoms at the expense of the Caliph's "empire". But to ensure their legitimacy as rulers they kept up a relationship of formal loyalty towards the Caliph. Such were the slave rulers Alaptigin and Subuktigin.

Amir Subuktigin (977-997 C.E.) made frequent expeditions into Hindustan, or more precisely into the Hindu Shahiya Brahman kingdom of Punjab which extended up to Kabul, "in the prosecution of holy wars, and there he

---

29. Andre Wink, *Al-Hind*, I, p.151, and reference. Dayaram Gidumal's Introduction to *Chachanama's* trs. by Kalichbeg, p.vii; M.Habib, *Collected Works*, ed. K.A. Nizami, II, pp. 1-35, esp. p. 32; Lal, *Early Muslims in India*, pp. 21-25.

conquered forts upon lofty hills, in order to seize the treasures they contained." When Jayapal, the ruling prince of the dynasty, had ascertained from reports of travellers about the activities of Subuktigin, he hastened with a large army and huge elephants to wreak vengeance upon Subuktigin, "by treading the field of Islam under his feet".[30] After he had passed Lamghan, Subuktigin advanced from Ghazni with his son Mahmud. The armies fought successively against one another. Jayapal, with soldiers "as impetuous as a torrent," was difficult to defeat, and so Subuktigin threw animal flesh (beef?) into the fountain which supplied water to the Hindu army.[31] In consequence, Jayapal sued for peace. But for greater gains, Subuktigin delayed negotiations, and Jayapal's envoys were sent back. Jayapal again requested for cessation of hostilities and sent ambassadors, observing: "You have seen the impetuosity of the Hindus and their indifference to death, whenever any calamity befalls them, as at this moment. If, therefore, you refuse to grant peace in the hope of obtaining plunder, tribute, elephants and prisoners, then there is no alternative for us but to mount the horse of stern determination, destroy our property, take out the eyes of our elephants, cast our children into the fire, and rush on each other with sword and spear, so that all that will be left to you, is stones and dirt, dead bodies, and scattered bones."[32]

Jayapal's spirited declaration convinced Subuktigin "that religion and the views of the faithful would be best consulted by peace". He fixed a tribute of cash and elephants on the Shahiya king and nominated officers to

---

30. Utbi, *Tarikh-i-Yamini*, E and D, II, pp.20-21.

31. *Ibid.*, p.20; Ufi, *Jamiul Hikayat*, p.181. Elliot's Appendix, on the authority of Abul Fazl, specifically mentions animal's flesh. p.439. The trick was common. The Fort of Sevana was captured by Alauddin Khalji by contaminating the fort's water supply by throwing a cow's head into the tank. See Lal, *Khaljis*, p.115.

32. Utbi, *op. cit.*, p.21.

collect them. But Jayapal, having reflected on the ruse played by the adversaries in contaminating the water-supply leading to his discomfiture, refused to pay anything, and imprisoned the Amir's officers. At this Subuktigin marched out towards Lamghan and conquered it. He set fire to the places in its vicinity, demolished idol temples, marched and captured other cities and established Islam in them. At last Jayapal decided to fight once more, and satisfy his revenge. He collected troops to the number of more than one hundred thousand, "which resembled scattered ants and locusts". Subuktigin on his part "made bodies of five hundred attack the enemy with their maces in hand, and relieve each other when one party became tired, so that fresh men and horses were constantly engaged...The dust which arose prevented the eyes from seeing... It was only when the dust was allayed that it was found that Jayapal had been defeated and his troops had fled leaving behind them their property, utensils, arms, provisions, elephants, and horses."[33] Subuktigin levied tribute and obtained immense booty, besides two hundred elephants of war. He also increased his army by enrolling those Afghans and Khaljis who submitted to him and thereafter expended their lives in his service.

Subuktigin's son Mahmud ascended the throne at Ghazni in C.E. 998 and in 1000 he delivered his first attack against India in continuation of the work of his ancestor. During the three hundred years between Muhammad bin Qasim and Mahmud Ghaznavi, Islamic Shariat had got a definite and permanent shape in the four well-defined schools of Muslim jurisprudence—Hanafi, Shafii, Hanbali and Malaki. The Quran and the six orthodox collections of Hadis were also now widely known. Mahmud himself was well-versed in the Quran and was considered its eminent interpreter.[34] He drew around himself, by means

33. Utbi, *op. cit.*, pp.22-23.

34. Bosworth, C.E., *The Ghaznavids* (Edinburgh, 1963) p.129; Utbi, *Kitab-i-Yamini*, trs. by James Reynolds (London, 1885): pp.438-39 and n.

of lavish generosity, a galaxy of eminent theologians, scholars, and divines so that on his investiture, when he vowed to the Caliph of Baghdad to undertake every year a campaign against the idolaters of India, he knew that *"jihad* was central to Islam and that one campaign at least must be undertaken against the unbelievers every year." Mahmud could launch forth seventeen expeditions during the course of the next thirty years and thereby fulfilled his promise to the Caliph both in letter and in spirit of Islamic theology. For this he has been eulogized sky-high by Muslim poets and Muslim historians. He on his part was always careful to include the Caliph's name on his coins, depict himself in his *Fateh-namas* as a warrior for the faith, and to send to Baghdad presents from the plunder of his Indian campaign.[35] The Caliph Al-Qadir Billah in turn praised the talents and exploits of Mahmud, conferred upon him the titles of *Amin-ul-millah* and *Yamin-ud-daula* (the Right hand) after which his house is known as Yamini Dynasty.

Let us very briefly recapitulate the achievements of Sultan Mahmud in the usual fields of Islamic expansionism, conversions of non-Muslims to Islam, destruction of temples and acquisition of wealth in order to appreciate the encomiums bestowed upon him as being one of the greatest Muslim conquerors of medieval India. In his first attack of frontier towns in C.E. 1000 Mahmud appointed his own governors and converted some inhabitants. In his attack on Waihind (Peshawar) in 1001-3, Mahmud is reported to have captured the Hindu Shahiya King Jayapal and fifteen of his principal chiefs and relations some of whom like Sukhpal, were made Musalmans. At Bhera all the inhabitants, except those who embraced Islam, were put to the sword. At Multan too conversions took place in large numbers, for writing about the campaign against Nawasa Shah (converted Sukhpal), Utbi says that this and

35. Hodivala, S.H., *Studies in Indo-Muslim History* (Bombay,1939).

the previous victory (at Multan) were "witnesses to his exalted state of proselytism."[36] In his campaign in the Kashmir Valley (1015) Mahmud "converted many infidels to Muhammadanism, and having spread Islam in that country, returned to Ghazni." In the later campaign in Mathura, Baran and Kanauj, again, many conversions took place. While describing "the conquest of Kanauj," Utbi sums up the situation thus: "The Sultan levelled to the ground every fort...., and the inhabitants of them either accepted Islam, or took up arms against him." In short, those who submitted were also converted to Islam. In Baran (Bulandshahr) alone 10,000 persons were converted including the Raja. During his fourteenth invasion in 1023 C.E. Kirat, Nur, Lohkot and Lahore were attacked. The chief of Kirat accepted Islam, and many people followed his example. According to Nizamuddin Ahmad, "Islam spread in this part of the country by the consent of the people and the influence of force." According to all contemporary and later chroniclers like Qazwini, Utbi, Farishtah etc., conversion of Hindus to Islam was one of the objectives of Mahmud. Wherever he went, he insisted on the people to convert to Islam. Such was the insistence on the conversion of the vanquished Hindu princes that many rulers just fled before Mahmud even without giving a battle. "The object of Bhimpal in recommending the flight of Chand Rai was that the Rai should not fall into the net of the Sultan, and thus be made a Musalman, as had happened to Bhimpal's uncles and relations, when they demanded quarter in their distress."[37]

Mahmud broke temples and desecrated idols wherever he went. The number of temples destroyed by him during his campaigns is so large that a detailed list is

---

36. For conversions at various places under Mahmud see Utbi, *Kitab-i-Yamini*, Eng. trs. Reynolds, pp.451-52, 455, 460, 462-63 and Utbi, *Tarikh-i-Yamini*, E and D, II, pp.27, 30, 33, 40, 42, 43, 45, 49. Also Appendix in E and D, II, pp.434-78.

neither possible nor necessary. However, he concentrated more on razing renowned temples to bring glory to Islam rather than waste time on small ones. Some famous temples destroyed by him may be noted here. At Thaneshwar, the temple of *Chakraswamin* was sacked and its bronze image of Vishnu was taken to Ghazni to be thrown into the hippodrome of the city. Similarly, the magnificent central temple of Mathura was destroyed and its idols broken. At Mathura there was no armed resistance; the people had fled, and Mahmud had been greatly impressed with the beauty and grandeur of the shrines.[38] And yet the temples in the city were thoroughly sacked. Kanauj had a large number of temples (Utbi's 'ten thousand' merely signifies a large number), some of great antiquity. Their destruction was made easy by the flight of those who were not prepared either to die or embrace Islam. Somnath shared the fate of *Chakraswamin*.[39]

The sack of Somnath in particular came to be considered a specially pious exploit because of its analogy with the destruction of idol of Al Manat in Arabia by the Prophet. This "explains the idolization of Mahmud by Nizam-ul-Mulk Tusi,[40] and the ideal treatment he has received from early Sufi poets like Sanai and Attar, not to mention such collectors of anecdotes as Awfi."[41] It is indeed noticeable that after the Somnath expedition (417H./ 1026 C.E.), "a deed which had fired the imagination of the Islamic world", Caliph al-Qadir Billah himself celebrated

38. Utbi, p.44; Farishtah, I, p.29 for temples at Mathura.

39. Alberuni, II, p.103.

40. *Siyasat Nama* (ed. Shefer), pp.77-80, 138-156.

41. Aziz Ahmad, *Studies in Islamic Culture in the Indian Environment* (Oxford, 1964), p.79.

Shah Waliullah considered Mahmud as the greatest ruler after *Khilafat-i- Khass*. He argues that "in reference to Mahmud historians failed to recognize that his horoscope had been identical to the Prophet's and that this fact had abled him to obtain significant victories in wars to propagate Islam" (Rizvi, *History of Sufism*, II, p.382 citing from Shah Waliullah, *Qurrat al-aynain fi tafil al-shaykhayan*, Delhi, 1893, p.324).

the victory with great eclat. He sent Mahmud a very complimentary letter giving him the title of Kahf-ud-daula wa al-Islam, and formally recognizing him as the ruler of Hindustan.[42] It is also significant that Mahmud for the first time issued his coins from Lahore only after his second commendation from the Caliph.

Mahmud Ghaznavi collected lot of wealth from regions of his visitations. A few facts and figures may be given as illustrations. In his war against Jayapal (1001-02 C.E.) the latter had to pay a ransom of 2,50,000 *dinars* for securing release from captivity. Even the necklace of which he was relieved was estimated at 2,00,000 *dinars* (gold coin) "and twice that value was obtained from the necks of those of his relatives who were taken prisoners or slain...".[43] A couple of years later, all the wealth of Bhera, which was "as wealthy as imagination can conceive", was captured by the conqueror (1004-05 C.E.). In 1005-06 the people of Multan were forced to pay an indemnity of the value of 20,000,000 (royal) *dirhams* (silver coin). When Nawasa Shah, who had reconverted to Hinduism, was ousted (1007-08), the Sultan took possession of his treasures amounting to 400,000 *dirhams*. Shortly after, from the fort of Bhimnagar in Kangra, Mahmud seized coins of the value of 70,000,000 (Hindu Shahiya) *dirhams*, and gold and silver ingots weighing some hundred maunds, jewellery and precious stones. There was also a collapsible house of silver, thirty yards in length and fifteen yards in breadth, and a canopy (*mandapika*) supported by two golden and two silver poles.[44] Such was the wealth obtained that it could not be shifted immediately, and Mahmud had to leave two of his "most confidential" chamberlains, Altun-

---

42. Farishtah, I, pp.30, 35.
43. Utbi, Reynolds, p.282.
44. The house was quite large, covering an area of about a thousand square feet. Hodivala also says that the canopy must have been what the old annalists of Gujarat call a Mandapika. It was a folding pavilion for being used in royal journeys, and not a throne (Hodivala, *op. cit.* p.143).

tash and Asightin, to look after its gradual transportation.[45] In the succeeding expeditions (1015-20) more and more wealth was drained out of the Punjab and other parts of India. Besides the treasures collected by Mahmud, his soldiers also looted independently. From Baran Mahmud obtained, 1,000,000 *dirhams* and from Mahaban a large booty. In the sack of Mathura five idols alone yielded 98,300 *misqals* (about 10 maunds) of gold.[46] The idols of silver numbered two hundred. Kanauj, Munj, Asni, Sharva and some other places yielded another 3,000,000 *dirhams*. We may skip over many other details and only mention that at Somnath his gains amounted to 20,000,000 *dinars*. [47] These figures are more or less authentic as Abu Nasr Muhammad Utbi, who mentions them, was the Secretary to Sultan Mahmud, so that he enjoyed excellent opportunities of becoming fully conversant with the operations and gains of the conqueror. He clearly notes the amount when collected in Hindu Shahiya coinage or in some other currency, and also gives the value of all acquisitions in the royal (Mahmud's) coins. A little error here or there does in no way minimise the colossal loss suffered by north India in general and the Punjab in particular during Mahmud's invasions.

The extent of this loss can be gauged from the fact that no coins (*dramma*) of Jayapal, Anandpal or Trilochanpal have been found.[48] The economic effects of the loss of

45. On return to Ghazni Mahmud ordered this impressive treasure to be displayed in the court-yard of his palace. "Ambassadors from foreign countries including the envoy from Taghan Khan, king of Turkistan, assembled to see the wealth... which had never been accumulated by kings of Persia or of Rum" (Utbi, Reynolds, pp.342-43; E and D, II, p.35).

46. Utbi, E and D., II, p.45, Reynolds, pp.455-57. I have elsewhere calculated that 70 *misqals* were equal to one seer of 24 tolas in the Sultanate period. See my *History of the Khaljis* (2nd ed. Bombay, 1967), pp.199-200. On the basis of the above calculation the weight of five gold idols comes to 10.5 maunds, each idol being of about 2 maunds.

47. Bosworth, *op. cit.*, p.78.

48. A. Cunningham, *Coins of Medieval India* (London, 1894), Reprint by Indological Book House (Varanasi, 1967), p. 65.

precious metals to India had a number of facets. The flow
of bullion outside India resulted in stablizing Ghaznavid
currency[49] and in the same proportion debasing Indian.
Consequently, the gold content of north Indian coins in
the eleventh and twelfth centuries went down from 120 to
60 grams.[50] Similarly, the weight and content of the silver
coin was also reduced. Because of debasement of coinage
Indian merchants lost their credit with foreign merchants.[51]

Outflow of bullion adversely affected India's balance
of trade in another way. India had always been a seller of
raw and finished goods against precious metals. She had
"swallowed up precious metals, both from the mineral
resources of Tibet and Central Asia and from trade with
the Islamic world..."[52] Now this favourable position was
lost. Indian merchants were even unable to ply their trade
because of disturbed political conditions. One reason
which had prompted Anandpal to send an embassy to
Mahmud at Ghazni with favourable terms to the Sultan
(C. 1012) was to try to normalize trade facilities, and after
an agreement "caravans (again) travelled in full security
between Khurasan and Hind."[53] But the balance of trade
for many years went on tilting in favour of the lands west
of the Indus.

Besides, the Ghaznavids collected in loot and tribute
valuable articles of trade like indigo, fine muslins, embroidered silk, and cotton stuffs, and things prepared from the
famous Indian steel, which have received praise at the
hands of Utbi, Hasan Nizami, Alberuni and many others.

49. J.R.A.S. 1848, pp.289, 307, 311; J.R.A.S., 1860, p.156; Bosworth,
pp.78-79.

50. A.S. Altekar in *Journal of the Numismatic Society of India*, II, p.2.

51. Muhammad Ufi, *Jami-ul Hikayat*, E and D, II, p.188; Thomas in
J.R.A.S. XVII, p.181.

52. Bosworth, *op. cit.*, pp.79, 149-52. Also Khurdadba, E and D, I, p.14,
and *Jami-ul-Hikayat*, E and D, II, p.68.

53. Utbi, *op. cit.*, Reynolds, 362; E and D, II, 36.

For example, one valuable commodity taken from India was indigo. From Baihaqi, who writes the correct Indian word *nil* for the dyestuff, it appears that 20,000 *mans* (about 500 maunds) of indigo was taken to Ghazna every year. According to Baihaqi, Sultan Masud once sent 25,000 *mans* (about 600 maunds) of indigo to the Caliph at Baghdad, for "the Sultans often reserved part of this (valuable commodity) for their own usage, and often sent it as part of presents for the Caliph or for other rulers".[54]

Mahmud's *jihad*, or the *jihad* of any invader or ruler for that matter, was accompanied by extreme cruelty. The description of the attack on Thanesar (Kurukshetra) is detailed. "The chief of Thanesar was... obstinate in his infidelity and denial of Allah, so the Sultan marched against him with his valiant warriors, for the purpose of planting the standards of Islam and extirpating idolatry... The blood of the infidels flowed so copiously that the stream was discoloured, and people were unable to drink it... Praise be to Allah... for the honour he bestows upon Islam and Musalmans."[55] Similarly, in the slaughter at Sirsawa near Saharanpur, "The Sultan summoned the most religiously disposed of his followers, and ordered them to attack the enemy immediately. Many infidels were consequently slain or taken prisoners in this sudden attack, and the Musalmans paid no regard to the booty till they had satiated themselves with the slaughter of the infidels... The friends of Allah searched the bodies of the slain for three whole days, in order to obtain booty..."[56] With such achievements to his credit, there is little wonder that Mahmud of Ghazni has remained the ideal, the model, of Muslims—medieval and modern.

---

54. Bosworth, *op. cit.*, pp.76, 120, 126; Hodivala, *op. cit.*, pp. 139-40, 176; Alberuni, pp. I, p.61; Fakhr-i-Mudabbir, *Adab-ul-Harb*, trs. in Rizvi, *Adi Turk Kalin Bharat* (Aligarh 1965), p.258; Utbi, *op. cit.*, p.33; *Taj-ul-Maasir*, E and D, II, p.227.

55. Utbi, E and D, II, pp.40-41.

56. *Ibid.*, pp.49-50.

Mahmud Ghaznavi had destroyed the Hindu Shahiya dynasty of Punjab. Alberuni, who witnessed its extinction says about its kings that "in all their grandeur, they never slackened in their ardent desire of doing that which is right,... they were men of noble sentiments and noble bearing".[57] On the other hand, the Ghaznavid rule in the Punjab was essentially militarist and imperialist in character, "whose sole business was to wage war against the Thakurs and Rajas (whereby) Mahmud sought to make the plunder of Hindustan a permanent affair".[58] The susceptibilities of the Indians were naturally wounded by an "inopportune display of religious bigotry", and indulgence in women and wine.[59] In such a situation, "Hindu sciences retired away from those parts of the country conquered by us, and fled to Kashmir, Benaras and other places".[60]

Sultan Mahmud's acts of Islamic piety like iconoclasm and proselytization were continued by future Muslim invaders and rulers and became a legacy of Muslim rule in India.

Mahmud was present with Subuktigin when the latter received the letter of Jayapal, cited above, emphasising the impetuosity of the Hindu soldiers and their indifference to death, and the Ghaznavids were convinced of their bravery and spirit of sacrifice. Years later Hasan Nizami, the author of *Taj-ul-Maasir* wrote about them like this: "The Hindus... in the rapidity of their movements exceeded the wild ass and the deer, you might say they were demons in human form."[61] Mahmud Ghaznavi therefore employed Hindu soldiers and sent them, along with Turks, Khaljis, Afghans and Ghaznavids against Ilak Khan when the lat-

57. Alberuni, II, p.13.
58. M.Habib, *Mahmud of Ghaznin*, p.95.
59. C.H.I., III, p.28.
60. Alberuni, I, p.22.
61. E and D, II, 208.

ter intruded into his dominions.[62] We learn from Baihaqi's
Tarikh-i-Subuktigin and "from other histories" that "even
only fifty days after the death of Mahmud, his son dis-
patched Sewand Rai, a Hindu chief, with a numerous
body of Hindu cavalry, in pursuit of the nobles who had
espoused the cause of his brother. In a few days a conflict
took place, in which Sewand Rai, and the greatest part of
his troops were killed; but not till after they had inflicted
a heavy loss upon their opponents. Five years afterwards
we read of Tilak, son of Jai Sen, commander of all the
Indian troops in the service of the Ghaznavid monarch,
being employed to attack the rebel chief, Ahmad Niyaltigin. He pursued the enemy so closely that many thousands fell into his hands. Ahmad himself was slain while
attempting to escape across a river, by a force of Hindu
Jats, whom Tilak had raised against him. This is the same
Tilak whose name is written in the *Tabqat-i-Akbari*, as
Malik bin Jai Sen, which if correct, would convey the
opinion of the author of that work, that this chief was a
Hindu convert. Five years after that event we find that
Masud, unable to withstand the power of the Seljuq
Turkomans, retreated to India, and remained there for the
purpose of raising a body of troops sufficient to make
another effort to retrieve his affairs. It is reasonable therefore to presume that the greater part of these troops consisted of Hindus. "Bijai Rai, a general of the Hindus... had
done much service even in the time of Mahmud."[63] Thus,
employment of Hindu contingents in Muslim armies, was
a heritage acquired by the Muslim rulers in India.

Another inheritance was acquisition of wealth from
Indian towns and cities whenever it suited the convenience or needs of Muslim conquerors, raiders or rulers. "It
happened," writes Utbi, "that 20,000 men from Mawaraun
nahr and its neighbourhood, who were with the Sultan

---

62. Utbi, *op. cit.*, p.32.
63. E and D, II, p.60.

(Mahmud), were anxious to be employed on some holy expedition in which they might obtain martyrdom. The Sultan determined to march with them to Kanauj..."[64] In other words, the Ghazis, to whom the loot from India had become an irresistible temptation, insisted on Mahmud to lead them to India for fresh adventures in plunder and spoliation. Even when Muslim Sultanate had been established, Muhammad Ghauri determined on prosecuting a holy war in Hind in 602 H. (1205 C.E.), "in order to repair the fortunes of his servants and armies; for within the last few years, Khurasan, on account of the disasters it had sustained, yielded neither men nor money. When he arrived in Hind, God gave him such a victory that his treasures were replenished, and his armies renewed".[65]

In brief, Mahmud was a religious and political imperialist through and through.[66] It took him more than twenty years to extend his dominions into Punjab. But he was keenly interested in acquiring territory in India,[67] and he succeeded in his aim. It is another matter that the peace and prosperity of Punjab was gone as suggested by Alberuni's encomiums of the Hindu Shahiya kings,[68] and it was superseded by despotism and exploitation.[69] Later chroniclers write with a tinge of pride that fourteen Ghaznavids ruled at Lahore and its environs for nearly two hundred years.[70] But there was progressive deterioration in their administration. However, the importance of his occupation of most part of the Punjab lies in the fact that Muslims had come to stay in India. And these Muslims helped in the third wave of Muslim onrush which swept northern India under Muhammad Ghauri.

---

64. Utbi, E and D, II, p. 41; Reynolds, p.450.

65. Juwaini, *Tarikh-i-Jahan Kusha*, E and D, II, p.389.

66. Hasan Nizami, *Taj-ul-Maasir*, E and D, II, pp.215-17.

67. Utbi, Reynolds, p.xxv.

68. Alberuni, II, p.13.

69. Bosworth, *op. cit.*, p.59; M.Habib, *Sultan Mahmud of Ghaznin*, p. 95.

70. Badaoni, *Muntakhab-ut-Tawarikh*, Bib. Ind. Text (Calcutta, 1868-69), I, p.8; Farishtah, I, p.21.

Third Invasion

Muhammad Ghauri's invasion was mounted 150 years after the death of Mahmud Ghaznavi. How the Ghauris rose on the ashes of the Ghaznavids may be recapitulated very briefly. Sultan Mahmud died in Ghazni on 20 April 1030 at the age of sixty, leaving immense treasures and a vast empire. After his death his two sons Muhammad and Masud contested for the throne in which the latter was successful. Masud recalled Ariyaruk, the oppressive governor of Punjab, and in his place appointed Ahmad Niyaltigin. Niyaltigin marched to Benaras to which no Muslim army had gone before. The markets of the drapers, perfumers and jewellers were plundered and an immese booty in gold, silver, and jewels was seized. This success aroused the covetousness of Masud who decided to march to Hindustan in person for a holy war. He set out for India by way of Kabul in November 1037. Hansi was stormed and sacked in February the next year, but the Sultan on return realised that the campaign had been counterproductive. During his absence Tughril Beg, the Seljuq, had sacked a portion of Ghazni town and seized Nishapur in 1037. Khurasan was rapidly falling into the hands of the Seljuqs and western Persia was throwing off the yoke of Ghazni. On the Indian side an army of 80,000 Hindus under Mahipal seized Lahore in 1043, but hastily withdrew on the approach of forces from Ghazni. But curiously enough it was neither the Seljuq danger nor the threat from the Indian side that uprooted the Ghaznavids. The Seljuqs were not interested in the hilly terrain of what is now called Afghanistan, and were spreading westward to Damascus and the Mediterranean. The power that actually ousted the Ghaznavids comprised the almost insignificant tribesmen of the rugged hills of Ghaur lying between Ghazni and Herat, with their castle of Firoz Koh (Hill of Victory). They had submitted to Mahmud in 1010 C.E. and had joined his army on his Indian campaigns. But when the power of the Ghaznavids declined they raised their head. To take revenge of the death of two brothers at the hands of the Ghazni ruler, a third, Alauddin Husain, carried fire and sword throughout the kingdom. The new Ghazni which had been built by Sultan Mahmud at the cost of seven million gold coins was burnt down by Husain (1151), which earned him the title of Jahan-soz (world burner). The very graves of the hated dynasty were dug up and scattered, "but even Afghan vengeance spared the tomb of Mahmud, the idol of Muslim soldiers". Near the modern town of Ghazni that tomb and two minarets (on one of which may still be read the lofty titles of the idol-breaker) alone stand to show where, but not what, the old Ghazni was.

Alauddin, the world-burner died in 1161, and his son two years later, whereupon his nephew, Ghiyasuddin bin Sam, became the chief of Ghaur. He brought order to Ghazni and established his younger brother Muizuddin on the ruined throne of Mahmud (1173-74). Ghiyasuddin ruled at Firoz Koh and Muizuddin at Ghazni. The latter is known by three names as Muizuddin bin Sam, Shihabud-din Ghauri and Muhammad Ghauri. Muhammad Ghauri entered upon a career of conquest of India from this city.

Muhammad Ghauri was not as valiant and dashing as Mahmud, but his knowledge about India and about Islam was much better. He now possessed Alberuni's *India* and Burhanuddin's *Hidaya*, works which were not available to his predecessor invaders. Alberuni's encyclopaedic work provided to Islamic world in the eleventh century all that was advantageous to know on India.[71] It provided infor-mation on Hindu religion, Hindu philosophy, and sources of civil and religious law. Hindu sciences of astronomy, astrology, knowledge of distance of planets, and solar and lunar eclipses, physics and metaphysics are all discussed by him. Ideas on matrimony and human biology are not

---

71. Hazard, *Atlas of Islamic History*, p.42.

ignored. Hindu customs and ceremonies, their cities, kingdoms, rivers and oceans are all described. But such a treatise, written with sympathetic understanding, evoked little
kindness for the Indian people in the Muslim mind, for to
them equally important was the *Hidaya*, the most authentic work on the laws of Islam compiled by Shaikh Burhan-
ud-din Ali in the twelfth century. The Shaikh claims to
have studied all earlier commentaries on the Quran and
the Hadis belonging to the schools of Malik, Shafi and
Hanbal besides that of Hanifa.[72] These and similar works
and the military manuals like the *Siyasat Nama* and the
Adab-ul-Harb made the Ghauris and their successors better
equipped for the conquest and governance of non-Muslim
India. There need be no doubt that such works were made
available, meticulously studied and constantly referred to
by scholars attached to the courts of Muslim conquerors
and kings.

Muhammad Ghauri led his first expedition to Multan
and Gujarat in 1175. Three years later he again marched
by way of Multan, Uchch and the waterless Thar desert
toward Anhilwara Patan in Gujarat, but the Rajput Bhim
gave him crushing defeat (1178-79).[73] The debacle did not
discourage Muhammad's dogged tenacity. It only spurred
him to wrest Punjab from the Ghaznavid, and make it a
base of operations for further penetration into Indian territory. He annexed Peshawar in 1180 and marched to
Lahore the next year. He led two more expeditions,[74] in
1184 and 1186-87, before Lahore was captured. By false
promise Khusrau Malik, a prince of the Ghaznavid dynasty, was induced to come out of the fortress, was taken
prisoner and sent to Ghazni. He was murdered in 1201.

72. It was translated into English by Charles Hamilton of the East India
Company and published in England in 1791. It is easily available in a recent
reprint.

73. Minhaj, p.116; *Indian Antiquary*, 1877, pp.186-189.

74. Habibullah, *The Foundation of Muslim Rule in India*, p.57.

Not a single member of the house of Mahmud Ghaznavi was allowed to survive and the dynasty was annihilated.

With Punjab in hand, Muhammad Ghauri began to plan his attack on the Ajmer-Delhi Kingdom. Muhammad bin Qasim had fought against the Buddhist-Brahmin rulers of Sind, and Mahmud of Ghazni against the Brahman Hindu Shahiyas of the Punjab. But now fighting had to be done with the Rajputs who had by now risen everywhere to defend their motherland against the repeated invasions of foreign freebooters. Muhammad Ghauri had already tasted defeat at the hands of Solanki Rajputs in Gujarat. Therefore, he made elaborate preparations before marching towards the Punjab in 587 H./1191 C.E. He captured Bhatinda, which had been retaken by the Rajputs from the possession of its Ghaznavid governor, and placed it in charge of Qazi Ziyauddin Talaki with a contingent of 1200 horse. He was about to return to Ghazni when he learnt that Prithviraj Chauhan, the Rajput ruler of Ajmer-Delhi, was coming with a large force to attack him. He turned to meet him and encountered him at Tarain or Taraori, about ten kilometers north of Karnal. The Rajput army comprised hundreds of elephants and a few thousand horse. The Muslims were overwhelmed by sheer weight of numbers and their left and right wings were broken. In the centre, Muhammad Ghauri charged at Govind Rai, the brother of Prithviraj, and shattered his teeth with his lance. But Govind Rai drove his javelin through the Sultan's arm, and had not a Khalji Turk come to his immediate assistance, Muhammad would have lost his life.[75] His rescue and recovery helped save his army which continued its retreat in good order. Prithviraj besieged Bhatinda but the gallant Ziyauddin held out for thirteen months before he capitulated.

75. Minhaj, p.118; Farishtah, I, p.57.

At Ghazni, Muhammad severely punished the Ghauri, Khalji and Khurasani amirs,[76] whom he held responsible for his defeat. Wallets full of oats were tied to their necks and in this plight they were paraded through the city. The Sultan himself was overcome with such shame that he would neither eat nor drink nor change garments till he had avenged himself. Next year he again started from Ghazni towards Hindustan with full preparations and with a force of one hundred and two thousand Turks, Persians and Afghans. On reaching Lahore, he sent an ambassador to Ajmer and invited Prithviraj to make his submission and accept Islam. The arrogant message met with a befitting retort, and the armies of the two once more encamped opposite each other on the banks of Saraswati at Tarain, 588 H./1192 C.E. The Rajput army was far superior in numbers. Prithviraj had succeeded in enlisting the support of about one hundred Rajput princes who rallied round his banner with their elephants, cavalry and infantry. To counter such a vast number Muhammad Ghauri "adopted a tactic which bewildered the Rajputs". "Of the five divisions of his army, four composed of mountain archers, were instructed to attack (by turns) the flanks and, if possible, the rear of the Hindus, but to avoid hand to hand conflicts and, if closely pressed, to feign flight."[77] He delivered a dawn attack when the Indians were busy in the morning ablutions; the Hindus had to fight the invaders on empty stomach. Explaining the reason for the empty stomach Dr. Jadunath Sarkar writes: "It was the Hindu practice to prepare for the pitched battle by waking at 3 0'clock in the morning, performing the morning wash and worship, eating the cooked food (*pakwan*) kept ready before hand, putting on arms and marching out to their appointed places in the line of battle before sunrise... But in the second battle of Naraina (also called Tarain, Taraori)

---

76. Habibullah, *op. cit.*, pp.60-61.
77. C.H.I., III, p.40; Farishtah, I, p.58.

the Rajputs could take no breakfast; they had to snatch up their arms and form their lines as best as they could in a hurry... In vain did they try to pursue the Turko-Afghan army from 9 o'clock in the morning to 3 o'clock in the afternoon at the end of which the Hindus were utterly exhausted from the fighting, hunger and thirst."[78]

When Muhammad found that the Rajput army was sufficiently wearied, he charged their centre with 12,000 of the flower of his cavalry. The Rajputs were completely routed. Govind Rai was killed. Prithviraj was captured[79] in the neighbourhood of the river Saraswati and put to death. Enormous spoils fell into the hands of the Muslim army.

With the defeat and death of Prithviraj Chauhan, the task of the invader became easy. Sirsuti, Samana, Kuhram and Hansi were captured in quick succession with ruthless slaughter and a general destruction of temples and building of mosques. The Sultan then proceeded to Ajmer which too witnessed similar scenes. Through a diplomatic move, Ajmer was made over to a son of Prithviraj on promise of punctual payment of tribute. In Delhi an army of occupation was stationed at Indraprastha under the command of Qutbuddin Aibak who was to act as Ghauri's lieutenant in Hindustan.[80]

Further extension of territory was in the logic of conquest. After Prithviraj, the power of Jayachandra, the Gahadvala chief, was challenged. Jayachandra had not come to the aid of Prithviraj hoping, perhaps, that after the defeat of the Chauhan ruler he himself would become the sole master of Hindustan. He was old and experienced, his capital was Kanauj, his dominion extended as far as Varanasi in the east, and he was reputed to be a very

78. Hindustan Standard, 14 March 1954, later reproduced in Jadunath Sarkar, *Military History of India*.

79. Minhaj, *Tabqat-i-Nasiri*, p.120.

80. Fakhr-i-Mudabbir, *Tarikh-i-Fakhruddin Mubarakshah*, p.23; Farishtah, p.58. Hasan Nizami's account in *Taj-ul-Maasir* is detailed.

powerful prince of the time.

The Sultan himself marched from Ghazni in 1193 at the head of fifty thousand horse and gave a crushing defeat to Jayachandra on the Jamuna between Chandwar and Etah, and Kanauj and Varanasi became part of Muhammad Ghauri's dominions. The usual vandalism and acts of destruction at Varanasi struck terror into the hearts of the people about the cruelty of the "Turushkas".

Incidental Fallout

The three waves of invasions under Muhammad bin Qasim, Mahmud of Ghazni and Muhammad of Ghaur, took about five hundred years to establish Muslim rule in India. For another five hundred years Muslim sultans and emperors ruled over the country. Invaders are cruel and unscrupulous by nature and profession, and there is nothing surprising about the behaviour of these Muslim invaders. But what is unusual is that these invaders left almost a permanent legacy of political and social turmoil in India because their aims and methods were continued by Muslims even after they had become rulers.

It was the practice of the invaders to capture defenceless people and make them slaves for service and sale. We shall deal with this phenomenon by Muslim conquerors and rulers in some detail later on. Here we shall confine to the taking of captives in the early years of Muslim invasions and how it led to rather strange occurrences. Many captives taken by conquerors like Mahmud of Ghazni were sold as slaves in Transoxiana, and the Arab Empire. But many people also fled the country to save themselves from enslavement and conversion. Centuries later they are today known as Romanies or Gypsies and are found in almost all European countries like Turkey, Yugoslavia, Hungary, Italy, Austria, Germany, Spain and Britain — and even in America. In spite of being treated as aliens in Europe, in spite of persistent persecution (as for example in Germany under Hitler), they are today around 6 millions.[81]

Their nomenclature is derived from *roma* or man. They also call themselves Roma *chave* or sons of Rama, the Indian God. Gypsy legends identifying India as their land of origin, Baro Than (the Great Land), are numerous and carefully preserved.[82] Researches based on their language, customs, rituals and physiogonomy affirm that it is Hindus from India who form the bulk of these people in Europe. "They are remarkable for their yellow brown, or rather olive colour, of their skin; the jet-black of their hair and eyes, the extreme whiteness of their teeth, and generally for the symmetry of their limbs."[83]

It is believed that the first exodus of the Roma out of India took place in the seventh century which coincides with the Arab invasion of Sind. In about 700 C.E. they are found serving as musicians of the Persian court.[84] Mahmud Ghazni took them away in every campaign. Their biggest group, according to Jan Kochanowski, left the country and set off across Afghanistan to Europe in the twelfth-thirteenth century after the defeat of Prithviraj Chauhan at the hands of Muhammad Ghauri.[85] Even today "a visit to the new community of Romanies (Gypsies) in Skojpe in the southeastern part of Yugoslavia is like entering a village in Rajasthan".[86]

"With regard to their language, a large number of the words in different dialects are of Indian origin... as their persons and customs show much of the Hindu character."[87] They are freedom loving and prefer tent life. Their

81. Singhal, D.P., *India and the World Civilization*, 2 vols. (Delhi,1972) I, p.234.
82. *Ibid.*, p.246
83. *Modern Cyclopaedia*, IV, p.319.
84. *Hinduism Today*, Malaysia Edition, August 1990, p.17.
85. Cited in Singhal, *op. cit.*, p.241.
86. Rakesh Mathur in *Hinduism Today*, *op. cit.*, August, 1990, p.1.
87. *Modern Cyclopaedia*, p.319.

marriages are simple, Indian type. There is no courtship
before marriage. Taking *parikrama* (rounds) around the fire
is wholly binding, just as in India. Originally they were
vegetarians. Holi and other Hindu festivals are celebrated
in Serbia and Spain. Most of them have converted to
Christianity but maintain Shiva's Trisula (trident) — sym-
bol of God's three powers of desire, action and wisdom.
Gypsies are divided into caste groups who live in separate
areas or *mohallas*. There are 149 sub-castes among the
Bulgarian gypsies. Their professions comprise working in
wood and iron, making domestic utensils, mats and bas-
kets and practising astrology, telling fortunes and sometimes indulging in tricks. Their talent for music is remarkable.[88] Their dance and music is voluptuous, of the Indian
dom-domni type. A classic example is the Gypsy women's
snake dance, which is still performed in Rajasthan. Their
language has many Indian words. They have *manush* for
man, *zott* for Jat, *Yak, dui, trin* for *ek, do, tin*. They have
lovari for *lohari* (smith), *Sinti* for Sindhi, *sui* for needle, *sa-
chchi* for true and *duur ja* for go away. We may close with
the old Gypsy saying: "Our caravan is our family, and the
world is our family which is a direct adaptation of the
Sanskrit saying *Vasudhaiva Kutumbakam.*"[89]

The Romanies or Gypsies left India or were taken
away from here centuries ago. Their history comes down
to our own times and is extremely absorbing. But their
transplantation cannot now be counted as a legacy of
Muslim conquest or rule in India. However, there are
other activities of Muslim conquerors and rulers like
converting people to Islam or breaking idols and temples
which are still continuing and which therefore form part
of Muslim heritage. We shall now turn to these.

---

88. Arnold, *The Legacy of Islam*, p. 17.
89. D.P. Singhal, *op. cit.*, Chapter on "Romanies: Lords of the Open
Country", pp.234-266, esp. pp.249, 255, 266; Rakesh Mathur, "Hindu
Origins of Romani Nomads" in *Hinduism Today, op. cit.*, August and
September, 1990.

Chapter 4

Muslim Rule in India

"The Great Mogol is a foreigner in Hindoustan. To maintain himself in such a country....he is under the necessity of keeping up numerous armies, even in the time of peace."

Francois Bernier

Theocratic State

The State that these Muslim invaders and rulers set up in India was a theocracy. This is the conclusion arrived at by Jadunath Sarkar,[1] R.P. Tripathi,[2] K.M.Ashraf,[3] T.P. Hughes,[4] the *Encyclopaedia of Islam* [5] and many others. "All the institutions that the Muslims either evolved or adopted were intended to subserve the law,"[6] observes Tripathi. On the other hand, I.H. Qureshi says that the "supremacy of the Shara (Islamic law) has misled some into thinking that the Sultanate was a theocracy."[7] Qureshi's contention may not be taken seriously, because he tries to eulogize every aspect of Muslim rule in India.[8] But even Mohammad Habib declares that "it (Muslim state in India) was not a theocratic state in any sense of the

---

1. *History of Aurangzeb*, III, pp.269-97.
2. *Some Aspects of Muslim Administration*, p.2.
3. *Life and Conditions of the People of Hindustan*, pp.138-42.
4. *Dictionary of Islam*, p.711.
5. Luzac & Co. (London, 1913-34), 1, p.959.
6. Tripathi, *op. cit.*, p 2.
7. *The Administration of the Sultanate of Delhi*, p.41.
8. Cf. Peter Hardy in Philips, *Historians of India, Pakistan and Ceylon*, p.302.

word" and that "its foundation was, non-religious and secular."[9]

Before analysing these two poles-apart views, let us first be clear about what theocracy means. According to the Oxford Dictionary the word theocracy is derived from the Greek *theos*, meaning God; and a state is theocratic when governed by God "directly or through a sacerdotal class". Theocracy envisages "direct intervention and authorship of God through revelation in government of society."[10] The Chambers Twentieth Century Dictionary defines theocracy as "that constitution of a state in which the Almighty is regarded as the sole soverign, and the laws of the realm as divine commands rather than human ordinances, the priesthood necessarily becoming the officers of the invisible ruler."[11]

The above premise makes three elements essential in a theocracy: (1) prevalance of the law of God, (2) authority of the soverign or ruler who promulgates this law, and (3) presence of a sacerdotal class or priesthood through which this law is disseminated. Let us examine to what extent these elements were present in the Muslim state in medieval India. We need not discuss the first two elements for, according to Dr. Qureshi himself, the Shara "is based on the Quran which is believed by every Muslim to be the word of God revealed to His prophet Muhammad...on these two rocks — the Quran and Hadis (the prophet's interpretations, traditions) is built the structure of Muslim Law....This Law was the actual sovereign in Muslim lands."[12]

So far as the third element is concerned, it is true that there was no 'ordained' or 'hereditary' Muslim priesthood in medieval India. But there was a scholastic class called

9. Introduction to the English trs. of Ziyauddin Barani's *Fatawa-i-Jahandari*, p.vi.

10. Concise Oxford Dictionary, p.1271.

11. 1950 Edition, p.1005

12. Qureshi, *op. cit.*, p.41.

the Ulama, who wielded great influence with the Sultan. About their education and orthodoxy, Dr. Yusuf Husain has this to say: "The institutions of higher learning....called Madrasa, had developed into centres of learning with a distinct religious bias. They were essentially schools of theology... These Madrasas were the strongholds of ortho-doxy and were subsidized by the state."[13] From amongst the products of these schools of theology were appointed jurists, advisers of Sultans and kings, and interpreters of the Shara (Islamic law). "The protection of Shariat," writes Ibn Hasan, "has two aspects: The propagation of the knowledge of Shara and its enforcement as law within the state. The one implies the maintenance of a class of schol-ars devoted to the study, the teaching and the propagation of that knowledge, and the other the appointment of one from those scholars....as an adviser to the king in all his acts of state. The scholars devoted to that knowledge are called Ulama and the one selected from among them is termed Shaikh-ul-Islam."[14] The Shaikh-ul-Islam was the representative of the Ulama and it was his duty to bring "to the notice of the King what he thought detrimental or prejudicial to the interest of his religion, and the king had little option in acting upon such an advice."[15] Henry Blochmann elaborates the position still further. "Islam has no state clergy," says he, "but we find a counterpart to our hierarchical bodies in the Ulemas about the court from whom the Sadrs of the provinces, the Mir Adls, Muftis and Qazis were appointed. At Delhi and Agra, the body of the learned had always consisted of staunch *Sunnis*, who believed it their duty to keep the kings straight. How great their influence was, may be seen from the fact that of all Muhammadan emperors only Akbar, and perhaps Alaud-din Khalji, succeeded in putting down this haughty

13. Yusuf Husain, *Glimpses of Medieval Indian Culture*, p.69.
14. Ibn Hasan, *The Central Structure of the Mughal Empire*, pp.255-56.
15. *Ibid.*, p.258.

sect."[16] No amount of arguments can obliterate the fact of the great influence of the priestly class (Ulama and Mashaikh) in the Muslim state.

Thus the law which obtained in medieval India was the Shara which was based on divine revelation. It was not a secular law. Muslim state could not be a secular state. In fact Islam and secularism are mutually exclusive. One has only to read the Quran and a few Persian chronicles of medieval times to realise the extent to which the Muslim state in India was theocratic both in spirit and in action.

The fundamental basis of the Islamic polity is the attainment of complete religious uniformity, to root out heresy and to extirpate infidelity — populations everywhere were to be converted into true believers.[17] The Quranic injuction is: "And when the sacred months (*Ramzan*) are passed, kill those who join other deities with God, wherever you shall find them. But if they shall convert....then let them go their way."[18] The prophet of Islam who had accorded some sort of religious toleration to the Jews of Medina, expelled them afterward to bring about a complete religious uniformity in that city, while Caliph Omar I (C.E. 634-644) expelled the Jews and Christians from the whole of Arabia.[19]

In India the decision of Muhammad bin Qasim to accord to the Hindus the status of *Zimmis* (protected people against payment of *jiziyah*) paved the way for subsequent Muslim rulers to follow the same precedent; else Hindus as idolaters could not be given this concession reserved for *Ahl-i-Kitab* (or the People of the Book)— Christians and Jews — and could only be given a choice between conversion and death. In all their discussions the

---

16. *Ain*, I, pp.xxxii-xxxiii.
17. Quran VIII, 39-40; English trs. by George Sale, p.172; Jadunath Sarkar, *Aurangzeb* (3rd Ed.), III, p.249.
18. Quran IX, 5, 6; Sale, p.179.
19. P.K.Hitti, *History of the Arabs*, pp.177, 179.

Ulama and Sufis never conceded the status of *Zimmis* to the Hindus. In this regard the declaration of the 'secular' Alim and Sufi, Amir Khusrau, may be taken as final: "Happy Hindustan, the splendour of Religion, where the Law finds perfect honour and security. The whole country, by means of the sword of our holy warriors, has become like a forest denuded of its thorns by fire... Islam is triumphant, idolatry is subdued. Had not the Law granted exemption from death by the payment of poll-tax, the very name of Hind, root and branch, would have been extinguished."[20] If the sultans treated Hindus as *Zimmis*, it was because of the compulsions of the Indian situation.

Even so, the Hindus, as *Zimmis*, became second class citizens in their own homeland and were suffered to live under certain disabilities. One of them was that each adult must pay a poll-tax called *jiziyah*. "Moreover, the main object in levying the tax is the subjection of infidels to humiliation[21] ...and...during the process of payment, the *Zimmi* is seized by the collar and vigorously shaken and pulled about in order to show him his degradation."[22] The *Zimmis* also had to suffer in respect of their mode of worship, payment of taxes, and on account of certain sumptuary laws.[23] Death awaited them at every corner, because, being idolaters they could be given a choice only between Islam and death.[24] "The State rested upon the support of the military class which consisted largely of the followers of the faith. They were treated as the favoured children of the state while various kinds of disabilities were imposed upon the non-Muslim...It is interesting to

20. *Ashiqa*, trs. E and D, III, pp.545-46.
21. *Encyclopaedia of Islam*, I,p.959; Tritton, *Caliphs and their non-Muslim Subjects*, p.21; Hitti, *History of the Arabs*, pp.119, 171, 228-45; R.P.Tripathi, *Some Aspects of Muslim Administration*, p.340.
22. Aghnides, *Muhammadan Theories of Finance*, pp.399-528.
23. Barani, pp.216-17; *Encyclopaedia of Islam*, I,pp.958-59.
24. Tripathi, *op. cit.*, p.340 citing Fagnan's French trs. of Abu Yusuf's *Kitab-ul-Kharaj*; Barani, p.291.

note that even (illiterate and unscrupulous) foreign adventurers were preferred just because they were Muslims to hold offices of importance and dignity which were denied to the Hindus."[25]

There are countless examples of prejudicial treatment meted out to non-Muslims under the theocratic government. Only a few may be mentioned here as an illustration. Amir Khusrau writes that under Jalauddin Khalji (1290-96), after a battle, "whatever live Hindu fell into the hands of the victorious king was pounded to bits under the feet of the elephants. The Musalman captives had their lives spared".[26] Similarly, Malik Kafur, the famous general of Alauddin Khalji (1296-1316), while on his expeditions in South India, spared the lives of Muslims fighting on the side of the Hindu Rai as they deserted to his army.[27] Rizqullah Mushtaqi is all praise for Sultan Sikandar Lodi (1489-1517) because under him the Muslims dominated and the Hindus were suppressed (musalman chira dast va hinduan ram).[28] It was not only so in the medieval period. Such discrimination is observed in theocratic states even today.

"When, in 1910, Boutros Pasha was murdered by an Egyptian Muhammadan for no personal provocation but for the political reason that he had presided over the court that sentenced the Denshawai villagers, and the guilt of the murderer was conclusively proved by evidence, the Chief Qazi of Egypt pronounced the judgement that according to Islam it is no crime for a Muslim to slay an unbeliever. This is the opinion held by the highest exponent of Islamic law in a modern civilized country."[29]

---

25. Lal, *Twilight of the Sultanate*, p.288.
26. *Miftah-ul-Futuh* (Aligarh text, 1954), p.22 (*za hindu harche amad zinda dar dast/bazere pae pilan khurd ba shikast/musalmanan-i-bandi gushta ra baz/bajan bakhshi chu isa gasht damsaz*).
27. Lal, *Khaljis*, p. 250.
28. *Waqiat-i-Mushtaqi*, fol. 40 a.
29. Jadunath Sarkar, *Aurangzeb*, III, p.151 note.

And here is a case of the year 1990. "Sunil Vadhera
was employed with M/s. Archirodo Construction (Over-
seas) Co., Riyadh. He died in an accident caused by a
Greek national of M/s. Saboo. The defender deposited
1,00,000 Saudi *riyals* or Rs. 4.65 lakh with the Saudi government as compensation for death. But the Shariat Saudi
court has ruled that as the 'deceased was a Hindu, as per
Shariat law he was entitled to Saudi *riyals* 6,666.66 only or
Rs.30,000'. This is just about one-fifteenth of the compensation that the parents would have got if their son was a
Muslim."[30]

The disabilities the Hindus suffered under this Islamic
or *Shariat* law are clearly mentioned in the Quran, the
Hadis and the *Hidaya*. It would be the best to go through
these works as suggested in Chapter 2. However, these are
also summarised in the *Encyclopaedia of Islam*,[31] T.P.
Hughes's *Dictionary of Islam*,[32] N.P.Aghnides's *Muhammadan Theories of Finance*,[33] Blochmann's translation of the
Ain-i-Akbari,[34] Ziyauddin Barani's *Tarikh-i-Firoz Shahi*[35]
and a host of other Persian chronicles, and there is no need
to repeat here 'zimmi', 'kharajguzar', 'jiziyah' syndrome.
The fact to be noted is that Shariat law continued to prevail throughout the medieval period.

The *Shariat* law was so brazenly prejudicial to the
interests of the vast majority of the non-Muslims (and
hence the wishful thinking that it did not prevail and that
the medieval state was 'secular'), that even the medieval
thinkers and rulers found it impracticable to enforce it in
full. When the nobles and Ulama of the Sultanate pressed
Shamsuddin Iltutmish to enforce the *Shara*, and give the
Hindus a choice between Islam and death, the latter asked

30. *Times of India*, 6.8.1990, under the caption: "Little value for his life."
31. Vol.1, pp.958-59.
32. pp.248, 711.
33. (New York, 1917), pp.399, 528.
34. Introduction.
35. *Tarikh-i-Firoz Shahi* (Calcutta, 1862), p.290.

for time.[36] Equally helpless (or shrewd) were Balban and Jalaluddin Khalji.[37] It was probably the experience of such rulers that prompted Ziyauddin Barani to advocate that if the enforcement of the *Shariat* was impossible or impracticable, new laws should be enacted by rulers. "It is the duty of a king," says he, "to enforce, if he can, those royal laws which have become proverbial owing to their principles of justice and mercy. But if owing to change of time and circumstances he is unable to enforce the laws of the ancients (i.e. ancient Muslim rulers), he should, with the counsel of wise men....frame laws suited to his time and circumstances and proceed to enforce them. Much reflection is necessary in order that laws, suited to his reign, are properly framed."[38] So that they in no way contravene the tenets of Islam. These laws Barani calls *Zawabits*.

Barani wrote in the fourteenth century. Perhaps he had in mind the rules of Alauddin Khalji about Market Control or his revenue regulations. Else, right up to the first half of the sixteenth century no king made any laws of the kind. No chronicler has made mention of any such laws. It was late in the sixteenth century that Akbar promulgated a number of regulations for "the real benefit of people." There were some tolerant monarchs in medieval India, and yet none except Akbar ever thought of enacting any laws which would have removed to some extent the disabilities imposed on the majority of the population. Between 1562 and 1564 he abolished the pilgrim tax, the *jiziyah* and the practice of enslaving prisoners of war. Restrictions were imposed on the manufacture and sale of liquor in 1582 and the same year child marriage was discouraged by fixing the marriage age at 14 for girls and 16

---

36. *Sana-i-Muhammadi* (Rampur Ms.) cited in *Medieval India Quarterly*, Vol.1, Pt. III, pp.100-105; K.A.Nizami, *Religion and Politics in India in the Thirteenth Century*, pp.315-16.

37. Barani, pp.70-79, 151, 216.

38. *Fatawa-i-Jahandari*, p.64.

for boys. In 1587 Akbar legalized widow remarriage and prohibited *Sati* for *Bal Vidhvas* in 1590-91. In 1601 he took the revolutionary step of permitting individuals to choose their religion and those who had been forcibly converted to Islam could go back to their former faith. But even Akbar did not 'codify' any laws as such for his successors to follow. His beneficial and equitable regulations remained, as they could remain, only for his empire and during his life-time. It is significant to note that even in the few reforms that Akbar ordered, many nobles and Ulama saw a danger to Islam.

So what Barani calls *Zawabits* were few and far between, and the *Shara* continued to be the supreme law prevalent in the Turkish and Mughal times. No wonder, contemporary chroniclers always eulogized the Indian Muslim kings as defenders of the Islamic faith. This tickled their vanity and prompted them to be strict in the enforcement of the law. It encouraged them to be iconoclasts, it made them patronize the Muslim minority and resort to all kinds of methods to obtain conversions, besides, of course, at the same time treating the non-Muslims unfairly to exhibit their love for their own faith. Secondly, the Ulama always tried to keep the kings straight. They considered it their sacred duty to see that the kings not only did not stray away from the path of religion and law, but also enforced it on the people. Such indeed was their influence that even strong monarchs did not dare suppress them. Others, of course, tried to walk on the path shown by this bigoted scholastic class. The third and the most important reason was that protestation of championship for Islam buttressed the claim of the king for the crown, for a ruler was not safe on the throne if he did not enforce the Shara. At the close of the Khalji regime, Ghiyasuddin declared himself as a champion of the faith, because the Ulama had been dissatisfied with Alauddin's policies and Ghiyasuddin with the activities of Nasiruddin Khusrau.

"The slogan of 'Islam in danger' so common yet so effective in the history of the Muslims, was started."[39] And this to a great degree won Ghiyasuddin Tughlaq the throne. The Ulama were equally dissatisfied with Muhammad bin Tughlaq. On his demise, Shaikh Nasiruddin Chiragh obtained from Firoz a promise "that he would rule according to the tenets of justice and law." Firoz Shah Tughlaq proved true to his word and "made religion the basis of his government."[40] A little later Amir Timur openly claimed to have attacked Hindustan with the avowed object of destroying idolatry and infidelity in the country.[41] Akbar's tolerance had exasperated the Muslim divines, and a promise was obtained from his successor, Jahangir, that he would defend the Muslim religion. Immediately after Akbar's death "Mulla Shah Ahmad, one of the greatest religious leaders of the age, wrote to various court dignitaries exhorting them to get this state of things altered in the very begining of (Jahangir's) reign because otherwise it would be difficult to accomplish anything later on."[42] Aurangzeb openly claimed to have fought "the apostate" Dara to re-establish the law of Islam. Thus, whether we consider the influence of the Muslim religious class (the Ulama), the application of the law of Islam (*Shara*), or the activities of the kings, it is clear beyond doubt that the medieval state was a theocratic state. No wonder that many contemporary and later Muslim writers praise the deeds of Aurangzeb with great gusto. The name of Akbar is obliterated: it does not find mention by a single Muslim chronicler after his death.

Why is then there a desire to escape from this fact? In modern times values of life have changed. Today, in an

39. Tripathi, *op. cit.*, p.56
40. Afif, p.29.
41. Sharafuddin Yazdi, *Zafar Nama*, II,p.15.
42. V.A.Smith, *Akbar the Great Mogul*, p.233. Smith writes on the authority of Du Jarric, III, p.133.
43. Sri Ram Sharma, *The Religions Policy of the Mughal Emperors*, p.61.

age of science and secularism, ideas of religious disabilities and persecution appear to be so out of tune with human behaviour, that we are made to believe that such disabilities were never there even in the past. Modern Indian government is based on the ideals of secularism. It tries to eschew religious controversies. It is felt that such was the position through the ages without realising that even now disabilities of non-Muslims are existing in many Islamic countries.

Fealty to Caliph

To maintain the Islamic character of the state, and to stabilize their own position as Muslim rulers, the Sultans of Delhi professed to be subservient to the Caliph. "Just as the Prophet is the viceregent of God and the Caliph is the viceregent of the Prophet," says T.W. Arnold, "the monarch is viceregent of the Caliph... No king of the east and the west can hold the title of Sultan unless there be a covenant between him and the Caliph."[44]

The Muslim Sultanate in Hindustan was carved out and maintained by the sword, but it derived sustenance also from some moral bases of political power. These consisted of the government's unqualified propagation of the Islamic religion, adherence to the *Shariat* law, regard for the Ulama and Sufis, and recognition of the supremacy of the Caliph. The sultans feigned to have trumped-up geneologies and on that basis claimed respect for the regime. The Ghaznavids and Ghaurids were plebians but to acquire legitimacy they sought high pedigrees, took grandiose titles, claimed divine origin for their kingship, and connected themselves with the old ruling families of Iran and Turan.[45] Balban sought his descent from Afra-

44. Arnold, *The Caliphate*, pp.173, 73, 101, 102; Qureshi, *op. cit.*, pp. 24, 25; Aziz Ahmad, *Islamic Culture in the Indian Environment*, p.11.

45. Eg. Minhaj-us-Siraj, *Tabqat-i-Nasiri*, Persian Text, Bib. Ind., Calcutta, pp.16 ff.

siyab, the legendary hero of Persia, and gave to his sons and grandsons names of old Persian princes. Every sultan took high-sounding titles, and the Ulama made him and the people believe that he was the shadow of God on earth. Fictitious geneologies counted in politics, high titles created awe, and divine right and religious fervour earned the respect of high and low.

Withal a very important moral basis for Muslim political power in Hindustan was the recognition the Indian sultan received from the Caliph, the respected head of the medieval Muslim world. The first four Caliphs were directly related to the Prophet. Muawiyah, the founder of the Ummayad Caliphate, was a cousin and Abbas, the founder of the Abbasid Caliphate, an uncle of Muhammad. There was therefore very great reverence for the Caliphs in the world of Islam. The Abbasids had built up a large empire with capital at Baghdad.[46] It is true that the Abbasid Caliphs did not enjoy any authority in the west. But the Muslim countries possessing an Islamic government and an Islamic civilization, were connected by such strong ties of common religion and common culture that their inhabitants felt themselves "citizens of a vast empire of which Mecca was the religious, and Baghdad the cultural and political centre...."[47] Its provinces were administered by their Turkish slave governors and Turkish mercenary troops. As the Caliphal empire disintegrated, in the third century of Islam, its provincial governors became independent.[48] But officially these were only slaves and their tenure of power was based on force and chance. They, therefore, thought it politic not to snap their connections with the Khalifa completely, to go on paying him tribute and seek from him recognision of their 'sovereignity.' The Caliphs too were eager to secure such

---

46. Ruben Levy, *The Baghdad Chronicle*, p.13.
47. J.H. Kramers in Sir Thomas Arnold, *The Legacy of Islam*, pp.79-80.
48. Ruben Levy, *The Social Structure of Islam*, p.282.

wealth as could be obtained from these self-manumitted, self-appointed rulers by granting investitures which cost the Caliphs nothing. Thus came into being a sort of an Islamic commonwealth under the aegis of the Khalifa.

The contacts of Muslim rulers of India with the Caliphs were of old. The Arab governors of Sind used to read the *khutba* in the name of the Ummayad Caliphs. Even in the distribution of the booty taken by the early Arab invaders, one-fifth was reserved for the Khalifa.[49] Under the jurisdiction of Saffah Abul Abbas, the first Abbasid Caliph, there were twelve provinces including Sind.[50] Even when Sind had reverted to a period of Hindu domination, the *khutba* continued to be read in mosques in the name of the Abbasid Caliph,[51] which boosted the morale of the few Muslims living there.

Mahmud Ghaznavi's campaigns in India had Caliphal blessings.[52] The introduction of Muslim rule in India was accordingly directly obliged to the Khalifa. Like the Ghaznavids, the Ghaurids were also alive to the importance of obtaining the confirmation of their sovereignty from the Caliphs of Baghdad. The earliest Muslim rulers of Hindustan were originally slaves, and it was recognised in all quarters that their position as rulers would be buttressed if they could receive caliphal recognition. Tajuddin Yilduz, the ruler of Ghazni, obtained the Caliph's sanction for his authority. After Yilduz and Qubacha had been destroyed by Iltutmish, the latter received the investiture from the Abbasid Caliph al-Mustansir Billah as a legal sanction of his monarchy.[53] It is not known if Iltutmish

49. Murray Titus, *Islam in India and Pakistan*, p.55; Al-Biladuri, E and D, I, p.201. Also E and D, I, Appendix, p.462.

50. Khuda Bakhsh, *Orient Under the Caliphs*, p.218.

51. Al Istakhri, E and D, I, p.28.

52. Bosworth, C.E., *The Ghaznavids*, pp.53, 54.

53. Minhaj, Raverty, I, p.616 and n. 4; Thomas, Edward, *Chronicles of the Pathan Kings of Delhi*, pp.46, 52. The patent of investiture was called *Manshur*, and the robe of honour such as turban, swords, ensigns and other gifts were called *Karamat*.

had requested the Khalifa for it and if so how much
wealth and presents he had sent. However, he was overwhelmed with happiness and "religiously bound himself
to the rules of obedience and submission". Iltutmish inscribed the Caliph's name on his coins and called himself
Nasir-i-Amirul-Mauminin (helper of the Islamic Caliph).[54]
This "fact fastened the fiction of Khalafat on the Sultanate
of Delhi, and involved legally the recognition of the final
sovereignty of the Khalifa, an authority outside the geo-
graphical limits of India, but inside the vague yet none the
less real brotherhood of Islam (1229)."[55] However, the
interesting point is that the Caliph at the same time conferred a patent of investiture also on Ghiyasuddin of
Bengal. What were his considerations for simultaneously
recongnising two sultans in Hindustan, is not known.
Perhaps whosoever sent presents and treasures was conferred with an investiture. But Iltutmish defeated Ghiyas
and forced him to recognise him (Iltutmish) as a superior
(Sultan-i-Azam).[56]

Such was the moral support derived from the Caliph's
recognition that even after the murder of the Baghdad
Caliph Al-Mustasim by the Mongols in 1258, his name
continued to appear on the coins of Indian sultans like
Ghiyasuddin Balban, Muizuddin Kaiqubad and Jalaluddin Khalji. Jalaluddin even called himself Yaminul Khilafat (Right hand of the Caliphate), reminiscent of Al-
Qadir's title to Mahmud Ghaznavi. The Abbasid Caliph of
Baghdad was no more, but the association of his name
was of such great import that it was not given up by the
Delhi rulers.

Alauddin Khalji (C.E. 1296-1316) made a departure
from the practice probably because he had built up a

---

54. Thomas, *Chronicles*, pp.168, 173. Also Amir Khusrau, *Aijaz-i-
Khusravi* (Lucknow, 1876), p.14.
55. Tripathi, R.P., *Some Aspects of Muslim Administration*, p.26.
56. Minhaj, Raverty, I, pp.610, 774 and n.

strong empire and also, because he had come to learn about the demise of the Abbasid Caliph. His son and successor Qutbuddin Mubarak Khalji went a step further. He himself assumed the title of Caliph. He had inherited a strong empire built up by Alauddin Khalji, and he was young. He might not have cared to pay homage to a dead Caliph, or even might have thought that if there could be Caliphs in Madinah, Dimishq (Damascus), Baghdad and Qurtubah (Cordova), and later on in Qahirah (Cairo) why not in India, which was, if Amir Khusrau's *Nuh Sipehr* at all reflects Qutbuddin's views, superior to all countries. But these are only conjectures; the real reasons for his assumption of Caliphal titles are not known. He appropriated to himself titles like Amir-ul-Mauminin and Imam-i-Azam, as well as the pseudo-Abbasid ruling name of Wasiq.[57] But this was an isolated case of assumption of Caliphal titles by an Indian sultan, and at that a profligate. Though not without some interest, it is hardly of any significance in the history of the Sultanate.

Nasiruddin Khusrau and Ghiyasuddin Tughlaq continued with the old pattern of loyalty to a universal Caliphate, while Muhammad Tughlaq did not rest content until he had made the discovery of the presence of the Abbasid Caliph Al-Mustakfi in exile at Cairo, and applied to him for investiture. His obvious motive was to strengthen his waning authority reflected in the recurrent rebellions in all parts of the country.[58] In such a situation he did not try to seek support in India from his (non-Muslim) people, but he attached such great importance to Caliphal recognition that he declared that all the sultans who had not applied for or received Caliphal investiture as usurpers (*Mutaghallib*). In 1343 he received the Caliphal

---

57. Thomas, *Chronicles*, pp.179-83.

58. Clearly seen in Ain-ul-Mulk Multani, *Qasaid-i-Badr Chach* (Kanpur, n.d.), pp.13,17, cited in Abdul Aziz, *op. cit.*, p.9. and trs. in E and D, III, p.569. Mahdi Husain lists 22 revolts during his reign (*Tughlaq Dynasty*, p.195).

edict and the robe of honour. His religious devotion to the Caliph and emotional behaviour towards the Caliph's envoys were so ludicurous as to call forth a contemptuous comment from the contemporary chronicler Ziyauddin Barani. "So great was the faith of the Sultan in the Abbasid Khalifas," says he, "that he would have sent all his treasures in Delhi to Egypt, had it not been for the fear of robbers."[59] But the Sultan must have sent a substantial amount, because when Ghiyasuddin, who was only a descendant of the extinct Caliphal house of Baghdad, visited India, Muhammad's bounty knew no bounds. He gave him a million *tankahs* (400,000 *dinars*), the fief of Kanauj, and the fort of Siri, besides such valuable articles as gold and silver wares, pages and slave girls. Withal one thousand *dinars* were given for head-wash, a bath-tub of gold, and three robes on which in place of knots or buttons there were 'pearls as large as big hazel nuts.'[60] If this was given to a scion of a house which had become defunct, how much more was sent to the living Caliph at Cairo can only be surmised. No wonder that because of the generosity of the Sultan, in his time the Caliphal investitures were received more than once.[61] Muhammad Tughlaq included the names of Abbasid Al-Mustakfi and his successors Al-Wasiq I and Al-Hakim in his *khutba*, and inscribed on his coins their names to the exclusion of his own.[62]

Such an attitude of subservience combined with munificence encouraged the Caliph to send to Muhammad's successor Firoz Tughlaq, a patent of investiture, entrusting to him the territories of Hind.[63] Although the honour was unsolicited, yet Firoz felt extremely happy as he confesses

59. Barani, p.493.
60. Ibn Battuta, p.73.
61. Ishwari Prasad, *A History of the Qaraunah Turks*, I, p.182 and n. 125.
62. Thomas, *Chronicles*, pp.207-16, 246-53, 259-60.
63. Barani, p.598; Afif, pp.274-76; Yahiya Sarhindi, *Tarikh-i-Mubarak Shahi*, Bib. Ind. Text, p.126.

in his *Futuhat-i-Firoz Shahi* that "the greatest and best of honours that I obtained through God's mercy was, that by my obedience and piety, and friendliness and submission to the Khalifa, the representative of the holy Prophet, my authority was confirmed; for it is by his (Caliph's) sanction that the power of the kings is assured, and no king is secure until he has submitted himself to the Khalifa, and has received a confirmation from the sacred throne."[64] Firoz Tughlaq's successors continued to inscribe the name of Al-Mutawakkil on their coins.

With the fall of the Tughlaq dynasty the name of the Caliph was dropped from Delhi coins. To the Saiyyad rulers, Timur and his successors were the real "Caliphs". "More than once, robe of honour and flag came from (Shah Rukh) to Delhi for Khizr Khan" and Mubarak Khan. In return annual tribute was sent to Shah Rukh.[65] Sultan Muhammad Saiyyad also remained loyal to him.[66] Henceforward it was Timur who provided source of inspiration to the Indian Muslim regime. Muslim regime in India depended for sustenance and strength not on the Indian people but on foreign Muslim Caliphs and potentates. For, while the Saiyyad Sultans were obliged to Amir Timur for installing them on the Delhi throne, the Mughal emperors descended directly from him. Timur or Tamerlane had carried fire and sword into Hindustan (1398-99) and his name revived horrendous memories among the Indian people, but to the Mughal emperors his name provided as good an inspiration for their Islamic rule in India as that of the Caliphs for the Delhi Sultans. Zahiruddin Muhammad Babur as a conqueror and a descendant of Amir Timur, assumed the title of Ghazi. But so also did

---

64. Translated in E and D, III, p.387.
65. Yahiya Sarhindi, *Tarikh-i-Mubarak Shahi*, p.218; Lal, *Twilight of the Sultanate*, pp.71, 93 and n. 50.
66. Muhammad Bihamad Khani, *Tarikh-i-Muhammadi*, Eng. trs. by Muhammad Zaki (Aligarh, 1972), p.95.

Jahangir, although "a true Indian,"[67] adopt the lofty title of "Nuruddin Mohammad Jahangir Padshah Ghazi."[68] Shahjahan, who was more Indian than even Jahangir, took the title of "Abul Muzaffar Shihabuddin Muhammad Sahib-i-Qiran-i-Sani (or Timur the Second)."[69] Right up to the end of the Mughal empire in India, the Mughal kings took pride in calling themselves descendants of Amir Timur and in belonging to the Chaghtai Turk clan of the Mongols. The last Mughal emperor Bahadur Shah Zafar asked Mirza Ghalib to write a history of the "Taimuria dynasty" on a payment of rupees six hundred annually as noted by the poet in his *Dastanbuy*. Furthermore, after the collapse of Mughal power early in the nineteenth century, the name of the Sultan of Turkey began to be mentioned in *khutba* in Indian mosques.

While the Mughal kings sought inspiration from the name of Timur and the Turkish Sultan, the people of India considered them as foreigners for that very reason. Bernier did not fail to notice that "the *Great Mogol* is a foreigner in *Hindustan*, a descendant of *Tamerlane*, chief of those Mogols from Tartary who, about the year 1401, overran and conquered the Indies, consequently he finds himself in a hostile country, or nearly so..."[70] In short, except for the confusion created by Indian-ness or foreign-ness of emperor Akbar,[71] the state remained basically foreign in character throughout the medieval period. The aim of the Caliphs in inspiring the Sultans of Delhi and that of Timur in invading India was the same, to spread Islam in idolatrous Hindustan.[72]

---

67. *Tuzuk-i-Jahangiri*, Eng. trs. Rogers and Beveridge, preface, p.x.
68. Beni Prasad, *A History of Jahangir*, p.113.
69. Banarsi Prasad Saksena, *History of Shahjahan of Dihli*, p.63.
70. Bernier, p.209.
71. Vincent Smith says: "Akbar was a foreigner in India. He had not a drop of Indian blood in his veins" (*Akbar the Great Mogul*, p.7).
72. Sharafuddin Yazdi, *Zafar Nama*, II, pp.29, 30.

Before closing the discussion on the Caliph's status in the eyes of the Delhi Sultans, an often-asked question may be attempted to be answered. Did the Caliphal recognition make the Sultanate of Delhi subservient to the Caliphs? Although it would be difficult to subscribe to the view that by receiving a formal Caliphal investiture, Iltutmish had made "the Delhi Sultanate a direct vassal" of the Caliphate,[73] yet as Firoz Tughlaq admitted, the Indian sultans were convinced that "it is by the Caliph's sanction that the power of the kings is assured; and no king is secure until he has submitted himself to the Khalifa". No wonder none of the sultans who ruled between Iltutmish and the later Tughlaqs repudiated this legal "vassalage" with the inexplicable exception of Mubarak Khalji. They all claimed to be the lieutenants of the Caliph, the supreme head of the world of Islam. Allegiance to the Caliph by India's Muslim kings gave the Khalifa prestige and wealth. It gave the Indian Sultans, many of whom were originally slaves, a status of honour in the Muslim world and satisfied the formalities of Muslim law.[74] Moreover, inclusion of the Caliph's name in the *khutba*, endeared the sultan to his Muslim subjects.[75] Besides, the way in which Caliphal envoys and investitures were received, indicates that this was not just lip subservience, and the extra-territorial allegiance to the Caliph provided a very strong moral and legal basis of political power to the Muslim regime in

---

73. Habibullah, A.B.M., *The Foundation of Muslim Rule in India* p.233.
74. Tripath, *op. cit.*, p.26.
75. It were not only the sultans of Delhi, but also of Jaunpur and Bengal who called themselves viceregents of the Abbasid Caliphs (Thomas, *Chronicles*, pp.194, 197, 321-322). The Caliph Al-Mustanjid Billah sent to Sultan Mahmud Khalji of Malwa robes of honour and a letter patent. Mahmud accepted the gifts of the Khalifa with due honour and gave in return to the envoy *tashrifat*, and a large amount of gold and silver. Even some rebels of the Delhi Sultanate received the Caliphal investure (Aziz Ahmad, *op. cit.*, p.10).

India. Timur's name and *Institutes* provided similar legitimacy and strength to Mughal emperors.

So that, in the Islamic state, Delhi was not the capital
of the empire; it was *Quwwat-ul-Islam*. The king was not
the ruler of the people; he was *Amir-ul-Mauminin*, "the
conqueror of infidels and shelterer of Islam." The army
was not the royal army; it was *Lashkar-i-Islam*. The soldier
was not a cavalry man or infantry man; he was *Ahl-i-Jihad*.
The law of the state was not any secular or humanitarian
law; it was *Shariat*, the law of Islam. The state was not an
end in itself, like the Greek state, but a means of sub-
serving the interests of Islam. Conquests were made,
shrines were broken, captives were taken, converts were
made — all in the name of Islam. The *raison d'etre* of the
regime was to disseminate the Islamic faith.[76]

Administrative Apparatus

This aim of the Muslim state could be achieved
through its administrative set up and military might.
Actually the theocratic nature of the state and fealty to the
Caliph formed the moral bases of the regime's authority;
administration and army its material strength. All these
components were alien and exotic and were implanted
from abroad. In its core the administration was Islamic
and was based on Quran and Hadis, though Persia also
contributed much to its development and application in
India.

The administrative system of Islam had evolved
gradually. In Arabia, in its earliest stages, the problem was
to provide the new converts made by Muhammad with
subsistence. They were indigent and poor, and to help
them, poor tax (*zakat*), voluntary contributions, and war-
booty (*ghanaim*) formed the revenue of the state at the
start. Muhammad was followed (632 C.E.) by a succession

---

76. Lal, K.S., *Early Muslim in India*, p.90.

of Caliphs at Medina.[77] According to Mawardi (who wrote in the fifth century of Islam), the Imamate, or Caliphate, was divinely ordained and the Khalifa inherited all the powers and privileges of the Prophet.[78] The four Schools of Islamic jurisprudence also made the Khalifa ecclesiastical as well as secular head of the Muslim world. The title of *Amir-ul-Mauminin* indicated and emphasised the secular, that of Imam the religious leadership of the Caliph.[79] His name had a hallow and a charm, and the institutions which developed under his rule became models of governance in the world of Islam. The Caliph Muawiyah (661-89 C.E.) transformed the republican Caliphate into a monarchy and created a governing class of leading Arab tribes.[80] These two institutions — kingship and nobility — became an integral part of Islamic polity. After the Umayyad came the Abbasid Caliphs. They established their capital in the newly built city of Baghdad situated on the borders of Persia. The Abbasids were more religious and devoted to the mission of Islam, but they came under the irresistible influence of superior Persian culture and Persian institutions. The Abbasid dynasty lasted for full five centuries (752-1258 C.E.), and under it different branches of administrative machinary were greatly elaborated and new departments and offices created. If the Quran contained almost nothing that may be called civic or state legislation, Persian theories and practices filled the lacuna. Persian court etiquette, Persian army organisa-

---

77. But as the Muslim empire expanded, Muawiyah founded the line of Umayyad Caliphs at Damascus (661 C.E.). The Abbasids who succeeded them, became Caliphs at Baghdad (750 C.E.) and Samarra (836 C.E.). Another line of Umayyad Caliphs ruled at Cordova or Qurtuba (756 C.E.). The Fatamid Caliphs were rulers in Cairo upto 1751 and the Ayyubids up to 1836.

78. Ruben Levy, *The Social Structure of Islam*, p.284.

79. Arnold, *The Caliphate*, p.33.

80. M. Habib, Introduction to Elliot and Dowson's *History of India as told by its Own Historians* (Aligarh reprint, 1952), II, p.6.

tion,[81] administrative system, postal service, conferment of robes of honour, and many similar institutions were all adopted and developed under the Abbasids.

The Turks brought these institutions into India, adding some more offices and institutions while keeping the core intact. Ziyauddin Barani openly asserts: "Consequently, it became necessary for the rulers of Islam (the Caliphs) to follow the policy of Iranian Emperors in order to ensure the greatness of True Word, the supremacy of the Muslim religion...overthrow of the enemies of the Faith... and maintenance of their own authority."[82] Therefore, when Fakhr-i-Mudabbir or Ziyauddin Barani[83] recommend the Sassanian pattern of governance to the Sultans of Delhi,[84] they neither saw anything new nor un-Islamic in their advice.

The four schools (*mazahib*) of Islamic jurisprudence also arose during the period of the Abbasids. Even in the compilations of Hadis the contribution of Persia was great. Of the Traditionists, only Imams Malik and Hanbal belonged to the Arab race; the rest were from Ajam, who sojourned in Arabia for years together collecting and compiling the *Hidaya*. In matters of law where the Quran and Hadis were silent, the jurisconsults resorted to *qiyas* or analogy, that is, the extension of an acknowledged principle to similar cases. Where *qiyas* was not possible, they appealed to reason[85] or judgement, known in Arabia as ra'y. Ra'y has become a technical term in Arabic jurisprudence. Consensus of opinion of the learned was known as *ijma*. The principle of *istihasan* (or "regarding as better") was developed by Abu Yusuf, disciple of Abu Hanifa, which gave him great freedom of interpretation and allowed him to adopt local customs and prejudices as part

82. *Fatawa-i-Jahandari*, p.39.
83. *Ibid*., pp.30-40.
84. Arnold, *The Caliphate*, p.202.
85. Habib, Introduction to E and D, II, pp.23-24.

of the general laws of Islam.[86] Mawardi felt himself compelled to admit that "the acts of administration were valid in view of the circumstances of the time."[87] In the case of any doubt about interpretation of rules, administrative manuals like Abul Hasan Al-Mawardi's *Ahkam-us-Sultaniya*, Abu Ali Nizam-ul-Mulk Tusi's *Siyasat Nama*, Jurji Zaydan's *Attamadun-i-Islami* or Fakhr-i-Mudabbir's *Adab-ul-Harb* (also known as *Adab-ul-Muluk*) were readily available for consultation and guidance.

In brief, Muslim administration had evolved in Muslim lands through centuries and was highly developed before it was brought to India by the Turkish Sultans. At the head was the monarch or Sultan. He appointed and was assisted by a number of ministers. A brief list of ministers and officers will give an idea of the framework of the central administration. At the top were four important ministers (and ministries) which formed the four pillars of the State.[88] These were Wazir (Diwan-i-Wazarat), Ariz-i-Mumalik (Diwan-i-Arz), Diwan-i-Insha and Diwan-i-Rasalat. The Wazir was the Prime Minister who looked after revenue administration. Ariz-i-Mumalik or Diwan-i-Arz was head of the army. He was known as Mir Bakhshi under the Mughals and was the inspector-general and paymaster-general of the army. Diwan-i-Insha was incharge of royal correspondence, and Diwan-i-Rasalat of foreign affairs and pious foundations. Mushrif-i-Mamalik was the accountant-general and Mustaufi the auditor-general. Sadr-i-Jahan, also called Sadr-us-Sudur, was the Chief Qazi. Under him served several Qazis and Miradls. Barid-i-Mumalik was minister in charge of reporting and espionage. There were officers of the royal household like Vakil-i-Dar (Chief Secretary), Amir-i-Hajib (Master of Ceremonies) and Barbak, 'the tongue of the sultan,' whose

---

86. Ruben Levy, *The Social Structure of Islam*, p.168.
87. *Ibid.*, p.258.
88. Barani, p.153.

duty it was to present petitions of the people to the king. There were dozens of other officers and hundreds of subordinates both in the Central administration and in the *Subahs* or provinces. However, here only a few top ministers and officers may receive detailed attention to enable us to appraise the working and spirit of the government.

The Central government was formed on the Persian model. As seen above, the Prime Minister was called Wazir and his ministry Diwan-i-Wazarat. All Muslim political thinkers attached great importance to this office. Fakhr-i-Mudabbir says that, "as the body cannot exist without life so also no regime can sustain without the Wazir."[89] Ziyauddin Barani declares that, "without a wise Wazir, kingship is vain... a king without a wise Wazir is like a palace without foundations. If the Wazir is wise the folly of the king does not lead to the ruin and the destruction of the kingdom."[90] The main business of the Wazir was finance, the Wazir's ministry or the Diwan-i-Wazarat cannoted the Revenue Department. Other duties and obligations of the Wazir included all the constructive functions of the state in a broad sense. He was to recommend promotions of officers, enlist and inspect the army and take steps to make the people prosperous, happy and contended. It was his duty also to look after men of piety and learning and protect the weak and the indigent, the widows and the orphans. In short, "Agriculture, Building, Charitable institutions, Intelligence Department, the *Karkhanas* and the Mint were all directly or indirectly under the Diwan-i-Wazarat."[91] It was his duty to organise the offices and make them efficient in their work. The Wazir in a word was the head of the entire machinery of the government.[92] The Diwan-i-Arz or the Ariz-i-Mumalik

---

89. *Adab-ul-Harb*, Br. Museum Ms. fol. 52(a).

90. *Fatawa-i-Jahandari*, p.10.

91. Lal, K.S., *History of the Khaljis*, 2nd Ed., p.157.

92. *Adab-ul-Harb, op. cit.*, fol.52 (a),56(b). Shams Siraj Afif goes even as far as to say: "If one wants to describe the work of the Diwan-i-Wazarat, one has to write a separate book" Afif, (pp.420-21).

was the controller-general of the military department.[93] The Ariz-i-Mumalik (Mir Bakhshi of the Mughals) had his provincial assistants and their duties comprised enlisting recruits, fixing their pay, inspecting the army and disbursing salaries to the troops.[94] The Diwan-i-Insha dealt with the correspondence between the sultan and the local governments, including all correspondence of a confidential nature. Since there was no typing, cyclostyling or printing in those days, dozens of hand-written copies of king's orders and *farmans* had to be prepared in this office for despatch to *iqtas* and *subahs*. The Diwan-i-Rasalat, as the term indicates,[95] looked after diplomatic correspondence, and as such this ministry was a counterpart of the present-day foreign office.

The Diwan which dealt with religious charities was presided over by the Sadr-us-Sudur. The Diwan-i-Qaza, or the department of justice, was presided over by the Chief Qazi, and the two offices of the Chief Qazi and the Chief Sadr were generally held by one and the same person. Administration of justice[96] was given a place of importance in Islamic polity, and there were elaborate rules about administering justice to civil and military men.[97] Similarly there were detailed rules about the functioning of the police department[98] and awarding of punishments.[99] One department of considerable importance was that of the Barid-i-Mumalik, who was the head of the State Information Bureau. Through this department the centre was kept informed of all that was happening all over the empire. A

---

93. For qualities of Ariz see *Fatawa-i-Jahandari*, p.24.

94. Barani, pp. 65, 319.

95. Steingass, *Persian English Dictionary*, p.574.

96. Wahed Husain, *Administration of Justice During the Muslim Rule in India* (Calcutta,1934), p.22.

97. M.Bashir Ahmad, *Administration of Justice in Medieval India* (Aligarh, 1941), p.117.

98. Barani, *Fatawa-i-Jahandari*, p.30.

99. Barani, p.313; Hasan Sijzi, *Favaid-ul-Fvad*, Lucknow text, pp.53-54.

net-work of news agents or intelligencers was spread out in all localities. They acted both as secret information agents as well as open news-reporters. There were also a large number of spies in every place and chiefly in the houses of the nobles to report their affairs to the Sultan.

The king's court, palace and household had an elaborate administrative set up of its own. The Vakil-i-Dar, or keeper of the keys of the palace gate was the most important.[100] The Amir-i-Hajib, also called Barbak[101] (or Lord Chamberlain) made arrangements for functions and ceremonies and enforced court etiquette. Other officers were Amir-i-Akhur (Master of the Horse), Shahna-i-Pilan, (Superintendent of the Elephants), the Amir-i-Shikar (Superintendent of the Royal Hunt), Sharabdar (Incharge of the Sultan's Drinks), Sar Chashnigir (Incharge of the Royal Kitchen), Sar Silahdar (Keeper of the Royal Weapons), Muhardar (Keeper of the Royal Seals), Sarjandar (Commander of the King's Bodyguards who were called Jandars),[102] and a host of others with specific duties and functions. Such an elaborate administrative system strengthened the position of the Sultan and roots of the Sultanate in India.

The provincial government was a miniature model of the central. The governors were called Walis and Muqtis. An expert in accounts called Sahib-i-Diwan was appointed in each province. He kept the local revenue records and submitted them to the Wazir. The army maintained by the governors and garrison commanders was subject to control and inspection by the provincial Ariz, who was responsible to the central government. Similary, administrative arrangement of *parganas*, *shiqqs* and later *sarkars* was

---

100. About the importance of and the risks involed in the office see Minhaj, *Tabqat-i-Nasiri*, Reverty, I, p.694. Also Yahiya, *Tarikh-i-Mubark Shahi*, p.72.

101. Barani, pp.34, 46, 61.

102. *Ibid.*, p.30.

also clearly laid down. During the Mughal period, some new offices were created while nomenclatures of some others were changed.[103] The administrative system also got the stamping of the Chingezi *Yassa* and the Institutes of Timur.[104] But the core of administration remained Islamic.

The Sultanate of Delhi, and more particularly the Mughal empire, possessed a highly unified and systematized bureaucratic apparatus the central point of which was the *mansab* or numerical rank. Mansab (introduced by emperor Akbar in 1573) defined the status and income of the holder, although titles of nobles in Persian, Turkish and Arabic sometimes make it difficult for us to form an idea of the exact grading. An elaborate bureaucratic administrative set up tends to be top-heavy and slow-moving. But the Turkish and Mughal administrative system was not so. Decision making was quick and so was action. It did not mean that the administration was all good. For example, if the theory of taxation was clear, there were just four taxes—*Kharaj*, *Jiziyah*, *Khums* and *Zakat*—and collection rates and procedures clearly defined.[105] But the taxes actually levied far exceeded these. Many *abwabs* (cesses) were cropping up from time to time so that, in spite of the measures taken by Alauddin Khalji, Firoz Tughlaq, Sher Shah and Akbar to increase and also keep control over the income of the state, "no system of assessment and collection could be discovered that was satisfactory both to the cultivator and the state."[106]

Just as the administrative system implanted in India had evolved in Iran and adjoining Islamic countries, important administrators also came from these regions to run it. With the establishment of Muslim rule, batches of Mus-

103. *Ain*, I, pp.5-6.
104. Tripathi, R.P., *Some Aspects of Muslim Administration*, pp.105-124.
105. N.P. Aghnides, *Muhammedan Theories of Finance*, pp.207, 399.
106. Mujeeb, *Indian Muslims*, p.43.

lims began to arrive in Hindustan from Central Asia, Persia, African Muslim countries and what is now called Afghanistan. India was rich and fertile as compared with their own lands and with the extension of Muslim political power in India, many emigrants — soldiers and administrators — attracted by the "abundance of wealth in cash and kind" — began to flock to Hindustan. Minhaj Siraj says that people from Persia (and adjoining countries) came to India in "various capacities."[107] Fakhr-ul-Mulk Isami, who had been Wazir at Baghdad for thirty years, but then had suffered some disappointment, arrived in India and was appointed Wazir by Sultan Shamsuddin Iltutmish.[108] Qazi Hamiduddin Nagori had also come from abroad. Thus from Wazir downwards the foreign Muslim elite filled all important offices in administration. Because of the Mongol upheaval twenty-five princes with their retinues from Iraq, Khurassan and Mawaraun Nahr arrived at the court of Iltutmish. During the reign of Sultan Balban fifteen more refugee princes came from Turkistan, Mawaraun Nahr, Khurasan, Iran, Azarbaijan, Rum and Sham.[109] From among these hundreds of officials must have been appointed to administrative positions in the Sultanate of Delhi. "The Abbasid tradition thus gained a firm footing in the administration of the Sultanate of Delhi."[110]

Balban had a weakness for things Persian. He introduced the Persian ceremonial in his court; his royal processions were organised on the Iranian pattern. His sons and grandsons were given Persian names of Kaimurs, Kai-Khusrau and Kaiqubad.[111] Thus under the Ilbari Sultans

---

107. Minhaj, *Tabqat-i-Nasiri*, Bib.Ind. (Calcutta, 1864), p.138.
108. Farishtah, I, p.67. Also Isami, *Futuh-us-Salatin*, Agra (1938), p.122.
109. Farishtah, I, p.75. Also A.B.M. Habibullah, *The Foundation of Muslim Rule in India*, p.272.
110. Qureshi, *op. cit.*, p.4.
111. Barani, pp. 27-29, 30-32, 127-28.

many Persian and Persian-knowing nobles and officers served as administrators and officers.[112] The Khaljis and Tughlaqs employed them too. Muhammad Tughlaq secured the services of many foreign nobles and patronised, among them, Khorasanis and Arabs.[113] In the medieval period, heredity and lineage were taken into account in the selection of officers and nobles, and as far as possible low-born Indian Muslims were not appointed to high offices. Foreign Muslims were generally preferred, not only in the Sultanate of Delhi or the Mughal Empire, but also in the independent kingdoms of Gujarat and Malwa and the Adil Shahi and Qutbshahi kingdoms of the Deccan.

With the coming of the Mughals, Persian element in administration became more prominent. Both Babur and Humayun depended upon Persia for help at one time or the other.[114] In their days of distress, they were served by Persian nobles with loyalty and distinction. In all his trials and tribulations of exile, Bairam Khan proved a valued guide to Humayun.[115] Bairam Khan's services in the restablishment of the Mughal empire, and management of the affairs of the government in the early years of Akbar's reign, are praiseworthy. The flow of immigration of Persian nobles and officers remained continuous under all the great Mughals — Akbar, Jahangir, Shahjahan and Aurangzeb. In Jahangir's reign Persian influence increased much more because of the powerful queen Nur Jahan. Her

112. Nigam, S.B.P., *Nobility under the Sultans of Delhi*, pp.106-107.

113. Barani, pp.462, 487-88.

114. At times there were tragically comic occasions in this situation. Sher Shah Suri sent an embassy to Shah Tahmasp requesting the extradition of Humayun, but the Suri envoy's ears and nose were out off by the order of the Shah and as a reprisal several Persians were mutilated in India (Aziz Ahmad, *Studies*, p.26, quoting Riazul Islam, *The Relations between the Mughal Emperors of India and the Safavid Shahs of Iran*, Ph.D. dissertation, Cambridge, 1957).

115. Cited in Sukumar Ray, *Humayun in Persia*, The Royal Asiatic Society of Bengal, Monograph Series, Vol. VI (Calcutta,1948), p.40.

father and brother, Itmad-ud-Daulah and Asaf Khan, rose to dizzy heights. Three of Shahjahan's chief nobles—Asaf Khan, Ali Mardan Khan and Mir Jumla—were Persian. Their meritorious services added to the glory of the Mughal Empire. Jadunath Sarkar sums up the situation thus: "The Persians were most highly valued for their polished manners, literary ability and capacity for managing the finance and accounts. There was always a keen desire on the part of the Mughal emperors to seduce to their service the higher officers of the Shah of Persia... For such officers, when they fell into disgrace in their homeland...a flight to India opened a road to honour, power and wealth."[116]

Persians alone did not monopolise high offices in the Mughal empire. Young Akbar, insecure on his throne, made overtures to the Ottoman Sultan, Sulaiman the Magnificent, for friendship so as not to remain dependent entirely on Persian goodwill. Qandhar was a bone of contention between the Persian Shah and the Mughal Emperor. Many Persian nobles while serving the Mughals, secretly sympathised with the Safavids. Because of suspicion, Mughal Emperors Shahjahan and the more orthodox *Sunni* Aurangzeb, began to favour Turani nobles, and a struggle between Irani and Turani nobility hastened the decline if not the fall of the Mughal Empire. With this background, it needs no reitreration that, by and large, Muslim administration drew neither on India's native tradition nor on native manpower and the development of Muslim administrative system and its implementation and execution in India owed much to foreign elements.

In the Sultanate of Delhi; in the independent Muslims kingdoms of Gujarat, Malwa, Bengal and the Bahmani kingdom; and in the Mughal empire, that is almost in the whole country Muslim administration based on Muslim law prevailed for five hundred years, at the minimum

---

116. *Mughal Administration*, Orient Longmans Edition, 1972, p.120.

from the end of the thirteenth to the end of the eighteenth
century. Therefore, it did not fail to leave its impress on
the administrative system of contemporary or later Indian
states. The Rajput, the Maratha and the Sikh kingdoms in
particular adopted many institutions and offices of Muslim administration. The British administration in India
was partially influenced by Muslim administration. Persian administrative terms were in common use in Indian
executive and judiciary right up to the middle of the
twentieth century. Therefore, the importance of the legacy
of Muslim administration in India has to be assigned its
proper place.

The Army

Like administration the core of the army of the Sultanate and the Mughal empire too was foreign. The establishment, expansion and continuance of Muslim political
power and religion in India was due to its army.[117] A very
important source of strength of this army was the constant
inflow of foreign soldiers from Muslim homelands beyond
the Indus. These may be called, for the sake of brevity, by
the generic terms Turks and Afghans. The Turks came as
invaders and became rulers, army commanders and soldiers. The warlike character of the Afghans attracted the
notice of the conquerors of India who freely enrolled them
in their armies. Mahmud Ghaznavi and Muhammad
Ghauri brought thousands of Afghan horsemen with
them.[118] Indian sultans continued the tradition. They had
a preference for homeland troops, or Muslim warriors
from the trans-Indus region. In the time of Iltutmish, Jal-

---

117. I have made a detailed study of this army in my article "The Striking power of the Army of the Sultanate" in the *Journal of Indian History*
(Trivandrum), Vol.LV,Part III, December 1977.

118. *Makhzan-i-Afghana*, N.B. Roy's trs. entitled Niamatullah's *History
of the Afghans* (Santiniketan, 1958), p.11; Sir Olaf Caroe, *The Pathans*,
Macmillan & Co. (London,1958),p.135; *Tabqat-i-Nasiri*, p. 315; Barani,
pp.57-58.

aluddin of Khawarism, fleeing before Chingiz Khan, brought contingents of Afghan soldiers with him. In course of time, many of them took service under Iltutmish.[119] Balban employed three thousand Afghan horse and foot in his compaigns against the Mewatis, and appointed thousands of Afghan officers and men for garrisoning forts like Gopalgir, Kampil, Patiali, Bhojpur and Jalali. In the royal processions of Balban hundreds of Sistani, Ghauri, Samarqandi and Arab soldiers with drawn swords used to march by his side. The Afghans had got accustomed to the adventure of soldiering in India. They joined in large numbers the armies of Mongol invaders as well as of Amir Timur when the latter marched into India. Like the Afghans, the Mongol (ethnically a generic term, again) soldiers too were there in the army of the Sultanate in large numbers. Abyssinian slave-soldiers and officers became prominent under Sultan Raziya. The immigration of foreign troops continued without break in the time of the Khaljis, Tughlaqs, Saiyyads and Lodis. Under the Saiyyad and Lodi rulers, they flocked into India like 'ants and locusts.' As conquerors, officers and soldiers these foreigners were all in pretty nearly the same stage of civilization. The Khurasanis or Persians were, for instance, more advanced and perhaps possessed milder manners than the Turks. But considering their 'imperial' point of view regarding Hindustan, this original difference of civilization was of little consequence. Their constant induction from Muslim lands contributed to the strength and maintenance of Muslim character of the army of the Sultanate.

Indians, or Hindus, too used to be enrolled. Ziyauddin Barani was against the recruitment of non-Muslims in the army,[120] but right from the days of Mahmud of Ghazni,

---

119. Jauhar, *Tazkirat-al-Waqiat* trs. C. Stewart, Indian Reprint, 1972, p.7.

120. *Fatawa-i-Jahandari*, pp.25-26.

Hindus used to join Muslim armies,[121] and lend strength to it.[122] Most of the Hindus in the army belonged to the infantry wing and were called Paiks. Some of these were poor persons and joined the army for the sake of securing employment. Others were slaves and war-captives. The Paiks cleared the jungles and were often used as "cannon fodder" in battle.[123] But others, especially professionals, joined the permanent cadre of infantry for combat purposes. Barbosa (early sixteenth century) says this about them: "They carry swords and daggers, bows and arrows. They are right good archers and their bows are long like those of England. They are mostly Hindus."[124] They were a loyal lot. Alauddin Khalji, Mubarak Khalji and Firoz Tughlaq were saved by Paiks when they were attacked by rivals and adventurers,[125] a phenomenon so common in Muslim history. But despite their loyalty the Paiks remained relegated to an inferior position.

There were also Muslim mercenaries or volunteers enrolled on the eve of a campaign. "The volunteer element in the army was known by the name of Ghazi. The Ghazis were not entitled to any salary, but relied mostly on 'rich pickings from the Indian campaigns.' Prospect of loot whetted their thirst for war, the title of Ghazi spurred their ego. The victories of the Ghaznavids had attracted these plundering adventures to their standards. The tradition of enrolling Ghazi merecenaries was continued by the Turk-

---

121. Utbi, *Kitab-i-Yamini* trs. by Reynolds, p.335-336. Also Shihabuddin al-Umri, *Masalik-ul-Absar*, E and D, III, p.576; Farishtah, I, p.18.

122. Bosworth, *op.cit., p.107.*

123. The infantrymen were so placed as to bear the first brunt of the enemy's attack. Consequently, the temptation to flee was great. But they could not leave their posts, for on the field of battle "horses are on their right and left...and behind (them) the elephants so that not one of them can run away" (Al-Qalqashindi, *Subh-al-Asha*, trs. Otto Spies, p.76).

124. Barbosa, *The Book of Duarte Barbosa*, I,p.181. It may be noted that when Alauddin Khalji, as Prince, marched against Devagiri, he had with him about 2,000 Paiks (Barani,*Tarikh,*pp.222).

125. Barani, pp.273, 376, 377.

ish sultans in India."[126] Right up to the Tughlaq times and beyond, merecenaries (Muslims says Afif for Firoz's times) joined the army for love of plunder and concomitant gains. These enthusiasts naturally added strength to the regular army, and also to its character.

Soldiers in permanent service, and the king's body-guards called Jandars, were largely drawn from his personal slaves.[127] Right from the days of Mahmud of Ghazni the pivot of the regular army was provided by the slave force (*ghilman, mamalik*).[128] Young slaves were obtained as presents, as part of tribute from subordinate rulers and as captives during campaigns. They were also purchased in slave markets in India and abroad. Captured or imported, they were broken in and brainwashed at an early age, their minds moulded and their bodies trained for warfare. The practice may sound cruel but it was eminently Islamic and was universal in the Muslim lands.[129] Compare, for example, the *Dewshirme* ('collecting boys') system of the Turkish empire according to which every five years, and sometimes every year, the Ottomans enslaved all Balkan Jewish and Christian boys aged 10-15, took them to Constantinople and brought them up in Islamic ideology. They were used for the further subjugation of their own people.[130] The value of the slave troops lay in their lack of roots and local connections and attachment to the master by a personal bond of fealty. The foundation of this relation was military clientship, the attachment of man to man, the loyalty of individual to individual, first by the

126. e.g. Minhaj, *Tabqat-i-Nasiri*, text, p.317; Barani, p.80; Afif, p.289; Fakhr-i-Mudabbir, *Adab-ul-Harb wa Shujaat*, Hindi trs. from photograph copy of the British Museum Ms. by S.A.A Rizvi in *Adi Turk Kalin Bharat* (Aligarh,1956), fol.109 b. Also Habibullah, *The Foundation of Muslim Rule in India*, pp.262, 265.

127. Minhaj, *Tabqat-i-Nasiri*, trs. by Raverty, 1,p.180.

128. C.E. Bosworth, *The Ghaznavids*, p.98.

129. Ira Marvin Lapidus, *Muslim Cities in the Later Middle Ages*, Harvard University Press (Cambridge, Massachusetts,1967), pp.6,44.

130. *Encyclopaedia of Islam* (1913-38), II, pp.952-53.

relation of chief to his companion and, if the warrior master succeeded in conquest and setting up a dominion, by the relation of suzerain to vassal. The devotion of man to man is the basis of the slave system, of feudalism, of imperialism of the primeval type, and of the success of medieval Muslim army. Slaves were collected from all countries and nationalities. There were Turks, Persians, Buyids, Seljuqs, Oghuz (also called Irani Turkmen), Afghans, Khaljis, Hindu etc. in the army of Mahmud. The success of the Ghaznavids and Ghaurids in India was due, besides other reasons, to the staunchly loyal slave troops.[131] This tradition of obtaining slaves by all methods and from all regions, was continued by the Delhi Sultans. In his campaign against Katehar Balban massacred all male captives except boys up to the age of eight or nine.[132] It was the practice with most sultans,[133] and making slaves of young boys by Muslim victors was common. As these slave boys grew in age, they could hardly remember their parents and remained loyal only to the king. Alauddin Khalji possessed 50,000 slave boys,[134] who, as they grew up, would have made his strong army stronger. Muhammad Tughlaq also obtained slaves through campaigns. Firoz Tughlaq commanded his "fief-holders and officers to capture slaves whenever they were at war". He had also instructed his Amils and Jagirdars to collect slave boys in place of revenue and tribute.[135] In short, the medieval Muslim slave-system was a constant supplier of loyal troops to the Muslim army, from India and abroad.

131. Lal, K.S., "The Ghaznavids in India," in *Bengal Past and Present*, Sir Jadunath Sarkar Birth Centenary Number, July-December 1970, pp.131-152.

132. Barani, pp.58-59; Farishtah, I, p.77.

133. For detailed reference from Persian sources see Lal, *Indian Muslims*, pp.23-26.

134. Afif, p.272.

135. *Ibid.*, pp.267-72.

Enrolment in the regular cadre depended on a number
of considerations like personal prowess, skill in weaponry
and family background. The times believed in the theory
of 'martial class.' Fakhr-i-Mudabbir advises that those
whose ancestors had not been soldiers should not be made
officers, Sawars or Sarkhails.[136] Ziyauddin Barani also
expresses similar views.[137] In practice recruitment of
troops was based on merit which was determined after a
severe test.[138]

Like the procedure of recruitment, the schedule of
training too was strenuous. If the Samanid traditions had
not been given up in India, the training of a slave-soldier
described in Nizamul-Mulk's *Siyasat Nama* should have
turned him into a veteran warrior in the course of a few
years. In the first year after his purchase, the *ghulam* was
trained as a foot-soldier, and was never permitted, under
penalties, to mount a horse. In the second year, he was
given a horse with plain saddle. After another year's training he received an ornamental belt, and so on. By the
seventh year alone was he fully trained and fit to become
a tent-commander.[139] The training of a boy-slave recruit in
the Sultanate might have been more or less similar. Details
about such training are not available in medieval Indian
chronicles, but Barani does hint at it when he speaks about
Balban's trained soldiers (*tarbiyat-yafta lashkar*).[140] For experienced soldiers constant campaigns, tournaments,
sports, *shikar* and regular reviews were enough to keep
them fit and alert.[141]

The Sultanate's army comprised both cavalry and infantry. It had an elephant corps. Camels and ponies and
other animals were also used for commissariat service. But

---

136. *Adab-ul-Harb*, fol. 49a.
137. Barani, *Fatawa-i-Jahandari*, p.2.
138. Ibn Battuta, p. 14. Also Barani, p.102.
139. Ruben Levy, *Social Structure of Islam*, p.74.
140. Barani, pp.51, 52.
141. Minhaj, p.225; Al-Qalqashindi, p.75; Afif, pp.317, 322.

the most important wing of the army was the cavalry. Cavalry comprises the man and his mount. In India, only in some places of eastern Punjab like the Shiwaliks, Samana, Sunnam, Tabarhind, Thanesar and the 'Country of the Khokhars,' good quality horses were found in sufficient numbers.[142] But these horses were inferior to the horses of West-Asia breed, and importation of war-horses from abroad became an imperative necessity for the Sultans of Delhi.[143] Medieval chroniclers speak of Yamani, Shami, Bahri and Qipchaqi horses as being in use by soldiers in India, and there was large-scale importation of horses into India from Arabia.[144] According to Ziyauddin Barani, Alauddin Khalji is said to have had 70,000 horses in his *paigahs* (stables) in Delhi.[145] The Arab geographer Ahmad Abbas Al-Umari states that Sultan Muhammad Tughlaq distributed to his retinue 10,000 Arab horses and countless others. Even Firoz Tughlaq, who is said to have neglected the army, maintained extensive *paigahs*.[146] Horses were a 'perishable' commodity and deaths and even epidemics among them were common.[147] Therefore, foreign breed war horses were constantly imported in India at great cost to keep the *paigahs* well stocked.

Alauddin Khalji (1296-1316) had under his command 475,000 horsemen,[148] and Muhammad Tughlaq's cavalry is said to have consisted of 900,000 soldiers.[149] Of course, the size of the army varied from time to time. The Saiyyads

---

142. Barani, p. 53.

143. Lal, "The Ghaznavids in India", *op.cit.*, pp.131-152, esp.157; Barani, pp. 57-58.

144. Simon Digby, *War Horse and Elephant in the Delhi Sultanate*, Orient Monographs (Oxford, 1971), pp.34-36; Barani, pp.461-62; Lal, *Twilight*, pp.131-32.

145. Barani, p.262.

146. Afif, pp.339-340.

147. Sharafuddin Yazdi, *Zafar Nama*, II,pp.59-70.

148. Farishtah, 1, p.200

149. Ahmad Abbas, *Masalik-ul-Absar*, E and D, III, p.576; Al-Qalqashindi, *Subh-ul-Asha*, p.66.

were weak and Lodis not so strong. But even in the newly
created kingdoms of the fifteenth century like Gujarat,
Malwa, Jaunpur etc. Muslim cavalry generally had an
edge over the armies of the neighbouring Rajas. Under
Alauddin Khalji the custom of branding horses and keeping a pen-picture of the soldier (*dagh-wa-chehra*) was
strictly followed.[150]

As against the cavalry of the Sultans, the Indian rulers
depended for military strength primarily on elephants.
But even in this sphere the Sultans excelled them in a short
time. The Sultans obtained for their *pilkhanas* elephants
from all possible sources, as plunder, as tribute from
subordinate rulers or provincial governors, by purchase
from the outside Muslim ruled territories, or by trapping
them directly from the forest regions. There is, and will
always be, a controversy about the real efficacy of the
elephant in medieval warfare. Still, the elephant occupied
an important place in warfare throughout the medieval
period. Heavily armoured, it could be used as a living
battering ram for pulling down the gates of a fortress.
Many of the strongest fortresses in India have elephant
spikes upon their doors to hinder such form of assault.
The elephant could also serve as a pack animal carrying a
very large load. Its gigantic size created a feeling of terror
in the enemy ranks.[151] War elephants could kill and destroy systematically.[152] And they looked awe-inspiring
and majestic.

Weapons, equipments, engines etc. for waging war are
mentioned in the *Sirat-i-Firoz Shahi*, and some other works.
There are manuals in the Persian language written right
from the tenth century onwards dealing elaborately with
the art of warfare. These would have provided guidance

150. Barani, p.145.

151. Price, Major David, *Memoirs of the Principal Events of Muhammadan History* (London 1921), III, p.252. Also Yazdi, *Zafar Nama*, II, pp.102 ff.

152. Barbosa, *The Book of Duarte Barbosa*, 1, p.118; Barani, p.53.

to the Indian Sultans on military matters. The *Qabus Nama*, for instance, written by Kaikaus in the year 475 H. (1082-83 C.E.) has three chapters—"On Buying Horses"; "On Giving Battle to the Enemy" and "On the Art of Controlling An Armed Force." Similarly, Nizam-ul-Mulk's *Siyasat Nama* written in 485 H. (1092-93 C.E.) contains two short chapters — "On Having Troops of Various Races" and "On Preparing Arms and Equipment for War and Expeditions."[153] In India Fakhr-i-Mudabbir and Ziyauddin Barani wrote on the theme.

What did the Muslim army look like? There are excellent pen-pictures by Fakhr-i-Mudabbir in his *Adab-ul-Harb* and Amir Khusrau in his *Khazain-ul-Futuh*, besides of course many others. Similarly, there are descriptions of the Rajput army. Padmanabh, in his *Kanhadade-Prabandh* (written about the middle of the fifteenth century) has this to say about the Rajput warriors: "They bathed the horses in the sacred water of Ganga. Then they offered them Kamal Puja. On their backs they put with sandal the impressions of their hands....They put over them five types of armour, namely, war armour, saddles acting as armour, armour in the form of plates, steel armour, and armour woven out of cotton. Now what was the type of Kshatriyas who rode these horses? Those, who were above twenty-five and less than fifty in age,... shot arrows with speed and were the most heroic. (Their) moustaches went up to their ears, and beards reached the navel. They were liberal and warlike. Their thoughts were good... They regarded wives of others as their sisters. They stood firm in battle, and struck after first challenging the enemy. They died after having killed first. They donned and used (all the) sixty-six weapons. If any one (of the enemy ranks) fell down they regarded the

---

153. Thomas, *Chronicles of the Pathan Kings of Delhi*, pp.78-79; "A Study of the Rare Ms. *Sirat-i-Firoz Shahi*" by S.M. Askari, *Journal of Indian History*, Vol. LII, April, 1974, Pt. I, pp. 127-146, esp. p.139; M.S. Khan, "The Life and Works of Fakhr-i-Mudabbir," *Islamic Culture*, April, 1977,pp. 138-40.

fallen person as a corpse and saluted it." Similar descriptions are found in the *Pachanika* of Achaldas and other books.[154]

The most graphic description of the Muslim army is by a Hindu, the famous Maithli poet Vidyapati of the fourteenth century. Vidyapati was patronised by Sultans Ghiyasuddin and Nasiruddin of Bengal. Writing about Muslim soldiers, he says: "Sometimes they ate only raw flesh. Their eyes were red with the intoxication of wine. They could run twenty *yojanas* within the span of half of a day. They used to pass the day with the (bare) loaf under their arm...(The soldier) takes into custody all the women of the enemy's city... Wherever they happened to pass in that very place the ladies of the Raja's house began to be sold in the market. They used to set fire to the villages. They turned out the women (from their homes) and killed the children. Loot was their (source of) income. They subsisted on that. Neither did they have pity for the weak nor did they fear the strong...They had nothing to do with righteousness... They never kept their promise... They were neither desirous of good name, not did they fear bad name..."[155] At another place he says: "Somewhere a Musalman shows his rage and attacks (the Hindus)....It appears on seeing the Turks that they would swallow up the whole lot of Hindus."[156]

A comparison of the two armies at once shows why the Muslim army was one up. It was, in one word, because of its strategy and tactic of terror, and it was because of this that Muslim state in India was like a police state.

The description of Vidyapati clearly shows how impressive and awe-inspiring the army of the Sultanate

---

154. Dashrath Sharma, Presidential Address, Rajasthan History Congress, Udaipur Session, 1969, Proceedings, pp.10-11. For detailed description also see *Kanhadade-Prabandh*, translated, introduced and annotated by V.S.Bhatnagar, pp. 21-22.

155. Vidyapati, *Kirtilata* (Indian Press, Allahabad, 1923), pp.70-72.

156. *Ibid.*, pp.42-44.

looked. The soldiers had excellent horses, magnificent armour, and fine costumes.[157] A soldier usually carried two swords.[158] Besides he had bows and arrows, maces and battle axes. The Muslim soldier was an enthusiastic fighter. Psychologically, he was a soldier of Allah. The word *Jihad* had a magic appeal for him. His enthusiasm for war was whetted by the promises of rewards, prospects of plunder and religious slogans.[159] Consequently, he exhibited great zeal and practised extreme ruthlessness and cruelty.[160] This cruelty gave the army of the Sultanate superiority over indigenous forces because it inspired terror wherever it went. The Turushka had become a bogey and everywhere inspired a paralysing fear.[161] As Ruben Levy points out, "the Turks have always been amongst the most active of Muslim peoples, and if they are not greatly given to pious exercise they are bigoted believers in this faith and excellent fighters in its cause."[162] The Afghans were equally ferocious. These and other Central and West Asian soldiers of "Allah, the Merciful, the Compassionate" were neither merciful nor compassionate and created consternation whenever they launched an attack. Balban in the thirteenth century held the conviction that no king could succeed against the army of Delhi, be he a Hindu Raja or a Rana (*Midanam ke pesh lashkar-i-dihli hech badshahi dast astad natawaned kard fikef rayan wa rajgan-i-hinduan*).[163]

But that is not entirely true. Local resistance against Muslim armies continued throughout, and hundreds of Hindu inscriptions claim victories for their kings. Battles

---

157. *Masalik,* E and D, III, p.567.

158. H.A.R. Gibb, *Ibn Battutah,* p.216; Ibn Battuta, trs. Mahdi Hussain p.108.

159. Afif, p.201.

160. *Adab-ul Harb,* 115 a, 158 b. After the massacre in Bengal, even Sultan Firoz Tughlaq had begun to weep (Afif, p.121). But such kind-hearted Sultans were rare.

161. Habibullah, *op.cit.,* pp.72-73.

162. *Social Structure of Islam,* p.25.

163. Barani, p.52.

between Muslim invaders from Delhi on the one hand and Rajput defenders on the other were always very hotly contested. For the Muslim army the going was tough from the very beginning; otherwise Fakhr-i-Mudabbir would not have declared that "peace is better than war,"[164] and "as far as possible war should be avoided because it is bitter fare."[165] Such statements from one who, while describing five types of warfare and considering war with the *kafirs* as the most righteous,[166] are not without significance.

In fact the army of the Sultanate suffered from a number of weaknesses. One was its heterogeneous character. Troops of the various racial groups, foreign and Indian, could not always pull together well nor were they all equally loyal to the regime.[167] Slaves, for instance, made good soldiers but "they are of one group and one mind and there can be no permanent security against their revolt."[168] The Afghans had been freely employed by Muhammad Ghauri, and Turkish Sultans of Delhi, but under the Saiyyads and Lodis the whole complexion of the army was changed from "Turk" to "Afghan". The Afghans were brave, sometimes even reckless. But traditional devotion to their own clan leaders was not conducive to discipline in the army.

Another weakness was that soldiers were habituated to plundering even in peace times. In war loot for the Musulmans was justified,[169] but when there was no war, the soldiers were enjoined to behave with the civilians and not to loot or destroy their property.[170] But exceptions apart, rowdyism and extortion had become the norms of

---

164. Fakhr-i-Mudabbir, *Adab-ul Harb wa Shujaat*, fol. 111a,
165. *Ibid.*, fols. 66 a-b.
166. *Ibid.*, fols. 131a-132a.
167. Fakhr-i-Mudabbir, *Tarikh-i-Fakhruddin Mubarak Shah*, pp.31-32.
168. Barani, *Fatawa-i-Jahandari*, pp.25-26.
169. Fakhr-i-Mudabbir, *Adab-ul-Harb*, fol. 154 a-b.
170. *Ibid.*, fol. 117a.

their behaviour.[171] The massacre of the people of Delhi by Amir Timur was a direct consequence of his soldiers' mis-behaviour with the market people.[172] The phenomenon repeated itself during Nadir Shah's invasion. As a result, sometimes the rough and disorderly behaviour of the armymen, especially of the temporary troopers, brought discredit to the regime. Again, keeping a large army on a permanent basis had to be ruled out for reasons of finance, security and convenience, and a large portion of the army of the Sultanate remained temporary with loot as its only source of sustenance. Often it was a string of military camps more interested in campaigns and booty-gathering than in administration. Alauddin's keeping an army of about five hundred thousand made him resort to collect-ing fifty percent of the produce as land revenue even when the imperial resources were large and gains and tribute from his conquests were immense. Other rulers were not financially so sound. The army, besides, could not all be stationed at Delhi; it was distributed all over the Sultanate under provisional governors and garrison com-manders.[173] And they could make use of it against the regime itself if they chose to revolt.

Thus the weaknesses in the army of the Sultanate were many. But since it won most of the battles and occupied the whole of northern India in the thirteenth century and penetrated into the South in the fourteenth, its superiority must be acknowledged. This superiority consisted first in the slave system. The system provided the Sultanate's army with loyal soldiers. The strict process of recruitment and hard training was another factor. Another reason for its having an edge over that of the local rulers was the constant and unbroken arrival of foreign troops from Turk

---

171. Amir Khusrau, *Khazain-ul Futuh*, Habib trs., pp.58-59.

172. Sharafuddin Yazdi, *Zafar Nama*, Bib. Ind., II, p.186; Hajiuddabir, *Zafarul Wali*, III,p.907.

173. Al-Qalqashindi, pp.66-67. Also Ibn Battuta, p.26.

and Afghan homelands. Rajputs could not replenish their manpower from a similar source. That is why if and when the contact of the Delhi Sultans with Muslim homelands was partially or wholly snapped (as for example because of the Mongol upheaval in Central Asia) the Rajput princes could contain Turkish expansion in India as the history of the Sultanate shows. The Ghazi element was peculiar to the Muslim army. While its cupidity resulted in too much cruelty in warfare, it added a very zealous element to the fighting forces. Islam gave them a unity of thought, interest and action. Man to man the Rajput was not inferior to the Turk, but on the basis of the evidence available, the armymen of the Sultanate, on the whole, had an upper hand over the indigeneous warriors. Their highly caparisoned cavalry was an additional strong point. Good quality horses in India were scarce and had to be imported by Hindu Rajas both in the South and the North. This placed Indian rulers at a disadvantage. The Turkish army had many engines of war. An elaborate army administrative system, constant inspection and reviews of troops too increased the striking power of the army of the Sultanate.

The discussion on the Muslim army of the Sultanate period (C. 1200-1526 C.E.) has been eleborate, deliberately. For the Muslim rule in India remained army rule and the army of the Mughal emperors (1526-1707-1857) was a continuation the Sultanate's with its merits and weaknesses. Francois Bernier says: "the *Great Mogol* is a foreigner in Hindoustan... Consequently he finds himself in a hostile country, or nearly so; a country containing hundreds of *Gentiles* to one Mogol or even to one Mahometan. To maintain himself in such a country... he is under the necessity of keeping up numerous armies, even in the time of peace."[174] Babur was a foreigner and so were Humayun

---

174. Bernier, p.209.

and even Akbar. With Akbar's accession, it is generally believed, that an era of government for the people had started.[175] But this view stands challenged by Bernier's statement. He wrote at a time when the Mughal Empire had reached the pinnacle of glory and when, it is believed, syncretism in society had become the order of the day. And yet he found the Mughal King a foreigner and his army an apparatus of oppression. The administration of the Sultanate and Mughal Empire was bureaucratic throughout. Over long periods this administrative system was dominated by immigrants from abroad, mainly West Asia and North Africa and this gave it much of the character of foreign and Islamic rule. Commenting on the list of *mansabdars* in the *Ain-i-Akbari*, Moreland says that while about 70 percent of the nobles were foreigners belonging to families which had either come to India with Humayun or had arrived at the court after the accession of Akbar, of the remaining 30 percent of the appointments which were held by Indians, rather more than half were Moslems and "rather less than half Hindus."[176] This high proportion of Muslim *mansabdars* belonging to families from foreign lands continued under Akbar's successors. Thus Bernier described the nobility under Aurangzeb as a medley of foreign elements like Uzbegs, Persians, Arabs, Turks and indigenous Rajputs. A medley, so that by playing the one against another, one group could be controlled and dealt with by the other — Irani by Turani, Shia by Sunni and so on.[177] The Rajputs could be put to manage all these by turns, or those other fellow Rajput Rajas who showed reluctance in making submission. Late in the seventeenth century, with the advance of the Mughal power in the Deccan, there was an influx of the Deccanis — Bijapuris,

---

175. Beni Prasad, *History of Jahangir*, Chapter on Mughal Government (pp.67-110), pp.74-75.

176. Moreland, *India at the Death of Akbar*, pp.69-70

177. Bernier, pp.209-211.

Hyderabadis. An interesting description of this composite Mughal nobility is given by Chandrabhan Brahman, who wrote during the last years of Shahjahan's reign.[178] And yet the regime remained exotic in nature. There was little trust existing between the various sections of the nobility and the Mughal King. Bernier did not fail to note that "the Great Mogol, though a Mahometan, and as such an enemy of the Gentiles (Hindus), always keeps in his service a large retinue of Rajas... appointing them to important commands in his armies." And still about the Rajputs, Bernier makes a startling statement. It debunks the generally held belief that the Mughal emperors trusted the Rajput *mansabdars* wholly, or the latter were always unsuspiciouly loyal to the regime. He says that the Rajput "Rajas never mount (guard) within a (Mughal) fortress, but invariably without the walls, under their own tents....and always refusing to enter any fortress unless well attended, and by men determined to sacrifice their lives for their leaders. This self devotion has been sufficiently proved when attempts have been made to deal treacherously with a Raja."[179] His statement reminds one of the successful flight of Shivaji from Mughal captivity to Maharashtra and of Durga Das with Ajit Singh to Marwar.

According to Bernier, the Mughals maintained "a large army for the purpose of keeping people in subjection...No adequate idea can be conveyed of the sufferings of the people. The cudgel and the whip compel them to incessant labour...their revolt or their flight is only prevented by the presence of a military force."[180] There is no need to wonder why cudgel and whip were used to compel people to incessant labour and prevent flight of peasants from the villages. One function of the army of course was to con-

178. *Guldasta*, Aligarh University Library, Sir Sulaiman Collection, Ms. No.666/44, fol. 4b-5a.
179. Bernier, pp.40, 210.
180. *Ibid*., p.230.

quer new regions and crush internal rebellions. Another was meant to coerce the recalcitrant land-holders (*zor talab*) and keep the poor peasants in subjection. For this second purpose there was a separate set of soldiery who could be called to service from regions and districts when so required. In the time of Akbar the number of such soldiers comes to a little more than forty-four lacs.[181] This force was organised on the quota system, each *Zamindar* or autonomous ruler being expected to produce on demand a fixed number of troops. "Ordinarily they received no stipends from the imperial government and were, there-fore, not required to submit to military regulations which governed the regular army."[182] It was mainly this cadre which kept the common people under subjection. In In-dia's climatic conditions, vagaries of monsoon, and resis-tance of freedom-loving though poor people[183] to oppres-sive foreign rule, made collection of revenue a perennial problem in medieval times. Right from the beginning of Muslim rule, regular military expeditions had to be sent yearly or half-yearly for realization of land-tax or reve-nue.[184] Under Afghan rulers like Sher Shah (who adopted the Sultanate model in general and Alauddin Khalji model in particular) the *Shiqdars* with armed contingents helped in the collection of revenue. The Mughals followed suit and troops were pressed into service for the collection of revenue. This constabulary carried long sticks mounted with pikes and was unscrupulous and tyrannical as a rule. Its oppressions inpired terror among the poor villagers.

---

181. *Report of the Indian Historical Records Commission,* Vol.V, 1923, pp.58ff; Elphinstone, Mountstuart, *History of India,* p.304; Saran, Parmatma, *Provincial Government of the Mughals,* pp.258-68; Tripathi, R.P., *Rise and Fall of the Mughal Empire* (Allahabad, 1960), p.234.

182. Tripathi, *loc.cit.*

183. See infra chapter 7.

184. For repeated references for the fifteenth century see Lal, *Twilight of the Sultanate,* especially the chapter entitled Revenue through Bayonet, pp. 73-83.

Bernier rightly observes that the government of the
Mughals was an army rule even in the time of peace.[185]
The rural fear of the *darogha saheb* and his men originated
neither in ancient nor in modern times. It is a legacy of the
medieval period.

Conclusion

It may be summarized in conclusion that the nature
of the Turco-Mughal state in India was theocratic and
military. The scope of the state activity was narrow and
limited. Generally speaking it discharged two main functions — the maintenance of law and order according to
Islamic norms, and the collection of revenue. In the medieval period both these functions meant suppression of the
people. Consequently, throughout the medieval period the
administration was army-oriented. It was not a secular
state, nor was it a welfare state except for some vested
Muslim interests. No attempt was made to build up a
national state in the name of a broad-based system working as a protective umbrella for all sections of the people.
It is a hypothetical belief that foreign Muslims who came
as invaders and conquerors but stayed on in India, made
India their home and merged with the local people. They
did not prove different from those conquerors (like
Mahmud Ghaznavi, Timur or Nadir Shah) who did not
stay on and went back. For, instead of integrating themselves with the mainstream of Indian national tradition, it
was their endeavour to keep a separate identity. To quote
from Beni Prasad: "By the fifteenth century the age of systematic persecution was past...but the policy of toleration
was the outcome of sheer necessity; it was the *sine qua non*
of the very existence of the government."[186] Else "the
Semitic conception of the state is that of a theocracy."[187]

185. Also Moreland, *The Agrarian System of Moslem India*,p.221.
186. Beni Prasad, *op. cit.*, p.75.
187. *Ibid.*, p.73.

Chapter 5

Upper Classes and Luxurious Life

"All the surplus produce...was swept into the coffers of the Mughal nobility and pampered them in a degree of luxury not dreamt of even by kings in Persia and Central Asia."

Jadunath Sarkar

Nobles and courtiers, army commanders and provincial governors, in fact all high officials of the Muslim government formed the upper classes. In 'civilian' upper classes could be counted the Ulama and the Mashaikh, scholars and historians, and some very rich Muslim merchants. A study of the high classes under two major categories — nobles, and Ulama and Mashaikh — would suffice to give a general idea of the life of Muslim upper classes, their composition, their corruption, their licence, their hopes and fears, and their high style of living.

The Nobles

The nobles constituted the ruling bureaucracy. In the early years of Muslim rule (1206-1399) foreign adventurers' and warriors monopolised appointments to high offices. In the beginning the Turks formed the bulk of the ruling elite. Besides, Persians, Abyssinians, Egyptians, Afghans and converted Mongols also continued to obtain high positions. Under the Lodi sultans (1451-1526), Afghan adventurers of various tribes and clans flocked to India like 'ants and locusts'. Even in the Mughal times (1526-

1707-1857) the imperial service remained predominantly foreign with Iranis and Turanis forming the core of the cadre. The Turanis hailed from Central Asia where the Turkish language was spoken. Iranis comprised the Persian speaking people and belonged to the region presently extending from Iraq and Iran to Afghanistan.

The Mughal nobles were also known as *Mansabdars*. The *Mansabdars* were not only government officers, but also the richest class in the empire. They formed a closed aristocracy; entrance into this class was not usually possible for the common people, whatever their merits. Naturally, therefore, the most important factor which was taken into account when nobles were appointed was heredity. The *Khanazads*, the scions of royalty and sons and descendants of *Mansabdars*, had the best claim to such appointments.

The Indian Muslim nobles, who were local converts, also rose to be officers in the upper cadres, but foreigners were always preferred. The fourteenth century Persian chronicler Ziyauddin Barani, who was born in India but traced his ancestry to a Turki Noble, credits the foreigner Turks with all possible virtues and the Indian Muslims with all kinds of imperfections.[1] The invectives he hurls on the converted Sultan Nasiruddin Khusrau Shah (C.E. 1320), are too well known to need repetition.[2] Muhammad Tughlaq always preferred foreign Muslims to Indians for appointment as officers. The rebellion of Ain-ul-mulk Multani (1339) during his reign was a symptom of the resentment felt by the India-born nobles against this policy of prejudice. In turn Khan-i-Jahan, a Telingana Brahmin convert, dominated the court of Sultan Firoz Tughlaq. The career of Mahmud Gawan, the minister of the Bahmani Sultan Muhammad III (1463-1482), illustrates both the

---

1. *Fatawa-i-Jahandari*, p.99.
2. Lal, *History of the Khaljis*, p.309.

reasons for which preference was given to foreigners and the jealousy it engendered. Foreign nobles looked down upon Indian Muslim nobles, and considered them as 'low-born', although not all foreign Muslims were of high lineage.

Right through the Muslim rule, low origin foreigners used to come as individuals and in groups to seek employment in India. Writing about the foreign element in the Mughal nobility in seventeenth century Bernier says that "the Omarahs mostly consist of adventurers from different nations who entice one another to the court; and are generally persons of low descent, some having been originally slaves, and the majority being destitute of education. The Mogol raises them to dignities, or degrades them to obscurity; according to his own pleasure and caprice."[3] W.H. Moreland, however, does not consider all foreign immigrants as of low descent. He says that in Mughal India "there were huge prizes to be won...and one need not wonder that the service should have attracted to the court the ablest and most enterprising men from a large portion of Western Asia."[4] High and low, foreign and Indian, the Muslim nobles after all belonged to one and the same cadre, and they tried to come closer together.[5] On the one hand, foreign Muslims used to become locals after the lapse of a few generations. Bernier writes that "the children of the third and fourth generation (of Uzbegs, Persians, Arabs and Turks)...are held in much less

---

3. Bernier, p.209.

4. Moreland, *India at the Death of Akbar*, pp.69, 71.

5. But sometimes neither the passage of time nor indeed death could remove the barriers. The remains of the Iranian Mir Murtaza Shirazi, who was earlier buried near the Indian Amir Khusrau, were ordered by Emperor Akbar "to be removed and buried elsewhere", on the representation of Shaikh-ul-Islam, who pleaded that the two deceased would find each other's company a torture (Ambashtya, B.P., Biographical Sketch of Badaoni in his Reprint of *Muntakhab-ut-Tawarikh* trs. by S.A.Ranking, Academia Asiatica, Patna, 1973, p.99).

respect than the new comers."[6] On the other hand, the low-born Indian Muslim became elitist with rise in economic status. There was a saying: "Last year I was a *julaha*, this year a *shaykh*; and the next year, if the harvest be good, I shall be a *saiyyad*."[7] "Belonging to Islam" was a great cementing force, and, whatever the colour of the skin, all Muslim nobles tried to feel as one, as belonging to the ruling elite, as searching for exotic roots. It was aristocratic on the part of the orthodox Muslim to feel that he was in India, but not of it. He durst not strike his roots deep into the native soil. He must import traditions, language and culture. His civil and criminal law must be derived from the writings of jurists and the decisions of judges in Baghdad and Cairo. The Muslim in India was an intellectual exotic; he considered it *infra dig* to adapt himself to his environment.[8]

Besides the competition between Indian and foreign Muslim nobles, there was also constant contest between Muslim and Hindu nobles. With the permanent establishment of Muslim rule, the policy of the sultans was generally to keep the Hindus excluded and appoint only Muslims. But the Hindus possessed native intelligence and experience, sons of the soil as they were, and many of the best Hindus had to be employed, especially during the Mughal period. The Hindus in a way were 'indispensable'. To them belonged, according to Badaoni, "half the army and half the land. Neither the Hindustanis (Indian Muslims) nor the Moghuls can point to such grand lords as the Hindus have among themselves." Bernier too did not fail to notice this.[9]

These nobles were in attendance on the king in the capital or in camp, and in outstations held civil and mili-

---

6. Bernier, p.209.
7. Titus, *Islam in India and Pakistan*, p.117.
8. Sarkar, *A Short History of Aurangzeb*, p.469.
9. Badaoni, II, p.339; trs. in *Ain*, I, p.214; Bernier, p.40.

tary assignments, as governors of provinces or commanders of the army. Indeed they were expected to cultivate versatility, there being no distinction between civil and military appointments and duties. Raja Birbal, after many years as court wit, met his death fighting Yusafzais as commander of troops on the frontier while Abul Fazl, the most eminent literary figure of the time, distinguished himself in military operations in the Deccan.

The nobles were called Umara and were graded as Khans, Maliks, Amirs and Sipehsalars in the Sultanate period, and as Mansabdars under the Mughals. According to Barani a Sarkhail commanded ten horsemen; a Sipehsalar ten Sarkhails; an Amir ten Sipahsalars; a Malik ten Amirs; and a Khan, ten Maliks.[10] According to the author of *Masalik-ul-Absar*, a Khan commanded more or less 100,000 troops, an Amir 10,000, a Malik a thousand, and so on.[11] The term Amir was normally used in a generic sense to denote a high officer. In Akbar's time and after, all the great men of the Mughal Empire were graded and appointed to a *mansab* (rank) in the imperial service. From the lowest rank, that of the commander of ten, upto the rank of 400 an officer was known as Mansabdar. From 500 onwards a noble was known as Amir, or Khan, or Khan-i-Azam. They were all generally spoken of as Umara.

The Umara were highly paid. Their remuneration was paid sometimes in the form of a cash salary, at others by the grant of a revenue assignment or *iqta*. "The *iqta* was basically a salary collected at source." According to the chroniclers of the Sultanate period every Khan received two lakh *tankahs*, every Malik from 50 to 60 thousand *tankahs*, every Amir from 40 to 50 thousand *tankahs*, and so on.[12] The salaries during the Mughal period were equally

---

10. Barani, p.145.

11. *Masalik-ul-Absar*, E and D, III,p.577. Also Hajiuddabir, *Zafarul Walih*, p.782.

12. Al-Qalqashindi, p.71; Ibn Battuta, p.129; Afif, pp.296-97 and 437-38.

high. It has been computed by expert opinion that a commandar of 5000 could count on at least Rs.18,000 a month under Akbar and his successor. He could even improve upon this amount if he practised judicious economy in his military expenditure and had the good fortune of securing a profitable *jagir*. A commander of 1000 could similarly count on receiving Rs.5000 a month (equal to from rupees 25,000 to 30,000 in 1914), while a commander of 500 would have received the equivalent of Rs.5000 to 6000 at the same rate. "While therefore the precise figures are uncertain, it appears to be reasonable to conclude that the higher ranks of the Imperial Service were remunerated on a scale far more liberal than that which now prevails in India (C. 1914), or for that matter in any portion of the world."[13]

Luxurious Life

Their high salaries and emoluments introduced into the lives of the Umara all the uses and abuses of luxury. They lived with such ostentation that it was not to be seen elsewhere in the world, and "the most sumptuous of European courts cannot compare in richness and magnificence with the lustre beheld in Indian courts."[14] Their splendid life-style may be studied in its two aspects — private inside the harem and public outside of it. They lived in magnificent mansions some costing four to six thousand gold *tankahs* (*dinars*) and provided with all amenities.[15] By the seventeenth century the Mahals of the nobles had gained in architectural excellence and constructional designs. At Agra, on the banks of the Jumna, "many persons have erected buildings of three or four storeys," writes emperor Jahangir[16] Asaf Khan's palace had a fair

---

13. Moreland, *India at the Death of Akbar*, p.68.
14. Manucci, II, p.330. Also Pelsaert, pp.1-5.
15. Ibn Battuta, p.141.
16. *Tuzuk-i-Jahangiri*, I,p.3.

Diwan Khana which was flanked by "diverse lodgings for his women neatly contrived with galleries and walks."[17] Asaf Khan's palace was exceedingly handsome and costly,[18] but the others were equally elegant.[19] The basic pattern of the mansions of the nobles was the same. One portion of the building was the Diwan Khana or the men's quarters but "the greater portion was occupied by their ladies and was called Zenan Khana."[20] "In the houses of the nobles the women's apartments are in the centre, and it is generally necessary to traverse two or three large courts and a garden or two before reaching there."[21] Bernier's observations about the houses of nobles of Delhi are similar to those of Pelsaert at Agra. They were spacious and along with "courtyards, gardens, trees, basins of water, small *jets d'eau* in the hall or at the entrance, and handsome subterraneous apartments which are furnished with large fans."[22] While encamping, their tents were made equally magnificient. "All the arcades and galleries were covered from top to bottom with brocade, and (even) the pavement with rich carpets."[23]

The nobles' ladies were numerous and spendthrift. Pelsaert says that "as a rule they have three or four wives...All live together... surrounded by high walls...called the *mahal*, having tanks and gardens inside. Each wife has separate apartments for herself and her slaves, of whom there may be 10, or 20, or 100, according to her fortune. Each has a monthly allowance for her (expenditure). Jewels and clothes are provided by the

---

17. William Finch in Foster, *Early Travels in India*, p.165.
18. Pelsaert, *Jahangir's India*, p.3.
19. *Ibid.*, p.56.
20. *Ibid.*, p.67. Also Foster, p.56.
21. Tavernier, *Travels in India*, I,p.393.
22. Bernier, p.247.
23. *Ibid.*, p.270.

husband according to the extent of his affection..."[24] Their Mahals were adorned with "superfluous pomp and ornamental dainties." The ladies made extensive use of gold and silver, for ornaments and jewellery, as well for their utensils and table service.[25] Even their bedsteads were "lavishly ornamented with gold and silver."[26] During the earlier period, there is also mention of gold bath-tubs and gold horse-shoes.[27]

For the security and supervision of these hundreds of ladies, dozens and dozens of maids and eunuchs were required. The harem paraphernalia cost tons of money. Furthermore, it was a fashion for the Umara to visit the houses of dancing girls, take them or call them to their own mansions and pay them handsomely.[28] Throughout the medieval times the nobility indulged in the expensive hobbies of women, wine, song and drugs. Chess and *chausar* they played at home; big game shooting, taming and flying birds, playing *chaugan* and practicing with swords were their outdoor recreations. Dozens of falconers, pigeon-boys and attendants were employed to keep their birds and horses in trim.[29] The nobles, their ladies, and even their slave-girls dressed in the best of cotton fineries and richest embroidered silks. Their food was rich and full of delicacies.[30] Their boon companions partook of it

---

24. Pelsaert, p.64. Some important ladies of royalty probably had their pay fixed on the lines of Mansabdars. William Hawkins, writing about 1611, says that the mother of the King, Mariyam Zamani, got an allowance of the *Mansab* of 12,000 (*Travels in India*, Edited by William Foster, London, 1921, pp.98-99). It is computed that the *Jagirs* of Nur Jahan, spread all over the country, "would have conferred on her the title of a commander of 30,000" (Blochmann, *Ain*, I, p.574). It is doubtful if any ladies of nobles got an allowance from the Court, but it was natural for the Umara themselves to fix monthly stipends for their favourite wives and concubines.

25. Pelsaert, p.67.

26. *Ibid.*, p.67. Also Manucci, I, p.87.

27. Ibn Battuta, pp.69, 73.

28. Peter Mundy, II, p. 218; Manucci, I, p.69.

29. Barani, p.318; Al-Qalqashindi, p.68.

30. Ashraf, *Life and Conditions of the People of Hindustan*, pp.282-83.

freely.[31] Most of the nobles "were soaked in wine and sunk in debauch" but they were also patrons of art and poetry. Since I have made a comprehensive study of the luxurious life of the medieval Muslim nobility in my monograph entitled *The Mughal Harem*, I shall refrain from repeating here what I have already stated therein in detail except reproducing one paragraph from the book. "The large establishment of wives and servants rendered the nobles immobile. No Indian scholars, engineers or travellers went abroad to learn the skills the Europeans were developing in their countries. While people from Europe were frequently coming to Hindustan, no Indian nobleman could go to the West because he could not live without his harem and he could not take with him his cumbersome harem to countries situated so far away. Europe at this time was forging ahead in science and technology through its Industrial Revolution, but the Mughal elites kept themselves insulated from this great stride because of inertia. Consequently, the country was pulled back from marching with progress, a deficiency which has not been able to be made up until now."[32]

Outside their mansions the Umara were extra ostentatious. Since they attained to highest honours "at court, in the provinces, and in the armies; and who are, as they call themselves, the Pillars of the Empire, they maintain the splendour of the court, and are never seen out-of-doors but in the most superb apparel; mounted sometimes on an

---

31. Afif, pp.145-46.

32. *The Mughal Harem*, Aditya Prakashan, New Delhi, 1988, p.203. Reacting to this statement, A.Jan Qaiser of the Aligarh Muslim University in his harsh review of the book observes: "Is Lal really ignorant of the fact that the Indians were being increasingly exposed to a number of European articles of technology and culture brought by the Europeans during the sixteenth, seventeenth and eighteenth century?" (*The Indian Historical Review*, 1991, p.346). The poor man does not realise that he is only confirming my assertion that the Indian nobles were being *only* exposed (whatever he may mean by the word) to articles *brought* by Europeans. On their own they were incapable of doing anything more.

elephant, sometimes on horseback, and not unfrequently in a *paleky* attended by many of their cavalry, and by a large body of servants on foot — not only to clear the way, but to flap the flies and brush off the dust with tails of pea--cocks; to carry the spitoon, water to allay the Omrah's thirst."[33]

Over and above the expenses on their "large establishment of wives, servants, camels and horses," the nobles were expected to present valuable gifts to the king on birthday anniversaries, Ids, Nauroz and other festivals, according to their pay and status. "Some of them, indeed take that opportunity of presenting gifts of extraordinary magnificance, sometimes for the sake of ostentatious display, sometimes to divert the king from instituting an inquiry into their excessive exactions, and sometimes to gain the favour of the king, and by that means obtain an increase of salary. Some present fine pearls, diamonds, emeralds and rubies; others offer vessels of gold set with precious stones; others again give gold coins..."[34] The king also gave some gift in exchange, but the presents of the nobles were much costlier and often extracted by the king. During a festival of this kind Aurangzeb, having paid a visit to Jafar Khan, the Wazir made a present to the king of gold coins to the amount of one hundred thousand crowns, some handsome pearls and a ruby about the value of which prevailed great "confusion among the principal jewellers, and it might have cost five hundred thousand crowns."[35] Thus the king sometimes took the initiative in contriving to extract costly presents and gathered huge amounts, for says Pelsaert, "from the least to the greatest right up to the King himself everyone is infected with insatiable greed."[36] Money spent on bribes and presents

---

33. Bernier, pp.213-14.
34. *Ibid.*, p.271.
35. *Ibid.*, p.272. Tavernier figures this ruby and also gives a full account of the incident (*Travels*, II, pp.127, 128).
36. Pelsaert, *Jahangir's India*, pp.57-58.

often proved profitable investment,[37] for, without presents the nobles could hardly expect timely response to his petition.[38] Not only were gifts presented to the king, means had to be found for making valuable presents, every year, to a Wazir, an eunuch or a lady of the seraglio, or to any other person whose influence at court the nobleman considered indispensable.[39]

Bribery and Corruption

Such high expenses of building spacious mansions, exchanging costly presents, maintaining a large harem of wives and concubines —in short, living in style at home and indulging in pompous display outside, could not be met by the aristocracy from their salaries alone. Therefore, the nobles augmented their income by other means. There were many sources from which extra amounts of money could come to their coffers, like enjoying a large military command, a profitable political appointment and a lucrative revenue assignment, and these were all inter-connected, all providing opportunities of corruption and exploitation.

Every nobleman or Mansabdar was alloted a quota of troops which he was expected to maintain. From the very beginning of Turkish rule the conquered land used to be distributed by the king among army officers, nobles, government officials and even soldiers as gifts, grants and rewards and also in lieu of personal salary, and for paying their soldiers. These grants were not hereditary, and were given as pay for military service. But in course of time the land-holders continued in possession of their land without rendering any military service. On inquiry it was found by Sultan Balban that about 2,000 cavalry officers had received villages in the Doab alone by way of pay during the

---

37. Moreland, *India at the Death of Akbar*, p.72.
38. Pelsaert, p.58.
39. Bernier, pp.230-31.

time of Iltutmish, but for the next forty years or more many of the grantees had become old and infirm, or had died. But their sons and even slaves continued to live off the lands as if they were an inheritance. Many of them were clever enough to get the assignments recorded in their own names in the books of the Ariz-i-Mumalik obviously by bribing the officials..."according to their means by wine, goats, chicken, pigeon, butter and food-stuffs from their villages"...to the Deputy Muster-Master and his officials.[40]

Sultan Balban tried to improve matters and so did many other rulers but corruption remained entrenched.

The salary of the soldiers and expenditure on their horses usually formed part of the pay of the Umara or Mansabdars who were expected to spend it on them. But this system gave the nobleman an opportunity to retain some money from every man's pay and prepare false returns of the horses he was supposed to provide. "Many of the lords who hold the rank of 5000 horse, do not keep even 1000 in their employ."[41] This practice was universal throughout the medieval period. It rendered the Amir's income very considerable, particularly when he was so fortunate as to have some good *jagirs* or suitable lands assigned to him. For some of the officers "received double, and even more than that, in excess of the estimated value of their grants".[42] There was thus the practice "which prevails too much at all times" of purchasing governorships against hard cash. Sometimes the king assigned a governorship to the highest bidder. The governor or farmer of revenue so appointed had to compensate himself by mercilessly fleecing the merchants and peasants of the province.[43] In this way many people without the smallest pat-

40. Barani, p.62.
41. Pelsaert, p.54.
42. *Masalik-ul-Absar*, E and D,III, p.577.
43. *Ain*, I, p.1.

rimony, some even originally wretched slaves, involved in debt, became great and opulent lords overnight. Bernier even complains that the Great Mogol did not select for his service "gentlemen of opulent and ancient families; sons of his citizens, merchants and manufacturers...affectionately attached to their sovereign...and willing to maintain themselves...by means of their own patrimony...Instead he is surrounded...by parasites raised by the dregs of society." That is how "the misery of this ill-fated country is increased."[44]

For many an Umara just looted both the government and the people all at once. In this regard certain misconceptions may be removed at the outset. It is generally believed that corruption flourishes in a democracy or a soft state where no one can be punished until proved guilty, and that despotic rulers would not brook it. Another idea repeatedly put forward is that it is poverty and low salaries that breed corruption, and that it is bound to be reduced in proportion to the rise in emoluments and standard of living.

However, on a study of the records of medieval times, when autocracy was the order of the day, we find that corruption was quite well-grounded, and people and the government were unabashedly cheated. Cheating of the people and the government are almost synonymous. In the fourteenth century too, those who cheated the people could not rest at that, and they took every opportunity of defrauding the government whenever an opportunity presented itself. One such opportunity came when Muhammad bin Tughlaq introduced his famous token currency. Another, when he struck upon the novel (now commonly practised) idea of having large-scale farm cultivation. An area of about 45 miles square (30 krohs) was set aside for intensive farming in which not a patch was to be left uncultivated at any time by changing crops constantly. A

44. Bernier, pp.230-31.

hundred *shiqdars* were appointed to supervise the project. They promised to cultivate thousands of *bighas* of land and also to reclaim waste land. Each one of them received fifty thousand *tankahs* in cash as advance (*sondhar*) from the State. But they turned out to be greedy and dishonest persons. They cheated the government, squandered the money on personal needs and did not care to cultivate the allotted area. In this way the State lost not less then 70,00,000 *tankahs* in all. Of the advance not even a hundredth or a thousandth part could be recovered and the avaricious *shiqdars* embezzled the whole amount.[45] And all this callousness was there about a measure which had been undertaken to ameliorate famine conditions.

A few more instances of corruption from the Sultanate period may be mentioned to appreciate the depth and extensivity of the malady. During the reign of Firoz Shah the profession of soldiers was made hereditary. Also old men were not retired on compassionate ground and efficiency of the army naturally suffered. Over and above this, corruption was galore in the Diwan-i-Arz. Horses of little value were brought to the Diwan and were passed as serviceable, obviously by greasing the palms of the clerks. In this reference a story narrated by Shams Siraj Afif is worth citing. Once the Sultan overheard a soldier complaining to a friend that because he did not have the necessary money to pay as bribe, he had not been able to get a fitness certificate for his horse at the Diwan-i-Arz. "The Sultan inquired how much was needed, and the soldier said that if he had a gold *tankah* he could get a certificate for his horse. The Sultan ordered his purse-bearer to give a *tankah* to the soldier." The trooper went to the Diwan-i-Arz with the *ashrafi* and paying it to the clerk concerned got the certificate.[46] He then returned and thanked the Sultan. Encouragement to corruption from the

---

45. Barani, p.499.
46. Afif, p.301.

head of the State was a matter of concern. But what else could Afif say but that Firoz Shah was a very kind-hearted and affectionate Sultan!

These cases of bribery, corruption and embezzlement concern government officials of not so high a status among the upper classes. But the highest nobles of the State indulged in them. The story of the deception of Kajar Shah, the Master of Mint, speaks for itself. It is so interesting that its incidents may be given in some detail. Firoz Tughlaq had issued several varieties of new coins and *shashgani* (or six-*jital*-piece) was one of them. As the coin went into circulation, it was reported to the Sultan by two courtiers that there was a deficiency of one grain of silver in the *shashgani*, and they prayed for an investigation. If what they had said was proved to be true, they pleaded, the officials responsible for debasement of the coin must take the consequences. The Sultan immediately directed the Wazir, Khan-i-Jahan Maqbul, to investigate the matter. Khan-i-Jahan was equally keen about the enquiry. Indeed he observed that "the coinage of kings was like an unmarried daughter, whom no one would seek after, however beautiful and charming she might be, if any aspersion had, rightly or wrongly, been cast upon her character. So also was the case with the royal coins; if any one honestly or falsely alleged a debasement of the currency, the insinuation would spread, the coinage would earn a bad name, and no one would take it."

The affair was as scandalous as it was unique. To hold an open inquest was ruled out because the bona fides of the government itself were in question. Therefore the Wazir decided on a secret investigation, and sent for Kajar Shah, the Master of Mint, and asked him if his officials had been covetous. Kajar Shah knew that his game was up and he thought it best to make a clean breast of it to the Wazir. Khan-i-Jahan could not displease the Sultan, who had insisted that the intrinsic value of the coin should be tested in his presence. But he also could not allow the government to get into disrepute, and now that he had known the truth, he thought it best to hush up the case. Therefore, he recommended to Kajar Shah to arrange the matter over with the goldsmiths that they so manage their performance before the king that the process of debasement of the *shashgani* may not be detected. The goldsmiths, charcoal dealers and stove (*angusht*) managers were all tutored and everything was given a fool-proof finish. Firoz Shah was requested to watch the operation sitting in a private apartment with Khan-i-Jahan Maqbul. Kajar Shah and his accusers were called in. The goldsmiths were also brought in. The charcoal dealers brought the stoves and placed them before the goldsmiths. Several *shashgani* pieces were placed in the crucible, which the goldsmiths put upon the fire. The Sultan meanwhile entered into a conversation with his minister, and while he was so engaged, the workmen adroitly picked up the required pieces of silver and surreptitiously threw them into the melting pot. After a while the crucible was taken off the fire and the contents were weighed; the *shashgani* was proved to be of full standard value. Kajar Shah was presented with a robe of honour and other favours. He was seated on an elephant and taken round the city so that people might understand that the *shashgani* was of full value. The 'honest' accusers were thus proved false and banished.[47]

Another instance. An important nobleman, Shamsuddin Abu Rija, the Auditor General (Mustaufi), had earned wide notoriety as a professional bribe-taker, embezzler and at that a tyrant. Shams Siraj Afif, historian contemporary of Firoz Shah, devotes thirty-five pages to record the crimes of Abu Rija.[48] The three years during which he held the office of the Auditor General, his hand of greed extended to all officers, Zamindars and Amils. Those who

---

47. Afif, pp.346-48.
48. *Ibid.*, pp.457-92.

gave him bribes, were permitted to go scot-free; others who did not, were implicated by him on one charge or another and punished. Nobody dared to raise a voice against his criminal breach of trust or his atrocities, because he was a hot favourite of the Sultan. Even before he was made the Mustaufi, he, as the deputy governor of Gujarat, had borrowed 90 thousand *tankahs* from the Provincial Treasury for his own use, but had not refunded the amount. To hide his improper gains he had built a new mansion in Delhi and had buried underground thousands of gold *Ashrafis*. At last the Sultan could not keep his eyes closed to Shamsuddin's black deeds because a number of nobles, including the Khan-i-Jahan, son of Khan-i-Jahan Maqbul, insisted that he should be brought to book. Shamsuddin's mansion was searched and his reserves of gold dug out. He was imprisoned and tortured so severely that he could never ride a horse again.[49] Strangely enough when Firoz's son Muhammad ascended the throne, he recalled Shamsuddin Abu Rija and reinstated him with all honours.[50]

But the one man who amassed probably the largest amount of wealth in the Sultanate period, escaped scot-free. This man was Bashir, a slave of Firoz Shah. He had originally come as a part of the dower of Firoz's mother. In course of time, and through the favour of Sultan Firoz, he rose into prominence and got the title of Imadul Mulk. His one passion was acquisition of wealth. Related to the sultan as he was, he soon accumulated crores of *tankahs*. Gunny bags required for storing the coin alone were estimated to cost 2,500 *tankahs*, the price of each bag being four *jitals*;[51] but Imadul Mulk objected to this extravagant

---

49. Barani, p.353.
50. Afif, p.492.
51. Afif, p. 439. The chronicler does not exaggerate. The wealth of Imadul Mulk was estimated at thirteen crores of *tankahs*. A *tankah* would buy 12 bags at the average rate of 48 *jitals* to a *tankah*. 2,500 *tankahs* would buy 30,000 bags and each bag would contain about 4,350 coins or one maund and 14 seers of silver in bullion.

outlay for bags and directed that pits should be dug in the ground and the money placed therein like as corn is stored. He had amassed thirteen crore *tankahs* but he was greedy about acquiring more.[52]

Just imagine thirteen crore *tankahs*. The total revenue of a year during Firoz's reign was six crore and seventy-five lac *tankahs*;[53] and one individual slave of the Sultan (Bashir-i-Sultani) had acquired wealth amounting to two years' total revenue of the country. Could corruption go further? "There were many rich Khans and Maliks in the time of Firoz Shah," writes Afif, "but no one was so rich as he; indeed there never had been one so rich in any reign or in any kingdom." Still the officers of the Revenue Department could not call him to account; they were indeed afraid of him, for he was a favourite of the Sultan. To please the Sultan, Imadul Mulk once presented him with a crore of *tankahs*. But twelve crores still remained with him. At his death, the Sultan ordered nine crores to be deposited in the State exchequer on the plea that "Bashir is my property (as his slave), and so his property is mine." Three crores were left with Imadul Mulk's son Ishaq who also got the title of his father. Afif adds that Ishaq himself was an extremely rich man and did not stand in need of his father's wealth.

The chronicler philosophises by saying: "These nobles accumulated so much wealth by lawful and unlawful means (*vajeh na vajeh*), and then leaving it undertook the last journey where they were to account for all this wealth."[54] But such ill-gotten gains at least created havoc in this world, because, according to Afif himself, "much of the trouble that came about in the time of Sultan Muhammad (son of Firoz) was due to the accumulation of such wealth in the hands of a few nobles."[55]

---

52. Afif, pp.440-41.

53. *Ibid.*, p.94.

54. *Ibid.*, p.440.

55. *loc. cit.* For the troubles of the post-Firoz decade see Lal, *Twilight of the Sultanate*, pp.2-6.

Thus there was corruption in the army, in civil administration and in the royal mint. Hoarding, black-marketing and bribery were commonly practised. Even the judiciary was not free from corruption, and that too during the reign of a strong and stern monarch like Alauddin. Talking of Qazi Hamiduddin Multani, Ziyauddin Barani cryptically remarks, "it would not be proper to write about his qualities in history." He also says that not "the godfearing and abstemious but corruptible, greedy and mundane" people were appointed as judges.[56] His one complaint was that judges used to stretch the meaning of the Quranic texts to carry out the wishes of the Sultans.[57] The indictment by Maulana Shamsuddin Turk of the judiciary of the day is also worth citing. The Maulana who hailed from Egypt, addressed a letter to Alauddin saying that "ill-fated wiseacres of black faces sat in mosques with abominable law books and made money by cheating both the accuser and the accused, and the Qazis...did not bring these facts to the notice of the king."[58] It is said that Shamsuddin Turk was opposed to Qazi Hamiduddin, and therefore wrote in such a way, but in *Mutla-i-Anwar*, Amir Khusrau also observes that the Qazis were ignorant of the principles of law. The appointment of Ibn Battuta, who did not know a word of law, as the Qazi of the capital by Muhammad bin Tughlaq, came to him as the greatest surprise.

Having studied some prominent cases of bribery, corruption and hoarding, of the nobles, and the rich upper class people in the Sultanate times, let us analyse their genesis and their prominent aspects. It is clear that corruption had nothing much to do with poverty or a low standard of living. During Balban's rule the nobility and armymen, who could not or would not perform their duties for which lands had been granted to them, were not

56. Barani, p.446.
57. *Ibid*., p.446.
58. *Ibid*., p.229.

poor. But they wanted their privileges to continue; about performing their duties they were not concerned. Fakhruddin, the Kotwal, who pleaded their case with the king was moved as much by compassion as by self-interest. He was himself old and in course of time stood to lose all privileges if the orders of Balban were not amended. The people who minted counterfeit coins found in the token currency of Muhammad bin Tughlaq a challenge to their intelligence and ingenuity, and took advantage of the golden opportunity provided by it to get rich. The officials of the Diwan-i-Arz who took a gold *tankah* for issuing the fitness certificate to the cavalryman in the days of Firoz were not poor; they were habitual bribe-takers. The *shiqdars* or officers who embezzled the money advanced to them for cultivation by Muhammad bin Tughlaq again, were not poor. The people who minted debased currency, the wholesalers and retailers who indulged in hoarding and black-marketing, men like Kajar Shah and Bashir-i-Sultani, did not do what they did because they were poor, but because they were greedy and opportunists. The object of the opportunists was to get rich, of the rich to get richer. Their luxurious life, their women and wine and their ambition to amass wealth, kept the torch of corruption burning.

Individual cases of corruption and embezzlement apart, the sure and perennial sources of extra income of the nobles were two—what they could save on their troops and what they could collect in addition to the nominal value of their assignments — and able and unscrupulous men made as much extra wealth as possible from both these. In the words of Shihabuddin Ahmad, "The *khans*, *maliks*, *amirs*, and *isfah-salars* receive the revenues of the places assigned to them by the treasury ....Generally speaking they bring in much more than their estimated value...Some of the officers receive double, and even more than that, in excess of the estimated value of their grants."[59] What this practice meant to the poor peasant would be discussed later.[60] The irony of the matter was that everyone knew about it, including the king himself. The king was even a party to the system for he allotted good lands to his favourites nobles. Even Sher Shah Suri, who is regarded as a friend of the agriculturists, changed his *amils* (revenue collectors) every year, or second year, and sent new ones, for he said that "there is no such income and advantage in other employments as in the government of a district. Therefore I (Sher Shah) send my good old loyal experienced servants to take charge of districts, that the salaries, profits, and advantages, may accrue to them in preference to others; and after two years I change them, and send other servants like to them, that they also may prosper...."[61]

In the Mughal period the same trends continued. Things might have improved under the able and shrewd Akbar, but only might. He too was part of the system. He too was surrounded by the same sort of people who were ready of speech and expert at intrigue. Corruption in the Mughal times was so widespread — in the army, in civil administration and even in judiciary — that narration of individual cases cannot just be done. Exceptions apart, the more important the Amir, the larger his expenses, and the greater his attempt at grabbing more and more wealth. "The biographical notices collected by Blochmann....afford instances of the possibilities which Akbar's service offered. Hakim Ali, for instance, came from Persia to India poor and destitute, but won Akbar's favour, and being his personal servant rose to the rank of 2000. Peshrau Khan again was a slave who was given to Humayun as a present; he rendered service in many different capacities and died a commander of 2000, leaving a fortune of 15 lakhs"

---

59. *Masalik-ul-Absar*, E and D, III,p.577.
60. See the Chapter on Lower Classes.
61. Abbas Sarwani, *Tarikh-i-Sher Shahi*, E and D, IV, p.414.

(equivalent to nearly a crore of rupees at modern values).[62] No one was immune from this temptation. Shaikh Ibrahim Chishti of Jaunpur died at Fatehpur, bidding farwell "to mountains of gold", 25 crores in cash taken into the treasury; "the rest" in the words of Badaoni, "fell to the share of his enemies — his sons and representatives."[63] Under Akbar's successor things were certainly bad. "Jahangir believed in frequent transfers, and the certainty of a speedy change meant increased activity in exploitation..."[64] Under Shahjahan and Aurangzeb the peasant was systematically fleeced.

"The exaction of official perquisites or gratuities...was the universal and admitted practice. Official corruption was, however, admitted in society to be immoral, and there were many officers above corruption." But the receiving and even demanding of presents by men in power was the universal rule and publicly acknowledged. Nur Jahan's father, when prime minister under Jahangir, was shameless in demanding presents. So also was Jafar Khan, one of the early Wazirs of Aurangzeb. Jai Singh offered a purse of Rs.30,000 to the Wazir for inducing the emperor to retain him in the Deccan command. Bhimsen expresses his disgust at having to pay everybody at Court in order to get or retain a petty civil office. The qazis grew enormously rich by taking bribes, the most notorious of them being Abdul Wahab. So also did many *sadars*. Even the emperor was not exempt from it. Aurangzeb asked an aspirant to a title, "Your father gave to Shahjahan one lakh of rupees for adding *alif* to his title and making him *Amir Khan*. How much will you pay me for the title I am giving you?"[65] Qabil Khan in two-and-a-half years of 'personal

---

62. Moreland, *India at the Death of Akbar*, p.71.
63. Ambashtya, Ranking's trs. of Badaoni's *Muntakhab-ut-Tawarikh*, Introduction.
64. Moreland, *op. cit.*, p.71.
65. Sarkar, *A Short History of Aurangzeb*, p.457.

attendance' on Aurangzeb amassed 12 lakhs of rupees in cash, besides articles of value and a new house for selling to suppliants his good offices. As Jadunath Sarkar says, "this pressure was passed from the emperor downwards; each social grade trying to sqeeze out of the class below itself what it had to pay as present to the rank above it, the cultivator of the soil and the trader being the victims in the last resort".[66]

Escheat

In short, the upper classes in the employment of the state were, by and large, ever busy in amassing wealth from all possible sources and enjoying it to their hearts' content. But only during their life-time. At the death of a noble, all his property, movable and immovable, was reclaimed by the government.[67] "Immediately on the death of the lord," writes Pelsaert, "who has enjoyed the king's *jagir*, be he great or small, without any exception — even before the breath is out of his body — the king's officers are ready on the spot, and make an inventory of the entire estate, recording everything to the value of a single pice, even to the dresses and jewels of the ladies, provided they have not concealed them." Concealing was very difficult. As a rule all the possesions of a noble, and his transactions were managed by his *diwan* and many other subordinates and accountants. Hence they could not be kept secret. When the noble died all his subordinates were detained, ordered to show all books and papers to the king's officers, and if there was any suspicion about their disclosure, they were tortured till they told the truth. "The king takes back the whole estate...except in a case where the deceased has done good service in his lifetime, when the women and children are given enough to live

---

66. *Ibid.*, pp.456-57 and note.
67. Moreland, *India at the Death of Akbar*, pp.72-73.

on, but no more," while most of the servants were left on the street "with a torn coat and a pinched face."[68]

On the face of it, forfeiture of the property of a deceased noble looks unjust, but in reality it was not. Under the escheat system the king saved the corrupt Amir and himself the bother of instituting an enquiry and presenting a charge-sheet. He let the grandee undisturbed to enjoy his ill-gotten wealth as long as he lived, but after his death acquired it in full. In his discretion the king sometimes left part of the wealth as pension to the widow and heirs, but generally the sons of an Amir had to start life anew. It was a bull-dozer law, and applied to both the innocent and the guilty. But there were hardly any innocent grandees. They knew very well about the law, and therefore spent so lavishly while in office, that in addition to their great income, most of them took huge amounts as loan from the State Treasury and the king was justified in recovering the loan from their property.

And after all, as per the convention, the king was the heir of the Umara. The Mughal emperors seem to have followed the Delhi Sultans in making a claim upon their nobles as if they were their slaves. We have seen how a high officer of the title of Imadul Mulk, was declared by Firoz Tughlaq as "Bashir is my property (as a slave) and so his property is mine". The Mughal claim to such succession is not elaborated in the *Ain-i-Akbari*, but is noticed by a number of European travellers from the time of Akbar onwards.[69] It was not declared in so many words but the Mughal nobles in status were not much better off than slaves. The grandees were prohibited from contracting marriage alliances without the emperor's permission. The noble was obliged, whatever be his rank, to fall prostrate on the ground in obeisance to his master. Although "the

---

68. Pelsaert, pp.54-55.
69. Pelsaert, pp.54-56; Bernier, pp.211-12; Manucci, II, p.417; Careri, p. 241.

price paid in human dignity was terrible", yet he paid it as his position, his promotion, indeed his very existence depended on the pleasure of the king. Manucci, writing about the last years of Aurangzeb says: "To get the *hazari* or pay of one thousand, it is necessary to wait a long time and work hard."[70]

This is one side of the coin. The other is that whether foreign or Indian, the nobles maintained a measure of individual independence. The pleasure of enjoying oneself with vigour and liberty amidst the chances of war and of life; the delights of activity without degrading labour; and the taste of an adventurous career full of uncertainty, inequality and peril, instilled in them a possionate desire of personal independence. There was a degree of brutality and an apathy for the weak and the poor. Nevertheless, at the bottom of this mixture of brutality, materialism and selfishness, lay the love of independence. It drew its strength from the moral nature of man, from a desire to develope one's own personality which the upper class elites loved and cherished in medieval India as is found to be the case in all ages. Their status might have been that of a servant of the ruling power, but they themselves felt as mini-rulers in their own assignments, and carried their swords like whipping sticks. Pelsaert noticed that the houses of the nobles at Agra were "hidden away in alleys and corners", and Bernier found that the dwellings of the Umara at Delhi were scattered in every direction. Manucci also observed that in Delhi many nobles "are very pleased to have their dwellings far from the royal palace". The reason was that these people enjoyed the pleasures of idleness and women's company away from mutual suspicion and court intrigues, and had it not been for official and court duties, the grandees would never have bothered to leave their houses at all, in order to enjoy uninterrupted

---

70. Beni Prasad, *History of Jahangir*, pp.72, 86; Manucci, II, p.372.

intimacy of their female beauties.[71]

The private and public life of the nobles, the system of seraglios, the widespread corruption, the custom of escheat, and so many other conventionalities of the upper classes, all left a legacy which is visible in many spheres of Muslim social life even now. Obviously, these cannot be discussed in any detail in a work of this size. A few observations, however, would indicate areas where such remnants of the legacy of Muslim rule could be found. For instance, becuse of escheat, writes Pelsaert, "everything in the (Mughal) kingdom is uncertain. Wealth, position, love, friendship, confidence, everything hangs by a thread.... The nobles build (mansions) with so many hundreds of thousands, and yet (because of escheat) keep them in repair only so long as the owners live... Once the builder is dead, no one will care for the buildings...one cannot contemplate without pity or distress...their ruined state."[72] Many old Muslim *havelis*, which have survived and are still inhabited bear out Pelsaert's statement.

Mughal corruption was of two kinds—polite custom, and outright bribery and embezzelement. In the first, a peson did not meet his senior or superior empty-handed; he presented some gift. This practice was not harmful. But the high corruption, bribery embezzelement, widely prevalent under Muslim rule, as averred by contemporary chroniclers and foreign visitors has never left the Indian scene, and the roots of the present day corruption may be traced to earlier times. Similarly, the sophistication associated with the Mughal court etiquette and the luxurious life of the harem is still to be seen in the graceful and refined behaviour of upper class Muslims, especially of their women. In the words of Jadunath Sarkar, "the general type of Muhammadan population...are more refined and

71. Pelsaert, pp.64-65; Bernier, p.247; Manucci, II, p.467; Lal, *The Mughal Harem*, pp.47-48.
72. Pelsaert, p.56. Also Bernier, p.227.

accustomed to a costlier mode of life, while Hindus of the corresponding classes, even when rich, are grosser and less cultured. The lower classes of Hindus, however, are distinctly cleaner and more intellectual than Muslims of the same grade of life."[73] But let us here keep confined to upper classes.

Ulama and Mashaikh

Muslim scholars and Sufi Shaikhs, though not all rich, also belonged to the upper classes because of the respect they enjoyed in society. Most of them were patronised by kings and nobles, many were actually in their employ. Some of them were very well-off.

The Ulama

Ulama (plural of alim or learned) used to be well-versed in the Muslim law. As such they assisted Muslim monarchs in administering their dominions according to the Shariat. That way they also helped the Muslims in organizing their lives according to the Shariat which comprehends not only beliefs and practices, public and personal law, and rules of behaviour but even includes dress and personal appearance. Acquiring knowledge for the sake of earning money was looked down upon;[74] hence tradition classified the Ulama into two categories, *Ulama-i-Akhirat* (the pious) and *Ulama-i-su* (the worldly). Knowledge was an extremely valuable ornament in an age when the educated were few and the Ulama were respected for their learning and ability.

Naturally, there was hardly any secular approach to education. Great emphasis was laid on theological education (*manqulat*). The most important subjects taught were Hadis, Fiqh (jurisprudence) and Tafsir (exegesis). The institutions of higher learning, called *madrasas*, were essen-

---

73. Sarkar, *A Short History of Aurangzeb*, pp.466-67.
74. Amir Ala Sijzi, *Favaid-ul-Fvad*, p.185.

tially schools of theology, with auxiliaries of grammar, literature and logic. "These *madrasas* were the strongholds of orthodoxy and were subsidised by the state."[75] A high value is placed on Muslim orthodoxy everywhere, because it is claimed that it maintains the identity of the community as against other communities. In actual practice it has served as a force against an integrated living, even coexistence, with other communities.

In a word, the Ulama were an orthodox lot. Those who were denied the life of affluence usually took to teaching (as *mutawalli*) in some mosque or under the thatched roof of their own mud houses.[76] Some other Ulama or *danishmands* became pious preachers and scholars. Very often they too had to work under indigent circumstances.[77] Some outstanding scholars were appointed as teachers in *madrasas* established by the Sultans. It was the ambition of the Ulama to join government service. There were many offices which the establishment could offer to a scholar. In official hierarchy of such appointments the post of the Sadr-i-Jahan came at the top, then followed Qazis (judges), Muftis (interpreters of law) Muhtasibs (censors of public morals), Imams (who led prayers) and Khatibs (reciters of the Quran). The Sadr-i-Jahan was the chief of the judicial department. He served as the Qazi-i-Mumalik (chief judge) and recommended to the king about the appointment of junior Qazis. The Shaikh-ul-Islam was in charge of the ecclesiastical affairs of the empire. All those saints, *faqirs* and indigent scholars who enjoyed state patronage were looked after by him. Normally, only well-read scholars were appointed as Khatibs and Imams. So also was the case with Muftis and Muhtasibs. Muslim public opinion did not approve of the appointment of less qualified persons to these posts.

---

75. Yusuf Husain Khan, *Glimpses of Medieval Indian Culture*, p.69, also p.74.
76. *Ibid.*, p.89. Also Hamid Qalandar, *Khair-ul-Majalis*, p.107.
77. Nizami, *Religion and Politics*, p.156.

The Ulama received salaries pertaining to the offices they held. Most of the Ulama dabbled in politics. They wielded influence with the kings and nobles as intepreters of Muslim law. Their presence was indispensable to a ruler who was generally uneducated. During the protracted struggle between the crown and the nobility which raged throughout the Sultanate period, they aligned themselves with one or the other of political groups. They always remained on the right side of the regime and forgot the community whom they were expected to help in times of economic distress and political oppression. In this way they encouraged political oppression on the one hand and on the other they preached the necessity of obedience and submission by the people even to an oppressor, taking shelter under the Quranic injunction: "Obey God and obey the Prophet, and those in authority among you."[78] Naturally, "an unholy alliance with them smoothed the path of king's depotism".[79] They themselves did not lag behind in obsequiousness. Their collaboration with and integration into the state apparatus made them subservient to the regime, "so much so that when Iltutmish nominated Raziya as his successor, there was not a single theologian in the Delhi Empire who could protest against this nomination on the grounds of Shariat."[80] The way they encouraged Sultans like Ruknuddin Firoz and Muizuddin Kaiqubad not to offer prayers or keep fasts during the month of Ramzan,[81] and live licentious lives, shows how servile they had become and how they "were wallowing in the dirty welters of politics." Of course the Ulama were openly critical of one another and, for this they have been criticised by their contemporary writers like Amir Khusrau, Zia Barani, Abdul Haq Muhaddis and Abdul

---

78. Quran IV, 59.
79. Habibullah, A.B.M., *The Foundation of Muslim Rule in India*, p.234.
80. Nizami, *op.cit.*, p.172.
81. Barani, p.54.

Qadir Badaoni.[82] Kings like Iltutumish and Balban and prince Bughra Khan are also critical of them.[83]

But in one thing they did not fail. They kept the rulers and the ruling class on the path of Islam and virtue by informing them "correctly" about their duty towards the non-Muslims. Some modern secularist historians blame the Ulama for making Muslim rulers intolerant through their orthodox advice. Such writers fail to realise that it was not safe for the Ulama to cheat the Sultans by giving wrong interpretation of their holy scriptures vis-a-vis the treatment of non-Muslims. I have not come across any instance where the Ulama deliberately gave a distorted version of their scriptures in this context. And why should they have done so? They were as much interested in seeing the Muslim state being run according to the Shariat as the Sultans. In short, they always interpreted their scriptures correctly and honestly when it came to the Hindus. So that a foreign visitor like Maulana Shamsuddin Turk, who is very critical of the Qazis of the day, condoned their faults for the reason that because of their right advice their king was prone to treating the Hindus terribly.[84] The lifestyle of the Ulama did not come in the way of serving Islam. Like other Muslims of the higher classes, it was normal for the Ulama to keep harems, live luxuriously and drink wine.[85]

Despite a few faults and a little criticism, therefore, the Ulama as a class were indispensable to the regime. They were advisers of the king and ran the establishment. It was from the Ulama class that the various officers of the government as well as religious institutions were chosen. It was through these people that the regime systematized

82. Amir Khusrau, *Mutla-i-Anwar* (Lucknow,1884), pp.55-60; Barani, p.317.

83. Barani, pp.94, 154-55, 550.

84. *Ibid.*, p. 299.

85. Badaoni, Ranking, I, p.187; Barani, p.446; Khusrau in *Mutla-i-Anwar*; Lal, *Early Muslims in India*, p.129.

the religious and social life of the Muslim community just as it organized the extension and administration of Muslim dominions in India through the nobility.

The Mashaikh

Equally influential, if not more, were the Sufi Mashaikh. In the early years of Muslim immigration, and more so with the establishment of Muslim rule in India, many Muslim *faqirs*, scholars and Sufi Mashaikh arrived in India. They entered Hindustan on their own or came with the invading armies. Later on, the disturbed conditions in Central Asia, consequent upon the Mongol upheaval also encouraged them to leave their homes in search of security. Many came to settle in India where peace and plenty and the protective arm of Muslim rule promised them all they wished.

Sufism may be defined as Islamic mysticism. In its early years in Central and West Asia, it was deeply influenced by Neo-Platonism, the monastic tradition of Buddhism and Christianity and the Vedantist and Yogic philosophy of Hinduism. All these were Islamized by the Sufis in such a way as to make them virtually unidentifiable. Nawbahar was a great Buddhist monastry in Balkh. The name of the city of Bokhara itself is derived from Vihar. Some Khurasan Sufis lived in caves like Buddhists. They were known as Shikafatiyah from the word Shikafat (cave). When Hindu and Buddhist thinkers and saints converted to Islam in Central and West Asia during the eighth to eleventh centuries they carried their thought and philosophy to Sufism. Ibn al-Arabi (1165-1241) wrote in his Diwan that idol-worship, Chritian ways and Kaaba were all acceptable to him as he believed in the religion of love.[86]

---

86. Rizvi, *History of Sufism*, I, pp.20, 33, 83, 88,; II, p.52; Singhal, *India and World Civilization*, I, pp.268-80; Tara Chand, *Influence of Islam on Indian Culture*, pp.70-75.

The Sufism that came to India in the twelfth century
with the Muslim Mashaikh did not, by and large, envisage
direct communion with God without the intermedium of
Islam. Just as the soul and body are one, in Islamic sufism
Tariqah and *Shariah* are so interrelated. Some Sufis believed in the doctrine of Wahadat-ul-Wajud, or the Unity
of Being which means "There is nothing but God, nothing
in existence other than He". This theory, propounded by
Shaikh Ibn al-Arabi and akin to Hindu Vedantism, was
developed later on in order to harmonise the doctrine of
mysticism with the teachings of orthodox Islam.

There were a number of Sufi orders or *silsila* as they
are called. Abul Fazl mentions as many as fourteen. But
four orders—Chishti, Suhrawardi, Qadiri and Naqsh-
abandi—became prominent in India. Of these only the
first two became more popular, for the latter two were
extremely orthodox and "legalistic in their strictness." By
the thirteenth century, northern India saw the flowering of
two Sufi orders, Chishti and Suhrawardi, and we will
concern ourselves with the Mashaikh of only these two orders. The founder of the Suhrawardi order was Shaikh
Bahauddin Zakariya. He was born near Multan in Sind in
578 H. (1182-83 C.E.). He and his disciples played a leading part in the north-west and "symbolically asked the
Chishtis not to dispute possession (of the region) with
them.[87] Shaikh Bahauddin Zakariya (and his successors)
mixed freely with the Sultans, took part in political affairs,
amassed wealth and accepted government honours".[88]

The Chishtis established themselves at Ajmer in Rajasthan, some parts of the Punjab, Delhi, U.P. and Bihar
and further east. They were probably the largest in number and represented what seems to be the most typical in
the Sufi way of life. The first great Chishti Shaikh was
Khwaja Muinuddin Chishti. He was born in Sijistan in

---

87. Amir Khurd, al-Kirmani, *Siyar-ul-Auliya*, p.61.
88. Nizami, *Religion and Politics*, p.226, also pp.220-229.

eastern Persia in C.E. 1141. He came to India a little before or after the battle of Taraori or Tarain (1192) and settled down at Ajmer.[89] There also he lies buried after his death in 1236. His mausoleum is a great centre of pilgrimage. He is known as Gharib Nawaz or Friend of the Poor and Nabi-ul-Hind or Prophet of India.[90] Shaikh Saiyyad Muhammad Gesu Daraz (he of the long locks) said that if people were unable to make the pilgrimage to Mecca, a visit once in their lives to the mausoleum of Muinuddin Chishti would convey the same merit.[91]

Shaikh Muinuddin is very famous today. But he was not known as such to his contemporaries. The three contemporary chroniclers—Hasan Nizami, Fakhr-i-Mudabbir and Minhaj do not refer to him at all. Early mystic records, the *Favaid-ul-Fuad* and *Khair-ul-Majalis* do not give any information about him. Barani makes no reference to him. Isami tells us only this much that Muhammad bin Tughlaq had once visited his grave.[92] In all probability his fame spread from the time of emperor Akbar (1556-1605 C.E.) who held his memory in great reverence and often paid visit to his *dargah* in Ajmer. However, the legend and fame of Muinuddin rests, as of all other Shaikhs, on the magic-like miracles (*karamah*) he is supposed to have performed.[93] It is difficult to say when the stories of the

89. It is claimed that Sufi Mashaikh either accompanied or followed rather than preceded the Muslim armies of invasion and lived under the protection and patronage of conquerors and kings (Titus, *Islam in India and Pakistan*, pp.124-25). For other claims see Lal, *Early Muslims in India*, pp.125, 152 n31. Akbar was a great devotee of Muinuddin Chishti. From 1567 to 1579 he made yearly pilgrimages to the Khwaja's *dargah* where he built a mosque. In Akbar's time, therefore, 'research' about the Khawaja's life must have been done and correct information collected. Abul Fazl's statement that the Khwaja came to India in 1192 and shifted to Ajmer in 1195 seems most probable (*Ain*, II, p.214).

90. Currie, P.M., *The Shrine and Cult of Muin-al-din Chishti of Ajmer*, OUP (Delhi, 1989), p.96.

91. Jafar Sharif, *Islam in India*, trs. Herklots, p.210.

92. K.A. Nizami, *Religion and Politics*, p.181.

93. Currie, *op.cit.*, pp.30-35.

miracles of Sufis began to be told but once this process
had begun, it could not be stopped. It became a criterion
by which Sufis were judged, and the common reason why
people believed in them.[94] They credited them with supernatural powers and feared and respected them. P.M.
Currie quotes Mohammad Habib to say that most of the
mystic records and Diwans are forgeries, "but regard for
public opinion has prevented them (Indian scholars) from
making a public declaration that these are forgeries."[95]
However, stories of miracles apart, "he (Muinuddin
Chishti) was Saiyid by descent. He did not depart in any
way from Sunna, the Ulama could not fault him, and he
performed the hajj."[96]

Shaikh Muinuddin Chishti had a number of disciples
two of whom, Shaikh Hamid and Qutbuddin, had earned
reverence of great and small. Shaikh Hamiduddin
Nagauri lived with his wife as a villager. Shaikh Qutbuddin Bakhtiyar Kaki came to Delhi in the reign of Iltutmish
and lived in a *khanqah* outside the city. He was very fond
of *sama* (devotional music). Once he was so overtaken by
wajd (ecstasy) that he collapsed and breathed his last.[97]
One of his principal disciples was Shaikh Fariduddin
Ganj-i-Shakar (1175-1265) popularly called Shaikh Farid.

Shaikh Farid lived in extreme poverty bordering on
starvation.[98] He trained a large number of disciples, established many *khanqahs* and raised the prestige of the Chishti
order. The greatest disciple of Shaikh Farid was Hazrat
Nizamuddin Auliya (1236-1325). He was born at Badaun.
In 1258 he settled at Ghayaspur near Delhi where his

---

94. For all kinds of miracles see *Siyar-ul-Auliya*, trs. Quddusi, pp. 87, 95,
102, 141, 156, 230, 251-52, 290, 298, 310, 341, 425, 533, 639-40, 649 and *Favaid-
ul-Fvad* trs. Ghulam Ahmad, pp.125, 126, 141, 143, 147, 151, 192, 338.

95. Currie, p.214.

96. *Ibid.*, p.95.

97. For an elaborate discussion on *sama, raqs* (dance) and *wajd* (ecstasy)
see *Siyar-ul-Auliya* trs. Quddusi, pp.729-791.

98. Amir Khurd, *Siyarul Auliya*, Persian text, pp.66-67.

shrine exists and a railway station is named after him. The Shaikh had a large circle of disciples who hailed from all sections of society, rich and poor, noble and plebian.[99] In his life of almost a century, Nizamuddin Auliya witnessed the reigns of seven Sultans, but he did not attend the *darbar* of any one of them. He was popularly known as *Mahbub-i-Ilahi* (Beloved of God). His popularity was due to his saintly virtues and service to humanity. His disciples included Amir Khusrau, Ziyauddin Barani and the renowned Shaikh Nasiruddin Chiragh-i-Delhi whom he appointed as his successor (Khalifa). Professor Mohammad Habib rightly calls Nasiruddin the last great saint of the Chishti *Silsilah* to have enjoyed an all India status.[100] This was the best period in India for Sufism in general and the Chishti *Silsilah* in particular. To this famous line of Sufis belongs Shaikh Salim Chishti, a contemporary of emperor Akbar, for whom the latter built a mausoleum in Fatehpur Sikri.

Many of the Sufi Mashaikh lived in poverty. Shaikh Hamiduddin (d. 1276 C.E.) lived in a small mud house in the city of Nagaur in Rajasthan. He eked out his meagre subsistence by cultivating a single *bigha* of land.[101] His wife spent her time in cooking and spinning like a peasant woman. He was a strict vegetarian. He refused to accept government gift of land and money from the muqta of Nagaur and Sultan of Delhi.[102] "Shaikh Muinuddin and Shaikh Qutbuddin Bakhtiyar never owned houses of their own. Shaikh Farid Ganj-i-Shakar built a small *kachcha* house only when his family had considerably increased... For many years during his early life Shaikh Nizamuddin Auliya had to wander from one quarter of the city to another in search of a house....Generally starvation condi-

99. Barani, pp.343-344.
100. Mohammad Habib, "Shaikh Nasiruddin Mahmud Chiragh-i-Delhi," *Islamic Culture*, April, 1946, pp.129-53.
101. Kirmani, *Siyar-ul-Auliya*, pp.156-57; Jamali, *Siyar-ul-Arifin*, p.13.
102. Nizami, *Religion and Politics*, pp.186-87.

tions prevailed in the houses of the Chishti saints....very
often these saints did not possess sufficient clothes to
cover their bodies."[103]

This is one side of the coin. The other is that Shaikh
Muinuddin's sons owned land, which may have been
granted to them directly or accepted by the Shaikh for
their sake.[104] Shaikh Fariduddin was destitute to the end of
his days, but gifts were received and distributed at his
khanqah.[105] The *khanqah* of Nizamuddin Auliya, probably
after he received money from Sultan Nasiruddin Khusrau,
"became an institution in which money, food and goods
circulated freely".[106] However, the Shaikhs who lived in
affluence were deemed to possess no less merit than those
who elected to remain destitute.[107]

The Sufi Mashaikh are also reported to have shunned
the company of the nobles and nearness to the court. But
that too was not always so. On the contrary, the attractions
of staying near the throne were compulsive. Sidi Maula
was a disciple of Shaikh Farid at Ajodhan.[108] He aspired
for name and fame and shifted to Delhi. Once in the
capital, Sidi Maula hurled himself headlong in the politics
of the court and, after many vicissitudes paid with his
life.[109] But Sidi was not alone in this pursuit. As K.A.
Nizami has pointed out, "Even Chisht the cradle-land of
the *silsilah* looked to Delhi for guidance in spiritual matters."[110] The Mashaikh mostly lived in cities and towns
where they were popular with kings and people and enjoyed the respectability of upper class elite. Shaikh Qutbuddin Bakhtiyar Kaki was much admired by the people

103. *Ibid.*, 199-201.
104. Mujeeb, *op.cit.*, pp.140-41.
105. *Ibid.*, p.147.
106. *Ibid.*, p.141-42.
107. *Ibid.*, pp.284, 301-302.
108. Badaoni, Ranking, I, pp.233-34.
109. Farishtah, I,pp.92-93; Barani, pp.209-12.
110. *Religion and Politics*, p.178.

of Delhi headed by Sultan Iltutmish himself. Muinuddin
Chishti was very much liked by the Muslims of Ajmer but
he was suspected of dabbling in politics which prompted
Prithviraj III to ask Ramdeva to expel him from Ajmer.[111]
Shaikh Nizamuddin Auliya used to hold his own *darbar*
which was often more awe-inspiring than even the court
of kings. The Shaikh was so popular with the people that
Sultan Alauddin Khalji began to entertain suspicions
about his influence and authority in Muslim society. With
a view to ascertain the real intentions of the Shaikh, and to
find out to what extent he was interested in seeking political power, the Sultan sent him a note seeking his advice
and guidance on certain political problems. The Shaikh
immediately surmised Alauddin's motives in sending the
letter, and replied that he had nothing to do with politics
and so could render no advice on political matters: he kept
busy with seeking God's grace for Muslim monarchs (*dua-
goee*). Only after this was the Sultan's mind set at rest.[112]
But to many he was popularly known as Sultan Nizamuddin and his resting place as Dargah Sultanji Saheb.[113]

Alauddin greatly respected Nizamuddin Auliya for
his supernatural powers and knack for correct predictions.[114] But his son Sultan Qutbuddin Mubarak Khalji
disliked him because of his political leanings. He even
declared a reward of a thousand *tankahs* for one who
would cut off Nizamuddin's head. Once when they
chanced to meet, the Sultan refused to acknowledge the
salutations of the saint[115] and even called Shaikh Ruknud-

111. Yusuf Husain Khan, *Glimpses of Medieval Indian Culture*, p.37; P.M.
Currie, *op.cit.*, pp.29-30.
112. Saiyyad Amir Khurd al-Kirmani, *Siyar-ul-Auliya*. Urdu trs.
Silsila-i-Tassavuf No. 130. Allah Wale-ki-Dukan, Kashmiri Bazar (Lahore,
n.d.), pp.118-20; Persian Text, pp.132 ff.
113. *Ibid.*, trs. Quddusi, Introduction, p.12, also pp.231-33.
114. Isami, *Futuh-us-Salatin*, p.277; Barani, pp.302, 330-32; Amir
Khusrau, *Deval Rani*, p.236.
115. Barani, p.396; Lal, *History of the Khaljis*, p.299.

din from Multan to eclipse Nizamuddin's popularity.[116] After Qutbuddin's death, Sultan Nasiruddin Khusrau ascended the throne at Delhi, but his authority was challenged by Ghazi Tughlaq. Khusrau Shah, to gain the support of the Shaikhs sent two or three lakhs of *tankahs* to each of them and five lakh *tankahs* to Nizamuddin Auliya. When Ghazi Tughlaq ascended the throne as Sultan Ghiyasuddin Tughlaq (1320 C.E.) he asked Nizamuddin to render the account of the amount he had received. The latter sent a reply, "seemingly insolent", that the money belonged to the *Bait-ul-mal* (Public Treasury) and therefore he had given it to the poor. The Sultan took umbrage at the Shaikh's answer. The relations between the two were sore also because of the Sultan's dislike of *sama* in which Nizamuddin freely indulged. In this scenario, Nizamuddin Auliya began to support Ghiyasuddin's son, Muhammad Tughlaq, who aspired for the throne. When Ghiyasuddin Tughlaq went on an expedition to Bengal, Nizamuddin Auliya prophesied that the Sultan would never come back from there. When the news of his return was received in Delhi, a worried Prince Muhammad rushed to Nizamuddin with the tiding at which the Shaikh uttered the famous words, "Delhi is still far off (*hanuz Delhi dur ast*)".[117] Nizamuddin Auliya was thus immersed in Delhi court politics, at least towards the end of his life (1320-25). But he was a Sufi. He had many disciples who were regular visitors to his *khanqah*. Such an one was Amir Khusrau.

Abul Hasan, popularly known as Amir Khusrau, was the most favoured disciple of Nizamuddin Auliya. He was a historian, a musician, a poet, a litterateur, a Sufi Shaikh,[118] and a full-fledged protege of Delhi Sultans. His

---

116. *Loc. cit.*

117. For detailed references see Ishwari Prasad, *A History of the Quraunah Turks in India*, p.43.

118. Barani, pp.351, 359; Lal, *History of the Khaljis*, pp.339-40, 361-63.

first patron was Prince Muhammad, son of Sultan Ghiyasuddin Balban. Thereafter for about forty years (1285-1325) he served a continuous succession of monarchs—Muizuddin Kaiqubad, Jalaluddin Khalji, Alauddin Khalji and Mubarak Shah Khalji—and his shrewdness was successful in keeping them all pleased. "The Sultan (Kaiqubad) flattered him by calling him 'the seal of authors' and promised to give him a big reward which would free him from all worldly cares ever afterwards."[119] His genius, if not character, helped him spend "the whole of his life in spinning yarn" (or writing many untruths).[120] Soon after, when Kaiqubad was murdered by Jalaluddin Khalji, he composed a new *masnavi*, *Miftah-ul-Futuh* in praise of his new patron. Six years later Jalauddin was murdered by his nephew and son-in-law Alauddin Khalji who marched into Delhi with the late king's head held aloft on the point of a spear and, writes Dr. Wahid Mirza, our poet Khusrau "was one of the first to offer his congratulations to the murderer whose hands were still red with the blood of his king, his uncle and his benefactor...The poet changed with changing time and turned with shifting wind."[121] No wonder, even Ghiya-suddin Tughlaq, who was hostile to Khusrau's *pir-o-murshid*, Nizamuddin Auliya, receives fulsome praise in Khusrau's *Tughlaq Nama*.

Amir Khusrau was very shrewd. When he found the reign of Qutbuddin Mubarak Khalji nothing to boast about, he wrote *Nuh Sipehr*, praising all things Indian, including the beauty of Indian women. In *Nuh Sipehr* he also wrote: "They have four books in that language (Sanskrit), which they are constantly in the habit of repeating. Their name is *Bed* (Vedas). They contain stories of their gods, but little advantage can be derived from their pe-

---

119. Ashraf, *Life and Conditions of the People of Hindustan*, p.114.

120. *Kulliyat-i-Khusrau*, pp. 245 and 674 cited in *ibid.*, p.114 and Dr. Wahid Mirza, *Life and Works of Amir Khusrau* (Calcutta, 1935), p.177.

121. Wahid Mirza, *op.cit.* p.87.

rusal."[122] This betrays the one-track mind of Muslim elite in general. This weakness was shared by almost all Sufi Mashaikh, debunking the belief that Sufi Mashaikh treated Hindus and Muslims on terms of equality or helped bring the two communities nearer to one another. They were keen on maintaining only orthodox Muslim rule and showed a general disregard for others. Since it was believed that Muhammad bin Tughlaq was not orthodox, Shaikh Nasiruddin Chiragh obtained a promise from Firoz Tughlaq before supporting the latter's claim to the throne, to the effect that he would rule according to the Shariat.[123] In 1409, when Raja Ganesh (Kans of Muslim chroniclers) obtained the throne of Bengal and sought to establish his authority by keeping the prominent Ulama and Sufis under control, Shaikh Nurul Haqq (Qutbul Alam) wrote to Sultan Ibrahim Sharqi of Jaunpur to come and save the Muslims of Bengal. Sultan Ibrabim responded to the call and Raja Ganesh, finding himself too weak to meet the challenge, came to the Shaikh and begged for his intercession, promising to agree to any conditions. Shaikh Nurul Haqq said he would intercede for him if he accepted Islam. The Raja retired in favour of his son Jadu, who ascended the throne as Sultan Jalaluddin Shah. Shaikh Nurul Haqq induced Sultan Ibrahim, much against his will, to withdraw his armies.[124] Shaikh Abdul Quddus combined spirituality with dogmatism. "His letters to Sultan Sikandar Lodi and Babur (1526-30) show that he was as anxious to maintain Muslim rule as any wordly Muslim, that he had no scruples in using the language of a courtier in asking the rulers...to establish the Shariah..."[125] "Akbar's attempt at secularizing the state" had

---

122. Extract trs. in E and D, III, p.563.

123. Afif, p.29.

124. Salim, Ghulam Husain, *Riyaz-us-Salatin*, trs. by Maulvi Abdus Salam, (Calcutta, 1902), p.112 ff.

125. M. Mujeeb, *op.cit.*, pp.297-98, citing from the *Maktubat-i-Quddusi*, pp.44, 335-37.

exasperated the divines, and Mulla Shah Ahmad and Shaikh Farid Bukhari exhorted court dignitaries to alter the state of things in the very beginning of Jahangir's reign, "otherwise it would be difficult to accomplish anything later on."[126] There are many other such instance.[127] It is understandable if disgruntled nobles and courtiers invited foreigners to "rescue Islam," but the Sufi Mashaikh by such actions compromised their image as "Indians first" and respectors of all people as equals. They were as opposed to "national integration" as any orthodox Muslim.

Similarly, many modern scholars have shown that some Sufi Mashaikh too resorted to aggressive and violent means in fighting infidelity.[128] Even Shaikh Muinuddin Chishti's "picture of tolerance is replaced by a portrait of him as a warrior for Islam."[129] Since I have studied this problem in detail elsewhere,[130] I would not like to repeat the cases of aggressive proselytization of Sufi Mashaikh mentioned therein. However, one shocking instance of forcible conversion not mentioned in my book referred to above, may be given here. Saiyyad Jalaluddin Bukhari Makhdum-i-Jahanian of Sind (d.1384) fell very seriously ill. Nawahun, the *darogha* of Uchch, called on him to enquire about his health. As a matter of courtesy and to raise his sinking spirits, Nahawun said: "May God restore your health...your holiness is the last of the saints as the Prophet Muhammad was the last of the prophets." Sayyid Jalaluddin Bukhari even on death-bed construed it as an expression of faith in Islam and demanded a formal declaration of conversion from him. Nawahun firmly de-

---

126. S.R. Sharma, *The Religious Policy of the Mughal Emperors*, p.61.

127. Greetz Clifford, *Islam Observed* (Chicago 1971).

128. Eaton, Richard Maxwell, *Sufis of Bijapur* (1300-1700), Chapter on Sufi Warriors; Currie, P.M., *The Shrine and Cult of Muin-al-din Chishti of Ajmer*, pp.1-19, 66-96; Rizvi, *History of Sufism*, II, pp.175n, 176.

129. Currie, p.94.

130. *Indian Muslims: Who Are They* (New Delhi, 1990), pp.58-60, 92-95.

clined to make any such declaration. Thereupon he was charged with apostasy. He fled to the court of Firoz Shah Tughlaq in search of asylum and redress. When Sayyid Jalaluddin Bukhari expired, his younger brother Sadruddin Raju Qattal, rushed to Delhi in order to persuade Firoz Shah to execute Nawahun. Though some scholars of the capital did not agree with the viewpoint of Raju Qattal, the latter prevailed upon Firoz Shah in obtaining his permission for Nawahun's execution as a renegade.[131]

Poor or rich, the Sufi Mashaikh lived as householders. Except Nizamuddin Auliya and Nasiruddin Chiragh, all Sufi Shaikhs married, and had large families. Since the word saint is associated with celibacy in people's minds of most religions, it would be pertinent to state that "marriage is enjoined on every Muslim, and celibacy is frequently condemned by Muhammad. 'It is related in the Traditions that Muhammad said: When the servant of God marries, he perfects half his religion'... Consequently in Islam, even the ascetic orders are rather married than single."[132]

Shaikh Muinuddin Chishti took two wives — Ummatullah and Asmatullah, and had three sons and one daughter. He had married in his old age "only to realize that his spiritual powers had greatly suffered on that account."[133] Shaikh Qutbuddin Bakhtiyar Kaki Ushi also married twice, late in life. He divorced one of his wives, soon after marriage, as her presence upset his programme of prayers. He had four sons.[134] Shaikh Farid had a number of wives and a large family. Shaikh Nasiruddin Chiragh is reported to have stated that Shaikh Farid had a number of wives (*harem bisyar bud*).[135] He had at least four wives and eight

---

131. Farishtah, II,pp.417-18; Jamali, *Siyar-ul-Arifin*, pp.159-60, English trs. in Nizami, *Religion and Politics*, p.179n.
132. Hughes, T.P., *Dictionary of Islam*, p.313.
133. Nizami, *Religion and Politics*, pp.202-203.
134. *Siyar-ul-Auliya*, p.50; Sijzi, *Favaid-ul-Fvad*, p.61.
135. *Siyar-ul-Auliya*, p.66.

children.[136] Shaikh Hamiduddin had led a very voluptuous life in his early years,[137] but when he joined the circle of Shaikh Muinuddin Chishti, he adopted the life of a mystic in all sincerity. He had a number of children. Shaikh Qutbuddin Husain Kirmani, uncle of the author of *Siyar-ul-Auliya*, used to put on the garments of the finest Chinese silks and Kamkhawab and always used to have pan in his mouth.[138] Shaikh Nizamuddin Auliya also relished betel.[139]

All this was normal life and all these were normal pleasures. But Sufi Mashaikh, known by many names like Wali, Shah, Qalandar, Murshid, Marabout, Shaikh, Faqir and Darwesh, indulged in all kinds of pleasures and luxuries. The case of Sidi Maula was exceptional. He had ready at hand brand new *tankahs* under every coverlet to spend. So many people dined at his *khanqah* that, if Barani is to be believed, "two thousand *man* of flour (*maida*), two to three hundred *man* of sugar and a hundred to two hundred *man* of vegetables used to be consumed in his kitchen every day."[140] But others were equally non-poor and generous. "We know that Shaikh Farid was destitute to the end of his days, but we also know that gifts were received and distributed. It could be said generally of every *khanqah* that even in the bad days a person... was sure to get some sort of a meal and, with luck, a share of money... in every *khanqah* ideals of austerity fought against satisfaction of physical needs,"[141] so that there was no dearth of money and parasites because of the well-to-do admirers of the Shaikh.

Sama or devotional music was a common feature of the *khanqah*. During *sama*, the Shaikhs and Qalandars placed

---

136. Nizamuddin Auliya, *Rahat-ul-Qulub*, p.3.
137. *Siyar-ul-Auliya*, p.156.
138. *Ibid.*, Urdu trs., p.188.
139. *Ibid.*, p.125.
140. Barani, p.209.
141. Mujeeb, *op. cit.*, p.147.

strong insistence on the practice of *Nazar-ilal murd* or gazing at good looking boys. One reason why Ghiyasuddin Tughlaq could not see eye to eye with Nizamuddin Auliya was the latter's fondness for *sama* and his ecstatic fits. The Sultan was free from unnatural lust (*lawatat*) and did not allow "handsome beardless boys" from coming near him.[142] In the *khanqahs* were also used drugs of the hashish family,[143] and even drinking was common.[144] Love affairs of sufis were of common occurrence. Ahmad Yadgar mentions the case of a *faqir* who fell for the newly wed bride of the son of Tatar Khan.[145] He relates another story about the love of a *darwesh* and a woman.[146] Love between a Hindu girl and a *darwesh* created flutter and tension.[147]

The Shaikhs used to marry in high families and possessed a clout which sometimes became a problem for Sultans. A sixteenth century Suhrawardi writer says[148] that Shaikh Sadruddin Arif had married a divorced wife of Prince Muhammad, the eldest son of Balban. The circumstances of this marriage are given as follows: The prince divorced his wife, whom he passionately loved, in a fit of fury. When he recovered his normal state of mind, he felt deeply pained for what he had done. Legally he could not take her back into his *harem* unless she was married to someone else and then divorced by him. A man of genuine piety was searched to restore the broken relationship. Shaikh Arif, the most outstanding saint of the town, prom-

---

142. Barani, p.443. For love of boys by Sufis also see *Tarikh-i-Salatin-Afghana* pp.29-30; *Akhbar-ul-Akhiyar*, p.187; Rizvi, *History of Sufism*, I, p.169; II, p.297.

143. Currie, *op.cit.*, p.7.

144. Mujeeb, *op.cit.*, pp.295-96, 315.

145. *Tarikh-i-Salatin-i-Afghana*, pp.53-54. Also *Waqiat-i-Mushtaqi*, 19(b)-20(a).

146. *Tarikh-i-Salatin-i-Afghana*, pp.102-10.

147. *Ibid.*, p.125.

148. Jamali, *Siyar-ul-Arifin*, p.135, cited in Nizami, p.226.

ised to marry the princess and divorce her the next day. But, after the marriage, he refused to divorce her on the ground that the princess herself was not prepared to be divorced. This incident led to bitterness between the saint and the prince. The latter even thought of taking action against the Shaikh, but a Mongol invasion cut short the thread of his life. Shaikh Salim Chishti had great influence with emperor Akbar, much more than Sadruddin Arif had in the time of Balban. And both Badaoni and Father Monserrate make unflattering comments about Shaikh Salim.[149] The Sufi Mashaikh lived a full-fledged life, different from saints of other religions. But among Indian Muslims their memory has always been cherished with utmost reverence.

It is said that saint-worship among Muslims is a practice unique to India. *Dargahs* of Sufis, real or figurative, are found all over the country and Muslims flock to them in large numbers. It is a legacy of medieval times. One reason for this can be that most Indian Muslims are converted Hindus, who, when their places of worship were converted into (*khanqahs* and later) *dargahs*, did not give up visiting them. For instance, at the most holy *dargah* of Shaikh Muinuddin Chishti, the Sandal Khana mosque is believed to have been built on the site of a Dev temple.[150] The other is that stories of miracles of saints give a hope and a chance to people to obtain fulfilment of their desires. Hence besides Muslims, a few Hindus also resort to such shrines.

149. Badaoni, trs. Ranking, II, p.113.
150. Currie, p.105.

Chapter 6

Middle Classes and Protest Movements

"There are very many merchants that are rich: but it is not safe for them that are so, so to appear, lest that they should be used as fill'd sponges."

Edward Terry

In the medieval period, the luxurious life of the upper classes and the poverty of the exploited peasants and workers attracted the attention of all foreign and Indian writers. These two sections of society were so prominent that the presence of the small, self-respecting, friend-of-the-people middle class was not even noticed by some contemporary writers. Francois Bernier is one of them. Writing in the middle of the seventeenth century, this renowned French visitor to India, found that in Delhi "there was no middle state. A man must be of the highest rank or live miserably."[1] Similar is the assertion of Tavernier about Burhanpur and Golkunda.[2]

Why did Bernier and Tavernier make such observations? Today most people (except the very poor) consider it a matter of satisfaction or even of pride to belong to the middle class. Ministers, Secretaries, Members of Parliament and high officers of Government, counterparts of medieval ruling class, call themselves not masters but servants of the people. Pride in belonging to high class has

---

1. Bernier, p.252.
2. Jean Baptist Tavernier, *Travels in India* trs. and ed. V. Ball, 2 vols. (London, 1889), I, p.152.

been replaced by humility in belonging to the middle class, and administrators and politicians, tradespeople and working men, officers and clerks, are all counted among the middle class. But in the Middle Ages ideas of equality, democracy, socialism and Marxism were not there. Consequently, it was not a fashion in medieval India to claim to belong to the middle class. This is probably what Bernier and Tavernier noted and also declared. In medieval India, rulers, nobles and high class people could never think of degrading themselves by belonging to any class other than the highest. In that age, levelling would have been revolting to the rich and probably embarrassing to the poor. In medieval society the ruling class and the subject people were two well-recognised strata.

But what applied to Mughal India applied also to the Pre-Revolution, Pre-Industrial seventeenth century France. There were there three recognized Estates; the first comprised the Clergy, the second the Nobility, and the third the Commoners. However, side by side with these categories was the yeomanry and the bourgeoisie, the "middle state" of Bernier. Did a corresponding middle state or middle class exist in India also, and Bernier missed to notice it, or was there no middle class in India at all in the medieval period?

The above cited statement of Bernier has been lifted out of context by many scholars, prompting some to deny the existence of a middle class in the pre-British period.[3] Therefore, Bernier has to be quoted at some length to understand why he said so. He gives a detailed description of Delhi and Agra and some other cities of Hindustan in a letter to Monsieur de la Mothe le Vayer dated 1st July, 1663.[4] In his description of Delhi, he writes about its citizens, its houses, *bazars*, food, fruit etc., and constantly

3. Misra, B.B., *The Indian Middle Classes* (Oxford,1961), pp. 1-65, esp.164.
4. Bernier, pp.239-99.

compares them with those of Paris. "In the *bazars* of the capital city of Delhi," writes he, "there are shops where meat is sold roasted and dressed in a variety of ways. But there is no trusting to their dishes, composed, for aught I know, of the flesh of camels, horses, or perhaps oxen which have died of disease. Indeed no food can be considered wholesome which is not dressed at home...But it would be unreasonable for me to complain....I send my servant to the king's purveyors in the Fort, who are glad to sell wholesome food, which costs them very little, at a high price I am willing to pay."[5] Pigeons were exposed for sale, capons were not, "these being wanted for their seraglios...good fish may sometimes be bought, particularly two sorts, called *sing-ala* and *rau* (Singi and Rohu). The former resembles our pike; the latter our carp...The *Omrahs* alone contrive to force the fishermen out at all times (to sell) by means of the *korrah*, the long whip always suspended at their door...Unquestionably the great are in the enjoyment of everything; but it is by dint of numbers in their service, by dint of the *Korrah*, and by dint of money. In Delhi there is no middle state. A man must either be of the highest rank or live miserably. My pay is considerable, nor am I sparing of money; yet does it often happen that I have not wherewithal to satisfy the cravings of hunger, the *bazars* being so ill-supplied, and frequently containing nothing but the refuse of the grandees. Wine, that essential part of every entertainment, can be obtained in none of the shops at Delhi, although it might be made from the native grape, were not the use of that liquor prohibited equally by the *Gentile* and *Mahometan* law.... To say the truth, few persons in these hot climates feel a strong desire for wine..."[6]

Bernier was only experiencing what Babur had witnessed a century ago. The latter notes in his memoirs that

5. *Ibid.*, p.252.
6. Bernier, pp.246-53.

in Hindustan they have "...no good flesh, no grapes or musk-melons, no good fruits, no ice or cold water, no good food or bread in their *bazars*..." And "every artisan there is follows the trade that has come down to him from his forefathers".[7] Bernier did not get food to his liking in the *bazar*, he could not get good wine, and for both these he himself provides correct explanations. What Bernier saw everyday in the *bazars* was the arbitrary ways of the nobles and their unfair use of force to get things at low prices. A hungry Bernier felt the pinch of non-availability of good food and heady wine in the open market, what he saw was the *Korrah* of the *Amirs*[8] and the wretched condition of the poor hawkers and fisherman. He missed to notice, at that point of time or in that mood at least, the middle or intermediate class, the accomplished artisans, hereditary craftsmen, rich jewellers and influential bankers or *sarrafs*. Most middle class people carried on with their hereditary crafts, in printing calico, stretching embroidery, or manufacturing jewellery. These worked mostly at home and did not exhibit their artistic products in show-cases in shops. That is why he wrote what he wrote in a limited context and perhaps under the influence of an empty stomach and thirsty throat when he could only see the rich *Umara* grabbing away the best fish and meat from the poor people with the help of the *Korrah*. There were no standard hotels serving good food in Delhi and Agra and other large cities where gentlemen like Bernier and Indians of his class could have dined without any doubt about the quality of food. But the Mughal gentry, as he himself noted, preferred to eat at home as the meats in the cooking joints in the *bazar* were sometimes adulterated. Also eating at home and not in hotels was also a matter of habit. Bernier's statement is a case of arriving at a major conclusion on the basis of a minor inconvenience.

7. *Babur Nama*, II,p.518.
8. The *Korrah* finds repeated mention in Bernier, eg.pp.228, 252, 256.

For, there has always been a middle class in society in every age, and medieval India was no exception. Among the Muslims the rich people who provided artisans, weavers, embroiderers and jewellers with raw materials to produce goods on order and paid wages, and merchants who dealt in goods, wholesale and retail, surely belonged to the middle class. There is no doubt that besides the two well-known sections of the rich and the poor, there were many who, in terms of wealth and income, could be placed between the two. There is evidence to show that in the contemporary Muslim society of the West Asian countries there were three categories of people — the *al-khassa* , *al-amma* (also called *al-raiyya*) and *al-nas*.There were "the people of great skill, specialists in medicine, architecture and accounting...and merchants who had at least a more than average fortune were also *al-nas*.[9] So middle class or common people, a word so often used by Ibn Battuta in the Indian context,[10] were interchangeable terms. Gustav Grunebaum also says: "The Muslim shares to a very high degree sensitivity about rank which is so characteristic of the Middle Ages. Not only is he rank conscious, but he is keenly concerned with expressing social distinctions through a delicate system of etiquette. Questions of precedence are of considerable importance. Mankind was divided into four orders by the Barmakid Wazir Al Fazl bin Yahiya (C. 8th century A.D.) — 1. King, 2. Wazir, 3. Aristocracy of Wealth, 4. The middle class...was connected with the above class by their culture. The rest of the population counted for nothing."[11]

In medieval times India was well advanced in manufacture, trade and commerce. Indian textiles and other manufactured goods had a market throughout the East

9. Ira Marvin Lapidus, *Muslim Cities in the Later Middle-Ages* (Cambridge, Mass., 1967), p.81.

10. Ibn Battuta, p.64.

11. Grunebaum, Gustav E. Von, *Medieval Islam*, p.171 cited in N.B. Roy, *History of the Afghans* (Santiniketan, 1958), p.92n.

and the West. India exported lot of goods and Indian ports served as clearing stations of trade between the East and the West. In industry and manufacture, whether it was of cloth, carpet or leather, or it was metal, ivory or gold, India held the supreme position. There were excellent ship-building and repairing yards (even for European ships) in India.[12] Mahuan, an interpreter attached to the Chinese envoy Chang Ho who visited Bengal in 1406, writes that "The rich build ships in which they carry on commerce with foreign nations."[13] Right from the thirteenth-fourteenth centuries, indeed from ancient times, manufacturing centres of all kinds of wares were spread all over the country.[14] India's position in the field of manufacture, industry and commerce, if not in science and technology, remained important throughout the medieval period.

There were, consequently, big manufacturers and merchants, foreign and Indian, living in the country. According to Yahiya Sarhindi a large number of Khurasani merchants who lived in Delhi possessed some of the best mansions in that prosperous city.[15] Barbosa says that Muslims, settled in Calicut, had large houses and many servants and they lived very luxuriously. About the Muslims at Rander he says, "they were well-dressed, had good houses, well-kept and furnished."[16] Della Valle has similar comments to make on the freedom of life in Surat, where there was open exhibition of riches and splendour.[17] Monopolists like Mir Jumla, Virji Vohra and, at a later date, Jagat Seth were renowned for their wealth. And they lived in the elitist fashion. "The exceptional position

---

12. Ibn Battuta, p.191; Varthema, p.152 ff; Mukerjee, R.K. *A History of Indian Shipping* (Orient Langmans, 1957), 2nd ed., pp.143-44.

13. J.R.A.S. 1895, pp.530-31.

14. Al Qalqashindi, p.51.

15. Yahiya Sarhindi, *Tarikh-i-Mubarak Shahi*, pp.107-108.

16. Barbosa, Duarte, *The Book of Barbosa*, II, p.73.

17. Della Valle, I, p.41.

on the coast is probably to be explained by the privileged status of the Moslem merchants...being free to live well....while the merchants of the interior (or Hindu merchants?) were very far from being free and....led the quiet and unostentatious life required by the circumstances of their position."[18] Muslim merchants were to be found at practically every seaport in India. Jews and Armenians and Parsis were few in numbers, but important in commercial life.[19] The horizons of Muslim freedom expanded in a country where "every man had a slight tincture of soldiership".

Urbanization helped in development of trade and commerce and the growth of middle class. There was rapid growth of towns and cities in medieval period. In the sixteenth-seventeenth centuries, India had hundreds of cities with a population of more than 100,000 and cities like Agra, Lahore and Cambay could boast of more than half a million people each.[20] Their middle class sections comprised traders, goldsmiths, jewellers, bankers (*sarrafs*), architects, scholars, merchants and many others. Small manufacturers and merchants too possessed gold and silver and its concomitant power. So also was the case with the other sections of middle class Muslims like the learned, such as physicians, mathematicians, architects, historians or chroniclers, and the Ulama. There were the *Saheb-i-Qalam va Saheb-i-Saif* (masters of the pen and the sword) and people belonging to or descended from distinguished families. Soldiers and warriors — neither the Khans or Maliks nor the common troops — that is, officers of the intermediate grade who, in the words of Abul Fazl, consumed "the straw and rubbish of strife" and kindled "the lamp of rest in this world of disturbances", too be-

---

18. Moreland, *India at the Death of Akbar*, p.265.
19. *Ibid.*, pp.23-24.
20. For details see Lal, K.S., *Growth of Muslim Population in Medieval India*, pp.58-62.

longed to this class. Other government officials like Qazis and Imams of *qasbas* (*as-hab-i-manasib*) as well as some sections of lesser note of Saiyyads and Sufis also comprised the middle class.

In contrast to the Muslim bourgeoisie, the life of the Hindu middle classes was different in many ways. They lived under the Muslim theocratic regime and paid the poll tax *Jiziyah* incumbent upon the non-Muslims. There were three rates of *Jiziyah*, 40, 20 and 10 *tankahs* imposed on three classes or income groups — the high, the middle and the low.[21] This in itself is a proof of the existence of a middle class among the Hindus. If Akbar abolished this tax, Aurangzeb reimposed it and the Hindu middle class paid the *Jaziyah* at the middle rate, or probably the high, for all through the medieval period they "possess almost exclusively the trade and the wealth of the country".[22] Pelsaert's description of the Hindu middle class is apt and elaborate. He writes: "First there are the leading merchants and jewellers, and they are most able and expert in their business. Next there are the workmen, for practically all work is done by Hindus, the Moslems practising scarcely any crafts but dyeing and weaving...Thirdly there are the clerks and brokers: all the business of the lords' palaces and of the Muslim merchants is done by Hindus — book-keeping, buying and selling. They are particularly clever brokers, and are consequently generally employed as such throughout all these countries."[23]

The life of the Hindu middle class was marked by moderation. Ostentatious living was as dangerous in their case as it was desirable in the case of Muslim merchants and courtiers. Nay, the Hindu "rich men study to appear indigent," says Bernier, and although "the profit be ever so great, the man by whom it has been made must still

---

21. Afif, p.383.
22. Bernier, p.225.
23. Pelsaert, pp.77-78.

wear the garb of indigence." Terry wrote that "there are very many private men in cities and towns, who are merchants or tradesmen that are very rich: but it is not safe for them that are so, so to appear, lest that they should be used as filled sponges."[24] Their traditional caution and the conditions of insecurity created by political conflict and the attitude of the administrators forced them to practice self-effacement. W.H. Moreland rightly observes that "they help us to understand the thrifty or even parsimonious scale of living which characterises so many of the commercial classes at the present day."[25] Thus apart from some great monopolists and bankers who belonged to the upper class, the trades-people in general were denied due regard in society and are mentioned by Muslim chroniclers with a contempt which is conveyed in words like *Dallal, Bania, Baqqal* etc. The treatment meted out to the lower class of traders and retailers by the rulers during the medieval period shares this contempt. The harshness with which Alauddin Khalji treated the traders, wholesalers and retailers, and made their 'flesh sore', has become proverbial.[26] Pelsaert too says that the condition of shopkeepers was good if they were not made victims of *bazar* officials. They had gold and silver in their houses but made exhibition of poverty lest they should be squeezed of their wealth at will.[27] In short, their style of living was unimpressive. This poor style of living was also an important factor in making the middle class of the medieval period invisible to foreign travellers like Bernier.

This unimpressive way of life was due to many other causes besides fear of being exploited and "sponged by the rich". Ibn Battuta, Nicolo Conti, Abdur Razzaq, Athnasius Nikitin and a host of others bear testimony to the

---

24. Terry, p.391.
25. Moreland, *op. cit.*, p.264.
26. Barani, pp.306-307.
27. See the views of Barbosa, Terry and Bernier in Moreland, *op. cit.*, pp. 264-65.

poor standard of living of the people even if they belonged to propertied and non-poor classes.[28] As late as the early nineteenth century David Macpherson observed: "Born and desiring to pass his life in the same country where his ancestors....were born and passed their lives, whose food is rice, whose drink is water or milk, to whom wine or strong liquor is an object of abomination....whose warm climate renders clothing, beyond what decency requires, intolerable, and whose light clothing is made by himself and his family from the cotton produced in his own fertile fields, whose customs and religion....render utterly inadmissible many articles of enjoyment and comfort...can never have any desire to acquire the produce or manufactures of Europe."[29] James Forbes even goes to the extent of declaring that the balance of trade with Europe was in India's favour because of Indian people's abstemious habits and simple life. "The commodities exported to Europe from India," says he, "far exceeded in value those imported from them thence; the natives of India, from the mildness of climate, and fertility of their soil, want but few foreign supplies, gold and silver have been always carried thither by European traders."[30]

In the process the Hindu middle classes helped in capital formation, even though on a limited scale, which the upper classes failed to do. An important contribution of the middle class, especially the Hindu middle class, was capital formation in medieval India. Apart from the accidents of war to which Muslims and Hindus were alike exposed, as witnessed during invasions of the Mongols in the Sultanate period or of Nadir Shah and Abdali in the Mughal times, it seems that the assets of the Hindu capitalist were safer than the wealth of the most powerful

28. Major, trs. Conti., p.23, Nikitin, p.12 and Abdur Razzaq.

29. Macpherson, *History of European Commerce with India* (London, 1812), p.391.

30. Forbes, James, *Oriental Memoirs* (London,1834), II,pp.158-159.

Muslim nobleman. The assets of Hindu elites could not be lost as a result of a court intrigue or fall from favour. On the contrary Muslim nobles, even Muslim kings, used to borrow large amounts from Hindu *Sahukars* who were known to possess wealth. The wealth of the Hindu could pass on from father to son without being divided up. It could not be taken away by the government under escheat. The Muslim officers and merchants believed in good and ostentatious living. The moment they came by some extra money, they raised their standard of living and set up larger establishments in proportion to their wealth. The Hindu was by nature thrifty. Fear of sponging by the government, kept the possessions of the Hindu capitalist concealed. It was this that made Hindu merchants *sahukars*, *sarrafs* and bankers during Muslim rule.

Middle Class Behaviour

In short, the poor style of living of the Hindu middle class of the medieval period made it rather invisible. Besides, it was very small in numbers. Traders, shopkeepers, jewellers, architects, all added up to a very small proportion of the population. With its small numbers, its influence was also limited. But the one chief characteristic of the middle classes was very much present in medieval India. In behaviour, the hall-mark of the middle classes is living with chin up, straight shoulder and chest thrown out, whether the income is less or more and whether it is categorized as lower, middle or upper middle class. The middle class has been found to be the custodian of society's undefined but ever increasing rights. It was so ever in the medieval period. It was generally the spearhead of any protest movement. It was respected in society, comprised the respectable citizens in the social milieu. One important identification of the middle classes is its representation of the people's rights and its readiness to fight for such rights. This distinguishes them from the upper and lower classes.

Muslim middle classes in general and Muslim scholars in particular lived as a privileged community under Muslim government. It was their own government and, by and large, they were at peace with the establishment. But that did not always deter them from protesting injustice. The lower middle classes like artisans, soldiers and the *bazar* people could remonstrate in a more candid way. Two examples of such protests, one each from the Sultanate and the Mughal periods, would suffice to bring home the point. The Ilbari sultans (of the so-called Slave Dynasty) had ruled from Delhi for almost a hundred years (1206-1290). Therefore when Jalaluddin Khalji ousted the last Ilbari prince, "the gentry, commoners and soldiers, rose in a body, poured out of the many gates of Delhi and assembled at the Badaon Gate" to march and rescue the abducted boy-king Shamsuddin. Malik Fakhruddin, the Kotwal of Delhi, succeeded in suppressing the tumult, but so apprehensive became the new Khalji king of the people's resentment that he did not venture to enter the city of Delhi for many months and made Kilughari the seat of his government.[31]

Bigger in nature was the protest lodged by the citizens of Delhi when the vanquished Prince Dara Shukoh was humiliated and later executed by Aurangzeb in 1658. Francois Bernier was present in Chandni Chowk and witnessed the event. He writes that "the crowd assembled upon this disgraceful occasion was immense; and everywhere I saw the people weeping and lamenting the fate of Dara."[32] In one of his letters Aurangzeb himself writes: "The fate of Dara Shukoh excited the passions of the misguided citizens of Delhi. They wept in sympathy with him and pelted the loyal Malik Jiwan who had brought him to justice with pots full of urine and excreta." Royal

31. Barani, pp.171-72.
32. Bernier, pp.98-100.

troops went into action and according to Khafi Khan, "several persons were knocked down and killed and many were wounded....If the Kotwal had not come forward with his policemen, not one of Malik Jiwan's followers would have escaped with life."[33]

As a king, Muhammad bin Tughlaq was unpopular with the Ulama. Critical of his action, some of them used to write anonymous letters containing complaints and abuses for the Sultan. They would seal the letters writing on the cover "By the head of His Majesty none except he should read the letter. These letters they used to throw into the council hall in the course of the night. When he (Md.Tughlaq) tore them open, he found abuses and scandals in the contents."[34] The art of drafting such letters in Persian was the speciality of the Ulama, and the king rightly became suspicious of this group of people. Ibn Battuta's account of Muslim bloodshed[35] and the executions of the Ulama under his orders is of a piece with that of Isami's in *Futuh-us-Salatin*.[36] In short, thinkers, scholars, Ulama and Qazis, sometimes openly, at others discreetly, did not refrain from criticising the sultan and his policies.[37]

There is an equally interesting example of such an independent protest in a seventeenth century work entitled *Tarikh-i-Salatin-i-Afghana* by Ahmad Yadgar. Writing about the strict rules of the Mughals about the law of escheat, and ruminating over the 'good old days' of the Lodi rule, Ahmad Yadgar says: "God be praised for endowing Sultan (Sikandar Lodi) with such a generous spirit (of permitting retention of any buried treasure discovered by someone). In these days (that is, of Mughal emperor Jahangir), if any one was to find even a few *tankahs*, our

33. Khafi Khan, *Muntakhab-ul-Lubab*, pp.245-46.
34. Ibn Battuta, p.94.
35. *Ibid.*, 83-93.
36. Persian Text, pp.158-60.
37. *Ibid.*, p.227.

rulers would immediately pull down his house to examine every nook and corner for more."[38] If a seventeenth century chronicler could make bold to write in such a way under the very nose of the mighty Mughals, it only shows that the Muslim middle class did sometimes gather courage to ventilate public grievances. But such occassions were rare. As pointed out earlier, the Muslim educated elite, the Ulama and Mashaikh, cooperated with the Muslim regime under which they enjoyed a privileged position.

Hindu Dissent

As compared with the Muslims, the problems of the Hindus were many and varied. They were unfairly taxed, their traders used to be harassed, their temples were broken and they were very often forcibly converted to Islam. There were so many disabilities that they could not take all the inequities lying down. They protested and resisted. Their dissent was often effective because it was made in the non-violent Hindu fashion.

Sultan Firoz Tughlaq (1351-1388), writes Shams Siraj Afif, "convened a meeting of the learned Ulama and renowned Mashaikh and suggested to them that an error had been committed: the *Jiziyah* had never been levied from Brahmans: they had been held excused, in former reigns. The Brahmans were the very keys of the chamber of idolatry, and the infidels were dependent on them (*kalid-i-hujra-i-kufr und va kafiran bar ishan muataqid und*). They ought therefore to be taxed first. The learned lawyers gave it as their opinion that the Brahmans ought to be taxed. The Brahmans then assembled and went to the Sultan and represented that they had never before been called upon to pay the *Jiziyah*, and they wanted to know why they were now subjected to the indignity of having to pay it. They were determined to collect wood and to burn

---

38. Ahmad Yadgar, *Tarikh-i-Salatin-i-Afghana*, Persian Text, p.36.

themselves under the walls of the palace rather than pay the tax. When these pleasant words (*kalimat-i-pur naghmat*) were reported to the Sultan, he replied that they might burn and destroy themselves at once for they would not escape from the payment. The Brahmans remained fasting for several days at the palace until they were on the point of death. The Hindus of the city then assembled and told the Brahmans that it was not right to kill themselves on account of the *Jiziyah*, and that they would undertake to pay it for them. In Delhi, the *Jiziyah* was of three kinds: Ist class, forty *tankahs*; 2nd class, twenty *tankahs*; 3rd class, ten *tankahs*. When the Brahmans found their case was hopeless, they went to the Sultan and begged him in his mercy to reduce the amount they would have to pay, and he accordingly assessed it at ten *tankahs* and fifty *jitals* for each individual".[39]

The protest of the Brahmans did succeed in getting some concessions from the King. He fixed their *Jiziyah* at a low rate although in status they belonged to the upper class. Secondly, he permitted other Hindus (shopkeepers and traders) to pay the tax on their behalf. But Aurangzeb (1658-1707) was more adamant because he himself knew the law well. His imposition of the *Jiziyah* provoked repeated protests. "On the publication of this order (reimposing the *Jiziyah*) by Aurangzeb in 1679," writes Khafi Khan, "the Hindus all round Delhi assembled in vast numbers under the *jharokha* of the Emperor...to represent their inability to pay and pray for the recall of the edict...But the Emperor would not listen to their complaints. One day, when he went to public prayer in the great mosque on the sabbath, a vast multitude of the Hindus thronged the road from the palace to the mosque, with the object of seeking relief. Money changers and drapers, all kinds of shopkeepers from the Urdu *bazar*, mechanics, and workmen of all kinds, left off work and

39. Afif, pp. 382-84.

business and pressed into the way....Every moment the crowd increased, and the emperor's equippage was brought to a stand-still. At length an order was given to bring out the elephants and direct them against the mob. Many fell trodden to death under the feet of elephants and horses. For some days the Hindus continued to assemble, in great numbers and complain, but at length they submitted to pay the *Jiziyah*."[40] Abul Fazl Mamuri, who himself witnessed the scene, says that the protest continued for several days and many lost their lives fighting against the imposition.[41] There were organized protests in many other places like Malwa and Burhanpur. In fact it was a countrywide movement, "and there was not a district where the people...and Muqaddams did not make disturbances and resistance."[42] Even Shivaji sent a strong remonstrance and translated into practice the threat of armed resistance he had posed. Similar objection was registered against pilgrim tax in Rajasthan, and when in 1694 it was ordered that except for Rajputs and Marathas, no Hindus were to be allowed to ride an Iraqi or Turani horse or an elephant, nor were they to use a palanquin, many Hindus defied it like in Multan and Ahmadnagar.[43] People's resentment against Aurangzeb was also expressed in incidents in which sticks were twice hurled at him and once he was attacked with bricks but escaped.[44]

These cases of open disapprobation of royal orders were the work mainly of the Hindu artisan and business classes. In spite of their modesty and humility they possessed the middle class temperament. As is well-known Indian manufactures were of excellent quality, often better

---

40. Khafi Khan, trs. E and D, VII, p.296.
41. Mamuri, pp.525-26.
42. Khafi Khan, Text, pp.278-79, 339.
43. S.R. Sharma, *Religious Policy of the Mughal Emperors*, p.143, quoting News Letter 11 December, 1694 and 18 April, 1694.
44. Saqi Mustaad Khan, *Maasir-i-Alamgiri*, trs. and annotated by Jadunath Sarkar (Calcutta, 1947), pp.78, 94, 95.

than European,[45] but this does not signify any social advancement of the manufacturers. Indeed, according to Bernier, they were either "wretchedly poor, or who, if rich assume appearance of poverty...a people whose grandees pay for a work of art considerably under its value and according to their own caprice, and who do not hesitate to punish an importunate artist or a tradesman with the *Korrah*, that long and terrible whip hanging at every Omrah's gate."[46] Bernier adds that the artisans could not venture to "indulge in good fare or to dress in fine apparel" even if they could afford to.[47] Manucci says that traders and merchants were sometimes wanting in courage and they could not claim any high status.[48] And yet these very people used to defy the ruler's orders. Their strength was known to the regime, that is why most kings used to treat them harshly. Ziyauddin declares them to be the most unscrupulous among the seventy-two classes, (believed to be inhabiting the world) and Alauddin Khalji visited them with dire punishments.[49] Even a mild king like Firoz Tughlaq did not treat them any better. Shams Siraj Afif writes that when Firoz Tughlaq was building the fort-city of Firozabad, he ordered that every trader who brought goods (grain, salt, sugar, cotton etc.) to Delhi, was to transport free of charge bricks and stones on his pack-animals from the old Delhi (Mehrauli) to the construction site at Firozabad. If the trader refused, government officials used to carry off his pack animals and clamp him in jail. But the traders were not to be cowed down and they more often than not refused to do *begar* (work without wages).[50] Such protests and resistance against government's injustice continued throughout the medieval period. Tavernier

45. Moreland, *India at the Death of Akbar*, pp.155-56.
46. Bernier, p.228.
47. Also Moreland, *op.cit.*, p.187.
48. Manucci, I,pp.143-44.
49. Barani, p.343.
50. Afif, pp.376-77.

writes similar things about Shahjahan. "All waggons which come to Surat from Agra or other places in the Empire and return to Agra and Jahanabad (Shahjahana-bad) are compelled to carry (the king's) lime which comes from Broach....It is a great source of profit to the Emperor (whose monopoly it was and) who sends it where he pleases."[51] Similarly, when Aurangzeb wanted more money and "ordained that the rupees or coined money of silver, not worth more than fourteen sols(sous) of France, or there-abouts, should pass as worth twenty-eight sols....the *sarrafs*, who are the money changers, resisted the royal orders, giving various excuses...." At last the king in anger sent for the money-changers in the city of Delhi, and when he found that they could not be brought round to his view he ordered one of the aged *sarrafs* to be thrown down the battlements. This terrified the *sarrafs* and they obeyed.[52]

It was only the terror created by the autocratic regime that suppressed these people. Else, they on their own, never failed to register their protests or go on *hartal*. Such demonstrations and protests, typical of the middle classes, were not confined to the capital city of Delhi alone. People fought for their rights all over the country. Let us take the case of Gujarat. Persecution forced a large number of Hindu merchants of Surat, led by Bhimji Parekh, in September 1669, to withdraw from Surat. An English communication of November 21 of that year is worth quoting at some length: "You have been formerly advised what unsufferable tyranny the *banias* endured in Surat by the force exercised by these lordly Moors on account of their religion...The Qazi and other Mughal officers derived large incomes from the Banias to redeem their places of idolatarous worship from being defaced and their persons from their malice and that the general body of the *banias*

---

51. Tavernier, *op.cit.*, p.35.
52. Manucci, II,pp.61-62.

began to groan under their affliction and to take up re-
solves of fleeing the country. Bhimji led a deputation of
five other *banias* (*panch?*) to Gerald Aungier, who later
became the maker of Bombay, to ask for asylum in Bombay. Aungier played it safe....He advised them to proceed
to Ahmadabad instead and from there make their general
humble requests to the King. Then on September 23rd and
24th all the heads of the *bania* families, of what condition
whatsoever, departed the town, to the number of 8,000
leaving their wives and children in Surat under charge of
their brothers, or next of kin. The Qazi was enraged at this
and called upon the governor to turn the *banias* back. The
Governor was inclined to side with the *banias* as he understood the important economic role they played in the life
of the city and replied that they were free to go wherever
they like." The *banias* then proceeded to Broach with the
result that "the people in Surat suffered great want, from
the *banias* having bound themselves under severe penalties not to open any of their shops without order from
their Mahager (*Mahajana*), or General Council, there was
not any provision to be got; the *tanksal* (i.e.mint) and
custom house shut; no money to be procured, so much as
for house expenses, much less for trade which was wholly
at a stand." The boycott lasted until December 20, 1669
when the *banias* returned to Surat on being assured by
Aurangzeb of safety of their religion. This incident clearly
shows how Aurangzeb's policy of religious persecution
had made his officers more zealous than the king himself.
It also shows the organizational capabilities of resistance
of the *banias* and the leading role played by Bhimji in this
affair.[53] Earlier in 1666, the merchants of Cambay complained to Aurangzeb against the oppressive local officials
and threatened to flee if their grievances remained unre-

53. B.G. Gokhale, "The Merchant Community in 17th Century
India", *Journal of Indian History*, Trivandrum, Vol.LIV, April 1976, Pt.I,
pp.117-141, esp. pp.126-27.

dressed. The Emperor thereupon ordered that there would be only two qanungos and two Chaudharis in place of the many reported, and they should treat the merchants well.[54]

Aurangzeb's policy of religious persecution of Hindus, in particular his destruction of temples, evoked universal Hindu discontent. It was an old practice, commencing from Muhammad bin Qasim's invasion of Sind,[55] to destroy temples during wars and in times of peace and convert them into mosques, and was continued throughout the medieval period. Aurangzeb also did the same in course of his wars in Bihar, Kuch Bihar etc. But when he started destroying temples in peace time on an unprecedented scale, he started a wave of general resentment and opposition. The history of resistance to such cases of temple destruction pertains to the whole country, but primarily to Gujarat, Mathura, Delhi, Banaras and many places in Rajasthan. "Soon after the order (about demolishing temples) was issued, reports of the destruction of temples from all over the empire began to arrive."[56] To make sure that his orders were faithfully carried out Aurangzeb instructed that reports of destruction of temples by *faujdars* and other officials, were to be sent to the court under the seal of the Qazis and attested by pious Shaikhs.[57]

"In August, 1669, the temple of Vishvanath at Banaras was demolished.[58] The presiding priest of the temple was just in time to remove the idols and throw them into a neighbouring well which thus became a centre of interest ever after. The temple of Gopi Nath in Banaras was also destroyed about the same time. He (Aurangzeb) is alleged to have tried to demolish the Shiva temple of Jangamwadi

54. Ali Muhammad Khan, *Mirat-i-Ahmadi*, I, p.263.
55. *Chachnama*, trs. Kalichbeg, p.190.
56. Sharma, S.R., *Religious Policy of the Mughal Emperors*, p. 133.
57. *Ibid.*, p.130.
58. *Maasir-i-Alamgiri*, p.88.

in Banaras",[59] but could not succed because of opposition.

Next came the turn of the temple of Keshav Rai at Mathura built at a cost of thirty-three lacs of rupees by Raja Bir Singh Bundela in the reign of Jahangir. The temple was levelled to the ground and a mosque was ordered to be built on the site to mark the acquisition of religious merit by the emperor.[60] No wonder that this created consternation in the Hindu mind. Priests and protesters from Brindaban fled the place with the idol of Lord Krishna and housed it in a temple at Kankroli in Udaipur state. A little later the priests of the temple of Govardhan founded by Vallabhachaya fled with the idols by night. After an adventurous journey they reached Jodhpur, but its Maharaja Jaswant Singh was away on imperial errands. Therefore, Damodar Lal, the head of the priesthood incharge of the temple, sent one Gopi Nath to Maharaja Raj Singh at Udaipur who himself received the fugitives on the frontiers of the state and decided to house the god at Sihar on 10 March, 1672.[61] In course of time the tiny village of Sihar became famous as Nathdwar after the name of its god, and Mewar of Mira Bai became a great centre of Vaishnavism in India.

The resistance gained in strength. In March 1671, a Muslim officer who had been sent to demolish temples in and around Ujjain was killed with many of his followers in the riot that followed his attempt at destroying the temples there. Aurangzeb's religious policy had created a division in the Indian society. Communal antagonisms resulted in communal riots at Banaras, Narnaul (1672) and Gujarat (1681) where Hindus, in retaliation, destroyed mosques.[62] Temples were destroyed in Marwar after 1678 and in 1680-81, 235 temples were destroyed in Udaipur.

---

59. Sharma, *op. cit.*, p.133.
60. *Maasir-i-Alamgiri*, pp.95-96.
61. Ojha, Gauri Shankar, *History of Udaipur*, I,p.35.
62. *Mirat-i-Ahmadi*, I, p.261.

Prince Bhim of Udaipur retaliated by attacking Ah-madnagar and demolishing many mosques, big and small, there.[63] Similarly, there was opposition to destruction of temples in the Amber territory, which was friendly to the Mughals. Here religious fairs continued to be held and idols publicly worshipped even after the temples had been demolished.[64] In the Deccan the same policy was pursued with the same reaction. In April 1694, the imperial censor had tried to prevent public idol worship in Jaisinghpura near Aurangabad. The Vairagi priests of the temple were arrested but were soon rescued by the Rajputs.[65] Au-rangzeb destroyed temples throughout the country. He destroyed the temples at Mayapur (Hardwar) and Ayodhya, but "all of them are thronged with worshippers, even those that are destroyed are still venerated by the Hindus and visited by the offering of alms."[66] Sometimes he was content with only closing down those temples that were built in the midst of entirely Hindu population, and his officers allowed the Hindus to take back their temples on payment of large sums of money. "In the South, where he spent the last twenty-seven years of his reign, Au-rangzeb was usually content with leaving many Hindu temples standing... in the Deccan where the suppression of rebellion was not an easy matter... But the discontent oc-casioned by his orders could not be thus brought to an end."[67] Hindu resistance to such vandalism year after year and decade after decade throughout the length and breadth of the country can rather be imagined than de-scribed.

63. Jaipur Records, XII, 72-74 cited in Sharma, *op. cit.*, pp. 135-36.
64. Jaipur Records, XVI, p.58.
65. Sharma, *op. cit.*, p.137.
66. Manucci, III, p.245.
67. For detailed references see Sharma, *op. cit.*, p.139.

Bhakti Movement

The most effective Hindu protest against atrocities was registered by the Bhakti Movement in medieval India. Bhakti means devotion to God. A *Bhakt* may worship Him at home, in the temple, all by himself through meditation, or in congregations through *Bhajan* and *Kirtan* (chorus singing). He need not go out into the streets to organize a movement. But this is exactly what happened at the behest of the socio-religious reformers in the fifteenth-sixteenth century. And the movement triumphed insofar as it succeeded in saving India from total Islamization. The Bhakta saints who spearheaded this movement belonged to all classes, but essentially the protest was a middle class movement and it was a strange combination of Renaissance, Reformation and dissent.

The Hindus resented conversion of their co-religionists by invaders and rulers by force. Many such converts used to return to their original faith at the first opportunity as vouched by Arabic and Persian chroniclers writing about Muhammad bin Qasim's invasion of Sind and Mahmud of Ghazni's campaigns in Hindustan. As early as in the time of Sultan Iltutmish (1210-1236), soon after the establishment of the Delhi Sultanate in 1206, some Ulama suggested to him to confront the Hindus with a choice between Islam and death. The Wazir Nizamul Mulk Junaidi replied: "But at the moment in India...the Muslims are so few that they are like salt (in a large dish). If such orders are to be enforced....the Hindus might combine...and the Muslims would be too few in number to suppress(them). However, after a few years when in the capital and in the regions and small towns, the Muslims are well established and the troops are larger, it will be possible to give Hindus, the choice of 'death' or 'Islam'."[68] On the other hand, Hindu saints used to assuage the outraged feelings of

68. Ziyauddin Barani, *Sana-i-Muhammadi in Medieval India Quarterly*, Aligarh, I, Part III, pp.100-105.

Hindus and encourage them reconvert to Hinduism. For instance Harihar and Bukka, sons of the Raja of Kampil converted to Islam by Muhammad bin Tughlaq, fled his court. At the instance of sage Vidyaranya they reverted to Hinduism and founded the Vijayanagar kingdom to resist the expansion of Muslim power in the South. Like Vidyaranya, there were scores of Bhakta saints who were helping people to resist injustice and retain their original religion. In Maharashtra, Namdeva in the fourteenth century declared that people were blind in insisting upon worshipping in temples and mosques, while His worship needed neither temple nor mosque.[69] Such courageous denunciations were infectious and these spread in Gujarat, Bengal, Punjab and Uttar Pradesh. Ramananda, Kabir, Nanak, Chaitanya, Raidas, Dhanna, Sain, Garibdas and Dadu Dayal and a host of others spoke out in the same idiom openly and repeatedly. They came from all classes of society — Raidas was a *chamar*, Sain was a barber while Pipa was a Raja, Raja of Gauranggarh — but they were all respected and listened to. Of these the three most important saints who turned Bhakti into a movement were Kabir, Nanak and Chaitanya.

Sant Kabir lived in U.P. from 1425 to about 1505, Guru Nanak in Punjab from 1469 to 1538 and Chaitanya Mahaprabhu in Bengal from 1486 to 1534. During this period, particularly after the invasion of Timur (1399 C.E.), northern India was broken up into a number of independent Muslim kingdoms like Gujarat, Malwa, Jaunpur and Bengal while the Sultanate of Delhi was ruled by the Saiyyads and Lodis. Sikandar Lodi (1489-1517) revived the strength of the Sultanate and was the strongest and most fanatical ruler of the dynasty. Babur conquered Hindustan from 1526 to 1530 and Akbar ascended the throne in 1556. Thus from the beginning of the fifteenth to the middle of the

---

69. Parasuram Chaturvedi, *Sant Kavya*, p.144.

232   THE LEGACY OF MUSLIM RULE IN INDIA

sixteenth century (1400-1556), India witnessed terrible
political upheavals resulting in large-scale massacres and
conversions. The division of the country into small kingdoms rendered the task of the Muslim rulers easy in
pressurising their Hindu subjects in their micro units into
accepting Islam. The local Sultans and nobles, in order to
control and demoralize the subject people, not only demolished their temples and imposed "legal" disabilities
upon them but also confronted them with the choice between Islam and death — a phenomenon which had been
going on since the days of Iltutmish in a rather haphazard
manner. It is therefore necessary to cursorily go through
this scenario to be able to make a correct appraisal of the
services of these great saints, and their disciples and followers, in saving Hindu society from succumbing to Muslim proselytization.

Punjab was always the first to bear the brunt of Muslim invasions directed against India, and Muslim invaders
were keenly interested in making converts. In the first half
of the fifteenth century the successors of Timur were
holding parts of Punjab to ransom. Under the Mongol
invaders too conversions used to take place on a large
scale.[70] Rebellions of Muslim adventurers were also creating anarchical conditions.[71] During this period and after,
therefore, the Muslim population of the Punjab swelled
considerably mainly due to proselytization. Added to this
were the large number of Afghans whom the Saiyyads
and Lodis had called from across the Indus with a view to
consolidating their position. Like in Punjab, in Sind also
the rule of the Turkish Sultans and the pressure of the
Mongols had combined to Islamise the northern parts. In
southern Sind the Summas became Muslims and Hindus
by turns, but ultimately they seem to have "adopted

70. Mohammad Habib, *Some Aspects of the Foundation of the Delhi Sultanate*, Dr. K.M. Ashraf Memorial Lecture (Delhi, 1966), p.20.
71. For details see Lal, *Twilight of the Sultanate*, pp.79-100.

Islam, and propagated the religion in their dominions".[72]
In Sind "compulsory conversions to Mahometanism were
not infrequent, the helpless Hindu being forcibly subjected
to circumcision on slight or misconstructed profession, or
the false testimony of abandoned Mahometans"[73] When
Humayun took refuge in Sind(1541),[74] Muslim population
in its cities had grown considerably.

There were Muslim kings in the Kashmir Valley from
the middle of the fourteenth century. However, it was
during the reign of Sikandar Butshikan (1394-1417) that
the wind of Muslim proselytization blew the hardest. His
bigotry prompted him to destroy all the most famous
temples in Kashmir and offer the Kashmiris the usual
choice between Islam and death. It is said that the fierce
intolerance of Sikandar had left in Kashmir no more than
eleven families of Brahmans.[75] His contemporary, the Raja
of Jammu, had been converted to Islam by Timur, by
"hopes, fears and threats".[76] The kingdom of Gujarat was
founded by Wajih-ul-Mulk, a converted Rajput in 1396.
One of its famous rulers, Ahmad Shah (1411-1442) was
responsible for many conversions. In 1414 he introduced
the *Jiziyah*, and collected it with such strictness, that it
brought a number of converts to Islam.[77] Mahmud
Beghara's exertions (1458-1511) in the field of proselytization were more impressive.[78] In Malwa there were large
number of Muslims since the days of Khalji and Tughlaq
sultans.[79] These numbers went on growing during the rule
of the independent Muslim rulers of Malwa, the Ghauris

72. C.H.I., III, p.501.
73. *Journal of the Asiatic Society of Bengal*, 1841, p.20. Also Thornton, *Gazetteer*, IV, p.296.
74. C.H.I., III, pp.501-502.
75. *Ibid.*, p.281.
76. Yazdi, *Zafar Nama*, II, pp. 168-69.
77. Farishtah, II, pp.184-85.
78. Farishtah, II, p.202; C.H.I., III,pp.305-06, 310.
79. Day, U.N., *Medieval Malwa* (Delhi, 1967), pp.6-7.

and Khaljis (1401-1562). The pattern of growth of Muslim population in Malwa was similar to that in the other regions but their harems were notoriously large, filled as they were with Hindu inmates.[80]

About the conversions in Bengal three statements, one each from Wolseley Haig, Dr. Wise and Duarte Barbosa, should suffice to assess the situation. Haig writes that "it is evident, from the numerical superiority in Eastern Bengal of the Muslims... that at some period an immense wave of proselytization must have swept over the country and it is most probable that the period was the period of Jalaluddin Muhammad (converted son of Hindu Raja Ganesh) during whose reign of seventeen years (1414-1431)...hosts of Hindus are said to have been forcibly converted to Islam".[81] With regard to these conversions, Dr. Wise writes that "the only condition he offered were the Koran or death....many Hindus fled to Kamrup and the jungles of Assam, but it is nevertheless probable that more Muhammadans were added to Islam during these seventeen years (1414-31) than in the next three hundred years".[82] And Barbosa writes that "It is obviously an advantage in the sixteenth century Bengal to be a Moor, in as much as the Hindus daily become Moors to gain the favour of their rulers".[83] The militant Mashaikh also found in Bengal a soil fertile for conversion, and worked hard to raise Muslim numbers.[84]

We may linger awhile in Bengal to have a clear picture of the spread of Islam through methods in which medieval Muslims took pleasure and pride while modern Muslims

---

80. *Ibid.*, p.244.
81. C.H.I., III, p.267.
82. *Journal of the Asiatic Society of Bengal*, 1894, Pt. III, p.28.
83. Barbosa, II, p.148.
84. Qanungo, K.R., *Historical Essays*, p.151; Abdul Karim, *Social History of Muslims in Bengal*, pp.136-38, 143-46; Qureshi, I.H., *The Muslim Community of the Indo-Pakistan Subcontinent* (610-1947), Monton & Co., S-Gravenhage, 1962, pp.70-71, 74-75.

maintain a studied silence.[85] The details of the conversion of Raja Ganesh bring out the importance of the role of force, of persuasion and of the Ulama and Sufis in proselytization. In 1409 Raja Ganesh occupied the throne of Bengal and sought to establish his authority "by getting rid of the prominent *ulama* and *sufis*".[86] Qutb-ul-Alam Shaikh Nurul Haqq wrote to Sultan Ibrahim Sharqi to come and save the Muslims of Bengal. Ibrahim Sharqi responded to the call, and Raja Ganesh, finding himself too weak to face the challenge, appealed to Shaikh Nurul Haqq for help. The latter promised to intercede on his behalf if he became a Musalman. The helpless Raja was willing, but his wife refused to agree. Ultimately a compromise was made by the Raja offering to retire from the world and permitting his son, Jadu, to be converted and ascend his throne. On Jadu being converted and enthroned as Jalaluddin Shah, Shaikh Nurul Haqq induced Sultan Ibrahim to withdraw his armies.[87] If a Raja of the

---

85. In a *majlis* held at the Khanqah of Shaikh Nizamuddin Auliya, the Shaikh averred that the Hindus are a very determined people and it is dificult to convert them through persuasion. He then narrated a story of the time of Hazrat Umar as an illustration. The king of Iraq was defeated and brought as a prisoner before the Caliph. Hazrat Umar gave him a choice between Islam and death. The king refused to become Musalman, at which the Caliph summoned the executioner. The king was very astute and he begged Umar to let him quench his thirst before he died. His request was granted, and as he was a king, a slave brought him water in a bowl of gold. This he did not accept, nor in a bowl of silver. He said that the water should be brought in an earthen cup. When this was done, the king requested the Caliph that until he had taken the water, he may not be killed. The plea was conceded. The king then dashed the cup to the ground. It was broken and its contents spilt. The king addressed the Caliph to keep his promise of not killing him until he had drunk the water. Hazrat Umar was as perplexed as he was impressed by the intelligence of the king. At last he handed him over to a 'respectable person' to bring him round to accepting Islam. In his company, over a period of time, the king's heart was changed and he agreed to be converted (Sijzi, *Favaid-ulFvad*, trs. Ghulam Ahmad Biryan, pp. 297-98).

86. M.Mujeeb, *op. cit.*, p.292.

87. Ghulam Husain Salim, *Riyaz-us-Salatin*, trs. Abdus Salam, pp.112 ff.

stature of Ganesh could not face up to the Ulama and the Sufis, other Rajas and Zamindars were still worse placed. Petty Rajas and Zamindars were converted to Islam, with their wives and children, if they could not pay land revenue or tribute in time. Such practice appears to be common throughout the whole country as instances of it are found from Gujarat[88] to Bengal.[89]

In Uttar Pradesh the region to the east and south of Delhi — Katehar, Doab, Bayana and Mewat — had become a problem tract in the fifteenth century, and there the Saiyyad and Lodi sultans contented themselves "with the ignoble but customary satisfaction of plundering the people, and obtaining converts in the bargain."[90] Muhammad Bihamad Khani, the author of *Tarikh-i-Muhammadi*, gives a clear idea of the keenness of the Muslim sultans and their subtle methods in obtaining converts. He writes that sultan Mahmud while fighting Rai Sumer in the vicinity of Irich "concluded that if he allowed his brave warriors to wage the war (outright), they would undoubtedly extirpate the infidels....but he deemed it fit to delay the operation (or advance slowly) in the hope that the infidels might accept Islam".[91]

Who could save the Hindus from extinction in such a scenario? Obviously, leaders of the society, the Brahmans. "What the Brahmans as protectors of their culture achieved in those days," writes Wilhelm von Pochhammer, "has never been properly recorded, probably because a considerable number of people belonging precisely to this class had been slaughtered. If success was achieved in preserving Hindu culture in the hell of the first few centuries, the credit undoubtedly goes to the Brahmans. They

---

88. C.H.I., III, pp.305-06.
89. Satya Krishna Biswas, *Banshasmriti* (Bengali, Calcutta, 1926), pp.6-10; Census of India Report, 1901, VI, Part I, Bengal, pp.165-181.
90. Lal, K.S., *Indian Muslims: Who Are They*, p.46.
91. Muhammad Bihamad Khani, *Tarikh-i-Muhammadi*, English trs. by Muhammad Zaki, pp.57-58.

saw to it that not too many chose the cowardly way of getting converted and that the masses remained true to the holy traditions on which culture rested..."[92] Muslim kings knew this and treated the Brahmans sternly, restricting their sphere of activity.[93] The Muslim Mashaikh were as keen on conversions as the Ulama, and contrary to general belief, in place of being kind to the Hindus as saints would, they too wished the Hindus to be accorded a second class citizenship if they were not converted. Only one instance, that of Shaikh Abdul Quddus Gangoh, need be cited because he belonged to the Chishtia *Silsila* considered to be the most tolerant of all Sufi groups. He wrote letters to Sultan Sikandar Lodi,[94] Babur[95] and Humayun[96] to re-invigorate the Shariat and reduce the Hindus to payers of land tax and *Jiziyah*.[97] To Babur he wrote, "Extend utmost patronage and protection to theologians and mytics...that they should be maintained and subsidized by the state....No non-Muslim should be given any office or employment in the Diwan of Islam. Posts of Amirs and *Amils* should be barred to them. Furthermore, in confirmity with the principles of the Shariat they should be subjected to all types of indignities and humiliations. The non-Muslims should be made to pay *Jiziyah*, and *Zakat* on goods be levied as prescribed by the law. They should be disallowed from donning the dress of the Muslims and should be forced to keep their *Kufr* concealed and not to perform the ceremonies of their *Kufr* openly and freely....They should not be allowed to consider them-

---

92. *India's Road to Nationhood: A Political History of the Sub-Continent* trs. by S.D.Marathe, Allied Publishers (Bombay, 1961).

93. Afif, pp.382-83; Farishtah, I, p.182; Dorn, *Makhzan-i-Afghana*, I, p.65.

94. *Maktubat-i-Quddusiya* (Delhi, 1871), pp.44-46.

95. *Ibid.*, pp.335-37.

96. *Ibid.*, p.338.

97. S.A.A.Rizvi, *Religious and Intellectual History of the Muslims in Akbar's Reign*, pp.63-64.

selves equal to the Muslims." He went from Shahabad to Nakhna where Sultan Sikandar was encamping. His mission was to personally remind the Sultan of the kingly duties and exert his influence over him and his nobles. He also wrote letters to Mir Muhammad, Mir Tardi, Ibrahim Khan Sherwani, Said Khan Sherwani, Khawas Khan and Dilawar Khan, making frantic appeals to them to live up to the ideals of Islam, to zealously uphold and strictly enforce the Shariat and extend patronage to the Ulama and the Mashaikh.[98] Such communications and advices did not go in vain. Contemporary and later chroniclers relate how Sikandar Lodi destroyed idols of Hindu gods and goddesses, and gave their pieces to Muslim butchers for use as meat-weights. Even as a prince he had expressed a desire to put an end to the Hindu bathing festival at Kurukshetra (Thanesar). Subsequently, he ordered that the Hindus, who had assembled there on the occasion of the solar eclipse be massacred in cold blood, but later on stayed his hand. In Mathura "and other places" he turned temples into mosques, and established Muslim *sarais*, colleges and *bazars* in the Hindu places of worship. The list of his atrocities is endless.[99] "Babur inherited his religious policy from the Lodis. Sikandar Lodi's fanaticism must have been still remembered by some of the officials who continued to serve under Babur....(who) was content to govern India in the orthodox fashion."[100]

The task of redeeming Hindu society, besides Brahmans, devolved on the Bhakta saints and they performed

---

98. For details see Zamiruddin Siddiqi, "Shaikh Abdul Quddus Gangoh and the contemporary rulers", paper read at the Indian History Congress, December, 1969.

99. Abdullah, *Tarikh-i-Daudi*, pp.39, 96-99; Dorn, Niamatullah's *Makhzan-i-Afghana*, pp.65-66, 166; Nizamuddin Ahmad, *Tabqat-i-Akbari*, I, pp.323, 331, 335-36; Farishtah, I, pp.182, 185-86; Ahmad Yadgar, *Tarikh-i-Salatin-i-Afghana*, pp.47, 62-63.

100. Sharma, *Religious Policy of the Mughal Emperors*, p.9. For atrocities committed on the Hindus, as depicted in their literary works, see *The Delhi Sultanate*, Bhartiya Vidya Bhavan, pp.631-36.

their obligation with a dedication that evokes our admiration and reverence. Their task was by no means an easy one. How to stop erosion in the Hindu society through Muslim proselyzation? If the trend was allowed to continue unabated, it would pose danger to the entire complex of the Hindu social structure. To check the penetration of Islam, particularly in the rural areas, the Hindu saints after Ramanand began to make Hinduism simple, straightforward and intelligible. They showed that there was nothing superior or inferior about one religion or the other, and there was no reason why Hindus should embrace a religion, implanted from abroad, when their own ancestral religion gave scope for infinite variety of worship and contained a philosophy and a message which could satisfy their social and spiritual needs. But their exhortations were devoid of ill-will towards any other religion or sect.

Kabir was more than sixty years of age when Sikandar Lodi ascended the throne and Nanak was twenty. Both saw the world around them and were dissatisfied with the unjust social and political order in which they lived. Not far from Nanak's home town of Talwandi, at Shahabad in the Ambala district, resided Shaikh Abdul Quddus Gangoh. Nanak must have heard about him and his fundamentalism which was shared by the Lodi monarch in equal measure, and it were the activities of Mashaikh like Abdul Quddus and Sultans like Sikandar Lodi which provoked the Bhakta saints to stand equal to them and confront and encounter them. Kabir openly declared: "I have come to save the devotee. I was sent because the world was in misery... The Almighty sent me to show clearly the beginning and the end."[101] Similarly Guru Nanak "regarded himself as...(having) received from His door-step the signs (aitan), the chapters (surahs) and the

---

101. Kabir: *Siddhant Dipika, Adi Mangal*, cited in Tara Chand, *Influence of Islam on Indian Culture*, p.151.

tradition (*hadis*) of the prophet".[102] He taught that "there is one God in the world and no other, and that Nanak the Caliph (or son) of God speaks the truth".[103] In language, sometimes soft and sometimes hard, they challenged the onslaught of Islam by claiming to have received message from God Himself. Kabir was conscious of his apostolic mission and challenged the concept that Islam was superior to Hinduism. There had been times under Muslim rule when, if one as much as said that Hinduism was as good as Islam, he was summarily executed.[104] Now Bhakta Kabir openly reiterated that "Mecca has verily become Kashi, and Ram has become Rahim".[105] So also asserted Guru Nanak when he declared that "There is no Hindu, there is no Musalman".[106] Most Hindu saints travelled widely and so did Guru Nanak, acquainting himself with different systems, orders and philosophies. He freely borrowed from Hindu classics and Muslim orders. He established the *Sangat* and the *Langar* after the way in the Muslim *Khanqahs*.

The Bhakta saints attempted to resist Islamism in two ways — by removing internal weaknesses of Hindu society and resisting proselytization. Both Kabir and Nanak denounced the caste system which was responsible for many evils in Hindu society. Nanak declared himself to be "with those who are low-born among the lowly,"[107] But like other Bhakta saints Kabir's "denunication of the caste system was as much an inspiration of Muslim example as response to its pull of conversion."[108] When Kabir de-

102. Khazan Singh, *The History and Philosophy of Sikhhism*, II, p. 350.
103. Tara Chand, *op. cit.* p.168.
104. Afif, p.388; Farishtah, I, 182.
105. Yugalanand, *Kabir Sahib ki Sakhi, Madhya ka Ang*.
106. Hughes, *Dictionary of Islam*, p.586.
107. Macauliffe, Max Arthur, *The Sikh Religion, Its Gurus, Sacred Writings and Authors*, 6 vols. (Oxford, 1909), I, 186.
108. Aziz Ahmad, *Studies in Islamic Culture in the Indian Environment*, p.146.

nounced caste and ritual of the Hindus, he also denounced the superstitions and rituals of the Muslims; or, conversely, the idea is best expressed in the words of his disciple Naudhan Pandit (whom Sikandar Lodi executed): "Islam was true, but his own religion was also true".[109] This was an open challenge to Muslim propagandism and proselytization. No wonder that Bhakti reformers were disliked by some Sufi Mashaikh, who looked upon them as competitors.[110] If a Muslim changed his religion he was liable to be condemned to death for apostasy. But under the influence of these saints many Muslims were converted to Bhakti Hinduism. Namdeva,[111] Ramdas, Eknath, Ramanand, Kabir, Nanak and Chaitanya and several other saints had Muslim disciples. Chaitanya openly converted Muslims to Bhakti Hinduism.[112] The *Bhaktamala* relates many instances of conversions that Pipa effected.

They also infused in the Mughal Emperors a spirit of tolerance. Babur appreciated the teachings of Guru Nanak,[113] and "on learning how much the people of the country prized their institutions, Akbar began to look upon them with affection."[114] But the influence of Bhaktas on Muslim royalty and nobility should not be overrated; the influence of Sufis like Gangoh on them was much more. There is a tendency to seek and find influence of Sufism on the Bhakti movement. But there is no evidence of such impulsion. Muslim Mashaikh were as keen on the spread of Islam as the Ulama. No Sufi could say with Kabir that "Mecca has verily become Kashi and Ram has become Rahim", or with Naudhan that Hinduism is as true as Islam. The Bhakti movement was an entirely

---

109. For details see Lal, *Twilight*, p.191.

110. S.A.A. Rizvi, *Muslim Revivalist Movements*, pp. 57-58.

111. M.G. Ranade, *Rise of the Maratha Power*, p.75.

112. D.C.Sen, *Chaitanya and His Age*, p.14; Abdul Karim *Social History of the Muslims in Bengal*, pp.150-202-204.

113. *Indian Antiquary*, III, 1874, 297-98.

114. Badaoni, II, 258.

Hindu reformist and resistance endeavour. All the Bhakta saints were Hindus. There is some controversy about Kabir's parentage, but "the whole background of Kabir's thought is Hindu."[115] If these Bhakta saints sometimes spoke in terms of Ram-Rahim, Krishna-Karim, Allah-Govind and Kashi-Kaba, it was to bring about Hindu-Muslim unity and to impress upon the neo-Muslims the futility of conversion. Else, they drew their inspiration from ancient Hindu philosophy and scriptures instilled into them by their Gurus or gained through intuitive consciousness.

Some Bhaktas confined themselves to purely Hindu language and lore with equal if not greater success. Such an one was Tulsidas. Through his *Ramcharitmanas*, he "slakes the thirst of those who are weary and heavy laden with the sorrow of the world."[116] Sometimes directly and at others symbolically he brings into focus contemporary problems of Hindu society, like the excruciating experience of exile in the forests (seen in next chapter), the relentless struggle of the righteous against *rakshasas*, the unflinching loyalty of the mace-warrior Hanuman (missing in contemporary scenario), the profound love among brothers (lacking in Mughal royalty), and above all the ultimate victory of truth over treachery (personified in Ravan). Tulsidasa's impulsion has been immense and lasting. His *Ramayan* is widely read with emotion. Ram, Hanuman and Anjaneya temples are spread all over the country and thronged with devotees.

So, from the very beginning of Muslim rule, from the thirteenth century onwards, from Namdeva in Maharashtra to Ramanand, Kabir, Nanak, Chaitanya and Tulsidas in North India, right upto the seventeenth century and threafter, a galaxy of middle class socio-religious reformers

---

115. Westcott, G.H., *Kabir and the Kabir Panth*, p.118. Also Ahmad Shah, *Bijak of Kabir*, p.40.
116. Tara Chand, *op. cit.*, p.145.

tried to help Indian society through sermon and song. They showed the futility of religious conflicts. They helped check excessive proselytization by attacking the caste system and reaching out to their audience in the languages of the common people throughout the country. Early Bhakta saints adhered to peaceful methods, but not all their disciples in later years. Kabir's followers spread out throughout North India and the Deccan. Jiwan Das was the founder of the Satnami sect which took up arms against the Mughals. The Sikh disciples of Nanak's successor Gurus, for varied reasons, fought against the Mughals and many times converted people by force. So did the Marathas.[117] According to Abdul Majid Khan it is because of Chaitanya's influence that large-scale conversions to Hinduism took place at the end of the eighteenth and beginning of the nineteenth century.[118] Hindu saint reformers continued to appear in a chain in the succeeding centuries of medieval India, infusing courage and confidence among the people. The present day strife for Ramjanmabhumi shrine is another legacy of *Hindu Bhakti* resistance to Muslim political and religious vandalism in the medieval age.

Conclusion

There were two major classes of society, the rulers and the ruled, the rich and the poor, the haves and the have-nots. In between these two, there was a middle class. The middle order in medieval India had certain peculiarities which made it different from the middle class of today. It was small in numbers and, therefore, sometimes it escaped notice especially of foreigners. With its small numbers its influence was also limited. Its life-style also

---

117. Khafi Khan, II, pp.115-118; Manucci, II, p.119.

118. Abdul Majid Khan, "Research about Muslim Aristocracy in East Pakistan" in *Social Research in East Pakistan*, ed. P. Bessaignet, Asiatic Society of Pakistan (Dacca, 1960), pp.23-25.

made it insignificant. But the middle class remained cus-
todians of public weal even in the medieval period. The
middle class people sometimes used to demonstrate and
protest, at others beg or purchase, if they did not actually
wrest concessions from the ruling classes. The Bhakti
Movement in medieval India was a middle class movement with far reaching consequences. It was an age of
religious conflict and violence. The Bhakta saints tried to
minimise it. Their mission was to save Hindu society from
ceaseless Muslim onslaught. How was it to live under a
polity hostile to its wellbeing? For an Akbar was a rare
phenomenon while Sikandars and Aurangzebs were
many. The *Girvan-Vanmanjari* of Dhuniraj[119] written in
1702-04 during the reign of Aurangzeb, brings out this
problem clearly. The book is written in the form of a cate-
chism between two Brahmanas discussing the correct
course of action to be adopted to put a stop to the injus-
tices of Aurangzeb. One of them advocates protest and
resistance. The other is of the view that such a course
would still more exacerbate the tyranny of the King, but if
they cooperated with the regime, they might obtain some
relief and minimise the tribulations of the Hindus under
the Mughal government. Centuries have rolled by, the
country has been partitioned on religious lines, and yet
the problem remains as a legacy of Muslim rule in India.
How to live with the Muslims who cannot but discriminate between the faithful and the infidels? Through appeasement or confrontation? Not a happy legacy indeed.

---

119. Text edited by U.P. Shah, Baroda, 1960.

Chapter 7

Lower Classes and Unmitigated Exploitation

"The Muslims dominate the infidels, but the latter fortify themselves in mountains...rugged places, as well as in bamboo groves...Hence they cannot be subdued...."

Ibn Battuta

Lower classes formed the bulk of the population. They were economically poor and socially degraded. They existed to provide food and apparel, services and comforts, to the higher classes, and resided in towns and villages. In urban areas these comprised all kinds of artisans from basket and rope makers to clothprinters, embroiders, carpet makers, silk-weavers, blacksmiths, tin workers, carpenters, oil-men, barbers, jugglers, mountebanks, street singers, brewers, tailors, betel leaf sellers, flower sellers, masons, stone-cutters, bullock-cart drivers, *doli*-carriers, water-carriers, domestic servants, *dhobis* and workers in a hundred other skilled and unskilled crafts.[1] In the villages there lived peasants and shepherds, besides a few artisans of the vocations enumerated above, although of inferior skill. The quality of work of the urban artisans and craftsmen used to be good. Let us take one example, that of stone-cutters and builders of edifices. Timur or Tamerlane, who invaded Hindustan in 1398, was highly impressed with Indian craftsmen and builders and on his return

---

1. Jaisi, *Padmavat*, pp.154,413; Pelsaert, p.60; Ashraf, *Life and Conditions of the People of Hindustan*, p.193.

home from India he took with him architects, artists and
skilled mechanics to build in his mud-walled Samarqand,
edifices like the Qutb Minar and the (old) Jama Masjid of
Delhi constructed by Firoz Shah Tughlaq.[2] Babur too was
pleased with the performance of Indian workmen and
described how thousands of stone-cutters and masons
worked on his buildings in Agra, Sikri, Biana, Dholpur,
Gwalior and Koil. "In the same way there are numberless
artisans of every sort in Hindustan."[3]

Despite this they were an exploited lot, and so were all
others, tillers of the soil in the villages and workmen in
towns. It is true that in the medieval times the concept of
welfare state was not widely prevalent, although it was
not entirely unknown, and many kings and nobles are
known to have tried to promote the general wellbeing of
the people. On a study of contemporary source materials,
it appears that the condition of the people of India up to
the fifteenth century was not deplorable. This is borne out
by the evidence provided by Indian writers and foreign
travellers from the eleventh to the fifteenth century. But
thereafter there is hardly any foreign visitor to India in sixteenth-seventeenth century in particular, who was not
struck by the extremely miserable existence of the lower
class people. Such a situation prevailed in all parts of the
country, north and south, east and west. We may attempt
a study of the economic and social condition of these
lower classes under two categories: (1) peasants and agriculturists, and (2) artisans and labourers, for better comprehension about their exploitation by the upper classes as
well as the government of the day.

---

2. Price, Major David, *Memoirs of the Principal Events of Muhammadan History* (London, 1921), III (I), p.267; Lamb, Harold, *Tamerlane the Earth Shaker* (London, 1929), p.272; Brown, Percy, *Indian Architecture* (Islamic Period), p.26; Lal, *Twilight of the Sultanate*, p.40.
3. *Babur Nama*, II, pp.518, 520.

Peasants and Agriculturists

The condition of the peasantry in India, up to the fourteenth century, was not bad. Contemporary Indian writers and foreign travellers do not generally talk about poverty; on the contrary they give an impression of the wellbeing of the tillers of the soil. Alberuni (eleventh century) has said many things about the Hindus, but nowhere does he say that the people were living in suffering or want. Minhaj Siraj, Ibn Battuta, Shihabuddin Abbas Ahmad, the author of *Masalik-ul-Absar*, Al-Qalqashindi, the author of *Subh-ul-Asha*, Amir Khusrau and Shams Siraj Afif (thirteenth-fourteenth centuries), even talk of the prosperity of the people. Even Barani is impressed with their wealth and conveys this impression when he feels delighted at the action of contemporary Muslim rulers against rich landlords and cultivators.[4] The decline of the political power of the Sultanate in the fifteenth century, saw a general recovery of people's strength and prosperity in good measure.

---

4. Only a few examples of this prosperity by writers of the fourteenth century may be cited. Shihabuddin says: "The general food of the Indians (Muslims) is beef and goat's flesh...it was a mere matter of habit, for in all the villages of India there are sheep in thousands" (E and D, III, p.583).

Ibn Battuta says: "When they have reaped the autumn harvest, they sow spring grains in the same soil in which autumn grains had been sown, for their country is excellent and the soil is fertile. As for rice they sow it three times a year......" (Mahdi Husain, trs., p.19). Shams Siraj Afif writing about the prosperity of Orissa at the time of Firoz Tughlaq's invasion says: "The country of Jajnagar was in a very flourishing state, and the abundance of corn and fruit supplied the wants of the army...the numbers of animals of every kind were so great that no one cared to take them...Sheep were found in such countless numbers..." (Afif, Persian text, pp.165-66. Also pp.180, 295).

For prosperity in the Deccan see Kincaid and Parasnis, *A History of the Maratha People*, I, p.37; Yule, *Ser Marco Polo*, II, p.323; Wassaf, Bombay text, pp.521-31.

About the prosperity of Vijayanagar countryside see Abdur Razzaq in *Mutla-us-Sadain*, E and D, IV, pp.105-6.

Also Barani pp. 216-17, 290-91; and Farishtah, Lucknow text, p.120.

But by the sixteenth and seventeenth centuries conditions are quite different. They change to such an extent that almost all foreign and many Indian writers are struck by the crushing poverty of the Indian peasant and do not fail to write about it. Athanasius Nikitin, Varthema, Barbosa, Paes, Nuniz, Linschoten, Salbank, Hawkins, Jourdain, Sir Thomas Roe, Terry and a host of others, all talk of the grinding poverty of the Indian people. It will serve no purpose to cite from each one of them, but one or two quotations may be given as specimens to convey the general trend of their impressions. Pelsaert, a Dutch visitor during Jahangir's reign, observes: "The common people (live in) poverty so great and miserable that the life of the people can be depicted or accurately described only as the home of stark want and the dwelling place of bitter woe......their houses are built of mud with thatched roofs. Furniture there is little or none, except some earthenware pots to hold water and for cooking......"[5] Salbank, writing of people between Agra and Lahore of about the same period, says that the "plebian sort is so poor that the greatest part of them go naked."[6] These two quotations would suffice to show how miserable the common people in the middle of the seventeenth century were. These and many others that follow lead one to the inescapable conclusion that the condition of the peasantry in India during the sixteenth and seventeenth centuries had considerably deteriorated.

It is pertinent to ask how the peasant during this period was reduced to such straits. India of the medieval times was mainly agricultural, and histories and legends of the times do not tire of singing in praise of the wealth and glory of the Great Mughals. Then how did the peasant become so miserably poor? Were there any ideas and actions of rulers which led to the impoverishment of the

---

5. Pelsaert, pp.60-61.
6. Quoted in Moreland, *India at the Death of Akbar*, pp.268-69.

agriculturists? Also, were there any ideas of the peasants themselves which taught them to reconcile themselves to their lot and did not prompt them to fight against their economic disablement? Contemporary chronicles do betray the existence of such ideas. That these have not yet been analysed by historians, does not mean that these ideas were not there. An attempt is being made here to discover such ideas and assess their effects.

To find the roots of the miserable condition of the agriculturists in the seventeenth century, one has naturally to look back to earlier times and, indeed, at the very nature of the Muslim conquest of India beginning with the thirteenth century. In the history of Muslim conquest, a unique phenomenon was witnessed in India. Contrary to what happened in Central Asia, Persia or Afghanistan, India could not be completely conquered, nor could its people be converted to the Islamic faith. On the other hand, a ceaseless resistance to the Muslim rule in the thirteenth, fourteenth and fifteenth centuries is clearly borne out by the records of the times. If Muslim chroniclers gloat over unqualified victories for their Turkish kings, there are a large number of inscriptions of Hindu kings who too lay exaggerated claim to military successes.[7] One thing which is clear beyond doubt is that throughout the Sultanate period (and also the Mughal period), there was stiff resistance to Muslim rule, and in one region or the other of the country, the authority of the Sultanate was being openly challenged.

Naturally, the Muslim kings gave much thought to finding some means to suppress the recalcitrant elements. Besides other things, one idea that struck Alauddin Khalji (1296-1316) was that it was "wealth" which was the "source of rebellion and disaffection." It encouraged defiance and provided means of "revolt". He and his

7. Liberally cited in A.B.M. Habibullah's *The Foundation of Muslim Rule in India*, First ed., Lahore, 1945.

counsellors deliberated that if somehow people could be impoverished, "no one would even have time to pronounce the word 'rebellion'."[8] How was this to be done? The Ulama would not have found it difficult to suggest a remedy. It is laid down in the *Hidaya* that when an "infidel country" is conquered, the Imam can divide it among the Muslims. He can also leave it in the hands of the original inhabitants, "exacting from them a capitation tax, and imposing a tribute on their lands." If the infidels are to lose their lands, their entire moveable property should also be taken away from them. In case they are to continue with cultivating the land, they should be allowed to retain "such a portion of their moveable property as may enable them to perform their business."[9] In India the conquered land was divided among Muslim officers, soldiers and Ulama in lieu of pay or as reward. Some land was kept under *Khalisa* or directly under the control of the regime. But in all cases the tiller of the soil remained the original Hindu cultivator. As an infidel he was to be taxed heavily, although a minimum of his moveable property like oxen, cows and buffaloes (*nisab*) was to be left with him.[10] The principle of the *Shariah* was to leave with him only as much as would have helped him carry on with his cultivation, but at the same time to keep him poor and subservient.

Bare Subsistence

According to W.H. Moreland "the question really at issue was how to break the power of the rural leaders, the chiefs and the headmen of *parganas* and villages...."[11] Sultan Alauddin therefore undertook a series of measures to crush them by striking at their major source of power—

8. Barani, pp.283-84.
9. Charles Hamilton's trs. of the *Hidaya*, Chapter IV.
10. Aghnides, *Muhammedan Theories of Finance*, pp.251-52, 253-54.
11. Moreland, *Agrarian System of Moslem India*, p.32 fn.

wealth.[12] But in the process, leaders and followers, rich and poor, all were affected. The king started by raising the land tax (*Kharaj*) to fifty percent. Under rulers like Iltutmish and Balban, it does not seem to have been above one-third of the produce. Furthermore, under Alauddin's system all the land occupied by the rich and the poor "was brought under assessment at the uniform rate of fifty per cent". This measure automatically reduced the chiefs practically to the position of peasants. The king also levied house-tax and grazing tax. According to the contemporary chronicler Ziyauddin Barani, all milk-producing animals like cows and goats were taxed. According to Farishtah, animals up to two pairs of oxen, a pair of buffaloes and some cows and goats were exempted.[13] This concession was based on the principle of *nisab*, namely, of leaving some minimum capital to enable one to carry on with one's work.[14] But it was hardly any relief, for there were taxes like *kari*, (derived from Hindi word *Kar*), *charai* and *Jiziyah*. The sultans of Delhi collected *Jiziyah* at the rate of forty, twenty and ten *tankahs* from the rich, the middle-class and the poor respectively.[15]

In short, a substantial portion of the produce was taken away by the government as taxes and the people were left with the bare minimum for sustenance. For the Sultan had "directed that only so much should be left to his subjects (*raiyyat*) as would maintain them from year to year... without admitting of their storing up or having articles in excess." Sultan Alauddin's rigorous measures were taken note of by contemporary writers both in India and abroad. In India contemporary writers like Barani, Isami and Amir Khusrau were inclined to believe him to

---

12. Barani, pp.216-17 and 291. Also Barani's *Fatawa-i-Jahandari*, pp.46-48.

13. Barani, p.287; Farishtah, p.109.

14. Aghnides, *Muhammadan Theories of Finance*, pp.251-54.

15. Afif, p.383.

be a persecutor of the Hindus. Foreigners also gathered the same impression. Maulana Shamsuddin Turk, a divine from Egypt, was happy to learn that Alauddin had made the wretchedness and misery of the Hindus so great and had reduced them to such a despicable condition "that the Hindu women and children went out begging at the doors of the Musalmans."[16] The same impression is conveyed in the writings of Isami and Wassaf.[17] While summing up the achievements of Alauddin Khalji, the contemporary chronicler Barani mentions, with due emphasis, that by the last decade of his reign the submission and obedience of the Hindus had become an established fact. Such a submission on the part of the Hindus "has neither been seen before nor will be witnessed hereafter." In brief, not only the Hindu Zamindars, who had been accustomed to a life of comfort and dignity, were reduced to a deplorable position, but the Hindus in general were impoverished to such an extent that there was no sign of gold or silver left in their houses, and the wives of *Khuts* and *Muqaddams* used to seek sundry jobs in the houses of the Musalmans, work there and receive wages.[18] The poor peasants (*balahars*) suffered the most. The fundamentalist Maulana Ziyauddin Barani feels jubilant at the suppression of the Hindus, and writes at length about the utter helplessness to which the peasantry had been reduced because the Sultan had left to them bare sustenance and had taken away everything else in *kharaj* (land revenue) and other taxes.[19]

But there was much greater oppression implicit in this measure. It was difficult to collect in full so many and such heavy taxes. "One of the standing evils in the revenue collection consisted in defective realization which

---

16. Barani, pp.291, 297-98.
17. Isami, *Futuh-us-Salatin*, Agra text, pp.569-70; *Tarikh-i-Wassaf*, Bombay Text, Book IV, p.448, Book V, pp. 646, 647.
18. Barani, p.288.
19. *Ibid*., pp.288, 305, 307.

usually left large balances,"[20] and unrealised balances used to become inevitable. Besides, lower revenue officials were corrupt and extortionate. To overcome these problems, Sultan Alauddin created a new ministry called the *Diwan-i-Mustakhraj*. The *Mustakhraj* was entrusted with the work of inquiring into the revenue arrears, and realizing them.[21] We shall discuss about the tyranny of this department a little later; suffice it here to say that in Alauddin's time, besides being oppressed by such a grinding tax-structure, the peasant was compelled to sell every maund of his surplus grain at government controlled rates for replenishing royal grain stores which the Sultan had ordered to be built in order to sustain his Market Control.[22]

After Alauddin's death (C.E. 1316) most of his measures seem to have fallen into disuse, but the peasants got no relief, because Ghiyasuddin Tughlaq who came to the throne four years later (C.E. 1320) continued the atrocious practice of Alauddin. He also ordered that "there should be left only so much to the Hindus that neither, on the one hand, they should become arrogant on account of their wealth, nor, on the other, desert their lands in despair."[23] In the time of Muhammad bin Tughlaq even this latter fear turned out to be true. The Sultan's enhancement of taxation went even beyond the lower limits of "bare subsistence." For the people left their fields and fled. This enraged the Sultan and he hunted them down like wild beasts.[24]

Still conditions did not become unbearable all at once. Nature's bounty to some extent compensated for the cru-

---

20. R.P. Tripathi, *Some Aspects of Muslim Administration*, p.262.

21. Barani, pp.288-89, 292.

22. For Alauddin's Market Control see Lal, *History of the Khaljis*, pp.197-225.

23. Barani, p.430.

24. Hajiuddabir, *Zafar-ul-Wali*; Barani, pp.479-80. For a detailed discussion on the Sultan's measures see Ishwari Prasad, *A History of the Qaraunah Turks in India*, pp.67-74.

elty of the king. If the regime was extortionist, heavy rains
sometimes helped in bumper production. Babur noted
that "India's crops are all rain grown".[25] Farming in north
India depended upon the monsoon rains coming from the
Bay of Bengal. Artificial irrigation was there on a very
limited scale, for irrigation "is not at all a necessity in
cultivating crops and orchards. Autumn crops (*Kharif*
season) grow by the downpour of the rains themselves;
and strange it is that spring crops (*Rabi* season) grow even
when no rain falls." Young trees are watered during two
or three years "after which they need no more (water-
ing)"[26] as the ground gets soaked with rain in the monsoon season. Ibn Battuta gives a detailed description of the
crops grown in India and adds: "The grains that have been
described are *Kharif* grains. They are harvested 60 days
after sowing. Thereafter *Rabi* grains like wheat, barley and
massoor are sown. These are sown in the very same field
in which *Rabi* grains (are harvested). The soil of this country is very fertile and is of excellent quality. Rice is sown
three times in the year. Production of rice is the largest in
the country. Sesame and sugar-cane are also sown with
Kharif."[27] Shams Siraj Afif writes that when, during the
monsoon season, "there were spells of heavy rains, Sultan
Firoz Tughlaq appointed officers to examine the banks of
all the water courses and report how far the inundations
had extended. If he was informed that large tracts had
been made fertile by the spread of waters, he was overwhelmed with joy. But if any village went to ruin (on
account of floods), he treated its officials with great severity."[28]

But the basic policy of impoverishing the people,
resulted in crippling of agricultural economy. By the

25. *Babur Nama*, II, p.487.
26. *Ibid.*, p.486. For Indian rains also Bernier, pp.431-34.
27. Ibn Battuta, pp.17-20.
28. Afif, pp.130-31.

Mughal period the condition of the peasantry became miserable; if there was any progress it was in the enhancement of taxation. According to W.H. Moreland, who has made a special study of the agrarian system of Mughal India, the basic object of the Mughal administration was to obtain the revenue on an ever-ascending scale. The share that could be taken out of the peasant's produce without destroying his chances of survival was probably a matter of common knowledge in each locality. In Akbar's time, in Kashmir, the state demand was one-third, but in reality it came to two-thirds.[29] The Jagirdars in Thatta (Sindh) did not take more than half. In Gujarat, according to Geleynsen who wrote in 1629, the peasant was made to part with three-quarters of his harvest. Similar is the testimony of De Laet, Fryer and Van Twist.[30] During Akbar's reign, says Abul Fazl, evil hearted officers because of sheer greed, used to proceed to villages and *mahals* and sack them.[31] Conditions became intolerable by the time of Shahjahan when, according to Manucci, peasants were compelled to sell their women and children to meet the revenue demand.[32] Manrique writes that the peasants were "carried off....to various markets and fairs, (to be sold) with their poor unhappy wives behind them carrying their small children all crying and lamenting...."[33] Bernier too affirms that the unfortunate peasants who were incapable of discharging the demands of their rapacious lords, were bereft of their children, who were carried away as slaves.[34] Here was also confirmation, if not actually the beginning, of the practice of bonded labour in India.

---

29. W.H. Moreland, *From Akbar to Aurangzeb*, pp.253-55.
30. Moreland in *Journal of Indian History*, IV, pp.78-79 and XIV, p.64.
31. Abul Fazl, *Akbar Nama*, Beveridge, II, pp.159-60.
32. Manucci, II, p.451.
33. Manrique II, p.272.
34. Bernier, p.205.

In these circumstances the peasant had little interest in cultivating the land. Bernier observes that "as the ground is seldom tilled otherwise than by compulsion....the whole country is badly cultivated, and a great part rendered unproductive.... The peasant cannot avoid asking himself this question: Why should I toil for a tyrant who may come tomorrow and lay his rapacious hands upon all I possess and value...without leaving me the means (even) to drag my own miserable existence?— The Timariots (Timurids), Governors and Revenue contractors, on their part reason in this manner: Why should the neglected state of this land create uneasiness in our minds, and why should we expend our own money and time to render it fruitful? We may be deprived of it in a single moment...Let us draw from the soil all the money we can, though the peasant should starve or abscond..."[35] The situation made the tax-gatherer callous and exploitative on the one hand and the peasant fatalistic and disinterested on the other. The result, in Bernier's own words, was "that most towns in Hindustan are made up of earth, mud, and other wretched material; that there is no city or town (that) does not bear evident marks of approaching decay."[36] Wherever Muslim despots ruled, ruin followed, so that, writes he, similar is the "present condition of *Mesopotamia, Anatolia, Palestine*, the once wonderful plain of *Antioch*, and so many other regions anciently well cultivated, fertile and populous, but now desolate...Egypt also exhibits a sad picture..."[37]

To revert to the Mughal empire. An important order in the reign of Aurangzeb describes the Jagirdars as demanding in theory only half but in practice actually more than the total yield.[38] Describing the conditions of the latter part of the seventeenth century Mughal empire, Dr. Tara

---

35. Bernier, pp.226-27.
36. *Ibid.*, p.227.
37. *Loc. cit.*
38. Moreland, *op. cit.*, p.255.

Chand writes: "The desire of the State was to extract the economic rent, so that nothing but bare subsistence. remained for the peasant." Aurangzeb's instructions were that "there shall be left for everyone who cultivates his land as much as he requires for his own support till the next crop be reaped and that of his family and for seed. This much shall be left to him, what remains is land tax, and shall go to the public treasury."[39]

Conditions could not always have been that bad. There were steps taken from time to time to help cultivation and ameliorate the condition of the agriculturists. Shamsuddin Iltutmish constructed a large tank called *Hauz-i-Shamsi*. Traces of Alauddin Khalji's *Hauz-i-Khas* and Firoz Tughlaq's irrigation canals still exist. Similar steps taken in Mughal times are also known. But such steps in aid of the development were taken because these could offer better means of increasing the revenue. Some steps which looked like helping the agriculturists, sometimes resulted in their perpetual penury. For example, a very common administrative measure of the medieval times was to advance loans to peasants to help them tide over their difficulties. But the important ideal entertained by rulers can be best summarized in the words of Sher Shah's instructions to his *Amils:* "Be lenient at the time of assessment, but show no mercy at the time of collection." This was, on the face of it, a good principle. But even Sher Shah Suri, renowned for his concern for the wellbeing of cultivators, was much more keen about the benefits to be drawn by his Afghan clansmen from the lands they administered. He sent his "good old loyal experienced servants" to districts which yielded good 'profits' and 'advantages' and after two years or so transfered them and sent "other servants like them that they may also prosper."[40] It was of course the peasant who paid for this prosperity.

39. Tara Chand, *History of Freedom Movement in India,* I, p.121. Also, Sir John Strachey, *India, Its Administration and Progress* (third Edition), p.126.
40. Abbas Sarwani, E and D, IV, p.414.

Collection of Arrears

We have earlier referred to the problem of collection of arrears. When agriculture was almost entirely dependent on rainfall and land tax was uniformly high, it was not possible for the peasants to pay their revenue regularly and keep their accounts ever straight with the government. The revenue used to fall into arrears. From the study of contemporary sources it is almost certain that there were hardly any remissions — even against conversion to Islam. Muslim rulers were very keen on proselytization. Sultan Firoz Tughlaq rescinded *Jiziyah* for those who became Muhammadan.[41] Sometimes he also instructed his revenue collectors to accept conversions in lieu of *Kharaj*.[42] Rajas and Zamindars who could not deposit land revenue or tribute in time had to convert to Islam.[43] Bengal and Gujarat provide specific instances which go to show that such rules prevailed throughout the Muslim-ruled regions.[44] But remissions of *Kharaj* were not allowed. On the other hand arrears went on accumulating and the kings tried to collect them with the utmost rigour. In the Sultanate period there was a full-fledged department by the name of the *Diwan-i-Mustakharaj*. The work of this department was to inquire into the arrears lying in the names of collectors (*Amils* and *Karkuns*) and force them to realize the balances in full.[45] Such was the strictness in the Sultanate period. Under the Mughals arrears were collected with equal harshness. The system then existing

---

41. Firoz Shah Tughlaq, *Fatuhat-i-Firoz Shahi*, English trs. E and D, III, p.368; Hindi trs. in Rizvi, *Tughlaq Kalin Bharat*, II, p.337.

42. Afif, pp.268-69; Ishwari Prasad, *Qaraunah Turks*, p.331; Badaoni, Ranking I, p.377.

43. For detailed references see Lal, *Growth of Muslim Population in Medieval India*, pp.160-161.

44. Lal, *Indian Muslims*, pp.50, 63-64; C.H.I., III, pp.305-306; Census of India Report, 1901, IV, Pt. I, Bengal, pp.165-181.

45. Barani, pp.288-89, 292; Tripathi, *Some Aspects of Muslim Administration*, p.262.

shows that the peasants were probably never relieved of the 'burden' of arrears. In practice it could hardly have been possible always to collect the entire amounts and the balance was generally put forward to be collected along with the demand of the next year. A bad year, therefore, might leave an intolerable burden for the peasants in the shape of such arrears. These had a natural tendency to grow It also seems to have been a common practice to demand the arrears, owed by peasants who had fled or died, from their neighbour. And peasants who could not pay revenue or arrears frequently became predial slaves.[46]

In short, between the thirteenth century when armies had to march to collect the revenue,[47] and the seventeenth century when peasants were running away from the land because of the extortions of the state, no satisfactory principle of assessment or collection except extortion could be discovered. The situation became definitely worse in the eighteenth and nineteenth centuries as attested to by contemporary historians Jean Law and Ghulam Hussain. It is this general and continued stringency that was the legacy of the Mughal empire and the Indian Muslim states which continued under the British Raj.

Another idea of the rulers of medieval India was to keep the prices of commodities of everyday necessity low. This idea too emanated in the time of Alauddin Khalji. It was either his own brain-child or that of his courtiers and Ulama. His passion for incessant conquests and constant invasions of Mongols had rendered maintenance of a large army unavoidable. Even if he had recruited the large number of soldiers on a moderate salary, the entire treasure of the state would have been exhausted in five or six years.[48]

---

46. Moreland, *India at the Death of Akbar*, pp.112-14 and *The Agrarian System of Moslem India*, pp.135-36, 146-47.

47. Barani, p.291; Yahiya, p.184. For detailed references see Lal, *Twilight of the Sultanate*, pp.73-75.

48. Barani, p.303.

Alauddin, therefore, decided to cut down the salary of soldiers; but to prevent their falling victim to economic distress,[49] he also decided to reduce the prices of commodities of daily use.

To the contemporary chronicler these prices were quite low and fluctuation, not even of a *dang* (small copper coin), was ever allowed whether in seasons of drought or of plenty. Indeed the 'low' and 'fixed' prices in the market were "considered to be one of the wonders of the age." But "when a husbandman paid half of his hard earned produce in land tax, some portion of the remaining half in other sundry duties, and then was compelled to sell his grain at cheap rates...to the government,[50] it does not speak well of the general condition of the peasantry in those days."[51] They could never have been happy in selling their grain cheap in the open market nor to the government itself at fixed rates without making profit. Profit is the greatest incentive to production, but it was completely checked by Alauddin's market regulations and the peasants seem to have lived a life of monotony and low standard.

Without caring to understand that low prices cripple production and impoverish the producer, many sultans after Alauddin Khalji took pride in competing with him in keeping prices low. But their actions led not only to the impoverishment of the peasantry but also of shopkeepers and businessmen. Shams Siraj Afif feels jubilant at describing and listing the low prices during the reign of Firoz Tughlaq, claiming that while Alauddin had to make strenuous efforts to bring down the prices, in the time of Firoz Tughlaq they remained low without resorting to any

---

49. *Ibid.*, p.304

50. Alauddin procured grain from the cultivators, and that too with great severity, to keep Government godowns ever replenished (Barani, pp.305, 307).

51. Lal, *History of the Khaljis*, pp.197, 290-91.

coercion.[52] "Like Alauddin, Sikandar Lodi also used to keep a constant watch on the price-level" in the market.[53] Abdullah, the author of *Tarikh-i-Daudi*, says that "during the reign of Ibrahim Lodi the prices of commodities were cheaper than in the reign of any other Sultan except in Alauddin's last days", and adds that whereas in Alauddin's time the cheapness of prices was maintained through compulsion, force and dire punishments, in Ibrahim's reign prices remained low 'naturally.'[54]

So Alauddin Khalji had pioneered the idea of maintaining prices of necessaries at cheap rates. It was followed by his successors up to the beginning of the sixteenth century, without perhaps caring for its implications on the condition of the peasantry. Historians of Sher Shah affirm that he was indebted to Alauddin in laying down his agrarian policy and Akbar adopted many measures of Sher Shah. During the Mughal period prices by and large went up,[55] although as late as in the reign of Aurangzeb, sometimes the prices reported were regarded as exceptionally cheap. But since the land revenue accounted for by far the larger portion of the peasant's surplus produce, it is obvious that this increase must have wiped out any possible advantage that the peasantry might have obtained through a rise in the prices.[56]

Besides these handicaps, the peasant suffered because there were no clear ideas about a regular commissariat service to maintain supply-line for the army during a campaign. There is evidence that camp-markets were sometimes established for the convenience of soldiers.[57] There are also situations on record when the soldiers were en-

---

52. Afif, p.294.
53. Nizamuddin Ahmad, *Tabqat-i-Akbari*, I, p.338; Farishtah, I, p.187.
54. Abdullah, *Tarikh-i-Daudi*, Bankipore Ms., fols, 223-24.
55. Abul Fazl, *Ain*, I, pp.65-71.
56. Moreland, *From Akbar to Aurangzeb*, pp.253-57.
57. Barani, pp.328-29; Afif, p.290; Farishtah, p.119.

couraged to loot the peasants to obtain grain.[58] Sher Shah took appropriate measures to see that agriculturists were not harassed by an army on march, but Babur noted that on the news of the arrival of an army the peasants used to leave their land, flee for life and establish themselves elsewhere. Encouragement to soldiers to loot was inherent in *khums* tax, through which the state obtained as its share one-fifth of the booty collected by the troops, while four-fifth was left with the soldiers.

And above all, one fact is clear in the chronicles of medieval India — any measures against the higher classes ultimately affected the peasants, because any loss to the former was surreptitiously transferred to the peasants. For, as Sir Thomas Roe (1615-19) wrote, the people of Hindustan lived "as fishes do in the sea — the great ones eat up the little. For first the farmer robs the peasant, the gentlemen robs the farmer, the greater robs the lesser and the King robs all."[59] Bernier corroborates the conclusion when he writes: "In eastern countries, the weak and the injured are without any refuge whatever; and the only law that decides all controversies is the cane and the caprice of a governor."[60]

Of all the ideas, motivations and actions mentioned above leading to the impoverishment of the peasantry, the one of leaving "nothing but bare subsistence", was the most atrocious. Writing about the times of Aurangzeb, Dr. Tara Chand rightly observes that "the policy (of leaving) bare subsistence was suicidal for it killed the goose that laid the golden eggs. It left no incentive for increasing the production or improving the methods of cultivation."[61] Consequently, there was a progressive deterioration in the living standards of the peasantry as decades and centuries

---

58. Afif, pp.112, 122, 289; Sharafuddin Yazdi, *Zafari Nama*, II, pp.87-88, 152-54, 156.
59. Cited in Moreland, *India at the Death of Akbar*, p.269.
60. Bernier, pp.235-36.
61. Tara Chand , *History of the Freedom Movement*, I, p.121.

passed. As said earlier, Alberuni, Barani, Ibn Battuta and Shams Siraj Afif talk about the prosperity of the people right up to the fourteenth century. R.H. Major in his translation of the works of Nicolo Conti, Athnasius Nikitin, Santo Stefano etc.,[62] only refers to the poverty of the Indian peasant in the fifteenth century. But Babur in the sixteenth century witnessed extreme poverty; he repeatedly talks about *langoti* as the only apparel and *khichri* as the only food.[63] Witnesses for the seventeenth century are unanimous in observing extreme poverty of the peasantry.

Resistance of the Peasantry

The idea of leaving only the bare minimum to the peasant and collecting the rest of his hard-earned produce in land revenue and other taxes, remained the basic policy of the rulers during the medieval times. Some chroniclers were aware of its evil effects. Shams Siraj Afif, writing in the days of Firoz Shah Tughlaq (1351-88) says that "Unwise regulations had been made in former reigns, and the *raiyyats* and subjects were oppressed in the payment of revenue. Several writers told the author of this work that it was the practice to leave the *raiyyat* one cow and take away all the rest."[64] Such a policy proved counter-productive. It not only harmed the agriculturists but also the Muslim regime, for, in place of minimising opposition, it actually encouraged resistance. In the unequal struggle between the poor peasantry and the mighty government carried on over a long period of time the tillers of the soil ultimately lost. But not without stiff resistance. Hindu Zamindars as the leaders and the peasants as their followers, both fought against the unjust demands of the king. Under Alauddin himself the *Khuts* and *Muqaddams* (Zamindars) avoided to pay taxes, did not care for the sum-

---

62. R.H. Major, *India in the Fifteenth Century* .
63. *Babur Nama*, II, p.519.
64. Afif, trs. E and D, III, pp.289-90.

mons of the *Diwan-i-Wazarat* or Revenue Department, ignored to call at his office and paid no heed to the revenue officials.[65] And the peasants, finding continuance of cultivation uneconomic and the treatment of the regime unbearable, left the fields and fled into the jungle from where they organized resistances. In this confrontation Zamindars played the role of leaders and the peasants joined under their banner.

Ibn Battuta describes this scenario. "The Muslims dominate the infidels," writes he, "but the later fortify themselves in mountains, in rocky, uneven and rugged places as well as in bamboo groves (or jungles)...which serve them as ramparts. Hence they cannot be subdued except by powerful armies."[66] The story of the resistance of the Hindus to Muslim dominance and injustice is repeated by many contemporary writers. Ziyauddin Barani says that if the Hindus "do not find a mighty sovereign at their head nor behold crowds of horse and foot with drawn swords and arrows threatening their lives, they fail in their allegiance, refuse payment of revenue and incite a hundred tumults and revolts."[67] Similar is the testimony of Amir Khusrau, Ibn Battuta, Vidyapati and the Muslim chroniclers of the fifteenth century.[68] In the fifteenth century, when the Sultanate of Delhi had grown weak, the tillers of the soil evaded, more than ever, payment of land tax, and revenue could be collected only through army sorties in regular yearly or half-yearly expeditions.[69] Such resistance continued throughout, for the Indian peasant had his own survival strategies. These comprised mainly of two options — to fight with determination as far as possible, but, if resistance proved of no avail, to flee and

---

65. Barani, p.291.
66. Ibn Battuta, p.124.
67. Barani, p.268.
68. Amir Khusrau, *Deval Rani*, p.50; Vidyapati, *Kirtilata*, pp.42-44, 70-72.
69. Lal, *Twilight*, pp. 70-106.

settle down elsewhere. Medieval Indian society, both
urban and agrarian, was to some extent an armed society.
In cities and towns the elite carried swords like walking
sticks. In villages few men were without at least a spear or
bow and arrows, and they were skilled in the use of these
arms. In 1632, Peter Mundy actually saw in the present
day Kanpur district, "labourers with their guns, swords
and bucklers lying by them while they ploughed the
ground".[70] Similarly, Manucci described how in Akbar's
days the villagers of the Mathura region defended themselves against Mughal revenue-collecting officers: "The
women stood behind their husbands with spears and
arrows, when the husband had shot off his matchlock, his
wife handed him the lance, while she reloaded the matchlock."[71] The countryside was studded with little forts,
some surrounded by nothing more than mud walls, but
which nevertheless provided centres of the general tradition of rebellion and agrarian unrest. Armed peasants
provided contingents to Baheliyas, Bhadauriyas, Bachgo-
tis, Mandahars and Tomars in the earlier period, to Jats,
Marathas and Sikhs in the later.

But as the people put up a continual resistance, the
Muslim government suppressed them ruthlessly. In this
exercise the Mughal emperors were no better than the pre-
Mughal sultans. We have often referred to the atrocities of
the Delhi sultans and their provincial governors. Abul
Fazl, Bernier and Manucci provide detailed accounts of
the exertion of the Mughals. Its summing up by Jahangir
is the most telling. In his *Tarikh-i-Salim Shahi* he writes:

"I am compelled to observe, with whatever regret, that
notwithstanding the frequent and sanguinary executions
which have been dealt among the people of Hindustan,
the number of the turbulent and disaffected never seems
to diminish; for what with the examples made during the

---

70. Mundy, *Travels*, II, p.90.
71. Manucci, I, p.134.

reign of my father, and subsequently of my own, there is scarcely a province in the empire in which, either in battle or by the sword of the executioner, *five or six hundred thousand human beings* have not, at various periods, fallen victims to this fatal disposition to discontent and turbulence. Ever and anon, in one quarter or another, will some accursed miscreant spring up to unfurl the standard of rebellion; so that in Hindustan never has there existed a period of complete repose."[72]

"In such a society," observes Kolf, "....the millions of armed men, cultivators and otherwise, were its (government's) rivals rather than its subjects."[73] This attitude was the consequence of the Mughal government's policy of repression. As an example, the exploits of one of Jahangir's commanders, Abdullah Khan Uzbeg Firoz Jung, can provide an idea of the excessive cruelty perpetrated by the government. Peter Mundy, who travelled from Agra to Patna in 1632 saw, during his four days' journey, 200 *minars* (pillars) on which a total of about 7000 heads were fixed with mortar. On his way back four months later, he noticed that meanwhile another 60 *minars* with between 2000 and 2400 heads had been added and that the erection of new ones had not yet stopped.[74] Abdullah Khan's force of 12,000 horse and 20,000 foot destroyed, in the Kalpi-Kanauj area, all towns, took all their goods, their wives and children as slaves and beheaded and 'immortered' the chiefest of their men.[75] Why, even Akbar's name stands besmeared with wanton killings. In his siege of Chittor (October 1567) the regular garrison of 8000 Rajputs was vigorously helped by 40,000 armed peasants who had shown "great zeal and activity". This infuriated the em-

---

72. *Tarikh-i-Salim Shahi*, trs. Price, pp.225-26.
73. Kolf, *Naukar, Rajput and Sepoy*, p.7.
74. Mundy, *Travels*, II, pp.90, 185, 186.
75. For action in this region in the reign of Akbar see Abul Fazl, *Akbar Nama*, II, pp.195-96.

peror to massacre 30,000 of them.[76]

In short, the Indian peasant was clear in his mind about meeting the onslaughts of nature and man. Attached to his land as he was, he resisted the oppression of the rulers as far as his resources, strength and stamina permitted. If conditions went beyond his control, he left his land and established himself in some other place. Indeed, migration or flight "was the peasant's first answer to famine or man's oppression." Babur's description of this process may be quoted in his own words: "In Hindustan," says he, "hamlets and villages, towns indeed, are depopulated and set up in a moment. If the people of a large town, one inhabited for years even, flee from it, they do it in such a way that not a sign or trace of them remains in a day or a day and a half. On the other hand, if they fix their eyes on a place in which to settle,......they make a tank or dig a well; they need not build houses or set up walls, *khas*-grass abounds, wood is unlimited, huts are made and straightaway there is a village or a town."[77]

Similar is the testimony of Col. Wilks about South India. "On the approach of a hostile army, the...inhabitants of India bury underground their most cumbrous effects, and...issue from their beloved homes and take the direction ...sometimes of a strong fortress, but more generally of the most unfrequented hills and woods." According to Amir Khusrau, "wherever the army marched, every inhabited spot was desolated... When the army arrived there (Warangal, Deccan), the Hindu inhabitants concealed themselves in hills and jungles."[78] This process of flight seems to have continued throughout the Mughal period, both in the North and the South. Writing

76. *Ibid.*, I, p.475.

77. *Babur Nama* trs. by Mrs. A.S. Beveridge, pp.487-88.

78. Erskine, *Babur's Memoirs* (Leyden and Erskine, pp.315 n 2) cites from Col. Wilks, *Historical Sketches*, Vol.I, p.309, note; Amir Khusrau, *Nuh Sipehr*, E and D, III, p.558.

of the days of Shahjahan, Bernier says that "many of the peasantry, driven to despair by so execrable a tyranny, abandon the country and sometimes fly to the territories of a Raja because they find less oppression and are allowed a greater degree of comfort."[79]

To flee was a good idea, when it is realized that this was perhaps the only way to escape from the cruel revenue demand and rapacious officials. Some angry rulers like Balban and Muhammad bin Tughlaq hunted down these escapists in the jungles, others clamped them in jails, but, by and large, the peasants did survive in the process. For, it was not only cultivators alone who fled into the forests, but often even vanquished Rajas and zealous Zamindars. There they and people at large organized themselves to defend against the onslaughts of the regime. For it was not only because cultivation was uneconomic and peasants left the fields; it was also a question of saving Hindu religion and Hindu culture. Under Muslim rule the two principal Muslim practices of iconoclasm and proselytization were carried on unabated. During the Arab invasion of Sind and the expeditions of Mahmud of Ghazni, defeated rulers, garrisons of captured forts, and civilian population were often forced to accept Islam. The terror-tactics of such invaders was the same everywhere and their atrocities are understandable. But even when Muslim rule had been established in India, it was a matter of policy with Muslim rulers to capture and convert or disperse and destroy the male population and carry into slavery their women and children. Minhaj Siraj writes that Sultan Balban's taking of captives, and his capture of the dependents of the great Ranas cannot be recounted.[80] In Katehar he ordered a general massacre of the male population above eight years of age and carried away women

---

79. Bernier's *Travels*, p.226, also quoted in Moreland, *India at the Death of Akbar*, p.135.
80. Minhaj, E and D, II, p.348.

and children.[81] Muhammad Tughlaq, Firoz Tughlaq, Sikandar Lodi, Sikandar Butshikan of Kashmir, Mahmud Beghara of Gujarat and emperor Aurangzeb were more enthusiastic, some others were lukewarm, but it was the religious duty of a Muslim monarch to capture people and convert them to Islam.

In these circumstances the defeated Rajas and helpless agriculturists all sought refuge in the forests. Forests in medieval India abounded. Ibn Battuta says that very thick forests existed right from Bengal to Allahabad. In his time rhinoceroses (*genda*) were to be found in the very centre of the Sultanate, in the jungles near Allahabad. There were jungles throughout the country. Even the environs of Delhi abounded in forests so that during the time of Balban, harassed Mewatis retaliated by issuing forth from the jungles in the immediate vicinity of the south-west of Delhi, attack the city and keep the king on tenter-hooks.[82] When Timur invaded Hindustan at the end of the fourteenth century, he had learnt about this resistance and was quite scared of it. In his *Malfuzat* he notes that there were many strong defences in India like the large rivers, the elephants etc. "The second defence," writes he, " consists of woods and forests and trees, which interweaving stem with stem and branch with branch, render it very difficult to penetrate the country. The third defence is the soldiery, and landlords and princes, and Rajas of that country, who inhabit fastnesses in those forests, and live there like wild beasts."[83]

Growth of dense forests was a cause and effect of heavy rains. Forests precipitated rainfall and rains helped in the growth of forests. Therefore, like forests, rains also helped the freedom loving "wild-beasts" living in the jungles in maintaing their independence and culture. It is

---

81. Barani, p.59; Farishtah, I, p.77.
82. Barani, p.56.
83. *Malfuzat-i-Timuri*, E and D, III, p.395.

truly said that in India it does not rain, it pours. The rainfall in the north and the northeastern India — Uttar Pradesh, Bihar and Bengal, including eastern Bengal (now Bangla Desh) and parts of Assam (the Hindustan of medieval times) — is in the following order: The average annual rainfall in U.P., Bihar and Bengal is 100 to 200 cms. (40 to 80 inches), in eastern Bengal and Assam it is 200 to 400 cms. and in some parts above 400 cms. (80 to 160 and above 160 inches). In all probability a similar average obtained in the medieval period also. Medieval chroniclers do not speak in quantitative terms: in their language "rivulets used to turn into rivers and rivers into seas during the rainy season." The situation is best depicted by the sixteenth century conqueror Zahiruddin Muhammad Babur himself in his memoirs *Tuzuk-i-Baburi* or *Babur Nama*. He writes about Hindustan: "Sometimes it rains 10, 15, or 20 times a day, torrents pour down all at once and rivers flow where no water had been."[84] Such intensity of rainfall had rendered precarious the grip of Turkish rulers in many parts. For example, the government at Delhi could not always maintain its hold on Bengal effectively. There were very few roads and hardly any bridges over rivers in those days, and the almost primitive medieval communication system used to break down during the rainy season. Local governors of the eastern region — Bihar and Bengal — did not fail to take advantage of this situation and used to declare independence. Governor Tughril Beg of Bengal "depended on the climate and waterlogged soil of the province to wear out the Delhi forces," for three years (1278-81).[85] Bengal almost remained independent till the middle of the sixteenth century.

---

84. *Babur Nama*, II, p.519.
85. Habibullah, A.B.M., *The Foundation of Muslim Rule in India*, pp.174, 185 n. 44.

In short, heavy rains and thick forests affected the mobility of the government's army, leaving the refugees safe in their jungle hide-outs and repulse any intrusion. Ibn Battuta describes how people used to fight behind barricades of bushes and bamboo trees. "They collect rain water" and tend their animals and fields, and remain so strongly entrenched that but for a strong army they cannot be suppressed.[86] Babur confirms this: "Under the monsoon rains the banks of some of its rivers and torrents are worn into deep channels, difficult and troublesome to pass through anywhere. In many parts of the plains (because of rains) thorny jungle grows, behind the good defence of which the people...become stubbornly rebellious and pay no taxes."[87] It was because of this that Muslim conquest could not penetrate the Indian countryside nor Muslim rule affect it. If there was any fear of attack, the villagers just fled and re-established themselves elsewhere, or returned after the storm was over.

SC, ST and OBC

Those who took to the jungle, stayed there, eating wild fruits, tree-roots, and the coarsest grain if and when available,[88] but surely preserving their freedom. But with the passing of time, a peasant became a tribal and from tribal a beast. William Finch, writing at Agra about 1610 C.E., describes how Jahangir and his nobles treated them — during *Shikar*. A favourite form of sport in Mughal India was the *Kamargha*, which consisted in enclosing a tract of country by a line of guards, and then gradually contracting the enclosure until a large quantity of game was encircled in a space of convenient size. "Whatever is taken in this enclosure" (*Kamargha* or human circle), writes Finch, "is called the king's *shikar* or game, whether men or

---

86. Ibn Battuta, p.124.
87. *Babur Nama*, II, p.487.
88. Badaoni, Ranking, I, p.377.

beasts... The beasts taken, if man's meat, are sold...if men they remain the King's slaves, which he sends yearly to Kabul to barter for horses and dogs: these being poor, miserable, thievish people, that live in woods and deserts, little differing from beasts."[89] W.H. Moreland adds: "Other writer (also) tell it besides Finch."[90] Even Babur, always a keen observer, had not failed to notice that peasants in India were often reduced to the position of tribals. "In our countries," writes he in his *Memoirs*, "dwellers in the wilds (i.e. nomads) get tribal names; here (i.e. Hindustan) the settled people of the cultivated lands and villages get tribal names."[91]

In short, the avalanche of Turco- Mughal invaders, and the policy of their Government turned many settled agriculturists into tribals of the jungles. Many defeated Rajas and harassed Zamindars also repaired to forest and remote fortresses for security. They had been defeated in war and due to the policy of making them *nest-o-nabud* (destroy root and branch), had been reduced to the position of Scheduled Castes /Tribes/Backward Classes. For example, many Parihars and Parmars, once upon a time belonging to the proud Rajput castes, are now included in lower castes. So are the "Rajputs" counted in Backward Classes in South India. Two examples, one from the early years of Muslim rule and the other from its closing years, would suffice to illustrate the point. In the early years of Muslim conquest, Jats had helped Muhammad bin Qasim in Sind; later on they turned against him. Khokhars had helped Muhammad Ghauri but turned hostile to him and ultimately killed him. This made the Turkish Sultanate ill-disposed towards them, and in course of time many of these Jats and Khokhars were pushed into belonging to low castes of to-day. For the later times is the example of

89. Finch, William, in Foster, *Early Travels*, p.154.
90. Moreland, *India at the Death of Akbar*, pp.27-28n.
91. *Babur Nama*, II, p.518.

the *Satnamis*. This sect was an offshoot of the Raidasis. Their stronghold in the seventeenth century was Narnaul, situated about 100 kms. south-west of Delhi. The contemporary chronicler Khafi Khan credits them with a good character. They followed the professions of agriculture and trade on a small scale. They dressed simply, like *faqirs*. They shaved their heads and so were called *mundiyas* also. They came into conflict with imperial forces. It began as a minor trouble, but developed into a war of Hindu liberation from the persecution of Aurangzeb. Soon some five thousand *Satnamis* were in arms. They routed the *faujdar* of Narnaul, plundered the town, demolished its mosques, and established their own administration. At last Aurangzeb crushed them by sending 10,000 troops (March, 1672) and facing a most obstinate battle in which two thousand *Satnamis* fell on the field and many more were slain during the pursuit. Those who escaped spread out into small units so that today there are about 15 million *Satnami* Harijans found in Madhya Pradesh, Maharashtra, Bihar and Uttar Pradesh.[92]

Thus were swelled the numbers of what are today called Scheduled Castes, Scheduled Tribes and Other Backward Classes (SC/ST/OBC). The eleventh century savant Alberuni who came to India in the train of Mahmud of Ghazni, speaks of eight castes/sections of *Antajya* (untouchable?), or workers in low professions in Hindustan such as fuller, shoemaker, juggler, fisherman, hunter of wild animals and birds. "They are occupied with dirty work, like the cleaning of the villages and other services."[93] In his time their number was obviously not large.Today the SC/ST alone comprise 23 percent of the population or about 156 million, according to 1981 census.

---

92. Their present religious head Mata Karuna Guru has withdrawn support from the Congress, says a press report of the *Times of India* date-lined Raipur 14 February, 1990.

93. Alberuni, I, pp.101-102.

Add to this the Other Backward Classes and they all count
to more than fifty percent. This staggeringly high figure
has been reached because of historical forces operating in
the medieval times primarily. Muslim rule spread all over
the country. Resistance to it too remained widespread.
Jungles abounded through out the vast land from Gujarat
to Bengal and Kashmir to Kanyakumari, and flight into
them was the safest safeguard for the weak and vulnerable. That is how SC/ST people are found in every state in
large numbers. During the medieval period, in the years
and centuries of oppression, they lived almost like wild
beasts in improvised huts in forest villages, segregated
and isolated, suffering and struggling. But by settling in
forest villages, they were enabled to preserve their freedom, their religion and their culture. Their martial arts,
preserved in their *Akharas,* are even now practised in different forms in many states. Such a phenomenon was not
witnessed in West Asian countries. There, in the vast open
deserts, the people could not save themselves from forced
conversions against advancing Muslim armies. There were
no forests into which they could flee, hide themselves and
organize resistance. Hence they all became Muslim.

In the Indian forest villages these "primitive" Hindus
continued to maintain themselves by engaging in agriculture and simple cottage industries. They also kept contact
with the outside world for, since they had remained
Hindu, they were freely employed by Rajas and Zamindars. They provided firewood and served as boatmen
and watchmen. The Hindu elite engaged them for guard
duty in their houses, and as *palki*-bearers when they travelled. Travelling in the hot climate of India was mostly
done at night, and these people provided guard to bullock
carts and other conveyances carrying passengers and
goods. There are descriptions of how these people ran in
front and rear of the carts with lighted torches or lanterns
in one hand and a *lathi* in the other. They also fought for

those Hindu leaders who organized resistance from remote villages and jungle hide-outs. The exaspertated and
starving peasantry sometimes took to highway robbery as
the only means of living. Raiding bands were also locally
formed. Their main occupation, however, remained me-
nial work, including scavenging and leather tanning. But
with all that, their spirit of resistance had made them good
fighters. Fighting kept their health replenished, compen-
sating for the non-availability of good food in the jungles.
Their fighting spirit made the British think of them as
thugs, robbers and bandits. But the British as well as other
Europeans also embarked upon anthropological and so-
ciological study of these poor forest people. In trying to
find a name for these groups, the British census officials
labelled them, in successive censuses, as Aboriginals
(1881), Animists (1891-1911) and as Adherents of Tribal
Religions (1921-1931).

These days a lot of noise is being made about helping
the SC/ST and OBCs by reserving their quotas in government jobs. It is argued that these people have been oppressed by high caste Hindus in the past and they should
now be helped and compensated by them. But that is only
an assumption. It is they who have helped save the Hindu
religion by shunning all comforts and taking to the life of
the jungle. That is why they have remained Hindu. If they
had been harassed and oppressed by high-caste Hindus,
they could have easily chosen to opt for Muslim creed
ever so keen on effecting proselytization. But they preferred to hide in the forests rather than do so. There is
another question. Was that the time for the Upper Caste
Hindus, fighting tenaciously to save their land, religion
and culture, to oppress the lower strata of Hindus whose
help they desperately needed in their struggle? The mind-
set of upper-caste/backward-caste conflict syndrome
needs reviewing as it is neither based on historical evidence nor supported by compulsions of the situation. The

present day isolated conflicts may be a rural politician/ plebian problem of no great antiquity.

Another relic of the remote past is the objection to the entry of men of lower class people into temples. In Islam slaves were not permitted to bestow alms or visit places of pilgrimage.[94] In India, according to Megasthenes, there were no slaves. But slavery (*dasta*) probably did exist in one form or the other. Were the *dasas* also debarred from entering temples and the practice has continued; or, was it that every caste and section had its own shrines and did not enter those of others? The picture is very blurred and origins of this practice are difficult to locate.

Above all, there is the question: Would the SC/ST by themselves accept to change their way of life and accept the assistance? Perhaps yes, perhaps no. An example may help understand the position. In June 1576 Maharana Pratap of Chittor had to face Akbar's armies in the famous battle of Haldighati. Rana Pratap fought with exemplary courage and of his soldiers only a little more than half could leave the field alive. In the darkness of the evening, the wounded Rana left the field on his favourite horse Chetak.[95] A little later, in October, Akbar himself marched in person in pursuit of the Rana, but the latter remained untraced and unsubdued. Later on he recovered all Mewar except Mandalgarh and Chittor. His nearest associates, the Bhil and Lohia tribals, had taken a vow that until their motherland was not freed, they would not eat in metal plates, but only on leaves; they would not sleep on bedsteads, but only on the ground; and they would renounce all comforts. The bravest among them even left Chittor, to return to it only when Mewar had regained independence. That day was not destined to come in their life-time. It was not to come for decades, for generations, for centuries. During these hundreds of years they lived as

---

94. Hughes, *Dictionary of Islam*, p.598.
95. Smith, *Akbar the Great Mogul*, p.108; C.H.I., IV, pp.115-16.

tribals and nomads, moving from city to city. On India regaining independence, Prime Minister Jawaharlal Nehru, who knew about these people's poignant history, decided to rehabilitate them in Chittor. In March 1955 an impressive function was arranged there and Pandit Nehru led the descendants of these valiant warriors back to their homes in independent Chittor in independent India. But most of them did not care to return. They live as nomads even today. The SC/ST and OBCs too may find their way of life too dear to relinquish for the modern "urban" civilised ways. Many welfare officers working in their areas actually find it to be so.

Slaves

The forest-village-dwellers, whether escapees or resisters, suffered untold privations. Still they had the satisfaction of being able to preserve their freedom, their religion and their culture. But all victims of aggresion were not so "lucky". Many vulnerable groups and individuals could not extricate themselves from the clutches of the invaders and tyranny of the rulers; they used to be captured, enslaved and even sold, not only in India but also outside the country. It was not only Jahangir, a comparatively kind hearted emperor, who used to capture poor people during his hunting expeditions and send them to Kabul in exchange for dogs and horses, all Muslim invaders and rulers collected slaves and exploited them as they pleased.

When Muhammad bin Qasim invaded Sind, he took captives wherever he went and sent many prisoners, especially women prisoners, to his homeland. Parimal Devi and Suraj Devi, the two daughters of Raja Dahir, who were sent to Hajjaj to adorn the harem of the Caliph, were part of a large bunch of maidens remitted as one-fifth share of the state (*Khums*) from the booty of war (*Ghanaim*). The *Chachnama* gives the details. After the capture of the fort of Rawar, Muhammad bin Qasim "halted there

for three day, during which time he masscered
6,000...men. Their followers and dependents, as well as
their women and children were taken prisoner." When the
(total) number of prisoners was calculated, it was found to
amount to thirty thousand persons (Kalichbeg has sixty
thousand), amongst whom thirty were the daughters of
the chiefs. They were sent to Hajjaj. The head of Dahir and
the fifth part of prisoners were forwarded in charge of the
Black Slave Kaab.son of Mubarak Rasti.[96] In Sind itself
female slaves captured after every campaign of the marching army, were married to Arab soldiers who settled
down in colonies established in places like Mansura,
Kuzdar, Mahfuza and Multan. The standing instructions
of Hajjaj to Muhammad bin Qasim were to "give no
quarter to infidels, but to cut their throats", and take the
women and children as captives. In the final stages of the
conquest of Sind, "when the plunder and the prisoners of
war were brought before Qasim...one-fifth of all the prisoners were chosen and set aside; they were counted as
amounting to twenty thousand in number... (they belonged to high families) and veils were put on their faces,
and the rest were given to the soldiers".[97] Obviously, a few
lakhs of women were enslaved and distributed among the
elite and the soldiers.

In the words of the Andre Wink, "From the seventh
century onwards, and with a peak during Muhammad al-
Qasim's campaigns in 712-13, a considerable number of
Jats [and also others] was captured as prisoners of war
and deported to Iraq and elsewhere as slaves. Some Jat
freemen became famous in the Islamic world, as for instance Abu Hanifa (699-767?), the founder of the Hanafite
school of law."[98]

96. *Chachnama*, E and D, I, pp.172-73; trs. Kalichbeg, p.154.
97. *Ibid.*, E and D, I, pp.173,181, 211.
98. Wink, *Al-Hind*, I, p.161.

So, from the days of Muhammad bin Qasim in the eighth century to those of Ahmad Shah Abdali in the eighteenth, enslavement, distribution and sale of captives was systematically practised by Muslim invaders. A few instances are necessary to have a clear idea of the monstrous practice of taking captives. When Mahmud Ghaznavi attacked Waihind (near Peshawar) in 1001-02, he took 500,000 persons of both sexes as captive. This figure of Abu Nasr Muhammad Utbi, the secretary and chronicler of Mahmud, is so mind-boggling that Elliot reduces it to 5000.[99] The point to note is that taking of slaves was a matter of routine in every expedition. Only when the numbers were exceptionally large did they receive the notice of the chroniclers. So that in Mahmud's attack on Ninduna in the Salt Range (1014), Utbi says that "slaves were so plentiful that they became very cheap; and men of repsectability in their native land (India) were degraded by becoming slaves of common shopkeepers (of Ghazni)".[100] His statement finds confirmation in Nizamuddin Ahmad's *Tabqat-i-Akbari* which states that Mahmud "obtained great spoils and a large number of slaves". Next year from Thanesar, according to Farishtah, "the Muhammadan army brought to Ghaznin 200,000 captives so that the capital appeared like an Indian city, for every soldier of the army had several slaves and slave girls".[101] Thereafter slaves were taken in Baran, Mahaban, Mathura, Kanauj, Asni etc. so that when Mahmud returned to Ghazni in 1019, the booty was found to consist (besides huge wealth) of 53,000 captives according to Nizamuddin. But Utbi is more detailed. He says that "the number of prisoners may be conceived from the fact, that each was sold for from two to ten *dirhams*. These were afterwards

---

99. *Tarikh-i-Yamini*, E and D, II, p.26; Elliot's Appendix, p.438; Farishtah, I, p.24.
100. Utbi, E and D, II, p.39.
101. Farishtah, I, p.28.

taken to Ghazna, and the merchants came from different
cities to purchase them, so that the countries of
Mawaraun-Nahr, Iraq and Khurasan were filled with
them". The *Tarikh-i-Alfi* adds that the fifth share due to the
Saiyyads was 150,000 slaves, therefore the total number of
captives comes to 750,000.[102]

This was the practice throughout the medieval period.
Furthermore, it was also a matter of policy with the
Muslim rulers and their army commanders to capture and
convert, destroy or sell the male population, and carry into
slavery women and children. Ibn-ul-Asir says that Qut-
buddin Aibak made "war against the provinces of
Hind...He killed many, and returned home with prisoners
and booty."[103] In Banaras, according to the same authority,
Muhammad Ghauri's slaughter of the Hindus was immense. "None was spared except women and children."[104]
No wonder that slaves began to fill the households of
every Turk from the very beginning of Muslim rule in
India. Fakhr-i-Mudabbir informs us that as a result of the
Muslim achievements under Muhammad Ghauri and
Qutbuddin Aibak, "even a poor householder (or soldier)
who did not possess a single slave before became the
owner of numerous slaves of all description (*jauq jauq
ghulam har jins*)..."[105]

In 1231 Sultan Iltutmish attacked Gwalior, and "captured a large number of slave"'.[106] Minhaj Siraj Jurjani
writes that Sultan Balban's "taking captives, and his capture of the dependents of the great Ranas cannot be recounted".[107] Talking of his war in Avadh against Trai-
lokyavarman of the Chandela dynasty (Dalaki wa Malaki

102. Lal, *Growth of Muslim Population in Medieval India*, pp.211-13. Also
Utbi, E and D, II, p.50 and n. 1.
103. *Kamil-ut-Tawarikh*, E and D, II, p.250.
104. *Ibid.*, p.251.
105. *Tarikh-i-Fakhruddin Mubarak Shah*, p.20.
106. *Tabqat-i-Nasiri*, Persian Text, p.175. Also Farishtah, I, p.66.
107. Minhaj, E and D, II, p.348.

of Minhaj), the chronicler says that "all the infidel wives, sons and dependents...and children...fell into the hands of the victors".[108] In 1253, in his campaign against Ranthambhor also Balban appears to have captured many prisoners. In 1259, in an attack on Haryana (the Shiwalik Hills), many women and children were enslaved.[109] Twice Balban led expeditions against Kampil, Patiali, and Bhojpur, and in the process captured a large number of women and children. In Katehar he ordered a general massacre of the male population of above eight years of age and carried away the women and children.[110]

The process of enslavement during war went on under the Khaljis and the Tughlaqs (1290-1414 C.E.). Of Alauddin Khalji's 50,000 slaves[111] some were mere boys,[112] and surely mainly captured during war. Firoz Tughlaq had issued an order that whichever places were sacked, in them the captives should be sorted out and the best ones should be forwarded to the court. His acquisition of slaves was accomplished through various ways—capture in war, in lieu of revenue and as present from nobles.[113] Soon he was enabled to collect 180,000 slaves. Ziyauddin Barani's description of the Slave Market in Delhi, (such markets were there in other places also), during the reign of Alauddin Khalji, shows that fresh batches of captives were constantly replenishing them.[114] The practice of selling slaves was well established and widely known. Amir Khusrau in the fourteenth century writes that "the Turks, whenever they please, can seize, buy, or sell any Hindu".[115] He is corroborated by Vidyapati in the next

---

108. *Ibid.*, p.367; Farishtah, I, p.71.
109. Minhaj, pp.371, 380-81.
110. Barani, p.59.
111. Afif, p.272.
112. Barani, p.318; Lal, *History of the Khaljis*, pp.214-15.
113. Afif, p.267-73.
114. Barani, pp.314-15.
115. Amir Khusrau, *Nuh Sipehr*, E and D, III, p.561.

century. The latter writes that the Muslim army commanders take into custody all the women of the enemy's
city, and "wherever they happened to pass, in that very
place the ladies of the Raja's house began to be sold in the
market."[116] Alauddin Khalji fixed the prices of such slaves
in the market, as he did for all other items of common use
like wheat and rice, horse and cattle. The sale price of boys
was fixed from 20 to 30 *tankahs*; the ill-favoured could be
obtained for 7 or 8. The slave boys were classified according to their looks and working capacity. The standard
price of a working girl was fixed from 5 to 12 *tankahs*, that
of a good looking girl from 20 to 40, and a beauty of high
family even from 1 thousand to 2 thousand *tankahs*.[117]
Under Muhammad bin Tughlaq, as per the information of
Shihabuddin al Umri, a domestic maid in Delhi could be
had for 8 *tankahs* and one deemed fit to be a concubine
sold for about 15 *tankahs*. "In other cities," says he, "prices
are still lower."[118]

Muhammad bin Tughlaq became notorious for enslaving captives, and his reputation in this regard spread far
and wide so that Umri writes about him thus: "The Sultan
never ceases to show the greatest zeal in making war upon
the infidels...Everyday thousands of slaves are sold at very
low price, so great is the number of prisoners."[119] Ibn
Battuta's eye-witness account of the Sultan's arranging
marriages of enslaved girls with Muslims on a large scale
on the two Ids confirms the statement of Al Umri. "First of
all," writes he, "daughters of *Kafir* (Hindu) Rajas captured
during the course of the year, come, sing and dance.
Thereafter they are bestowed upon Amirs and important
foreigners. After this the daughters of other *Kafirs* dance
and sing...the Sultan gives them to his brothers, relatives
sons of Maliks etc. On the sixth day male and female

---

116. Vidyapati, *Kirtilata*, pp.72-74.
117. Barani, pp.313-15.
118. *Masalik-ul-Absar*, E and D, III, p.580.
119. *Loc. cit.*

slaves are married."[120] It was a general practice for Hindu girls of good families to learn the art of dancing. It was a sort of religious rite. They used to dance during weddings, festivals and *Pujas* at home and in temples. This art was turned ravenous under their Muslim captors or buyers.

In short, female slaves were captured or obtained in droves throughout the year. Such was their influx that Ibn Battuta appears having got bored of them when he wrote: "At (one) time there arrived in Delhi some female infidel captives, ten of whom the *Wazir* sent to me. I gave one of them to the man who had brought them to me, but he was not satisfied. My companion took three young girls, and I do not know what happened to the rest."[121] "Thousands (*chandin hazar*) of non-Muslim women (*aurat va masturat*) were captured during the yearly campaigns of Firoz Tughlaq" and under him the Id celebrations were held on lines similar to those of his predecessor.[122] Their sale outside, especially during the Hajj season, brought profits to the state and Muslim merchants. Their possession within, inflated the harems of Muslim kings and nobles beyond belief.[123]

Some feeble attempts were sometimes made by some kings to put a stop to this inhuman practice. The Mughal emperor Akbar, for example, abolished the custom of enslaving helpless women and children in times of war.[124] Jahangir ordered that "a government collector or *Jagirdar* should not without permission intermarry with the people of the *pargana* in which he might be",[125] for abduction and

---

120. Ibn Battuta, p.63, Hindi version by S.A.A. Rizvi in *Tughlaq Kalin Bharat*, Part I, Aligarh, p.189.

121. *Ibid.*, p.123.

122. Afif, p.265. Also pp.119-20.

123. *Ibid.*, p.144. Also Lal, K.S., *The Mughal Harem*, pp.19-38, 167-69, 170 and *Growth of Muslim Population*, p.116.

124. *Akbar Nama*, II, p.246; Du Jarric, *Akbar and the Jesuits*, pp.152-59. Also pp.28, 30, 70, 92.

125. *Tuzuk-i-Jahangiri*, I, p.9.

forced marriages were common enough. But there was
never an abjuration of the policy of enslavement as mainly
it was not the Mughal emperors but the Mughal nobility
who must have taken the lion's share of the state's enslavement, deportation and sale. To make the long and
painful story short, it may just be mentioned that after the
Third Battle of Panipat (1761), "the plunder of the (Maratha) camp was prodigious, and women and children who
survived were driven off as slaves — twenty-two thousand (women), of the highest rank in the land, says the
Siyar-ul-Mutakhkhirin."[126]

The above study points to some hard facts about enslavement of Hindus under Muslim rule. It is not pertinent here to make a detailed study of the Muslim slave
system which was an institution as peculiar as it was
unique. Examples of men like Iltutmish and Balban are
cited to show how well the slaves fared in the Islamic state
and society, how well they were brought up and how
easily they could rise to the highest positions in life. "Iltutmish received nourishment like a son" in the house of his
master.[127] Firoz Tughlaq and his nobles too treated their
slaves in a similar fashion.[128] But it is the captured and
enslaved victims who felt the pinch of slavery. Here only
their sufferings may be briefly recapitulated under three
separate sections—the fate of men, of women and of children. Of the men captives, the Muslim regime did not
have much use. Male prisoners were usually put to the
sword, especially the old, the overbearing and those bearing arms, as had happened during Muhammad bin
Qasim's invasion, Ghauri's attack on Banaras, Balban's
expedition to Katehar, Timur's campaign in Hindustan or
Akbar's massacre at Chittor.[129]

---

126. Rawlinson, H.G., in C.H.I., IV, p.424 and n.
127. Muhammad Aziz Ahmad, *Political History and Institutions of the
Early Turkish Empire of Delhi*, pp.147-48, 159.
128. Afif, pp.272-73.
129. Barani, p.59; Yazdi, *Zafar Nama*, II, p.92; *Malfuzat-i-Timuri*, E and
D, III, p.436; Nizamuddin Ahmad, *Tabqat-i-Akbari*, I, p.255; Farishtah, I,
p.77; *Akbar Nama*, II, p.475.

Of the captured men, those who could fetch good price were sold in India and outside. A lucrative trade in Indian slaves flourished in the West Asian countries. Many chroniclers aver that an important export item of commerce abroad comprised of Indian slaves who were exchanged for horses. If the trade in slaves was as brisk as the horse-trade, then many thousands of people must have been deported from India each year. For example, over the years from the eleventh to the early years of the nineteenth century, three quarters of the population of Bukhara was of mainly Indian slave extraction. The Hindu-Kush (Hindu-killer) mountain ranges are so called because thousands of Indian captives "yoked together" used to die while negotiating them. Ibn Battuta himself saw Indian slaves being taken out of the country.[130]

Many of the slaves who were not sold by their captors, served as domestic servants, as artisans in the royal *Karkhanas* and as Paiks in the army. The Paiks cleared the jungles and prepared roads for the army on march. They were also sometimes used as human "shields" in battle.[131] But others, especially professional soldiers captured in war and willing to serve the Muslim army, joined the permanent cadre of the infantry, and were known for their loyalty.[132] Alauddin Khalji, Mubarak Khalji, and Firoz Tughlaq were saved by Paiks when attempts were made on their lives.[133]

Child captives were preferred to grown up men. It may be recollected that in his campaigns in Katehar, Balban massacred mercilessly, sparing only boys of eight or nine.[134] The age factor is material. As these boys grew in

130. Ibn Battuta, p.71; Jahangir, *Tarikh-i-Salim Shahi*, p.165; Burnes, *Travels into Bokhara*, I, p.276; II, p.61.
131. Al-Qalqashindi, *Subh-ul-Asha*, p.76.
132. Barbosa, *The Book of Duarte Barbosa*, I, p.181; Barani, *Fatawa-i-Jahandari*, p.25.
133. Barani, pp.273, 376, 377.
134. *Ibid.*, pp.58-59.

years, they gradually forgot their parents and even their native places and developed loyalty only to the king. They could thus be reared as Janessaries were brought up in the Ottoman Empire. The price-schedule of Sultan Alauddin Khalji is evidence of the importance attached to boy-slaves. In his time, while the price of a handsome slave was twenty to 30 *tankahs* and that of a slave-servant ten to 15 *tankahs*, the price of a child slave (*ghulam bachchgan naukari*) was fixed at 70 to 80 *tankahs*.[135] Therefore during a campaign it was aimed at capturing lots of children. But no Hindus wished their children to become slaves, and in the face of an impending defeat Hindu mothers used to burn their little children in the fire of *Jauhar*[136] rather than let them fall into the hands of the enemy to lead the life of perpetual bondage and sometimes meet a most detestable death.[137]

The women captives in Muslim hands were treated as objects of sex or for making money through sale. Al Umri writes that "in spite of low prices of slaves, 200,000 *tankahs* and even more, are paid for young Indian girls. I inquired the reason...and was told that these young girls are remarkable for their beauty, and the grace of their manners."[138]

This was the position from the very beginning. It has been mentioned before that Muhammad bin Qasim sent to Hajjaj some thirty thousand captives many among whom were daughters of chiefs of Sind. Hajjaj forwarded the prisoners to Caliph Walid I (C.E. 705-15). The latter "sold some of those daughters of the chiefs, and some he granted as rewards. When he saw the daughter of Rai

---

135. *Ibid.*, p.314.

136. Sharma, G.N., *Mewar and the Moghul Emperors*, pp.56, 76-77. Also Smith, *Akbar the Great Mogul*, p.64.

137. "After his (Firoz Tughlaq's) death, the heads of these his favoured slaves were cut off without mercy, and were made into heaps in front of the *darbar*" (Afif, p.273).

138. *Masalik-ul-Absar*, E and D, III, pp.580-81.

Dahir's sister, he was much struck with her beauty and charms...and wished to keep her for himself". But as his nephew Abdullah bin Abbas desired to take her, Walid bestowed her on him saying that "it is better that you should take her to be the mother of your children". Centuries later, in the time of Jahangir, Abdullah Khan Firoz Jung expressed similar views when he declared that "I made prisoners of five lacs of men and women and sold them. They all became Muhammadans. From their progeny there will be crores by the day of judgement".[139] The motive of having progeny from captured women and thereby increasing Muslim population was at the back of all marriages, abductions and enslavements throughout the medieval period.

One recognised way of escape from sex exploitation in the medieval period was *Jauhar* or group-self-immolation. *Jauhar* also was naturally resorted to because the motives and actions of the victors were never in doubt. For example, before Qasim could attack the Fort of Rawar many of the royal ladies themselves voluntarily immolated themselves. The description of the holocaust in the *Chachnama* is like this: "Bai, the sister of Dahir, assembled all her women and said...'God forbid that we should own our liberty to these outcast cow-eaters. Our honour would be lost...there is nowhere any hope of escape; let us collect wood, cotton and oil...and burn ourselves. ...If any wish to save herself she may.' So they went into a house, set it on fire and burnt themselves."[140] It is those of the lesser mettle who used to save themselves and used to be captured. The repeated *Jauhars* at one place, Chittor, during the attacks of Alauddin Khalji, Bahadur Shah of Gujarat and Emperor Akbar have become memorable for the spirit shown by the Rajputnis. Captured and enslaved women

---

139. *Chachnama*, trs. Kalichbeg, pp.153-54; Shah Nawaz Khan, *Maasir-ul-Umara*, I, p.105.

140. *Ibid.*, trs. Kalichbeg, p.155.

often had to lead a life of misery and dishonour as happened with Deval Devi, daughter of Raja Karan Baghela of Gujarat.[141]

As the legacy of this scenario, Indian girls are still being sold to West Asian nationals as wives, concubines and slave girls. For example, all the leading Indian newspapers like *The Indian Express, The Hindustan Times* and *The Times of India* of 4 August 1991, flashed the news of a sixty year old "toothless" Arab national Yahiya H.M. Al Sagish "marrying" a 10-11 year old Ameena of Hyderabad after paying her father Rs. 6000, and attempting to take her out of the country. Al Sagish has been taken into police custody and the case is in the law-court now. Mr. I.U. Khan has "pointed out that no offence could be made out against his client as he had acted in accordance with the Shariat laws. He said that since this case related to the Muslim personal law which permitted marriage with girls who had attained puberty (described as over 9 years of age), Al Sagish could not be tried under the Indian Penal Code (IPC). Besides Ameena's parents had not complained." (*Times of India,* 14 August 1991).

But this is not an isolated case. I was in Hyderabad for about four years, 1979-1983. There I learnt that such "marriages" are common. There are regular agents and touts who arrange them. Poor parents of girls are handsomely paid by foreign Muslims for such arrangements. Every time that I happened to go to the Hyderabad Airlines office or the Airport (which was about at least once a month), I found bunches of old bridegrooms in Arab attire accompanied by young girls, often little girl brides. "A rough estimate indicated that as many as 8000 such marriages were solemnised during the past one decade in

141. She was captured by Malik Kafur and brought to Delhi. She was first married to Khizr Khan, then Mubarak Khalji married her forcibly. She was later on taken by Khusrau Shah—too much for a Hindu maiden (Lal, *History of the Khaljis,* pp.234-36, 298-99).

Hyderabad alone." (*Indian Express Magazine*, 18 August 1991). In short, the sex slave-trade is still flourishing not only in Hyderabad but in many other cities of India after the medieval tradition.

Artisans and Labourers

After a brief survey of the misery and exploitation of the peasants, backward classes and slaves, let us look at the condition of artisans and labourers. In the medieval period, as sometimes even now, the work and vocation of agriculturists approximated, bordered, converged and telescoped into many other subsidiary professions. A peasant, when he was free from his field, in terms of time and seasons, or was compelled to leave his village, generally worked as basket-maker, weaver or water-carrier in his village or in the town nearby temporarily or after migrating to it. With the passage of time some of these agriculturalists became efficient and skilled craftsmen while the majority remained engaged in unskilled jobs. In urban setting their life-style may have improved a little— only a little in the medieval age—but they all remained an exploited lot. There was hardly any contemporary foreign visitor to India who was not struck by the extremely miserable existence of the lower class people. Such a situation obtained in all parts of the country, north and south, east and west.

Athnasius Nikitin, who travelled in the Deccan between 1470 and 1474 says that "the land is overstocked with people: but those in the country are very miserable..."[142] Durate Barbosa (1600-1615) was horrified by the poverty existing on the Malabar coast and says that some of the lower classes in the region were so poor that they lived on roots and wild fruits and covered themselves with leaves. His near contemporary Varthema (1504-06)

---

142. Nikitin in Major, *India in the Fifteenth Century*, p.14.

and the later visitor Linschoten wrote in a similar strain. Writing around the year 1624, Della Valle gives glimpses of life in Surat by pointing out that the people were numerous, wages were low, and slaves cost practically nothing to keep. Similar is the testimony of Pyrard.[143] The Portuguese writer Paes (wrote in 1520) and Nuniz (1536-37), confirm the assertion that the mass of the people were living in the greatest poverty and distress. In the seventeenth century John De Laet (1631) summarised the information he had collected from English, Dutch and Portuguese sources regarding the Mughal empire as a whole. "The condition of the common people in these regions (south and west) is," says he, "exceedingly miserable"; wages are low; workmen get only one regular meal a day, the houses are wretched and practically unfurnished, and people have not got sufficient covering to keep warm in winter.[144]

This about the south and west. About the east and north, Bengal and the region between Agra and Lahore, Joseph Salbank (1609-10) writing of the thickly populated country between Agra and Lahore observes that while the nobles "are said to be very wealthy...the plebian sort, is so poor that the greatest part of them go naked." In this regard, and for the urban scene in particular the testimony of Pelsaert (1620-27) and Bernier (1656-68) is of immense value. They lived and wrote mainly about Agra and Delhi respectively. Pelsaert laments "the utter subjection and poverty of the common people—poverty so great and miserable that the life of the people can be depicted or accurately described only as the home of stark want and the dwelling place of bitter woe."[145] He continues: "There are three classes of people who are indeed nominally free, but whose status differs very little from voluntary slav-

---

143. Moreland, *India at the Death of Akbar*, pp. 267-8 and n.
144. *Ibid.*, p.269.
145. Pelsaert, p.60.

ery—workmen, peons or servants and shopkeepers. For the workmen there are two scourges, the first of which is low wages. Goldsmiths, painters (of cloth or chintz), embroiderers, carpet makers, cotton or silk weavers, blacksmiths, copper-smiths, tailors, masons, builders, stonecutters, a hundred crafts in all—any of these working from morning to night can earn only 5 or 6 *tackas* (*tankahs*), that is 4 or 5 strivers in wages. The second (scourge) is (the oppression of) the Governor, the nobles, the *Diwan*, the *Kotwal*, the *Bakshi*, and other royal officers. If any of these wants a workman, the man is not asked if he is willing to come, but is seized in the house or in the street, well beaten if he should dare to raise any objection, and in the evening paid half his wages, or nothing at all. From these facts the nature of their food can be easily inferred... For their monotonous daily food they have nothing but a little *khichri*...in the day time, they munch a little parched pulse or other grain, which they say suffices for their lean stomachs... Their houses are built of mud with thatched roofs. Furniture there is little or none, except some earthenware pots to hold water and for cooking... Their bedclothes are scanty, merely a sheet or perhaps two...this is sufficent in the hot weather, but the bitter cold nights are miserable indeed, and they try to keep warm over little cowdung fires...the smoke from these fires all over the city is so great that the eyes run, and the throat seems to be choked."[146] In 1648 the capital shifted from Agra to Delhi, but the story of exploitation remained the same. Bernier writes that "...grandees pay for a work of art considerably under its value, and according to their own caprice."[147] "When an *Omrah* or *Mansabdar* requires the services of an artisan, he sends to the *bazar* for him, employing force, if necessary, to make the poor man work; and after the task is finished, the unfeeling lord pays, not according to the

146. *Ibid.*, pp.60-61.
147. Bernier, p.228.

value of the labour, but agreeably to his own standard of fair remuneration; the artisan having reason to congratulate himself if the *Korrah* has not been given in part payment."[148]

The artisans and craftsmen in the permanent service of the monarch and the principal *Omarahs* were a little better off than the casual wage earners. They tended to preserve the arts for they were paid more and regularly. Akbar sanctioned the following daily wages for workers and artisans—2 *dams* (copper coins, 1/40 of *Rupia*) for ordinary labourers, 3 to 4 *dams* for superior labourers, 3 to 7 *dams* for carpenters and 5 to 7 *dams* for builders. According to Moreland carpenters and builders got, in Akbar's days, equivalent to about one rupee per day on the average, and they were rather better off than the modern workmen of the United Provinces, if not Punjab in the early years of the twentieth century. But there are many buts. It is not certain if the workmen got full sanctioned rates. Then for the slightest mistake they were heavily fined. "If a horse lost condition, the fines came down to the water carriers and sweepers employed in the stable. When an elephant died through neglect, the attendants (some of whom drew less than three rupees a month) had to pay the price of the animal."[149] During the process of investigation and impositon of punishment some money had to be paid to middlemen and Mughal officers. Naturally, such artisans and workers "can never become rich, and he feels it no trifling matter if he have the means of satisfying the cravings of hunger and of covering his body with the coarsest raiment".[150]

"Peons or servants are exceedingly numerous in this country," writes Pelsaert, "for every one—be he mounted soldier, merchant or king's official—keeps as many as his

---

148. *Ibid.*, pp.256, 288.
149. *Ain*, I, pp.148-49, 139, 235; also Moreland, pp.190-91 n.
150. Bernier, p.229.

position and circumstances permit. Outside the house, they serve for display, running continually before their master's horse; inside, they do the work of the house, each knowing his duty," like the *bailwan*, the *farrash*, the *masal-chi*, the *mahawat* etc.[151] Edward Terry (1616-19), Pelsaert and many others note that men stood in the market places to be hired and many of them were paid very low wages or even paid in kind, "for most of the great lords reckon 40 days to the month, and pay from 3 to 4 rupees for that period: while wages are often left several months in arrears, and then paid in worn-out clothes or other things." Such fleecing was naturally responded to by cunning and "very few of them serve their master honestly; they steal whatever they can; if they buy only a pice-worth of food, they will take their share or *dasturi* (commission)."[152]

Transporters and coolies were no better off. On land, elephants, camels, horse, bullocks and donkeys were the main means of conveyance of kings, nobles, landlords and big merchants. Agricultural products were transported from fields to the markets in the cities in bullock carts. Grain was also carried and sold by roving merchants (*banjaras*) on mules in places which were not easily accessible. Big merchants with their merchandise generally moved only in large convoys[153] using chariots, horses, bullock carts, mules, camels, and even buffaloes, depending on the terrain. The government officials with treasures also travelled in convoys and under proper escorts.[154]

Transport between rural and urban areas, between cities and within the city was provided by coolies, horses, bullock carts and *dola* or *doli*. In the days of Firoz Tughlaq, hire for a bullock cart was 4 to 6 *jitals*, and 12 *jitals* for a horse. A *dola* which was carried by *kahars* cost half a

151. Pelsaert, pp.61-62.
152. *Ibid.*, p.62-63.
153. Barani, p.316.
154. Ibn Battuta, p.151.

tankah. The *dola* or palanquin was the common conveyance of ladies of high rank. But this sophisticated means of transport was also being brought into more and more use by the old and infirm and the ease loving elite. When Qutbuddin Mubarak Khalji (1316-20) felt miserable without the company of his favourite Khusrau Khan, he sent orders to the latter to return from the Deccan as quickly as possible (about C.E. 1320), and Khusrau Khan was taken in a palanquin post haste from Devagiri to Delhi. And Sikandar Lodi's boast, "if I order one of my slaves to be seated in a palanquin, the entire body of nobility would carry him on their shoulders at my bidding",[155] clearly indicates that besides ladies, the use of palanquin had also become a fashion with men of means. In the fifteenth century *Ekka* and *Tonga* had also come into vogue,[156] but for long journeys the horse was the common conveyance.[157] A footman's services could be requisitioned for 5 *tankahs* a month,[158] and a man could travel from Delhi to Agra spending only one *Bahloli*, which sufficed for him, his horse and his small escort/retinue during the journey.[159] A large number of people were engaged on this work, and they plied a brisk trade.[160] In the Mughal times comparatively better roads added some sort of sophistication to land travel.

Those employed by the Government on the work of transport and communication were not ill paid. Ibn Battuta's description of the same pertains to government's communication system which facilitated smooth running of administration. According to Barani and Ibn Battua

155. Passage in *Tarikh-i-Daudi* as trs. by N.B. Roy in Niamatulah's *History of the Afghans*, p.134.
156. Ahmad Yadgar, *Tarikh-i-Salatin-i-Afghana*, p.24 and n, also p.33.
157. *Ibid.*, 45.
158. A Sikandari silver *tankah* was equal to 30 copper *Bahlolis* (Thomas, *Chronicles of the Pathan kings of Delhi*, p.336).
159. *Tarikh-i-Daudi*, Allahabad University Ms., fols. 137-38.
160. Afif, p.136.

there were two types of news-carriers: the mounted runners (*Aulaq*) and the foot runners (*Dhava*). The administration of the Sultanate, Sur and Mughal governments "was
greatly facilitated by an efficient postal service which
connected different parts of the empire."[161] According to
Pelsaert, postmen carrying their master's letters could
cover 25 to 30 *Kos* a day, but that was also because they ate
opium regularly.[162]

To sum up, Professor Mohammad Habib in his review
of G.N. Sharma's *Social Life in Medieval Rajasthan* (1500-
1800) has this to say about artisans and workers and their
wages in northern India of the Mughal times: "The industries of Rajasthan were well-developed, (but) further progress was made impossible owing to the low social position
assigned to the worker, forced labour or *begar* and administrative oppression of all types. 'The cultivator had to be
satisfied with a meagre reward for the hard work of
himself and his family'. The inventories of thefts committed show that a well-to-do peasant had two dhotis and
two turbans for himself, four saris costing about Rs. 2-4 for
his wife and some ten utensils costing Rs.25." The wages
recorded tell the same sad tale. "The account papers (1693-
1791 A.D.) of the construction of the palaces of Jaipur and
Kotah show that skilled labourers got annas 6 to 8 and a
supervising architect Rs.1/2 per day." The wages of unskilled labourers as mentioned in the Kotah records of
1689 A.D. vary from one anna to two annas. Payment was
sometimes made in grain—14 *Chataks* daily for skilled
workers and 2 to 4 *Chataks* for women workers. The
Bikaner *Bahis* throw some light on wages—a *chaukidar* Rs.2
per month, grooms, sweepers and gardeners Rs.1 to Rs.3
per month. "From the point of view of wages the prospects of government officials were not very encouraging."
The pay of officers of position, according to the Bikaner

---

161. Lal, *History of the Khaljis*, pp.167-77.
162. Pelsaert, p.62.

Bahi (V.S.1764) varied from Rs.21 to Rs.28 per month. An accountant's pay according to the Kotah records was Rs. 135 per year. An ordinary clerk could be engaged for Rs. 60 per year, while a senior clerk's pay was about Rs.235 a year. A *Kotwal* was generally paid Rs. 15 to 20 a month. Such low wages would only be possible with the low price of grain. According to Dr. Sharma 10 maunds of wheat could be purchased for Rs. 14 to 16; the same quantity of millet for Rs. 11 to 12 and of barley for Rs. 9 to 10.

The low scale of both grain prices and wages proves only one thing—the thorough exploitation of the peasants and the workers. But this was an Indian—and not a Rajasthani—misfortune. Tavernier, for example, could on his journey from Surat to Agra get 50 guards at Rs.4 per month each. The states and the governing classes tried to appropriate the whole surplus value of labour. Still the condition of the workers and peasants was probably better in Rajasthan than in the Mughal empire.[163] The situation in the Mughal empire is summed up by W.H. Moreland like this: "In several instances the lowest grades of servants were entitled to less than two rupees monthly (65 *dams* for a sweeper, 60 for a camel-driver, 70 for a wrestler, and so on), while the bulk of the menials and of the ordinary foot-soldiers began at less than three rupees. The minimum for subsistence at the court is probably marked by the lowest grade of slaves, who were allowed one *dam* daily, equivalent to three-quarters of a rupee monthly in the currency of the time...artisans were, as a rule badly off, and they can scarcely have been able to pay high wages to their journeymen... The facts available regarding the wages paid by travellers and merchants come almost entirely from the south and west of India. Terry insists on the excellence of the servants obtained for five shillings, or say two rupees

---

163. Review of Dr. G.N. Sharma, *Social Life in Medieval Rajasthan* (1500-1800) by Mohammad Habib, *Medieval India, A Miscellany*, Vol.II, Aligarh, 1972, pp.342-43.

a month, and he adds that they would send half this sum home; probably this statement relates to servants hired in Surat, but in any case it refers to this part of the country, as Terry went no farther north than Mandu. Valle, writing of Surat about ten years later put the rate at not more than three rupees, while De Laet's informants gave him from three to four rupees, which could be supplemented in some cases by commission charged on purchases. A messenger between Surat and Masulipatam was in 1641 allowed seven or eight *mahmudies* (say something between three and four rupees) for the journey... These instances appear to justify the conclusion that early in the seventeenth century foreigners could secure capable servants for somewhere about three rupees a month. What this represents in real wages is uncertain... (But) The rates struck Europeans as extraordinarily low, and taken with those which prevailed in the northern capital they enable us to understand the great development of domestic employement which...characterised the life of India at this period."[164] The important point to note is that servants, messengers and escorts were in great demand. Any journey seems to have been inconceivable without a certain number of them. William Hawkins, who was in India in Jahangir's reign, found that "almost a man cannot stir out of doors throughout all his dominions without great forces, for they are all become rebels". Tavernier said that, in about 1660, "to travel with honour in India, one hired 20 to 30 armed men, some with bows and arrows and others with muskets. They cost Rs.4 a month".[165] The profession must have been well organised and yet the wages were miserably low.

The economic position of artisans was no better. Bernier writing to Colbert, said: "No artisan can be expected to give his mind to his calling in the midst of a

---

164. Moreland, *India at the Death of Akbar*, pp.192-93.
165. Foster, *Early Travels*, pp.113,114; Tavernier, I, p.38.

people who are either wretchedly poor, or who, if rich, assume an appearance of poverty, and who regard not the beauty and excellence but the cheapness of an article; a people whose grandeess pay for a work of art considerably under its value and according to their own caprice... For it should not be inferred that the workman is held in esteem, or arrives at a stage of independence. Nothing but sheer necessity or blows from a cudgel keeps him employed; he never can become rich, and he feels it no trifling matter if he have the means of satisfying the cravings of hunger and of covering his body with the coarsest garment. If money be gained it does not in any measure go into his pocket, but only serves to increase the wealth of the merchant." Bernier's description is corroborated by what Thevenot was told about the same period of the state of the arts in Delhi.

The story of the exploitation of the poor, both rural and urban, is unending. And the guiding principle of this pernicious practice was to leave the people with bare subsistence. No foreign traveller fails to notice it with disapproval if not actual disgust. It would appear that the lords and the upper classes in Turco-Mughal India derived a cynical pleasure in oppressing the poor. The result was as expected. Artisans, workers and labourers became lazy. Scarcely any one made an effort to climb the ladder to better prospects,[166] so that "for a job which one man would do in Holland, here passes through four men's hands before it is finished."[167] Such exploitation in the Mughal period provided droves of *khidmatgars* to British officers and men when they established and ran their Raj in this country.

---

166. Bernier, p.228; Moreland, *India at the Death of Akbar*, p.187.
167. Pelsaert, p.60.

Poorest of the poor

Before closing, a word may be said about the exploitation of the poorest of the poor, the beggars and the handicapped. Muslim law decrees mutilation as punishment for certain crimes and a large number of healthy people were blinded, mutilated and made "physically handicapped" under Muslim rule. The punishments of sultans like Balban and Muhammad bin Tughlaq were terribly severe. Alauddin Khalji had ordered that if any shopkeeper sold any article short-weight, a quantity of flesh equal to the deficiency in weight was to be cut off from his haunches.[168] Firoz Tughlaq lists some of the punishments "for common offences", which were prevalent before his time. These comprised of cutting of hands and feet, noses and ears, putting out eyes, pulverizing the bones with mallets, burning parts of the body, nailing the hands and feet, hamstringing etc., etc.[169] As seen earlier, many cultivators and labourers were also reduced to the position of beggars from the Sultanate through Mughal times because of high rate and severity of collection of *Kharaj*.

All such unfortunate people could only resort to begging for a living. They were sometimes given doles and meals by kind-hearted people: free feeding (*langar*) was common for the poor beggars. But sometimes even such helpless people were exploited by the rich who extracted their pound of flesh even from them. An Amir by the name of Saiyyad-ul-Hijab was very close to Sultan Firoz Shah Tughlaq. He used to help all and sundry, but for a consideration. "It is narrated," says Shams Siraj Afif, "that one day a helpless *faqir* (beggar) approached him for assisting him get some help from the Sultan." The nobleman gave him necessary guidance for achieving his purpose. The *faqir* did as advised, and the Sultan ordered that the

---

168. Barani, p.316.
169. Firoz Shah, *Fatuhat-i-Firoz Shahi*, Aligarh, 1954, p.2.

suppliant be given one *tankah* per day from the Zakat fund. But the help rendered was not gratuitous. "The said Amir," continues Afif, "after rendering help to the needy used to extract something by way of *shukrana*."[170] No further comment is necessary.

170. Afif, pp.446-50.

Chapter 8

The Legacy of Muslim Rule in India

"Muslim rule should not attract any criticism. Mention of destruction of temples by Muslim invaders and rulers should not be mentioned."

Circular, Boards of Secondary Education

The end of Muslim rule in India was as spasmodic as its beginning. It took five hundred years for its establishment (712-1206) and one hundred and fifty years for its decline and fall (1707-1857). The benchmarks of its establishment are C.E. 712 when Muhammad bin Qasim invaded Sind, 1000 when Mahmud of Ghazni embarked upon a series of expeditions against Hindustan, 1192-1206 when Prithviraj Chauhan lost to Muhammad Ghauri and Qutbuddin Aibak set up the Turki Sultanate at Delhi, and 1296 when Alauddin Khalji pushed into the Deccan. The stages of its downfall are 1707 when Aurangzeb died, 1739 when a trembling Mughal Emperor stood as a suppliant before the Persian invader Nadir Shah, 1803 when Delhi was captured by the British, and 1858 when the last Mughal ruler was sent to Rangoon as a prisoner of the "Raj".

For five centuries—thirteenth to seventeenth—however, most parts of India were under Muslim rule, though with varying degrees of effectiveness in different regions of the country. But at no single point of time was the whole country ruled exclusively by the Muslims. On the other hand the five hundred year long Muslim rule did not fail to influence Indian political and cultural life in all its facets. Muslim rule apart, Muslim contact with India can be counted from the seventh century itself. Naturally, the interaction of Muslim culture with the Hindu way of life, backed by the superimposition of Muslim rule in India, gave rise to a sort of a common Indian culture. But only a sort of, there is a superficial veneer about it. On the face of it the influence of Islam on Indian culture is to be seen in all spheres of life, in architecture, painting, music, and literature; in social institutions like marriage ceremonies, in eating habits, in gourmet and cuisine, sartorial fashions and so on. In actual fact, Hindus and Muslims lead their own lives, mostly in isolation from one another's, except for personal friendships. Even living together for a thousand years has not welded Hindus and Muslims into one people. Why is it so?

Because Islam believes in dividing humanity into believers and Kafirs, the Muslim community (Ummah) is enjoined not to cooperate on the basis of equality or peaceful coexistence with Kafirs. To them it offers some alternatives—conversion to Islam, or death, or slavery. At the most it allows survival on payment of a poll-tax, *Jiziyah*, and acceptance of a second class status, that of *Zimmi*. As a matter of fact, Muhammadans invaded India to turn it into a land of Islam and spread their culture. Islamic culture is carrier culture, borrowed from exotic streams. The main contribution of Islamic culture is Quran and Hadis. It invaded Indian culture not to co-exist with it but to wipe it out. Its declared aim was Islamization through Jihad. But in spite of repeated endeavours through invasions and centuries of Muslim rule, India could not be turned into a Muslim country. Had India been completely converted to Islam, its people, like those of Iran or Libya, would have taken pride in organising Islamic revolutions, spearheading pan-Islamic movements and espousing right-or-wrong Islamic causes. Or, had Hindus the determination and the wherewithal to throw out Islam from India as was done by the Christians in some countries like Spain, there would have been no Muslim problem in India today. But here Muslims stay put, and yet a thousand years of Muslim contact failed to Islamize India. India, therefore, provides a good study to evaluate the achievements and failures, atrocities and beneficences, fundamentalism and "secularism" of Muslim rule and Muslim people. In the appraisement of Muslim rule, Muslim religion also cannot escape scrutiny, for the former was guided by the latter, the one being inseparable from the other. This makes the assessment of the legacy of Muslim rule in India an extremely controversial subject. Its contribution comprises of both bitterness and distrust on the one hand and on the other a composite common culture. We shall take up the common culture first.

So much has already been written about the development of Indo-Muslim composite culture, its 'give and take' and its heritage, that it is neither necessary nor possible to touch upon all its aspects. Therefore only a few areas may be taken up—like music and architecture—in which Muslims have made special and substantial contribution. In other branches of fine arts like painting, the story too is familiar. Many Mughal paintings bear the touch of Ajanta or its regional variations, while Rajput and Pahari *Qalam* adopted a lot from Muslim miniature style and art of portraiture. Equally important is the Muslim contribution in the sphere of jewellery, textiles, pottery etc. In the fields of sport and athletics, again, Muslim participation has been both extensive and praiseworthy.

Music

It is in the domain of music in particular that the contribution of Muslims is the greatest. It is, however, difficult to claim that it is really Muslim. What they have practised since medieval times is Hindu classical music with its *Guru-Shishya parampara*. The *gharana* (school) system is the extension of this *parampara* or tradition. Most of the great Muslim musicians were and are originally Hindu and they have continued with the tradition of singing an invocation to goddess Saraswati or other deities before starting their performance.

Be that as it may, all Muslim rulers and nobles had musicians — singers and players on instruments — in their courts.[1] They patronised the meritorious by giving them high salaries and rich rewards. They got a number of books on music translated from Sanskrit into Persian. Some of them used to get so much involved in poetry and music that sometimes it was done at the cost of state work. There are many reasons for this phenomenon. The Indian system of notation is perhaps the oldest and most elaborate.[2] There are *ragas* meant to be sung in winter, in summer, in rains and in autumn. There are month-wise *ragas* meant to be sung during the twelve months of the year (*baramasa*). There are *ragas* meant for singing in the morning, early noon, afternoon and in the evenings. There are *ragas*, it is claimed, that can light a lamp or bring about downpour of rain. Then there are *ragas* and *raginis* designated for dance. Dance in its art form is as elaborate as music, and is based on Hindu *natya-shastra*. Sculptures of dancers and musicians carved on ancient and medieval temples, now mostly surviving in south India, bear testimony to their excellence, popularity and widespread practice.

In such a situation Muslims could add little to this art from outside. Officially music and dance are banned in Islam. Muslim ruling classes therefore could only patronise Hindu classical music in its original form. Some rulers were patrons of artistes, others practised it themselves,

---

1. Barani, pp.199-200.
2. Gaurishankar Hirachand Ojha, *Madhya Kalin Bharatiya Sanskriti*, pp.193-94.

many others collected musicians from all over the country. That is how Mian Tansen could earn so much renown. Amir Khusrau is also credited with composing songs some of which are popular to this day. Under the Khaljis there were concerts and competitions arranged between Hindustani and Karnatak musicians.[3] Indian classical music flourished throughout the medieval period, although classical Indian dancing drifted from the aesthetic and religious sphere into the *salons* of courtesans and dancing girls.

Abul Fazl writes about the Mughal emperor Akbar that "His Majesty pays much attention to music and is the patron of all who practice this enchanting art".[4] About Tansen he says that "a singer like him had not been in India for the last one thousand years." Tansen was originally a Gaur Brahman of Gwalior and he had been trained in the school established by Raja Man Singh Tomar of Gwalior (C.E. 1486-1518). The Raja was the author of a treatise on music entitled *Man Kutuhal*. He also got the *Ragadarpan* translated into Persian. Similarly, during the reign of Firoz Tughlaq (1351-88) was composed *Ghunyat-ul-Munya* by a Muslim scholar of Gujarat. Under the patronage of Sikandar Lodi was written the *Lahjat-i-Sikandar Shahi* by one Umar Yahiya. Yahiya was a scholar of Arabic, Persian and Sanskrit and his work is based on many Sanskrit treatises like *Sangit Ratnakar*,[5] *Nritya Ratnakar*, *Sangit Kalpataru* and the works of Matang.[6]

Most Muslim rulers, nobles and elite passionately patronised Indian classical music and dance and therefore there is no need to mention their names or those of their musicians. But Vincent Smith aptly notes that "the fact that many of the names are Hindu, with the title Khan

---

3. Beale, T.W., *Oriental Biographical Dictionary*, p.145. Also Amir Khusrau's *Ghurrat-ul-Kamal*.
4. *Ain*, I, p.681.
5. By Sarang Deva, a contemporary of Alauddin Khalji (1296-1316).
6. *Islamic Culture*, 1954, pp.411, 415.

added, indicates that the professional artists at a Muhammadan court often found it convenient and profitable to conform to Islam."[7] There is another interesting fact noticeable. The Indian classical music which became "national" music about the time of Akbar in Agra holds the field even to this day. Political or religious barriers have failed to divide musicians and lovers of music into narrow or antagonistic camps, as the Hindu classical music remains the common legacy of both Hindus and Muslims.[8]

Medieval Monuments

But if music unites, many monuments of the medieval period revive bitter memories in the Hindu mind.These are found almost in every city, every town and even in many villages either in a dilapidated state or under preservation by the Archaeological Survey of India. Many of these have been converted from Hindu *temples* and now are extant in the shape of *mosques, Idgahs, Dargahs, Ziarats* (shrines) *Sarais* and *Mazars* (tombs) *Madrasas* and *Maktabs*. Throughout the Muslim rule destruction of Hindu shrines and construction of mosques and other building from their materials and at their very sites went on as a normal practice. From the Quwwal-ul-Islam mosque in Delhi built out of twenty-seven Hindu and Jain temples in the twelfth century to the Taj-ul-Masajid built from hundreds of Hindu and Jain temples at Bhopal in the eighteenth century, the story is the same everywhere.

For temples were not broken only during war, but in times of peace too. Sultan Firoz Shah Tughlaq writes: "I destroyed their idol temples, and instead thereof raised mosques...where infidels and idolaters worshipped idols, Musalmans now, by God's mercy, perform their devotion

---

7. Smith, *Akbar the Great Mogul*, p.306.
8. For details and reference, see Lal, *History of the Khaljis*, pp.334-39; *Twilight of the Sultanate*, pp.241-44; *The Mughal Harem*, pp.124ff, 167ff. Also Smith, *op.cit.*, pp.306-07.

to the true God."⁹ And so said and did Sikandar Lodi, Shahjahan,¹⁰ Aurangzeb and Tipu Sultan. Shams Siraj Afif writes that some sovereigns like Muhammad Tughlaq and Firoz Tughlaq were "specially chosen by the Almighty from among the faithful, and in the whole course of their reigns, whenever they took an idol temple, they broke and destroyed it."¹¹

Why did Muslim conquerors and rulers break temples? They destroyed temples because it is enjoined by their scriptures. In the history of Islam, iconoclasm and razing other peoples' temples are central to the faith. They derive their justification and validity from the Quranic Revelation and the Prophet's *Sunna* or practice. Shrines and idols of unbelievers began to be destroyed during the Prophet's own time and, indeed at his behest. Sirat-un-Nabi, the first pious biography of the Prophet, tells us how during the earliest days of Islam, young men at Medina influenced by Islamic teachings used to break idols. However, desecration and destruction began in earnest when Mecca was conquered. Umar was chosen for destroying the pictures on the walls of the shrine at Kabah. *Tarikh-i-Tabari* tells us that raiding parties were sent in all directions to destroy the images of deities held in special veneration by different tribes including the images of al-Manat, al-Lat and al-Uzza.¹² Because of early successes at home, Islam developed a full-fledged theory of iconoclasm.¹³ India too suffered terribly. Thousands of Hindu shrines and edifices disappeared in northern India by the

9. *Fatuhat-i-Firoz Shahi*, E and D, III, pp.380-381.
10. Abdul Hamid Lahori, *Badshah Nama*, Bib. Ind. Text, I, p.402; J.N. Sarkar, *History of Aurangzeb*, III, pp.290-291.
11. Afif, E and D, III, p.318.
12. Arun Shourie et al, *Hindu Temples: What Happened to Them*, New Delhi, 1990, pp.30-31.
13. Margoliouth, D.S., *Mohammed and the Rise of Islam*, pp.24, 377-409; Hitti, P.K., *The Arabs*, p.28; Gibbon, Edward, *Decline and Fall of the Roman Empire*, II, pp.649-660.

time of Sikandar Lodi and Babur. Since the wreckage of
Hindu temples became scarcer and scarcer to obtain, from
the time of Akbar onwards many Muslim buildings began
to be constructed, not from the debris of Hindu temples,
but from materials specially prepared for them like pillars,
screens etc. Alauddin Khalji's Alai Darwaza at Delhi,
Akbar's Buland Darwaza at Fatehpur Sikri and Adil
Shah's Gol Gumbaz at Bijapur are marvels of massive
elegance, while Humayun's tomb at Delhi and Taj Mahal
at Agra are beauteous monuments in stone and marble.
Any people would be proud of such monuments, and the
Indians are too. But for an if. If there was no reckless
vandalism in breaking temples and utilizing their materials in constructing Muslim buildings which lie scattered
throught the country, Hindu psyche would not be hurt.
Will Durant rightly laments in *Story of Civilization* that
"We can never know from looking at India to-day, what
grandeur and beauty she once possessed." Thus in the
field of architecture, the legacy is a mix of pride and de-
jection. With impressive Muslim monuments, there is a
large sprinkling of converted monuments which are an
eye-sore to the vast majority of the population.

Conversions and Tabligh

Similar is the hurt felt about forcible conversions to
Islam, another legacy of Muslim conquest and rule in Hindustan.

Impatient of delay, Muslim invaders, conquerors and
kings openly and unscrupulously converted people to
Islam by force. Muhammad bin Qasim invaded Sind in
C.E. 712. Whatever place he captured like Alor, Nirun,
Debal, Sawandari, Kiraj, and Multan, therein he forcibly
converted people to Islam. Mahmud Ghaznavi invaded
Hindustan seventeen times, and every time he came he
converted people from Peshawar to Mathura and Kashmir
to Somnath. Such was the insistence on the conversion of

the vanquished Hindu princes that many rulers just fled before Mahmud even without giving a battle.[14] Al Qazwini writes in his *Asar-ul-Bilad* that when Mahmud went "to wage religious war against India, he made great efforts to capture and destroy Somnath, in the hope that the Hindus would then become Muhammadans".[15] The exploits of Mahmud Ghaznavi in the field of forced prose-lytization were cherished for long. His example was pre-sented as the model before all good Muslim rulers, as early as the fourteenth century by Ziyauddin Barani in his *Fatawa-i-Jahandari* and as late as the close of the eighteenth century by Muhammad Aslam in his *Farhat-un-Nazirin*.[16] There were forcible conversion both during the war and in peace. Sikandar Butshikan in Kashmir to Tipu Sultan in Mysore, Mahmud Beghara in Gujarat to Jalaluddin Mu-hammad in Bengal, all Muslim rulers carried on large-scale forcible conversions through *jihad*.

This *jihad* never ceased in India and forcible conver-sions continued to take place, not only in the time of Mahmud Ghaznavi, Timur or Aurangzeb, but throughout the medieval period. It is argued that the aim of Muham-madans is to spread Islam, and it is nowhere laid down that it should be propagated only through peaceful means. Others point out that a choice was always there—Islam or death. Some others, seeking civilizational modes, assert that conversions were effected in peaceful ways by Sufi Mashaikh. Many others say that Sufis were not interested in proselytization. Whatever the means employed, Islam being a proselytizing religion, Muslim conquerors, rulers, nobles, Sufis, Maulvis, traders and soldiers all worked as its missionaries in one way or the other. But the most abundant, extensive and overwhelming evidence in con-temporary Persian chronicles is about forced conver-

14. Elliot's trs. II, p.49.
15. Elliot's trs. I, p.98.
16. Eng. trs. Elliot, VIII, p.171.

sions.[17]

During the medieval period, forcible and hurried conversions to Islam left most of the neo-Muslims half-Hindus. With his conversion to Islam the average Muslim did not change his old Hindu environment and tenor of life. The neo-Muslims' love of Hinduism was because of their attachment to their old faith and culture.[18] High class converted Hindus sometimes went back to Hinduism and their old privileges.[19] At others the various classes of which the new Muslim community was composed began to live in separate quarters in the same city as described by Mukundram in the case of Bengal. Their isolation gave them some sort of security against external interference. On the other hand "Indian Islam slowly began to assimilate the broad features of Hinduism".[20] Such a scenario obtained throughout the country. A few examples would suffice to bring out the picture clearly.

In the northwest part of the country the Ismaili Khojas of the Panjbhai community were followers of the Agha Khan. They paid *zakat* to the Agha Khan, but regarded Ali as the tenth incarnation of Vishnu. Instead of the Quran, they read a manual prepared by one of their *Pirs*, Sadr-uddin. Their prayers contained a mixture of Hindu and Islamic terms. The Zikris and Dais of Makran in Baluchistan, read the Quran, but regarded the commands of Muhammad to have been superseded by those of the Mahdi, whom they followed. They set up their Kaba at Koh-i-

17. Those interested in detailed references may see my book *Growth of Muslim Population in Medieval India*, Research Publication, New Delhi, 1973, pp.14, 97-146, 159-164. Also my *Indian Muslims: Who Are They*. For justification of force in spread of Islam, Shah Walliullah, *Tafsir-i-Fath-ur Rahman*, cited in Harsh Narain, *Myths of Composite Culture*, p.57.

18. Amir Khusrau, *I'jaz-i-Khusravi*, 5 Parts, Lucknow, 1875-76, I, p.169.

19. As the Hindu reformers discovered, "the fire of Brahmanical spirit burns in a Brahman up to six generations". See Gupta in *Journal of the Department of Letters*, Calcutta University, cited in Ashraf, *Life and Conditions of the People of Hindustan*, p.194 n.

20. Ashraf, *op. cit.*, p. 191.

Murad, and went there on pilgrimage at the same time as the orthodox Muslims went to Mecca.[21]

In Gujarat, where Islam appeared early in the medieval period, besides Khojas and Mahdawis, there were a number of tribal or sectarian groups like Sidis, Molislams, Kasbatis, Rathors, Ghanchis, Husaini Brahmans, Shaikhs and Kamaliyas whose beliefs and practices could not be fitted into any Islamic pattern. The Sidis were descendants of Africans imported as slaves mainly from Somaliland. The Molislams, Rathors and Kasbatis were segments of converted Rajput tribes, who did not give up worshipping their Hindu gods or observing their Hindu festivals. The Rathors claimed to be *Sunnis* but did not perform the daily prayers or read the Quran. The Ghanchis found mainly around Godhra were believed to abhor all other Muslims and to be well inclined towards Hindus.[22] Near Ahmedabad, the Shaikhs and Shaikhzadas of Gujarat adopted both Hindu and Muslim rituals in marriage, employing the services of a *Faqir* and a Brahman. The half-converted *Sunni* Rathors of Gujarat intermarried with Hindus and Muslims, which was characteristic of Kasbatis also. In Gujarat, north of Ahmedabad, tribals like Kolis, Bhils, Sindhis, though converted to Islam, remained aboriginals in customs and habits.[23]

In the coastal towns and western Rajasthan, the Husaini Brahmans called themselves followers of *Atharvaveda* and derived their names from Imam Husain. They did not eat beef. The men dressed like Muslims, but put on *tilak*. They did not practice circumcision. At the same time they fasted during Ramzan and followed other Muslim practices. They held Khwaja Muin-ud-din Chishti of Ajmer in special reverence. The Shaikhs and Shaikh-

21. Imperial Gazetteer of India, Provincial Series, Baluchistan, p.30.
22. Gazetteer of Bombay Presidency, Vol.III, Baroda (Bombay, 1899), p.226. Also Vol. VII, Baroda, p.72.
23. Gazetteer of the Bombay Presidency, Vol. IX, Pt. II, pp.64, 69.

zadas did not practice circumcision but put on *tilak* mark. They did not eat with the Muslims but buried their dead like the Muslims. The Kamaliyas did not circumcise, and except that they buried the dead all their ceremonies were Hindu. The Momnas of Cutch professed to belong to the *Shia* sect of the Muslims but they did not eat flesh, did not practice circumcision, did not say the daily prayers or keep the fast of Ramzan.

In Madhya Pradesh, in district Nimar, was a sect known as Pirzada. Their supreme deity was the tenth incarnation of Vishnu. Their religious book was compiled from the religious literature of the Hindus and Muslims. The Pirzadas were Muslims, though for all intents and purposes they were Hindus.[24] "Of the Muslims living in the rural areas of what was formerly known as the Central Provinces and Berar, and in the districts of Thana, Ahmadnagar and Bijapur, it could be said generally that they were three-fourths Hindu."[25] The Qasais of Thana, Ahmadnagar and Bijapur abhorred beef-eating to such an extent that they would not even touch a beef-butcher, and they avoided mixing with Muslims, though a Qazi was engaged for marriage ceremonies and funerals. In Ahmadnagar, the butchers or *Baqar Qasabs* and the *Pinjaras* or cotton carders still worshipped Hindu gods and had idols in their houses.[26] In Bijapur, in addition to the *Qasabs* and *Pinjaras*, the *Baghbans* (gardeners), *Kanjars*, poulterers, rope-makers and grass-cutters, though professing to be Muslim, had such strong attachment to their old faith, that they did not associate with other Muslims and openly worshipped Hindu gods. This was not so only with the very low classes. Some Deshmukhs and Deshpandes of Buldana professed the Muslim religion, but employed

---

24. Central Provinces District Gazetteers, XIV, Nimar (Allahabad, 1908), p.63.
25. M. Mujeeb, *The Indian Muslims*, pp.17-18.
26. Central Provinces District Gazetteers, XIII, p.296.

Brahmans in secret to worship their old tutelar deities.[27]

In Southern India, especially along the sea-coast, Islam came directly from Arabia through Arab traders. Still the Muslims were very largely affected by environment generally in dress and food, manners and customs. The South does not, of course, form a homogeneous unit, the Muslims of Mysore and Bangalore being much closer culturally to those of Hyderabad than to the Moplahs and Navayats of Kerala, who are geographically much nearer. But the divergence is in manners and customs, and not in belief.

In Uttar Pradesh, and in the central parts of Bihar, there were fairly large semi-converted neo-Muslim tribes. North of the Ganga in the district of Purnea, while there were educated and orthodox Muslims also, the dividing line between the religious beliefs and practices of the lower class Hindus and Muslims was very thin indeed. In every village could be found a shrine dedicated to the worship of goddess *Kali* and almost in every house a *Khudai Ghar*, and in their prayers the names of both *Allah* and *Kali* were invoked. A part of the Muslim marriage ceremony was performed at the shrine of the goddess *Bhagwati*. The most popular deity among both Hindus and Muslims was *Devata Maharaj*. In the Barasat and Bashirhat sub-divisions of 24-Parganas the Muslim woodcutters and fishermen venerated *Mubrah* (*Mubarak*?) Ghazi. In the Chittagong district, Pir Badar was venerated by Hindu as well as Muslim sailors as their guardian saint.

In western India, midway between Thatta and Mirpur Sakro in Sind was followed the cult of Pir Jhariyon, saint of trees. In the east, in 24-Parganas, *Rakshaya Chandi* (*Kali*) was worshipped in the form of trees which would be smeared with vermillion.[28] Between the two extreme

27. Central Provinces District Gazetteers, XVII, Seoni (Allahabad, 1907), p.221.
28. Bengal District Gazetteers, XXXI, 24-Parganas (Calcutta, 1914), pp.74-76.

points tree worship was common throughout the country.
There was snake worship too. The Hindus celebrated *Nag
Panchami*, the Bengali sub-caste of Muslims living in the
Kishangunj sub-division built shrines for *Baishahari*, the
snake-goddess.

Back in the west, in Karnal a large number of Muslim
peasants were, till 1865, worshipping their old village deities, though as Muslims they repeated the *kalima* and practised circumcision.[29] In Bharatpur and Alwar, Meos and
Minas continued with their Hindu names or suffixed them
with Khan, and celebrated not only Diwali and Dashehra
but most important Janamashtami. Because of geohistoric
traditions of proximity to Mathura and Vrindavan,
Krishna is integrated into Muslim consciousness at folk
level in the Brij and Mewat area — but not eleswhere. Few
Meos and Minas could recite the *kalima*, but they went on
pilgrimage to the tombs of Salar Mas'ud Ghazi at Bahraich
and Muin-ud-din Chishti at Ajmer. The Meos, like the
Hindus, did not marry within the *gotra* or family group
having the same surname, and their daughters were not
entitled to inherit.[30] The Minas worshipped Bhairon, a
form of Shiva, and Hanuman. A little to the south, in Jaora
in Central India, Muslim cultivators followed Hindu customs in their marriages, worshipped *Shitla* or deity of
small-pox and fixed *toran* (decorated band) on the door
during wedding. In Central India, again, around Indore,
Muslim Patels and Mirdhas had Hindu names, dressed
exactly like Hindus and some of them recognised *Bhawani*
and other Hindu deities. The Nayatas of Khajrana, converted by their urban neighbours, continued with their
Hindu ways.[31]

---

29. Mujeeb, *op.cit.*, p.10.
30. Alwar Gazetteer, pp.37ff., 70.
31. Indore State Gazetteer (Calcutta, 1908), p.59. For references to Gazetteers and some additional information on observance of Hindu manners
and customs by neo-Muslims, see Mujeeb, *op. cit.*, pp.9-25.

This is an assortment of the religious beliefs of mainly uneducated, lower class, rural-based Indian Muslims. But the facts have been placed in the past tense, because conditions may have changed during the last few years for as a religious community Indian Muslims are being continuously turned into firm believers in "pure" Islam. Ordinarily there should be nothing unusual or strange in the above picture. There are local, environmental and traditional influences among Muslims everywhere. Even in urban areas, even among educated Muslims, such distinctions exist, and Muslims of Aligarh, Hyderabad and Srinagar are different from each other in many ways. Many Christians of Eastern Europe had converted to Islam during the period of the Ottoman empire. They have not discarded their European way of life. In India, however, Muslims who continue to retain their old traditions and habits are considered to be only half-converted. If left alone they might help in religious syncretization which is traditional to India. But persistent efforts are made by upper class educated Muslims to turn them into *pucca* (confirmed) Musalmans. The process is called *Tabligh*. This is due as much to the fear of these half-converts reverting to their old faith as to the determination to turn Indian Muslims into the Arabic brand.

Only one or two cases of *tablighi* endeavour may be discussed in some detail. We have spoken of the Molislams of Gujarat. Molislams or Maula-i-Salaam are so called as they bear the *Mohar* or stamp of Islam. Else they are Hindus and are known as Garasiyas. Originally Rajputs, they were converted in the time of Sultan Mahmud Beghara (1458-1511). They are about two lakhs in number and live mainly in Bharuch, Kheda and Ahmedabad. Many of the Garasiyas have both Hindu and Muslim names. They have retained their Hindu customs and traditions. In their marriages *mandap*-setting ceremony and *garba*-type dance are prominent. Their mar-

riages are performed both by Maulvis and Brahmans. But
recently efforts have been made to wean them away from
their Hindu ways and turn them into confirmed Muslims.

Similarly, in Mewat, converts to Islam have ever remained half-Hindu. Many such converts do not have even
Muslim names: they have only Hindu names like "Ram
Singh, Ram Din and Jai Singh". Islamic fundamentalists
fearing that some of them might revert to their original
faith have organised repeated preachings to make them
into *pucca* Muslims. Some modern works throw light on
this activity. Shah Muhammad Ramzan (1769-1825) was a
crusading *tablighi* of Haryana. He found that the converted
Rajputs and Jats (Muslim Rajputs and Maula Jats) were in
no way different from their Hindu counterparts in culture,
customs and celebrations of religious festivals. They were
not only *pir-parast* (Guru-worshippers) and *qabr-parast*
(Grave-worshippers); they were also idol-worshippers.
Muslim Rajputs worshipped in Thakurdwaras. They celebrated Holi, Diwali and other Hindu festivals with zeal
and dressed in the Hindu fashion. Shah Muhammad
Ramzan used to sojourn in areas inhabited by such converted Rajputs, dissuade them from practising Hindu rites
and persuade them to marry their cousins (real uncle's
daughters which converts persistently refused to do).
They equally detested eating cow's flesh. To induce them
to eat beef, he introduced new festivals like Mariyam ka
Roza and 'Rot-bot'. On this day, observed on 17 Rajjab, a
'pao' of roasted beef placed on a fried bread, was distributed amongst relatives and near and dear ones. Shah Muhammad also encouraged such people to build mosques in
large numbers. Such endeavours have ruled out the possi-
bility of reconversion and have helped in the "Islamization"of neo-Muslims. Curiously enough, this *tablighi*
was killed by his co-religionist Bohras at Mandsaur in
Madhya Pradesh.

Another *tablighi*, Muhammad Abdul Shakur, was more
vituperative against the prevalence of Hindu customs

among the Muslims. He raved against the barbarous (*wahshiana*) dress of the Hindus like *dhoti, ghaghra* and *angia* and advocated wearing of "*kurta, amama, kurti, pyjama* and *orhni* (or long Chadar)". He attacked Hindu marriage cutoms practised by Muslims and warned women against participating in marriages with their faces uncovered. He insisted on women observing *parda* and was shocked to find that even after a thousand years of their conversion during the expeditions of Mahmud of Ghazni, Indian Muslims were living like Hindus. In the end he exhorted the senior Mewati Muslims thus: "Oh Muslims, the older people of Mewat, I appeal to you in a friendly way, doing my *tablighi* duty, to give up all idolatrous and illegal (*mushrikana*) ways of the Hindus....Islam has laid down rules for all social and cultural conduct...follow them."[32]

Such *tablighis* are still busy in their mission in Mewat and other regions. Along with this, fresh conversions to Islam are also going on from Ladakh to Gujarat and from Kerala to Assam, creating tensions in society. A report in the *Times of India* datelined New Delhi 14 August 1989 says: "When Pakistan *zindabad* slogans were raised first time on the streets of Leh recently, it came as a shock to the Buddhist people of Ladakh. Said Mr. P. Stobdan, a scholar from Ladakh now working in Delhi: 'For centuries, the Ladakhi Buddhists and Muslims lived together in harmony. Even inter-marriages were common among them. What had destroyed the secular traditon of Ladakh was the systematic attempt at conversion of Buddhists to Islam.' But above all was the fear of the proselytizing drive which threatened to 'eliminate the 84 per cent Buddhists

---

32. Manzur-ul-Haqq Siddiqi, *Massir-ul-Jadad*, published by al-Maktaba al-Saifia, Shish Mahal Road, Lahore, 1964, pp.94-115, esp. pp.98, 106, Muhammad Abdul Shakur, *Aslah-i-Mewat*, Sadar Bazar, Delhi, 1925, pp.2-3, 35-40. Also see K.C. Yadav, "Urdu Sahityakaron ki Haryanvi ko den", in *Harigandha*, September-October, 1989, pp.26-28 for similar literature.

as a religious group'. Within the framework of this new consciousness, according to Mr. Stobden, "the Ladakhis considered themselves to be patriotic citizens of India, the land of the Buddha. However, because of the policy of appeasement of the Centre towards the Kashmiris and the consequent neglect of Ladakhis, a sense of disillusionment was growing among people of the region."

In Assam and other regions of the east, Bangladeshis are being brought in large numbers to raise Muslim numbers. In Kerala and Tamilnadu, Gulf money is being openly utilized for proselytization work. The 1980 conversions in Meenakshipuram provide a classic example.

There are stages of conversion and exploitation. First, non-Muslims are converted to Islam through means which are neither mysterious nor edifying. Then, after conversion, they are treated as inferior Muslims or riff-raff. No effort is made to improve their economic condition. The sole concentration is on increasing Muslim numbers through more and more conversions and unrestricted procreation. Lastly, their leaders inculcate in them a spirit of alienation towards their ancestral society, culture and religion as well as their native land.

It would be worthwhile to note that a substantial number of Muslim students start their education in *madrasas* attached to mosques. Most of those in other schools do not proceed beyond the IInd or IIIrd class. And the remaining drop out after matriculation. There may be various reasons for it but primarily they are religious, for money received from abroad is spent on building mosques and making converts rather than on secular education. The Muslim child from the first day learns of *"momins"* and *"kafirs"*. He is taught that the main aim of his life is devotion to Islam which obliquely tells him of *"Dar-ul-Islam"* and *"Dar-ul-Harb"*. In a very subtle way he learns that to kill or convert a *kafir* is a *"kar-e-sawab"*, a pious act. A tempting picture of heaven is projected before his mind and he learns about the fairies waiting for him there if he goes there as a *"ghazi"* or martyr.[33] Indian Muslims do not always attempt to sort out their problems within the country. They look to Pakistan for inspiration and support. Through Pakistan they look to the whole Umma. That is what makes them aggressive and violent even when they are in a minority. That is why they dare break temples in Kashmir and Bangladesh even to-day. For accomplishing such tasks petro-dollars received from abroad and fundamentalism at home are brought into full play. The tensions generated by this process in various parts of the country is a permanent legacy of Muslim rule in India.

Muslim Fundamentalism

Iconoclasm, proselytization, *tabligh* and Islamization in general have been due to Muslim fundamentalism. Muslim fundamentalism finds no virtue in any non-Muslim culture, it only believes in destroying every other culture and superimposing Muslim culture.

It is, therefore, necessary to understand the meaning of the word "fundamentalism" because it is loosely and unintelligibly applied to both Hindu and Muslim faiths and their followers are unwittingly called fundamentalists day in and day out. The Oxford Concise Dictionary defines fundamentalism as "maintenance, in opposition to modernism, of traditional orthodox beliefs such as the inerrancy of scripture..." and fundamental as "base or foundation, essential, primary, original". Hindus and Muslims can both be fanatics, but it is only Muslims (and

---

33. For the traditional education of Muslim children in *Madrasas*, see Ram Gopal, *Indian Muslims, op.cit.,* pp.55-57. For their learning "political fanaticism" see S. Maqbul Ahmad, "Madrasa System of Education and Indian Muslim Society", in *Indian and Contemporary Islam,* ed. by S.T. Lokhandwala, Simla, 1971, p.32.

For conversions in Meenakshipuram, Puliangudi and other places, see *Politics of Conversion* ed. by Devendra Swarup, Deendayal Research Institute, New Delhi, 1986, pp.7-70.

Christians) who can be fundamentalists. For the Muslim sticks to the "traditional orthodox belief" that there is no God but Allah and Muhammad is His Prophet. No Muslim can question this belief. As Ishtiaq Husain Qureshi says: "The Quran is believed by every Muslim to be the Word of God revealed to his Prophet Muhammad."[34] This Word of God cannot be amended, it cannot be changed, because "Not even the Prophet could change the revelation".[35] "There are no local variations of the Muslim Law."[36] It is this which is fundamentalism. There is nothing compared to it in Hinduism where every thing can be questioned and all kinds of religious innovations and digressions are accepted. "This (Muslim) Law was the sovereign in Muslim lands: no one was above it, and all were ruled by it."[37] Under Islamic law a non-Muslim could not be accorded full citizentship of the state. Only against payment of *Jiziyah* could he receive protection of life.[38] *Jiziyah* also seems to have been an instrument of humiliation for the *Zimmis* (non-Muslims).[39] Muslim rulers not only followed the Islamic law to the best of their own ability and the knowledge of the Ulama, they kept the non-Muslims under all kinds of disabilities and thraldom.

It is not widely known that the Turco-Mughal Muslim rule saw to it that Muslims should not come closer to the Hindus, and that the one should dominate the other.[40] Ziyauddin Barani the historian, Ibn Battuta the foreign traveller and Vidyapati the poet did not fail to notice the insulting attitude of the Muslims towards the Hindus.[41]

34. I.H. Qureshi, *Administration of the Sultanate of Delhi*, p.42.
35. *Loc. cit.*
36. *Ibid.*, p.43.
37. *Ibid.*, p.42. Also Khuda Bakhsh, *Essays Indian and Islamic*, p.51.
38. Aghnides, N.P., *Muhammadan Theories of Finance*, pp.399, 528.
39. Tritton, A.S., *Caliphs and their Non-Muslim Subjects*, p.21. Also Hitti, *History of the Arabs*, pp.119, 171.
40. Amir Khusrau, *Deval Rani Khizr Khan*, Persian Text, p.50.
41. Barani, p.262; Ibn Battuta, p.124; Vidyapati, *Kirtilata*, pp.42-44, 70-72.

The inferior status accorded to the non-Muslims under Islamic law kept the Hindus and the Muslims apart. For example, although monotheism, iconoclasm and proselytization have no spiritual sanction or superiority, the Muslim rulers turned temples into mosques and converted people to Islam by force. But the Hindus were not permitted to convert *Muslims to Hinduism*. Such was the policy of the Muslim rulers in this regard that even if a Hindu proclaimed or preached that Hinduism was as good as Islam, he was awarded capital punishment.[42] This was the general policy. Only Akbar was liberal insofar as he permitted those Hindus who had been forcibly converted to Islam and wished to return to their original faith, to go back to Hinduism. But only Akbar, not even all his officers in his extensive empire. Jahangir did not permit people to embrace Hinduism even of their own free will.[43] Under Shahjahan, apostasy from Islam had again become a capital crime, and so also any critical comment on Muhammad.

Inter-communal marriages would have encouraged equality but these were partially banned in the medieval period, partially insofar as that while Muslims married Hindu women freely, the rulers would not permit Muslim girls to marry Hindus. Contrary to general belief, Hindus have had no inhibitions about marrying women of other nationalities and religions. There is the well-known instance of Chandragupta Maurya marrying the daughter of Seleucus Nikotor. Of course, Chandragupta was a king and kings used to contract such alliances. But throughout the medieval period, Hindus used to marry non-Hindus and foreigners without prejudice in Southeast Asia or countries to which they migrated. Even today Hindus marry in America, Britain, Germany and other countries which they visit or to which they migrate. Similarly, they

---

42. Afif, p.388; Farishtah, I, p.182; Dorn, pp.65-66.
43. *Tuzuk-i-Jahangiri*, I, p.171.

had no hesitation in marrying Muslim women in the
medieval period. As has been pointed out on many occasions earlier, handsome women captives were kept mainly
for sex. They were known as *kanchanis, kanizes* and concubines. Their exchange among Muslim nobles too was
common. Even Hindu nobles were glad to take Muslim
women. According to *The Delhi Sultanate,* quoting
Nizamuddin Ahmad, Musalman women were taken by
the Rajputs and sometimes taught the art of dancing and
singing and were made to join the *akharas.*[44] Muslim
women from the palace of Malwa Sultan entered, between
1512-1518, the household of his *nayak* or captain Medini
Rai. Sultan Mahmud Sharqi (1436-58) was accused of
handing over Muslim women to his *kafir* captains. Similarly, the Muslim ruler of Kalpi and Chanderi, shortly
after 1443, had made over Muslim women to some of his
Hindu captains. "Clearly Malwa was not an exception." In
Kashmir, according to Jonraj, Shah Mir had gone to the extent of marrying his daughters to his Brahman chiefs.[44]
This shared pleasure cemented the bonds of friendship.

But Muslim rulers were more strongly entrenched, and
they, from the very beginning, discouraged Hindus from
taking Muslim women. Even Sher Shah, who is considered to be a liberal king, broke his promise with Puran
Mal of Raisen because of the latter's "gravest of all offences against Islam" in keeping some Muslim women in
his harem.[45] The Mughals freely married Hindu princesses, but there is not a single instance of a Mughal princess being married to a Rajput prince, although so many
Mughal princesses died as spinsters. Akbar discouraged
all types of inter-communal marriages.[46] When Jahangir

44. *The Delhi Sultanate,* Bharatiya Vidya Bhawan, p.582, quoting
Tabqat-i-Akbari, III, p.597; Lal, *Mughal Harem,* p.159; Nizamuddin, *Tabqat-
i-Akbari,* III, pp.453-56; Kolf, *Naukar, Rajput and Sepoy,* p.161.
    45. C.H.I., IV, pp.52, 57.
    46. 'The object of Akbar's order was evidently to prevent a woman
from doing what she liked; for, according to the Muhammadans, women
are looked upon as *naqis-ul-aql",* deficient in mind (*Ain,* I, p.220 and n.4).

learnt that the Hindus and Muslims intermarried freely in Kashmir, "and both give and take girls, (he ordered that) taking them is good but giving them, God forbid". And any violation of this order was to be visited with capital punishment.[47] Shahjahan's orders in this regard were that the Hindus could keep their Muslim wives only if they converted to Islam. Consequently, during his reign, 4,000 to 5,000 Hindus converted in Bhadnor alone. 70 such cases were found in Gujarat and 400 in the Punjab.[48]

Sometimes Hindus took back Hindu girls forcibly married to Muslims.[49] Many Hindu Rajas and elite kept Muslim women in their seraglios, sometimes as a reprisal as it were. Hindus continued to take Muslim women wherever they felt strong. Such were the Marathas. Khafi Khan and Manucci both affirm that the Marathas used to capture Muslim women because, according to them, "the Mahomedans had interfered with Hindu women in (their) territories".[50] So did the Sikhs. But marriages are not made this way. The dominance of the Muslims kept matrimonial engagements a one-way traffic. There was no option for the Hindus but to scruplously avoid marrying Muslim women. How long could they go on suffering humiliation on this account? With all their weaknesses, the Hindus have after all been a proud people.[51] Centuries of Muslim rulers' policy brought rigidity in Hindu behaviour also. He stopped marrying Muslim women and shut his door to reentry of Muslim converts. Today it is observed that the Hindu has a closed mind. He does not marry a Muslim woman for even if he does so, she would not be welcome in his family. The genesis of this situation is the result of

47. *Tuzuk-i-Jahangiri*, II, p.181.
48. S.R. Sharma, *Conversion and Reconversion to Hinduism*, p.12.
49. Farishtah, I, p.311.
50. Khafi Khan, II, pp.115-118; Manucci, II, p.119.
51. Alberuni, I, pp.19-23. Also Nicolo Conti in Sewell, *A Forgotten Empire*, p.84.

centuries of Muslim rulers' practice of prohibiting Hindus from marrying Muslim girls.

In short, the policy of Muslim rulers was to keep the Muslim minority in a privileged position and see to it that there was no integration between the two communities. Muslim rulers were so allergic to the prosperity of the Hindus that they expressed open resentment at the Hindus dressing well,[52] riding horses or travelling in palanquins like Muslims.[53] Many rulers of the Sultanate and Mughal time enforced regulations requiring Hindus to wear distinguishing marks on their dresses so that they may not be mistaken for Muslims.[54] Qazvini say that Shahjahan had ordered that Hindus should not be allowed to dress like Muslims.[55] The *Fatawa-i-Alamgiri* also recommended that the Hindus should not be allowed to look like Muslims.[56] Many local officers also issued similar orders in their *Jagirs*.[57] All these regulations were in accordance with the tenets of Islam. The order of the Prophet was, "Do the opposite of the polytheists and let your beard grow long."[58]

Partition of the Country

During the eighteenth century the Mughal empire fell on bad days; in the nineteenth it rapidly declined. But the Muslims could not forget the privileged position they had enjoyed in the medieval period. With the decline of the

---

52. Sharma, *Religious Policy of the Mughal Emperors*, pp.5, 143, 147 for detailed references.

53. Barani, p.219.

54. Sharma, p.5.

55. Qazvini, *Badshah Namah*, p.445. Shaikh Shamsuddin Yahiya wrote a *Risala* (treatise) on the dress of the *Zimmis*. The work is no longer extant. See Nizami, *Religion and Politics*, p.318.

56. *Fatawa-i-Alamgiri*, Nawal Kishore Press (Lucknow), III, pp.442-45.

57. Badaoni, Persian Text, II, p.223.

58. Jafar Sharif, trs. Herklots, *Islam in India*, p.304. Also Hughes, *Dictionary of Islam*, p.40 citing *Mishkat*, XX, iv.

Muslim political power at the Centre and in Muslim ruled provinces, a dilemma stared them in the face. They had to live on terms of equality with the Hindus. Worse still, these Hindus were in a majority. They could not think of living under the "dominance" of the Hindu majority. Three examples of this attitude, one each from the eighteenth, nineteenth and twentieth century will suffice to illustrate the point.

(1) After Aurangzeb's death when Muslim power started to disintegrate, the Sufi scholar Shah Waliullah (1703-1763) wrote to the Afghan King Ahmad Shah Abdali, inviting him to invade India to help the Muslims. The letter said: "...In short the Moslem community is in a pitiable condition. All control of the machinery of the government is in the hands of the Hindus because they are the only people who are capable and industrious. Wealth and prosperity are concentrated in their hands, while the share of Moslems is nothing but poverty and misery... At this time you are the only king who is powerful, far-sighted and capable of defeating the enemy forces. Certainly it is incumbent upon you to march to India, destroy Maratha domination and rescue weak and old Moslems from the clutches of non-Moslems. If, Allah forbid, domination by infidels continues, Moslems will forget Islam and within a short time, become such a nation that there will be nothing left to distinguish them from non-Moslems."[59]

(2) Nawab Wiqar-ul-Mulk (1841-1917) of the Aligarh School of Muslim Politics who is generally regarded as one of the makers of modern Muslim India, was Sir Syed Ahmed's loyal follower. He also became the Secretary of the Aligarh College. According to *Tazkirah-i-Wiqar* the Wiqar-ul-Mulk said: "We are numerically one-fifth of the

---

59. *Shah Waliullah ke Siyasi Maktubat*, ed. by Khaliq Ahmad Nizami reproduced in English in Khalid Bin Sayeed's *Pakistan: The Formative Phase*, Pakistan Publishing House, Karachi, p.2.

other community. If, at any time, the British Government ceases to exist in India, we shall have to live as the subjects of the Hindus, and our lives, our property, our self-respect and our religion will all be in danger... If there is any device by which we can escape this it is by the continuance of the British Raj, and our interests can be safeguarded only if we ensure the continuance of the British Government."[60]

(3) About half a century later, Laiqat Ali Khan voiced his demand at a meeting with Lord Wavell on 24 January 1946 that the British resolve the transfer of power problem by imposing a solution on the basis of Pakistan. Wavell told him in reply that in such a case, the British would have to stay on in India to enforce this imposed solution. According to an entry in Wavell's journal of the same date Liaqat Ali said that "in any event we (the British) would have to stop for many years yet, and that the Moslems were not at all anxious that we should go."[61]

Thus highly educated and important Muslim leaders like Shah Waliullah, Wiqar-ul-Mulk and Liaqat Ali Khan preferred to live under the rule of foreigners like the Afghans and the British than to live as a free people with the Hindus just because the latter happened to be in a majority. Is it therefore any wonder that the majority of Muslims were not interested in joining the freedom struggle for India's independence? The leadership of Mahatma Gandhi was acceptable to them only in the context of the Khilaft movement. Else, he was declared as a leader of the Hindus only. And what the Ali brothers said about the Mahatma vis-a-vis an ordinary or even an anti-social Muslim has become proverbial as indicative of

---

60. Reproduced by A.H. Albiruni in *Makers of Pakistan and Modern Muslim India*, Muhammad Ashraf, Lahore, p.109.

61. Wavell, *The Viceroy's Journal* ed. by Penderel Moon, Oxford University Press, p.206.

the Muslim attitude towards non-Muslims in India.[62] Of course, today Muslims in India swear by democracy and secularism

The idea of Pakistan was as old as the Muslim rule in India. M.A. Jinnah is reported to have said that the seeds of Pakistan were planted when the first Hindu converted to Islam in India. Zulfiqar Ali Bhutto reiterated the same conclusion in still clearer terms. Wrote he, "The starting point of Pakistan goes back a thousand years to when Mohammed-bin-Qasim set foot on the soil of Sind and introduced Islam in the sub-continent... The study of Mughal and British periods will show that the seeds of Pakistan took root in the sub-continent from the time Muslims consolidated their position in India. The creation of two sovereign states of India and Pakistan merely formalised this existing division."[63] Jinnah and Bhutto were not historians. But Aziz Ahmad in a historical analysis in his *Studies in Islamic Culture in the Indian Environment* arrives at the same conclusion. However, whatever the point of time or the genesis of Partition, never before was India geographically divided on religious basis in the course of its long history. The creation of Pakistan in 1947 showed the way to other ambitious or aggrieved identities in

---

62. Maulana Muhammad Ali wrote:... Some Mussulman friends have been constantly flinging at me the charge of being a...Gandhi-worshipper... Since I hold Islam to be the highest gift of God, therefore, I was impelled by the love I bear towards Mahatmaji to pray to God that he might illumine his soul with the true light of Islam... As a follower of Islam I am bound to regard the creed of Islam as superior to that professed by the followers of any non-Islamic religion. And in this sense, the creed of even a fallen and degraded Mussulman is entitled to a higher place than that of any other non-Muslim irrespective of his high character, even though the person in question be Mahatma Gandhi himself" (*Young India*, 10.4.1924).

Gandhiji's reaction was: "In my humble opinion the Maulana has proved the purity of his heart and his faith in his own religion by expressing his view. He merely compared two sets of religious principles and gave his opinion as to which was better" (*Navajivan*, 13.4.1924).

63. *The Great Tragedy*, a pamphlet published in September, 1971 in the wake of Bangladesh War.

Kashmir, Punjab and Assam to clamour for secession. The partition of the country may, perhaps, have been the logical legacy of Muslim rule in India, but the cinder fuelled by the original separatists is posing an unsurmountable problem for India's unity and integrity.

Communal Riots

One of the immediate causes of Partition was the Direct Action or the unleashing of widespread communal violence in the country. But there was nothing new or unique about it. The history of communal riots is synchronous with the advent of Muslims in India. For the next hundreds of years invaders and rulers committed 'all sorts of atrocities on the people and the atmosphere was surcharged with aggression and violence. But one day the Hindus struck back. The opportunity came when Nasiruddin Khusrau Shah ascended the throne of Delhi (1320). Khusrau Shah was a Hindu convert. He belonged to the Barwari class of Gujarat and they were known for their bravery.[64] Qutbuddin was very much 'enamoured' of him. It was customary in those days, says Ibn Battuta, that when a Hindu accepted Islam, the sultan used to present him with a robe of honour and a gold bangle.[65] Khusrau Khan pleaded with the sultan that some of his relations wanted to embrace Islam and in this way collected about 40,000 Barwaris in the capital.[66] One day they killed Qutbuddin Khalji and started rioting and killing.[67] Copies of the Quran were torn to pieces and used as seats for idols which were placed in the niches (mehrabs) of the mosques. A later but otherwise reliable chronicler, Nizamuddin Ahmad, says that some mosques were also broken.[68] The

---

64. Barani, p.379; Farishtah, I, pp.124, 126; Ibn Battuta, Def. and Sang, III, p.198.
65. Ibn Battuta, op.cit., III, pp.197-98.
66. C.H.I., III, p.123.
67. Barani, p.408.
68. Tabqat-i-Akbari, Persian Text, I, p.187.

Barwaris had known the Muslims breaking temples and destroying religious books of the Hindus. This they had done on a large scale in Gujarat itself about twenty years ago.[69] In the Delhi rioting, they paid the Muslims back in the same coin. Their King Khusrau Shah even forbade cow-slaughter.[70] But in the end this rioting was brought under control by Ghazi Malik.

It is often asserted that unlike during British rule, there were no communal riots under Muslim rule. This is only partially true; firstly, because the Hindus could not always respond to Muslim violence with symmetrical force in the medieval period; and secondly, details given by chroniclers about communal conflicts cannot be easily separated from those of perennial political strife and resistance during Muslim rule. Persian chroniclers repeatedly aver that Muslims were dominant and domineering during the medieval period while the Hindus were kept systematically suppressed.[71] But just because of this, because of the treatment accorded to non-Muslims and sometimes their reaction to it, there were Hindu-Muslim riots. And this situation is understandable. But why were there *Shia-Sunni* riots under Muslim rule just as they have always been there.[72] It is for the reason that a psyche geared to aggression and violence cannot rest in peace without fighting. When non-Muslims are not there to fight, *Sunnis* and *Shias* call each other *Kafir* and attack each other.

But ultimately the brunt of all such riots was borne by the Hindus. For instance, this is how Pelsaert describes the situation prevalent in the time of Jahangir (1605-27) during

69. For details and references see Lal, *History of the Khaljis*, p.70.
70. Ibn Battuta, p.47; Yahiya Sarhindi, *Tarikh-i-Mubarak Shahi*, p.87.
71. Barani. pp.216-17;290-91. Amir Khusrau, *Miftah-ul-Futuh*, E and D, III, p.539. Also *Nuh Sipehr*, E and D, III, p.559, 561. Firoz Shah, *Fatuhat-i-Firoz Shahi*, E and D, III, pp.380-81; Rizquallah, *Waqiat-i-Mushtaqi*, fol. 40a; Dorn, *Makhzan-i-Afghana*, pp.65-66; Farishtah, I, pp.147-48; Also Lal, *Twilight of the Sultanate*, p.194, n.176.
72. C.H.I., III, p.59.

Muharram. "The outcry (of mourning) lasts till the first quarter of the day; the coffins (*Tazias*) are brought to the river, and if the two parties meet carrying their biers (it is worse on that day), and one will not give place to the other, then if they are evenly matched, they may kill each other as if they were enemies at open war, for they run with naked swords like madmen. No Hindu can venture into the streets before midday, for even if they should escape with their life, at the least their arms and legs would be broken to pieces..."[73]

Jafar Sharif's description of the Muharram scene for the eighteenth-nineteenth century is still more detailed. Writes he: "Whenever the Muharram...chances to coincide with Hindu festivals, such as the Ramnavmi or the birth of Rama, the Charakhpuja, or swing festival, or the Dasahra, serious riots have occurred as the processions meet in front of a mosque or Hindu temple, or when an attempt is made to cut the branches of some sacred fig-tree which impedes the passage of the cenotaphs. Such riots, for instance occurred at Cuddapa in Madras in 1821, at Bhiwandi in the Thana District, Bombay, in 1837. In the case of some disturbances at Hyderabad, it is said that Hindus, who act as Muharram Faqirs (who erect them, *Tazias*, themselves and become *Faqirs* during Muharram), sometimes take the part of Mussulmans against their co-religionists."[74]

According to a contemporary Sufi, Shaikh Abdur Rahman Chishti, the "the subservience of the Hindus to Islam" under Shahjahan was thorough and complete.[75] However, communal riots had become common from the time of Aurangzeb because of his religious policy. Rioting went on for days together in Varanasi when Vishvanath and other temples were destroyed there in 1669. Here is

73. Pelsaert, p.75.
74. Herklots, *Islam in India*, pp.166-67.
75. Rizvi, *History of Sufism*,II, p.369.

the description of the communal riots as narrated in a contemporary work:

"The infidels demolished a mosque," writes the author of the *Ganj-i-Arshadi*, "that was under construction and wounded the artisans. When the news reached Shah Yasin, he came to Banaras from Mandyawa and collecting the Muslim weavers, demolished the big temple. A Sayyid who was an artisan by profession agreed with one Abdul Rasul to build a mosque at Banaras and accordingly the foundation was laid. Near the place there was a temple and many houses belonging to it were in the occupation of the Rajputs. The infidels decided that the construction of a mosque in the locality was not proper and that it should be razed to the ground. At night the walls of the mosque were found demolished. Next day the wall was rebuilt but it was again destroyed. This happened three or four times. At last the Sayyid hid himself in a corner. With the advent of night the infidels came to achieve their nefarious purpose. When Abdul Rasul gave the alarm, the infidels began to fight and the Sayyid was wounded by the Rajputs. In the meantime, the Mussulman residents of the neighbourhood arrived at the spot and the infidels took to their heels. The wounded Muslims were taken to Shah Yasin who, determined to vindicate the cause of Islam. When he came to the mosque, people collected from the neighbourhood. The civil officers were outwardly inclined to side with the saint but in reality they were afraid of the royal displeasure on account of the Raja, who was a courtier of the Emperor and had built the temple (near which the mosque was under construction). Shah Yasin, however, took up the sword and started for *Jihad*. The civil officers sent him a message that such a grave step should not be taken without the Emperor's permission. Shah Yasin, paying no heed, sallied forth till he reached Bazar Chau Khamba through a fusillade of stones... The doors (of temples) were forced open and the idols thrown down.

The weavers and other Mussulmans demolished about 500 temples. They desired to destroy the temple of Beni Madho, but as lanes were barricaded, they desisted from going further."[76]

Temple destruction in Māthura, Ujjain, Rajasthan and many other parts of the country was always followed by communal rioting. "In March, 1671, it was reported that a Muslim officer who had been sent to demolish Hindu temples in and around Ujjain was killed with many of his followers in the riot that had followed his attempts at destroying the temples there. He had succeeded in destroying some of the temples, but in one place, a Rajput chief had opposed this wanton destruction of his religious places. He overpowered the Mughal forces and destroyed its leader and many of his men. In Gujarat somewhere near Ahmedabad, Kolis seem to have taken possession of a mosque probably built on the site of a temple and prevented reading of Friday prayers there. Imperial orders were thereupon issued to the provincial officers in Gujarat to secure the use of the mosque for Friday prayers".[77] So, as a measure of retaliation sometimes mosques were destroyed by Hindus and Sikhs when their shrines were desecrated and razed. This was done as seen earlier by the *Satnamis* and by the Sikhs when they rose against the fanatical policy of Aurangzeb.[78] Hindus had learnt to do it in imitation of their Muslim rulers since the days of Sultan Nasiruddin Khusrau Shah.

---

76. Faruki, *Aurangzeb*, pp.127-28 citing from *Ganj-i-Arshadi*, reproduced in Sharma, *op.cit.*, p.144 n.12.

The Vishvanath temple site was never relinquished by the Hindus even after its desecration by Aurangzeb. The present one was built by the Maratha Rani Ahilya Bai in 1785. The Sikh Maharaja Ranjit Singh (d. 1839) got its *shikharas* covered with gold plates.

77. Sharma, *Religious Policy of the Mughal Emperors*, p.134, also pp.133-38, writing on the basis of News Letter of 27 March, 1670 and *Mirat-i-Ahmadi*, I, p.261.

78. C.H.I., IV, pp.245,322.

Attack on Hindu honour and religion were common, evoking, naturally, violent response. Jadunath Sarkar writes: "The prime minister's grandson, Mirza Tafakhkhur used to sally forth from his mansion in Delhi with his ruffians, plunder the shops in the *bazar*, kidnap Hindu women passing through the public streets in litters or going to the river, and dishonour them; and yet there was no judge strong enough to punish him, no police to prevent such crimes."[79] Such ruffians were dealt with directly by the Hindu public, resulting in communal rioting. The king was busy in suppression of Hindu religion, and the Hindus in fighting for their rights. In brief, as noted by Sharma, "The Holi ceased to be celebrated by imperial orders issued on 20 November, 1665. It was not a police order alone, promulgated for the purpose of keeping peace and order during the Holi days as Sir Jadunath Sarkar has suggested. Raja Bhim of Banera and Kishen Singh while serving in south India in 1692, made arrangements for the celebration of the Holi. The censor tried to stop the celebration (but failed). He reported the matter to the emperor by whose orders the celebrations were stopped. In 1704, 200 soldiers were placed at the disposal of the censor for the purpose of preventing the celebration of the Holi. Of course the emperor was not always able to stop the celebrations" as the people had learnt to fight back in the streets. And their resistance was not always easy to crush. "In the South where he spent the last twenty-seven years of his reign, Aurangzeb was usually content with leaving many Hindu temples standing as he was afraid of arousing the feelings of his Hindu subjects in the Deccan where the suppression of rebellions was not an easy matter. An idol in a niche in the fort of Golkunda is said to have been spared by Aurangzeb. But the discontent occasioned by his orders could not thus be brought to an end."[80]

79. Sarkar, *A Short History of Aurangzeb*, p.452.
80. Sharma, *op. cit.*, p.139, 142.

From then on to this day Hindu-Muslim communal riots have gone on and on. The occasions are the same. Coincidence of a Hindu and a Muslim festival falling on the same day, music before mosque, chance sprinkling of coloured-water on a Muslim even by a child, coming out of the mosque on Friday after hearing a hot sermon, and now political sabre-rattling of direct action. During the early years of the twentieth century communal riots were a common feature in one or the other part of the country. Pakistan was created as much by the ambition of the Muslim politicians as by the violence of their Direct Action. After that there was some respite. But from 1970 onwards communal riots in India have again become an yearly feature. The riots in 1970 in Aligarh and in 1971 in Moradabad were trend-setters as it were.

Every riot is followed by an Inquiry Committee, but its report is never published. Take U.P. for instance. A report in the *Times of India* of 13.12.1990 from Lucknow says: "At least a dozen judicial inquiry reports into the genesis of communal riots in the state have never seen the light of the day. They have been buried in the secretariat-files over the past two decades. The failure of the successive state governments to publish these reports and initiate action has given credence to the belief that they are not serious about checking communal violence... There were other instances when the state government instituted an inquiry and then scuttled the commissions. In the 1982 and 1986 clashes in Meerut and in the 1986 riots in Allahabad, the judicial inquiries were ordered only as an 'eye-wash'..." Judicial inquiries are ordered as an eye-wash because the perpetrators of riots are known but cannot be booked. In a secular state it is neither proper to name them nor political to punish them. Inquiry committee reports are left to gather dust, while those who should be punished are pampered and patronised as vote-banks in India's democratic setup. Therefore communal riots in India as a legacy of Muslim rule may continue to persist. If these could help in partitioning the country, they could still help in achieving many other goals.

In brief, Hindu-Muslim composite culture is seen in the domain of music, film industry, sports, army life and Indian cuisine, while Muslim iconoclasm, proselytization, fundamentalism and continuous communal riots repeatedly remind us of the chasm that separates the two communities. Actually it is manifested only in personal friendships and neighbourhood loyalties. It is conspicuous by its absence in the history of Indian philosophy. Jaisi, Rahim, Raskhan and Dara Shukoh, though no conventional philosophers, are rare phenomenon. Recognized leading lights of Islamic philosophy like Shaikh Ahmad Sarhindi, Shah Waliullah and Shah Ismail Shahid, find no place in the histories of Indian philosophy. The issue of composite culture was finally settled in 1947. "In 1947," writes Harsh Narain, "Muslim society succeeded in extorting recognition as a separate culture and nation and getting the country vivisected on that basis. It is another matter that... we go on harping on the theme of the truncated India's belonging to Hindus and Muslims alike and its culture's being a composite culture, a culture composed of Hindu and Muslim religio-cultural traditions."[81]

Medieval Legacy and Modern Politics

Whether Indian leaders accepted Partition willingly or not, they should have realised the necessity of clearly understanding the two-nation theory in all its aspects, in all its implications, at least in post-Partition years. Muslims were more or less clear about the policies that were to be followed in the newly established state of Pakistan. They pushed out the Hindu minority to the extent possible, broke most of the temples, and in course of time

81. Harsh Narain, *Myths of Composite Culture and Eqality of Religions*, p.24.

Pakistan was declared an Islamic State. Bangladesh also followed suit. But in the residual India no thought was given to the formulation of practicable policies of the newly independent State. The old mindsets continued. The policy of the Indian National Congress before Partition was alright. It appeased the Muslims to somehow save the country from division. But after the country was partitioned on Hindu-Muslim basis, continuance of the old policy of appeasement showed bankruptcy of political acumen and a betrayal of the implicit trust reposed by the people in the Congress—in particular Jawaharlal Nehru. With all his knowledge of history he could not understand Islam and its fundamentalism. It appeared that his life-long contact with its followers and the bitter fruit of Partition had no lessons for him.

Pandit Nehru's family tradition, political training and social intercourse[82] made him (what was jocularly called) the greatest nationalist Muslim of India. It is said that he even felt small because of his Hindu lineage. He himself stated that by education he was an Englishman, by views an internationalist, by culture a Muslim; he happened to be a Hindu only by the accident of birth. He mistook Indian nationalism as Hindu communalism, and this confusion has come to the Indian National Congress Party as an inheritance. For example in a public meeting in August 1947, he declared that "As long as I am at the helm of affairs, India will not become a Hindu state. If they do not subscribe to my views and are not prepared to cooperate with me, I shall have no way except to resign from the Prime Ministership..." Almost the same views were expressed in his letter to Dr. Kailash Nath Katju on 17 November, 1953. He wrote: "What real Hinduism is may be a matter for each individual to decide, in practice the

---

82. Henry Sender, *The Kashmiri Pandits: A Study of Cultural Choice,* Oxford University Press, 1988. Also review of this book by Ratan Watal in Express Magazine, 15 January, 1989.

individual is certainly intolerant and is more narrow-minded than almost any person in any other country... The Muslim outlook may be, I think, often worse, but it does not make very much difference to the future of India."[83] This assessment has proved to be incorrect.

On 30 December, 1949, addressing a meeting under the auspices of the Secular Democratic Front at Farrukhabad, Pandit Nehru said that the talk of Hindu culture would injure India's interests and would mean the "acceptance of the two-nation theory which the Congress had opposed tooth and nail". Again, addressing the students at Lucknow University on 16 September, 1951, he said that the ideology of Hindu Dharma was completely out of tune with the present times, and if it took root in India, it would "smash the country to pieces". Nehru's pro-western, pro-Muslim leanings were very well-known. Hindus did not protest because they loved and respected Nehru. They had full faith in him. Hindus did not even care because they thought they were in such vast majority. Hindus did not make a noise because in the flush of freedom they remained, as usual, casual and indifferent to any future Muslim plans. But every society wants some security, some piece of land as its homeland under the sun. This law of human existence is supereme. Every country worth the name has some core element or force in it called the nation, which is its backbone and the source of all strength in it. Such a force in India is the Hindu force. This force has always been active in the day-to-day life of this nation, but has shown itself more markedly and spectacularly and has sprung into action with redoubled energy during the last few years. Rigmarole of language apart, India is a Hindu nation. As Dr. Gopal Krishna observes, "It seems to me that for a student of history and a man of long political experience, Nehru's understanding of eth-

83. *India's Minorities*, Publications Division, Ministry of Information and Broadcasting (New Delhi, 1948), pp.1 ff.

nic/religious plurality (of India) and its political pressures
was amazingly shallow. His outraged reaction to displays
of communal antagonism was aesthetic rather than
thoughtful. To describe persistent mass group behaviour
as 'barbaric' did not suggest any understanding of the behaviour itself."[84]

The Muslims who stayed on in India after Partition did
not take much time to discover that most policies of the
Nehru Goverment were anti-Hindu. For them it was a
political windfall. Soon enough they asserted that they
were being discriminated against by the dominant Hindu
majority. Pre-Partition psychology and slogans reap-
peared. Hindus have a stake in India. This is the only
country which they can call their own and for which they
are prepared to make any sacrifice. Muslims have no such
inhibitions. They can and do look outside as well. There is
a tendency to explain Muslim communalism in terms of
the intrigues of the British Government and failings of the
Indian National Congress, but Muslim politics is not a
passive product. It has its own aims, aspirations, ambi-
tions and dynamism. It dreams of a pan-Islamic state
which could go on expanding. On the one hand the
Muslim minority truly professes allegiance to India and
on the other, and equally truly, even after forty years of
Independence, looks to Pakistan for directions. Pakistan
on its part avows friendship with India and at the same
time strives for confederal alliance with neighbouring
Muslim States against India.[85] The medieval concept of
Dar-ul-Harb and *Dar-ul-Islam* has never ceased to be. According to Deoband *Fatwas*, even free India is a *Dar-ul-
Harb*.[86]

---

84. Gopal Krishna, *"Nation Building In Third World"*, a series of four
articles, *Times of India*, 26 to 29 December, 1988.
85. Speech by the Pakistan Army Chief at the Staff College at Quetta
on 26.10.1988.
86. *Fatawa-i-Deoband*, Vol. II, p.269 cited in Harsh Narain, *op. cit.*, p.44.

After Partition, Pakistan solved its minority problem without much ado. But Indian leaders failed to do so. Contrary to the Benthamite doctrine of the greatest good of the greatest number, to Gandhiji the last man was his first concern. Even after the vivisection of the country he remained more concerned with the "difficulties" of the Muslim minority than anything else. Ram Gopal, while discussing the problem of Muslims before Partition, summarises the Hindu attitude contained in a resolution of V.D. Savarkar who proposed to secure the Muslim rights thus: "When once the Hindu Mahasabha not only accepts but maintains the principles of 'one man and one vote' and the public services go by merit alone added to the fundamental rights and obligations to be shared by all citizen alike irrespective of any distinction of race or religion...any further mention of minority rights is on principle not only unnecessary but self-contradictory. Because it again introduces a consciousness of majority or minority on a communal basis."[87]

In brief, the Muslim minority problem has continued and will continue also because of the fact that two theocratic states have been established in the east and west of India. With inspiration received from these two fundamentalist states, the Indian Muslim is prone to succumb to extra-territorial allurements. A Hindu cannot be a fundamentalist because there is nothing fundamental or obligatory in his socio-religious life, but be can be a fanatic, a greater fanatic than all, when the only country he loves and belongs to, is broken up and is threatened to be broken up again and again. This is Hindu backlash. And since Indian leaders have not only not been able to solve the Muslim minority problem in India, and talk in the same uncertain idiom in which they spoke in pre-Partition days, Hindu anger cannot but be fanned.

87. Ram Gopal, *Indian Muslims: A Political History* (1858-1947), pp.264-65.

In this scenario the Nehruvian Government continues to pursue the pre-Partition policies of the Indian National Congress. Actually there is no minority problem in India; it is Muslim problem. It is generally not realised that whenever there is mention of words like National Integration, National Mainstream, National Unity, Community Identity, Sectional Separatism, Minority Rights, Minority Commission, fundamentalism, secularism etc., we mainly think about only one thing — the Muslim problem in India. Minorities have been living in India from long past, minorities like Jews, Christians and Zoroastrians for example, but they have not posed a minority problem as such. They have always lived according to Indian cultural traditions and within the parameters of Indian national unity. But with the Muslims, the problem of their absorption into the Indian mainstream continues even after Partition.

National Integration

There are ethnic, religious and linguistic groups in all large countries of the world like America, Russia and China, and so also there are in India. But America and Russia never talk about national integration: at least they never make a fetish of it. As Gopal Krishna in his series of articles on *"Nation Building in Third World"*, referred to above, has said, "A modern state rests on the citizenship principle, where all the citizens, irrespective of any specificities of birth, occupation, religion, sex, etc., constitute the political community. Ideally there are no majorities or minorities, except on particular issues; people of course have interests, but these are pursued in harness with the general interest." But in India the government arrogates to itself obligations which are better left to the society itself. National Integration is a fallacious conception. The very words imply that we are a disintegrated people who need to be united or integrated into a nation. At the same time it is repeatedly asserted that there is a basic Indian unity in the midst of diversity. India undoubtedly presents a cultural peagantry of exuberant variety with an underlayer of basic unity. This unity, however, has its source and derives its strength not from political but from cultural sources. Regional languages, climate, dresses and food of the people may be different but most Indian ceremonies and festivals are associated with religion and culture. That is how they are common and sometimes similar throughout the country from Bengal to Kashmir and Kashmir to Kanya Kumari. Gods and Goddesses, festivals and ceremonies sometimes have different names in different parts of the country but they are the same and are celebrated with equal enthusiasm everywhere. But Indian Muslims who are mainly Hindu-converts, keep away from these. If Muslims of Indonesia can perform the Ramayana as a national cultural festival, why Indian Muslims cannot do it in India. It is not the Government appointed National Integration Council but the people's will alone that can bring about national integration.

Similar is the case with regard to minorities. There are minorities in all countries, but it is only in India that there is a Minorities Commission — emphasising thereby that minorities *have* problems *here* only. This by itself is an instigation to the minorities (read Muslims) to put forth all kinds of demands based on trumped up grievances. Social cohesion has to be left to the society itself for a healthy natural growth. The sooner the Government gives up the slogans of national integration and minorityism, the better for the country. Justice M.H. Beg, Chairman of the Minority Commision, rightly recommended winding up of the Commission.

In Muslim countries the nature of the state is generally Islamic if not totally theocratic. Secularism is prevalent in most advanced countries of the world. India too is a secular country. The Indian state gives equal status to all religions. It means that people of all faiths can practice their religious rites with equal freedom and without interference from others or the state. Secularism should not be a tool for demanding privileges, asserting rights, claiming more jobs (in proportion to population, whether qualified or not) and "establishment of a minorities finance development corporation with an initial asset of Rs. 100 crore." Some political parties encourage such demands for gathering votes. All this makes India the only country in the world where "reservations in jobs" and not merit counts, thus making small a country otherwise great. This is one side of the coin. The other is that "secularism" in India is a stick to beat the majority community with, as it is an instrument for the appeasement of the minorities. For all practical purposes, secularism in India is very welcome to the Muslims. With Islamic regimes established to the east and west (Bangladesh and Pakistan), secularism means that the Muslim minority in India can have the cake and eat it too.

In this combination of national integration, minorityism, secularism and a common civil code, the most damaging to the Muslim interests is their resistance to the enactment of a common civil code. On the other hand, there is a lurking fear among many Muslims that national integration is a ploy to submerge their religious and cultural identity by tempting them into the national mainstream and placing them under a common civil code. That is what makes them so keen to stick to their Personal Law. On the face of it, it is very satisfying for Muslims to see that they have their own separate laws; that through them they are enabled to preserve their separate identity. In actual practice separateness makes them different from others. Difference leads to inequality. Inequality can either make them a little superior or a little inferior to others. Being in a minority they cannot be superior in a democratic set up. In Muslim countries non-Muslims are generally given an inferior status. In India Muslims on their own by insisting on preserving their personal law make themselves "lesser" citizens. Once they realise that because of their Personal Law they cannot claim equality with other citizens, they will not come in the way of enactment of a common civil code.

An early warning against perpetuating the minority complex was sounded in a memorandum submitted to the Constituent Assembly's committee on minorities by Rajkumari Amrit Kaur, a leading member of the Christian community. She said: "The primary duty of the committee appointed to look into the problem of minorities is to suggest such ways and means as will help to eradicate the evil of separatism, rather than expedients and palliatives which might, in the long run, only contribute to its perpetuation." She added, "Privileges and safegurds really weaken those that demand them..." A distinguished member of another minority community, Muhammad Currimbhoy Chagla, wrote in his autobiography in 1973: "I have often strongly disagreed with the government policy of constantly harping upon minorities, minority status and minority rights. It comes in the way of national unity, and emphasises the differences between the majority community and minority. Of course it may serve well as a vote-catching device to win Muslim votes, but I do not believe in sacrificing national interests in order to get temporary party benefits. Although the Directive Principles of the State enjoin a uniform civil code, the Government has refused to do anything about it on the plea that the minorities will resent any attempt at imposition." The false equation of secularism and minorityism of the Congress is repeated in the policies of the National Front Government.[88]

---

88. G.N.S. Raghavan, *"Secularism or Minorityism"*, in *Statesman*, 19.11.89.

Politics of Minorityism

Whichever political party has been in power at the Centre during the last forty-three years, whosoever has been the Prime Minister — Nehru or Gandhis, Morarji Desai or V.P.Singh — the Nehruvian Congress culture has spared no effort to woo the Muslim minority. In this attempt it was even decided to manipulate and distort our country's history. The justification for rewriting Indian history, particularly medieval Indian history, from the 'nationalist' point of view lay in the plea that British historians have deliberately distorted Indian history with a view to highlighting Hindu-Muslim differences. We have already discussed this allegation earlier in Chapter 2. The British rulers and their historians only took advantage of the prevailing situation. For example, Monstuart Elphinstone, a Governor of Bombay, suggested in his Minute dated 14 May 1859: *"Divide et Impera* was the old Roman motto, and it should be our". Given the circumstances, it would have been foolish of any imperialist power not to follow such a policy. But for achieving this aim there was no need for them to distort Indian history. British historians had just to reiterate what the Muslim chroniclers themselves had written about the "glorious achievements" of their kings and conquerors. Their stories needed no proof: they stood confirmed by the hundreds of vandalised medieval monuments. The mistake lay with the misjudgement of our Congress-culture Government and the so-called secularist and Stalinist historians. They chose to treat history as a handmaid of politics to please the Muslim minority. They instructed their text-book writers to eschew mention of unpalatable historical facts like destruction of temples and forced conversions by Muslims in history, language and social science. But perpetration of lies has proved counter-productive. It has encouraged Muslims to ask for proof as to when Babur or Aurangzeb broke this or that temple, knowing full well that such shrines were actually vandalised and razed.

As a consequence of all this, it is now being generally realised, though not admitted, that organisations like the National Integration Council and Minorities Commision are all there for appeasement rather than for grappling with the basic issues. It is now being felt that the best qualification for becoming a member of the National Integration Council is to be capable of denouncing Hindus and Hinduism. If minorities were suffering in India, Christians, Parsis, Jews too would have complained. But in our secular democracy not only are they feeling safe but also contributing their mite in development of the country. The biggest joke is that it is the "largest minority" of Muslims (75 millions according to 1981 census) that feels unsafe. To please it the Government is coerced, history is falsified and Hindus castigated, and yet Muslims cannot be brought to join the national mainstream. They insist on having a separate identity with separate laws.

In a democracy all citizens have equal rights. Words like majority and minority are out of place. The moment these words are uttered in the Indian context, they create the impression that minority is weak and helpless and majority strong and tyrannical. Institutions like the Minorities Commission and National Integration Council breed vested intrests as they continue to harp upon real or imaginary minority grievances. That is probably why the late Justice M.H. Beg recommended that the Minorities Commission should be done away with, but it suited the politicians not to do so. A fear psychosis is created vis-a-vis the Hindus, who although in majority, have not been known for possessing cohesion. It is well known that this fear is created by politicians who can go to any length to ensure their vote-banks. No leader has bothered to find out what effect the policy of appeasement of Muslims has on other sections of society.

The crux of the problem is the legacy of Muslim rule in India. Directly associated with it is the problem that the religion of the largest minority has certain peculiarites. It believes that there is one 'chosen religion' and one 'chosen people'. In an Islamic state, no consideration is given to people of other faiths. Non-Muslims cannot construct a Christian church or a Hindu temple in Saudi Arabia or Iran, or say their prayers in public. During the month of Ramzan no food is available to non-Muslims in hotels or restaurants, although fasting is compulsory only for the Muslims. After the conquest of Mecca, "a perpetual law was enacted (by Muhammad himself) that no unbeliever should dare to set his foot on the territory of the holy city."[89] Where Muslims rule, they may declare the state secular or Islamic, they may treat the minorities with dignity or as *Zimmis*, follow the Islamic laws or prohibit polygamy. No non-Muslim can demand anything from them. They consider it entirely their own business to do what they like to do in their own country. But elsewhere their demands know no limits.[90]

No wonder that in India Muslims want separate schools for their children and claim Urdu as their language. They want their Personal Law (which mainly means polygamy),[91] and resist enactment of a uniform

---

89. Gibbon, *op.cit.*, II, p.685.

90. A news item in the *The Statesman* of Sunday, 6 August 1989, entitled "Muslims in Britain displaying militancy" and datelined London, August 5, underscores the problem. It says that Muslims in Britain are displaying increasing militancy. "The Muslim community is demanding that its way of life be respected in Britain and instead of integration, many want separation... They are concentrating on the right to have Muslim schools and official recognition for Islamic family laws which permit polygamy... These demands they placed before the Home Secretary Mr. Douglas Hurd while protesting against Salman Rushdie's controversial novel *Satanic Verses*. That turned out to be an excuse or occasion to put claims quite unrelated to the book. Later reports indicate that they are striving to establish a non-territorial Muslim Kingdom in Britain."

91. "The reason why the Muslims do not insist upon chopping off the hands of thieves and stoning adulterers to death is that the courts imparting justice are not Shariat courts. The Shariat law prescribes certain qualifications for the judges which the present judicial set-up does not fulfil" (A correspondent from Aligarh in a letter to the Editor, *Times of India*, 17.8.91). Of course for contracting four marriages no permission is required from non-Shariat Indian law-courts.

civil code for all. They are against family planning so that their population may grow unchecked. In short, in countries where Muslims are in a minority and the state is not Islamic, they insist on living an alienated, unintegrated and "superior" life by agitating for concessions specified by their Islamic *Shariat*. No amount of falsification of history can humour them into living with others on terms of equality. Therefore Congress-culture politicians and pseudo-secularists should at least inform the minority whose cause they espouse, but to whom they never dare read a lecture, that secularism and fundamentalism are mutually exclusive, and that in the Indian secular state the Muslims cannot practise their fundamentalism. Furthermore, they can also be told that history can no longer be distorted, that it cannot be made the handmaid of politics, and that therefore they need to feel sorry if not actually repentant about the past misdeeds of Muslims.

Sometime back the East German Ambassador to Poland publicly apologised to the Poles for the ill-treatment meted out to them by Germans during the last war. Two years ago, the Japanese Government officially apologised to the Chinese Government for the atrocities committed by the Japanese on the Chinese population in the 30's during China-Japan war. Recently on 23/24 May, 1990, during a visit to South Korea, emperor Akihito of Japan apologised to South Koreans for the same reason. Nearer home, the Caste Hindus are doing their best to make amends for their alleged or actual ill-treatment of backward classes through administrative, legislative and "reservation" methods. But such a gesture appears to be out of tune with Muslim culture and creed. Not that politicians of other communities are entirely selfless: no politicians are angles. Still it is felt that the Muslim minority community, misguided by its leaders, thinks and works only for its own narrow interests. The interest of the country is not its concern because it is not an Islamic country. That is why there is need to appeal to the Muslims to join the national "mainstream". Indian Muslims were originally Hindus. As Hindus they were part of the country's social and political mainstream. Conversion to Islam wrenched them away from it because Islam and Islamic theology enjoin upon Muslims to keep separated and segregated from non-Muslims. To integrate is not their obligation. To strive for national integration is the duty of the Government and the Hindus. And so it has been through the centuries. It is significant that Bhakta saints of the medieval period who preached integration were all Hindus. Even Sant Kabir. It is they who preached that Hinduism is as good as Islam and *vice versa*. No Muslim Ulama or Sufi can say such a thing. No Muslim gives any other religion a status of equality with Islam. Such an assumption is against the tenets of his creed.

Therefore, eversince the appearance of Muslims in India, there has been a struggle between Muslim communalism and Hindu nationalism, to use the modern phraseology. Today on the side of Muslim communalists are Marxists, pseudo-secularists, progressives etc. They have chosen the safe side because they know that it is easy to decry Hindus and Hinduism but very unsafe to criticise Muslims or Islam. But the great pundits of modernity and secularism have exhausted their volleys. The Hindu is now regaining his self-respect dwarfed over centuries. His no-nonsense stance has made the secularists and progressives panicky. They have recently propounded a new theory. They say that while the fundamentalism of the minority community harms only that community, the communalism of the majority community harms the whole nation.[92] The Hindu does not care to seek elaboration of such shiboleths. His watchword of Indianization,

_____

92. Professor Shaharyar in a Seminar at Aligarh as reported in *Qaumi Awaz* dated 23 November, 1989. And V.M. Tarkunde's article *Hindu Communalism* in *The Times of India* of 30 May, 1990.

considered in certain circles to have anti-Muslim implications, asserts a staunch opposition to disintegration. India is on the march. It is not going communist, nor communalist. India is steadily going Indian. It is to be watched if Indian Muslim or Muslim Indian leadership will contribute to this endeavour or only continue to cherish and preserve the legacy of Muslim rule in India.

Bibliography

Original Sources

Abdullah, *Tarikh-i-Daudi*, Bankipore Ms. Text, ed. by S.A. Rashid, Aligarh.

Abdul Hamid Lahori, *Badshah Nama*, Bib. Ind., 2 vols., Calcutta, 1898.

Abdul Haqq Dehelvi, *Akhbar-ul-Akhiyar*, Delhi, 1309 H.

Abdur Razzaq, *Mutla-us-Sadain*, trs. in E and D, IV. Also see Major under foreign Travellers' Accounts.

Abul Fazl, Allami, *Ain-i-Akbari*, 3 vols., Vol.I trs. by H. Blochmann and ed. by D.C. Phillot, Asiatic Society of Bengal, Calcutta, 1939; Vol.II trs. by H.S. Jarret and annotated by Jadunath Sarkar, A.S.B., Calcutta, 1939; Vol.III, trs. by Jarret and Sarkar, Calcutta, 1948.

Abul Fazl, Allami, *Akbar Nama*, Bib. Ind. Text, 3 vols., English trs. by Henry Beveridge, Calcutta, 1948.

Afif, Shams Siraj, *Tarikh-i-Firoz Shahi*, Bib. Ind., Calcutta, 1890.

Ahmad Yadgar, *Tarikh-i-Salatin-i-Afghana*, Bib. Ind., Calcutta, 1936.

Ain-ul Mulk Multani, *Qasaid Badr Chach*, Kanpur, n.d.

Alberuni, Abu Raihan Muhammad., *Alberuni's India*, Eng. trs. by Edward Sachau, 2 vols., Trubners Oriental Series, Kegan Paul, London, 1910.

Al Biladuri, *Futuh-ul-Buldan* (written 9th cent. C.E.), trs. in E and D, Vol.I.

Al Istakhri, *Kitab-ul-Aqalim* (written C.E. 951), trs. in E and D, Vol.I.

Al Kufi, *Chach Nama*, trs. in E and D, I. Also by Mirza Kalichbeg Fredunbeg, Karachi, 1900, Delhi reprint, 1979.

Al Masudi, *Muruj-ul-Zuhab* (written C.E. 941), trs. in E and D, I.

Al Qalqashindi, *Subh-ul-Asha*, trs. by Otto Spies as *An Arab Account of India in the 14th century*, Aligarh, 1935.

Ali Muhammad Khan Bahadur, *Mirat-i-Ahmadi*, Calcutta, 1928; English trs. by Lokhandvala, 2 vols., Oriental Institute, Baroda, 1965.

Amin Qazvini, *Badshah Nama*, Ms. Raza Library, Rampur.

Amir Khurd, see Kirmani.

Amir Khusrau, Abul Hasan, *Deval Rani*, Aligarh, 1917.

Amir Khusrau, Abul Hasan, *Tughlaq Nama*, ed. by Hashim Faridabadi, Aurangabad, 1933.

Amir Khusrau, Abul Hasan, *Ghurrat-ul-Kamal*, published by Yasin Ali, Delhi.

Amir Khusrau, Abul Hasan, *Khazain-ul-Futuh*, see Habib under Modern Works.

Amir Khusrau, Abul Hasan, *Mutla-i-Anwar*, Lucknow, 1884.

Amir Khusrau, Abul Hasan, *Aijaz-i-Khusravi*, 5 parts, Lucknow, 1876.

Amir Khusrau, Abul Hasan, *Miftah-ul-Futuh*, Aligarh Text, 1954.

Amir Khusrau, Abul Hasan, *Afzal-ul-Favaid* (compilations of conversations of Shaikh Nizamuddin Auliya), Persian Text, Rizvi Press, Delhi, 1305 H.; Urdu trs. in *Silsila-i-Tasawwuf* No. 81, Allah Wale Ki Dukan, Kashmiri Bazar, Lahore.

Babur, Zahiruddin Muhammad, *Babur Nama or Tuzuk-i-Baburi*, trs. from Turki by Mrs. A.S. Beveridge, 2 vols., Luzac & Co., London, 1922; trs. from the Persian version by John Leyden and William Erskine as *Memoirs of Babur*, London, 1926.

Badaoni, Abdul Qadir Ibn-i-Muluk Shah, *Muntakhab-ut-Tawarikh*, ed. by Ahmad Ali, Persian Text, Bib. Ind., 3 vols., Calcutta, 1864-67; English trs. by George S.A Ranking, A.S.B., Calcutta, 1898.

Baihaqi, Khwaja Abul Fazl, *Tarikh-i-Subuktgin* (written 1089 C.E.), trs. in E and D, II.

Bakhtawar Khan, *Mirat-i-Alam* (written 1078 H/1666 C.E.), trs. in E and D, VII.

Barani, Ziyauddin, *Tarikh-i-Firoz Shahi*, Bib. Ind., Calcutta, 1864.

Barani, Ziyauddin, *Fatawa-i-Jahandari*, English trs. by Afsar Begum and Mohammad Habib, Kitab Mahal, Allahabad, 1960.

Barani, Ziyauddin, *Sana-i-Muhammadi*, trs. in *Medieval India Quarterly*, Vol.I, pt.III.

Bihamad Khani, Muhammad, *Tarikh-i-Muhammadi*, British Museum Ms. Rotograph copy in Allahabad University Library, English trs. by Muhammad Zaki, Aligarh, 1972.

Chandrabhan Brahman, *Guldasta*, Sir Sulaiman Collection Ms. No. 666/44, Aligarh Muslim University Library.

Devalsmriti, published by Anandasrama Sanskrit Series, Poona; English trs. by M.N. Roy in *Journal of the Bihar and Orissa Research Society*, 1927.

Dhuniraj, *Girvan-Vanmanjari* (written 1702-04 C.E.), Text ed. by U.P. Shah, Baroda, 1960.

Fakhr-i-Mudabbir, *Tarikh-i-Fakhruddin Mubarak Shah*, ed. by Sir Denison Ross, London, 1927.

Fakhr-i-Mudabbir, *Adabul Harb wa Shujaat*, Photocopy British Museum, Add. 1653; Hindi trs. in Rizvi, *Adi Turk Kalin Bharat*.

Fatawa-i-Alamgiri, Urdu trs., Nawal Kishore Press, 3 vols. Lucknow.

Farishtah, Muhammad Qasim Hindu Shah, *Gulshan-i-Ibrahimi*, also known as *Tarikh-i-Farishtah*, Persian Text, Nawal Kishore Press, Lucknow, 1865.

Firoz Shah Tughlaq, *Fatuhat-i-Firoz Shahi*, Aligarh, 1954.

Hamid Qalandar, *Khair-ul-Majalis* (compilation of conversations of Shaikh Nasiruddin Chiragh Dihli), Text ed. by K.A. Nizami.

Hajiuddabir, *Zafar-ul-Wali bi Muzaffar Wali, An Arabic History of Gujarat*, ed. by Sir Denison Ross, 3 vols., London, 1910, 1921.

Hasan Nizami, *Taj-ul-Maasir*, trs. by S.H. Askari in *Patna University Journal* (Arts), Vol.18, No.3, 1963. Also in E and D, II.

Hidaya Kitab al Siyar wail Jihad, Mujtabai Press, Delhi, 2 vols., 1331, 1332 H. Also see Hamilton under Modern Works.

Ibn Battuta, *The Rehla of Ibn Battuta*, English trs. by Agha Mahdi Husain, Oriental Institute, Baroda, 1953. Abridged Translation by H.R.A. Gibb, Broadway Travellers Series, London, 1929. French trs. as *Ibn Batoutah's Voyages*, ed. by C. Defremery and B.R. Sanguinetti, Paris, 1857.

Ibn Hauqal, *Ashkalal-ul-Bilad* (written 976 C.E.), trs. in E and D, I.

Ibn-ul-Asir, Shaikh Abul Hasan Ali, *Kamil-ut-Tawarikh* (written 12th century C.E.), trs. in E and D, II.

Idrisi, *Nuzhat-ul-Mushtaq* (written 12th century C.E.), trs. in E and D, I.

Isami, Khwaja Abdullah Malik, *Futuh-us-Salatin*, ed. by Agha Mahdi Husain, Educational Press, Agra, 1938.

Jahangir, Nuruddin Muhammad, *Tuzuk-i-Jahangiri* or *Memoirs of Emperor Jahangir*, trs. by Rogers and Beveridge, Delhi reprint, 1968. See also Price for *Tarikh-i-Salim Shahi*.

Jaisi, Malik Muhammad, *Padmavat*, ed. by R.C. Shukla, Indian Press, Allahabad, 1935.

Jamali, Maulana Hamid Ibn Fazlullah, *Siyar-ul-Arifin*, Rizvi Press, Delhi, 1311 H.

Jauhar, *Tazkirat-ul-Waqiat*, trs. by C. Stewart, Indian reprint, 1972.

Kalhana, *Rajatarangini*, trs. by M.A. Stein, Westminister, 1900.

Kamboh, Muhammad Saleh, *Amil Saleh*, Bib. Ind., 3 vols., Calcutta, 1923, 1927, 1939.

Kanz-ul-Mahfuz (written 1150 H.), trs. in E and D, VIII.

Khafi Khan, Muhammad Hashim, *Muntakhab-ul-Lubab*, ed. by Kabir-ud-din Ahmad, Bib.Ind., Calcutta, 1869, 1925.

Kirmani, Saiyyad Muhammad Mubarak, also known as Amir Khurd, *Siyar-ul-Auliya*, Muhibbul Hind Press, Delhi, 1309 H./1891 C.E.; Urdu trs. by Allah Wale ki Dukan, Silsila-i-Tassawuf No.130, Kashmiri Bazar, Lahore, n.d.; Urdu trs. by Aijaz-ul-Haqq Quddusi, Seema Offset Press, Jama Masjid, Delhi, 1985.

Mamuri, Abul Fazl, *Tarikh-i-Aurangzeb*, continuation of Sadiq Khan's *Shahjahan Nama*. B.M. Or. 1671.

Minhaj Siraj Jurjani, *Tabqat-i-Nasiri*, Bib. Ind., Calcutta, 1864; English trs. by Major H.R. Raverty, London, 1881.

Mir Masum, *Tarikh-i-Masumi* also called *Tarikh-i-Sind*, ed. by Daudpota, Bhandarkar Oriental Institute, Poona, 1938.

Muhammad Aslam, *Farhat-un-Nazirin* (written 1770-71 C.E.), trs. in E and D, VIII.

Muhammad Bihamad, see Bihamad

Muhammad Sharif Hanafi, *Majlis-us-Salatin*, trs. in E and D, VII.

Muhammad Ufi, *Jami-ul-Hikayat*, trs. in E and D, II.

Mustaad Khan, Saqi, *Maasir-i-Alamgiri*, trs. and annotated by Jadunath Sarkar, Calcutta, 1947.

Niamatullah, *Makhzan-i-Afghana*, trs. by Nirodbhushan Roy as *History of the Afghans*, Santiniketan, 1958. Also B. Dorn's trs., 2 parts, London, 1829-36.

Nizamuddin Ahmad, *Tabqat-i-Akbari*, Bib. Ind., 3 vols., Calcutta, 1927-35. Also trs.by B. De.

Nizamuddin Auliya, *Rahat-ul-Qulub*, Urdu trs., Allah Wale ki Dukan, Lahore.

Nizamul Mulk Tusi, *Siyasat Nama*, ed. by Shefer, Tehran.

Nurul Haqq, *Zabdut-Tawarikh* (written about close of Akbar's reign), trs. in E and D, VI.

Padmanabh, *Kanhadade Prabandh*, translated and annotated by V.S. Bhatnagar, Aditya Prakashan, New Delhi, 1991.

Price, Major David, trs. of *Tarikh-i-Salim Shahi* under the title of *Memoirs of the Emperor Jahangir, written by himself*, London, 1829; Indian edition, Bangabasi Press, Calcutta, 1906. Also see Price under Modern Works.

Qazvini, see Amin.

Ranking, see Badaoni.

Razi, Amin Ahmad, *Haft Aqlim*, ed. by H. Hatley, Abdul Muqtadir and M.Mahfuzul Haq, Bib. Ind., Calcutta, 1939.

Reynolds, see Utbi

Rizqullah Mushtaqi, *Waqiat-i-Mushtaqi*, Photo copy of the British Museum Ms. Ad. 11633.

Salim, Ghulam Husain, *Riyaz-us-Salatin*, ed. by Abdul Haqq Abid, Bib. Ind., Calcutta, 1890-98; English trs. by Abdus Salam, Calcutta, 1902-04.

Sarwani, Abbas, *Tarikh-i-Sher Shahi*, trs. in E and D, IV.

Shah Nawaz Khan, Samsam-ud-daula, and his son Abdul Hayy, *Maasir-ul-Umara*, trs. by H. Beveridge and Baini Prasad, 3 vols., Calcutta, 1911-14.

Shihabuddin al Umri, *Masalik-ul-Absar fi Mumalik-ul-Amsar* (written in middle of 14th century), trs. in E and D, III; Hindi trs. in Rizvi, *Tughlaq Kalin Bharat*.

Sijzi, Amir Hasan Ala, *Favaid-ul-Fvad*, being conversations of Shaikh Nizamuddin Auliya, Nawal Kishore Press, Lucknow, 1302 H., Delhi, 1856; Urdu trs. by Ghulam Ahmad Khan Biryan, Manzoor Book Depot, Bulbuli Khana, Delhi, 1984.

Sirat-i-Firoz Shahi, Anonymous, Photostat Ms. in Bankipore Library. Extract trs. by K.K. Basu under the title of *Firoz Tughlaq and His Bengal Campaign* in the *Journal of Bihar and Orissa Research Society*, Vol.XXVII. Extract of Text and English trs. in J.R.A.S., Vol.VIII, 1942.

Sikandar bin Muhammad, *Mirat-i-Sikandari*, Bombay, 1308 H.
Sujan Rai, *Khulasat-ut-Tawarikh*, ed. by Zafar Hasan, Delhi, 1918.

Timur, Amir, *Malfuzat-i-Timuri*, trs. in E and D, III.

Utbi, Abu Nasr Muhammad, *Kitab-i-Yamini*, trs. by James Reynolds, London, 1858. Also in E and D, II.

Vidyapati, *Kirtilata*, Indian Press, Allahabad, 1923.

Wassaf, Abdullah, *Tajziat-ul-Amsar wa Tajriyat-ul-Asar*, also called *Tarikh-i-Wassaf* (written 1327 C.E.), Bombay, 1877.

Yahiya Sarhindi, *Tarikh-i-Mubarak Shahi*, Bib. Ind., Text edited by M. Hidayat Husain, Calcutta, 1931; English trs. by K.K. Basu, Baroda, 1932.
Yazdi, Sharafuddin, *Zafar Nama*, 2 vols., Bib. Ind., Calcutta, 1885-88.

Zakaria al Qazvini, *Asar-ul-Bilad* (written 13th century C.E.), trs. in E and D, I.

Foreign Travellers' Accounts

Barbosa, Duarte, *The Book of Duarte Barbosa*, 2 vols., Hakluyt Society, London, 1918-21.
Bernier, Francois, *Travels in the Mogul Empire* (1656-1668), revised by V.A. Smith, Archibald Constable, Oxford, 1934.

De Laet, John, *The Empire of the Great Mogol*, trs. by Hoyland and Banerjee, Bombay, 1928.
Della Valle, *The Travels of Pietro Della Valle in India*, trs. by Edward Grey, 2 vols., Hakluyt Society, London, 1892.
Du Jarric, *Akbar and the Jesuits*, see Payne.

Finch, William, see Foster
Foster, William, *Early Travels in India* (1583-1619), contains narratives of Fitch (pp.1-47), Mildenhall (pp.48-59), Hawkins (pp.60-121), Finch (pp.122-87), Withington (pp.188-233), Coryat (pp.234-87) and Terry (pp.288-322), London, 1927.

Foster, William, *English Factories in India* (1618-69), 13 vols., Oxford, 1906-27.

Hakluyt, Richard, *Principal Navigations, Voyages, Traffiques, and Discoveries of the English Nation*, Glasgow, 1903-05.
Heber, Reginald, *Narrative of a Journey through the Upper Provinces of India*, Second ed., 3 vols., London, 1828.

Ibn Battuta, see under Original Sources

Major, R.H., *India in the Fifteenth Century* (contains extracts from narratives of Nicolo Conti, Santo Stefano, etc.), Hakluyt Society, London, 1857.
Manrique, *Travels of Frey Sebastian Manrique*, trs. by Eckford Luard, 2 vols., Hakluyt Society, London, 1927.
Manucci, Niccolao, *Storia do Mogor*, trs. by W. Irvine, 4 vols., John Murray, London, 1906.
Marco Polo, see Yule
Mundy, Peter, *Travels of Peter Mundy in Asia*, ed. by R.C. Temple, Hakluyt Society, London, 1914.

Payne, C.H., *Akbar and the Jesuits*, contains in trs. Du Jarric's account of the Jesuit Missions to the Court of Akbar, London, 1926.
Pelsaert, Francisco., *Jahangir's India*, trs. by W.H. Moreland and P. Geyl, Cambridge, 1925.

Tavernier, *Travels in India*, trs. and ed. by V. Ball, London, 1925.
Terry, Edward, *A Voyage to East India*, London, 1655.
Thevenot, *Indian Travels of Thevenot and Careri*, ed. by Surendra Nath Sen, New Delhi, 1949.

Varthema, *The Itinerary of Ludovico di Varthema of Bologna*, ed. by Sir Richard Temple, London, 1928.

Yule, Sir Henry, and H. Cordier, *The Book of Ser Marco Polo*, 2 vols., New York, 1903.

Modern Works

Abdul Karim, *Social History of Muslims in Bengal,* Asiatic Society of Pakistan, Dacca, 1959.

Acton, Lord, *The Study of History,* Macmillan & Co., London, 1905.

Aghnides, Nicholas P., *Muhammadan Theories of Finance,* New York, 1916.

Ahmad Shah, *Bijak of Kabir,* Hamirpur, 1917.

Albairuni, A.H., *Makers of Pakistan and Modern Muslim Indians,* Muhammad Ashraf Publishers, Lahore.

Ambashtya, B.P., Biographical sketch of Badaoni in reprint edition of Abdul Qadir Badaoni's *Muntakhab-ut-Tawarikh,* trs. by S.A. Ranking, reprinted by Academia Asiatica, Patna, 1973.

Arnold, T.W., *The Preaching of Islam,* Westminister, 1896.

Arnold, T.W., *The Caliphate,* London, 1924.

Arnold, T.W., and Guillaume A., eds., *The Legacy of Islam,* Oxford, 1931.

Ashraf, Kunwar Muhammad, *Life and Conditions of the People of Hindustan,* A.S.B. Journal, Calcutta, 1935.

Askari, S.M., *A Study of the Rare Ms. of Sirat-i-Firoz Shahi* in *Journal of Indian History,* Vol. LII, April, 1974.

Aziz Ahmad, *Studies in Islamic Culture in the Indian Environment,* Oxford, 1964.

Bashir Ahmad, M., *Administration of Justice in Medieval India,* Aligarh, 1941.

Beale, T.W., *Oriental Biographical Dictionary,* London, 1910.

Beni Prasad, *A History of Jahangir,* Third ed., Allahabad, 1940.

Bharatiya Vidya Bhavan, see Majumdar, R.C.

Bhatnagar, V.S., see Padmanabha under Original Sources.

Biswas, Satya Krishna, *Banshasmriti* (Bengali), Calcutta, 1926.

Bosworth, C.E., *The Ghaznavids: Their Empire in Afghanistan and Eastern Iran,* 994-1040, Edinburgh University Press, 1963.

Brown, Percy, *Indian Architecture* (*Islamic Period*), Third ed., Taraporevala, Bombay, n.d.

Burnes, Sir Alexander, *Travels into Bokhara, together with a Narrative of a Voyage on the Indus,* 3 vols., Karachi reprint, 1973.

(*The*) *Cambridge History of India,* Cambridge University Press.
  Vol. I, ed. by E.J. Rapson, Cambridge, 1922.

Vol. III, ed. by Wolseley Haig, Delhi reprint, 1958.
Vol. IV, ed. by Richard Burn, Cambridge 1937.
Vol. V, ed. by H.H. Dodwell, Delhi reprint, 1963.
Caroe, Sir Olaf, *The Pathans,* Macmillan & Co., London, 1958.
Chaturvedi, Parasuram, *Sant Kavya,* Kitab Mahal, Allahabad, 1952.
Crone, Patricia and Cook, Michael, *Hagarism: The Making of Islamic World,* Cambridge University Press, Cambridge, 1977.
Crooke, William, *Tribes and Castes of North Western Provinces and Oudh,* Calcutta, 1896.
Cunningham, Alexander, *Coins of Medieval India,* London, 1894, Varanasi reprint, 1967.
Currie, P.M., *The Shrine and Cult of Muin-al-din Chishti of Ajmer,* Oxford, Delhi, 1989.

Day, U.N., *Medieval Malwa,* Delhi, 1965.
Denison Ross, *Islam.*
Digby, Simon, *War Horse and Elephant in the Delhi Sultanate,* Orient Monographs, Oxford, 1971.
Devahuti, "Significance of Contemporary Dharma-Shastras and Indigenous Historical Literature for study of Hindu-Muslim Encounter in Early Middle Ages" in *Historical and Political Perspectives,* Indian History and Culture Society, Books and Books, New Delhi, 1982.
Devendra Swarup (ed.), *Politics of Conversion,* Deendayal Research Institute, New Delhi, 1986.
Dorn, Benhard, *History of the Afghans,* being trs. of *Makhzan-i-Afghana,* Oriental Translation Fund, London, 1829.
Durant, Will, *The Story of Civilization,* Vol.I, *Our Oriental Heritage,* New York, 1972.

Easton, Stewart C., *The Heritage of the Past,* Rinehart and Co., New York, 1957.
Eaton, Richard Maxwell, *Sufis of Bijapur* (1300-1700), Princeton, 1978.
Elliot, H.M. and Dowson, J., *History of India as told by its own Historians,* 8 vols., London, 1867-77; Vol.II, Aligarh reprint, 1952.
Elphinstone, Mountstuart, *The History of India,* 2 vols., London, 1843.
Encyclopaedia Britannica
Encyclopaedia of Islam, Luzac & Co., 1913-38.
Encyclopaedia of Social Sciences, 1949 reprint.

Faruki, Zahiruddin, *Aurangzeb and His Times*, Delhi reprint, 1980.

Forbes, A.K., *Rasmala*, ed. by G.H. Rawlinson, Oxford, 1924.

Forbes, James., *Orient Memoirs*, 2 vols., 2nd ed., London, 1934.

Francklin, W., *A History of the Reign of Shah-Aulum*, first published 1798, Allahabad, 1915.

Fuhrer and Smith, *The Sharqi Architecture of Jaunpur*, Calcutta, 1889.

Gazetteers, Imperial and Provincial Series.

Gazetteers of Alwar, Trubner & Co., London, 1878.

Gibb, H.R.A., *Mohammedanism: A Historical Survey*, Oxford University Press, London, 1949.

Gibbon, Edward, *Decline and Fall of the Roman Empire*, 2 vols., Everymans Library ed., n.d.

Gokhale, B.G., "The Merchant Community in the 17th century India", *Journal of Indian History*, Trivandrum, Vol. LIV, 1976.

Gopal Krishna, "Nation Building in Third World", series of four articles in *The Times of India*, New Delhi, 26-29 December, 1988.

Greetz, Clifford, *Islam Observed* (Religious Development in Morocco and Indonesia), University of Chicago Press, 1971.

Grunebaum, Gustav E. von, *Medieval Islam*, Chicago, 1946.

Guillaume, A., *Islam*, Penguin Books, 1954.

Guillaume, A., *The Life of Muhammad*, Oxford, 1958.

Guillaume, A., see also Arnold.

Habib, Mohammad, *Sultan Mahmud of Ghaznin*, Delhi reprint, 1951.

Habib, Mohammad, *Some Aspects of the Foundation of the Delhi Sultanate*, K.M. Ashraf Memorial Lecture, Delhi, 1966.

Habib, Mohammad, *Campaigns of Alauddin Khilji*, being trs. of Amir Khusrau's *Khazain-ul-Futuh*, Bombay, 1933.

Habib, Mohammad, "Chishti Mystic Records of the Sultanate Period", in *Medieval India Quarterly*, Aligarh, Vol.I, No. 2.

Habib, Mohammad, Introduction to E and D, II, Aligarh, 1951.

Habib, Mohammad, "Shaikh Nasiruddin Mahmud Chiragh-i-Dehli", in *Islamic Culture*, April, 1946.

Habib, Mohammad, Review of G. N. Sharma's *Social Life in Medieval Rajasthan*, in *Medieval India, A Miscellany*, Vol. II, Aligarh, 1972.

Habib, Mohammad, *Collected Works*, entitled *Politics and Society During Early Medieval Period*, edited by K.A. Nizami, Vol. I, 1974; Vol. II, 1981.

Habibullah, A.B.M., *The Foundation of Muslim Rule in India*, Revised ed., Allahabad, 1961, first published, Lahore, 1945.

Hall, D.G.E., *A History of South-East Asia*, Macmillan & Co., London, 1955.

Hallam, *The Middle Ages*, fifth ed., London, 1829.

Hamilton, Charles, trs., *Hidayah*, 4 vols., London, 1791.

Harsh Narain, *Myths of Composite Culture and Equality of Religions*, Voice of India, New Delhi, 1991.

Havell, E.B., *History of Aryan Rule in India*, London, 1918.

Hazard, H.W., *Atlas of Islamic History*, Princeton, 1954.

Herklots, see Jafar Sharif.

Hitti, P.K., *The Arabs: A Short History*, Macmillan & Co., London, 1948.

Hitti, P.K., *History of the Arabs*, London, 1951.

Hodivala, S.H., *Studies in Indo-Muslim History*, Bombay, 1939.

Hughes, T.P., *Dictionary of Islam*, W.H. Allen & Co., London, 1885.

Ibn Hasan, *The Central Structure of the Mughal Empire*, London, 1936.

Indian Antiquary.

Indian Historical Quarterly.

Indian History Congress Proceedings.

Indian Heritage, Vol. I, Bharatiya Vidya Bhavan, Bombay, 1955.

India's Minorities, Publications Division, Government of India, New Delhi, 1948.

Ira Marvin Lapidus, *Muslim Cities in the Later Middle Ages*, Cambridge, Mass., 1967.

Ishwari Prasad, *A History of the Qaraunah Turks in India*, Vol. I, Indian Press, Allahabad, 1936.

Ishwari Prasad, *History of Medieval India*, Fourth impression, Allahabad, 1940.

Ivanow, W., *Brief Survey of Evolution of Ismailism*, Bombay, 1942.

Jafar Sharif, *Islam in India or the Qanun-i-Islam*, trs. by G.A. Herklots, ed. by William Crooke, London, 1875, 1921.

Journal of the (Royal) Asiatic Society of Bengal.

Kane, P.V., *History of Dharmashastra*, 5 vols., Bhandarkar Oriental Research Institute, Poona, 1946-1968.

Karim, A.K. Nazmul, "Muslim Social Classes in East Pakistan" in *Changing Society in India and Pakistan*, Universtiy of Dacca, 1956.

Kennedy, Melville T., *The Chaitanya Movement*, Calcutta, 1925.

Kennedy, Pringle, *A History of the Great Mughals*, Calcutta, 1905, 1911.

Khan, Abdul Majid, "Research about Muslim Aristocracy in East Pakistan" in Pierre Bessaignet (ed.) *Social Research in East Pakistan*, Dacca, 1960.

Khan, M.S., "The Life and Works of Fakhre Mudabbir" in *Islamic Culture*, April, 1977.

Khazan Singh, *The History and Philosophy of Sikhism*.

Khuda Bakhsh, *Essays, Indian and Islamic*, London, 1927.

Khuda Bakhsh, *Orient under the Caliphs*, Calcutta, 1921.

Kincaid, C.A. and Parasnis, D.B., *A History of the Maratha People*, 2 vols., Oxford, 1922.

Kolf, Dirk H.A., *Naukar, Rajput and Sepoy: The ethnohistory of the military labour market in Hindustan* (1450-1850), Cambridge University Press, 1990.

Lach, Donald F., *Asia in the Making of Europe*, Vol. I, Bks I and II, Chicago University Press, Chicago, 1965.

Lal, K.S., *History of the Khaljis*, New Delhi, 1980, first published 1950.

Lal, K.S., *Twilight of the Sultanate*, New Delhi, 1980, first published, 1963.

Lal, K.S., *Studies in Medieval Indian History*, Ranjit Publishers, Delhi, 1966.

Lal, K.S., *Growth of Muslim Population in Medieval India*, Research Publications in Social Sciences, New Delhi, 1973.

Lal, K.S., *The Mughal Harem*, Aditya Prakashan, New Delhi, 1988.

Lal, K.S., *Early Muslims in India*, Books & Books, New Delhi, 1984.

Lal, K.S., *Indian Muslims : Who Are They*, Voice of India, New Delhi, 1990.

Lal, K.S., "The Ghaznavids in India", in *Bengal Past and Present*, Sir Jadunath Sarkar Birth Centenary Number, July-December, 1970.

Lal, K.S., "Striking Power of the Army of the Sultanate" in the *Journal of Indian History*, Vol. LV, Pt. III, December, 1977.

Lamb, Harold, *Tamerlane the Earth Shaker*, Thornton, London, 1929.

Lanepoole, Stanley, *Medieval India under Muhammadan Rule*, T. Fisher Unwin, London, 1926, first published, 1903.

Lapidus, see Ira Marvin.

Levy, Ruben, *The Social Structure of Islam*, Cambridge, 1957.

Levy, Ruben, *The Baghdad Chronicle*, Cambridge, 1929.

Logan, W., *Malabar*, Madras, 1951.

Lokhandvala, S.T. (ed.), *Indian and Contemporary Islam*, Simla, 1971.

Macauliffe, Max Arthur, *The Sikh Religion, Its Gurus, Sacred Writings and Authors*, 6 vols., Oxford, 1909.

Macpherson, *History of European Commerce in India*, London, 1812.

Mahdi Husain, *Tughlaq Dynasty*, Thacker Spink & Co. Calcutta, 1963.

Mahdi Husain, *Shah Namah-i-Hind* or trs. of Isami's *Futuh-us-Salatin*, 3 vols., Aligarh, 1976-77.

Majumdar, R.C., Raychaudhuri, H.C., and Datta, K.K., *An Advanced History of India*, Macmillan & Co. London, 1958.

Majumdar, R.C. (ed.), *The Classical Age*, Bharatiya Vidya Bhavan, Bombay, 1954.

Majumdar, R.C. (ed.), *Struggle for the Empire*, Bombay, 1957.

Majumdar, R.C. (ed.), *The Delhi Sultanate*, Bombay, 1960.

Majumdar, R.C., "Study of Indian History", in *Journal of the Bombay Branch of Asiatic Society*, 1957.

Manzur-ul-Haqq Siddiqi, *Maasir-ul-Jadad*, al-Maktaba al Saifia, Shish Mahal Road, Lahore, 1964.

Margoliouth, D.S., *Mohammed and the Rise of Islam*, London, 1905, Indian reprint, 1985.

Marx, Karl, *Economy, Class and Social Revolution*, trs. and ed. by Z.A. Jordan, Nelson Paperback, 1972.

Mathur, Rakesh, "Hindu Origins of Romani Nomads", in *Hinduism Today*, Malaysia edition, August, September, 1990.

Mazumdar, B.P., *The Socio-Economic History of Northern India* (1030-1194 A.D.), Calcutta, 1960.

Misra, B.B., *The Indian Middle Classes*, Oxford, 1961.

Misra, S.C., *Muslim Communities in Gujarat*, Asia Publishing House, Bombay, 1964.

Misra, S.C., *The Rise of Muslim Power in Gujarat*, Bombay, 1963.

Mitra, R.C., *The Decline of Buddhism in India*, Visvabharati, 1954.

Modern Cyclopaedia, 8 vols.

Moreland, W.H., *India at the Death of Akbar*, Macmillan, London, 1920.

Moreland, W.H., *From Akbar to Aurangzeb*, Macmillan, London, 1923.

Moreland, W.H., *The Agrarian System of Moslem India*, London, 1929.

Morris-Jones, W.H., *The Government and Politics of India*, New Delhi, 1989.

Moses, Angelo, "Cow-protection in Mughal India", in *The Modern Review*, Calcutta, May, 1948.

Muhammad Abdul Shakur, *Aslah-i-Mewat*, Sadar Bazar, Delhi, 1925.

Muhammad Aziz Ahmad, *Political History and Institutions of the Early Turkish Empire of Delhi* (1206-1290 A.D.), New Delhi, 1949, 1972.

Mujeeb, M., *The Indian Muslims*, George Allen and Unwin, London, 1967.

Mukerjee, Radhakumud, *A History of Indian Shipping*, Orient Longmans, 1957.

Mukerjee, Radhakumud, *Economic History of India* (1600-1800), Kitab Mahal, Allahadab, 1967.

Murray, H.J.R., *A History of Chess*, Oxford, 1913.

Naqvi, Hamida Khatoon, *Urbanisation and Urban Centres under the Great Mughals*, 1556-1707, Simla, 1971.

Naqvi, Hamida Khatoon, *Agricultural, Industrial and Urban Dynamics under the Sultans of Delhi*, New Delhi, 1986.

Nazim, M., *The Life and Times of Sultan Mahmud of Ghazna*, Cambridge, 1931.

Nigam, S.B.P., *Nobility under the Sultans of Delhi*, New Delhi, 1967.

Nizami, K.A., *Some Aspects of Relgion and Politics in India during the Thirteenth Century*, Aligarh, 1961.

Nizami, K.A., *Shah Waliullah ke Siyasi Maktubat*, reproduced in English translation in Khalid bin Sayeed's *Pakistan : The Formative Phase*, Pakistan Publishing House, Karachi.

Ojha, Gauri Shankar Hirachand, *Udaipur ka Itihas*, Ajmer, 1928-32.

Ojha, Gauri Shankar Hirachand, *Madhya Kalin Bharatiya Sanskriti*, Hindustani Academy, Allahabad, 1928.

Orme, Robert, *A History of the Military Transactions of the British Nation in Indostan*, 3 vols., Fourth ed., London, 1803.

Phillips, C.H. (ed.), *Historians of India, Pakistan and Ceylon*, London, 1961.

Price, Major David, *Memoirs of the Principal Events of Muhammadan History*, 3 vols., London, 1921. Also see Price under Original Sources.

Pochhammer, Wilhelm von., *India's Road to Nationhood: A Political History of the Sub-Continent*, trs. by S.D. Marathe, Allied Publishers, Bombay, 1961.

Qanungo, K.R., *Historical Essays*, Agra, 1968.

Qureshi, Ishtiaq Hussain, *The Muslim Community in the Indo-Pakistan Subcontinent*, Monton & Co., 'S Gravenhage, 1962.

Qureshi, Ishtiaq Hussain, *Administration of the Sultanate of Delhi*, Fifth ed., New Delhi, 1971, first published, Lahore, 1942.

Rabbi, Dewan Fazle, *The Origin of the Muhammdans of Bengal*, Thacker Spink & Co., Calcutta, 1895.

Ram Gopal, *Indian Muslims: A Political History* (1858-1947), Asia Publishing House, Bombay, 1959.

Ram Swarup, *Understanding Islam through Hadis*, Indian reprint, New Delhi, 1983.

Ramanayya, N. Venkata, *The Third Dynasty of Vijayanagar*, University of Madras, 1935.

Ranade, M.G., *Rise of Maratha Power*, Publications Division reprint, New Delhi, 1961.

Rao, R.P., *Portuguese Rule in Goa*, Asia Publishing House, Bombay, 1963.

Raverty, H.G., *Notes on Afghanistan*, London, 1886. Also see Minhaj under Original Sources.

Ray, Sukumar, *Humayun in Persia*, The Royal Asiatic Society of Bengal, Calcutta, 1948.

Report of the Indian Historical Records Commission, Vol. V., 1923.

Risley, H.H., *The Tribes and Castes of Bengal*, Bengal Secretariat Press, Calcutta, 1891.

Rizvi, Saiyyad Athar Abbas, *Muslim Revivalist Movements in North India in the Sixteenth and Seventeenth Centuries*, Agra Universtiy, Agra, 1965.

Rizvi, Saiyyad Athar Abbas, *Religious and Intellectual History of the Muslims in Akbar's Reign*, Munshiram Manoharlal, New Delhi, 1975.

Rizvi, Saiyyad Athar Abbas, *A History of Sufism in India*, 2 vols., 1978, 1983.

Rizvi, Saiyyad Athar Abbas, *Adi Turk Kalin Bharat*, Aligarh, 1965.

Rizvi, Saiyyad Athar Abbas, *Tughlaq Kalin Bharat*, 2 parts, 1956, 1957.

Rizvi, Saiyyad Athar Abbas, *Uttar Timur Kalin Bharat*, Part II, Aligarh, 1959.

Saksena, Banarsi Prasad, *History of Shahjahan of Dihli*, Second Impression, Allahabad, 1961.

Saran, Parmatma, *Provincial Government of the Mughals*, Kitabistan, Allahabad, 1941.

Saran, Parmatma, *Studies in Medieval Indian History*, Ranjit Publishers, Delhi, 1952.

Saran, Parmatma, *Resistance of Indian Princes to Turkish Offensive*, Sita Ram Kohli Memorial Lectures, Punjabi University, Patiala, 1967.

Sarkar, Jadunath, *History of Aurangzeb*, 5 vols., Calcutta, 1912-25.

Sarkar, Jadunath, *Fall of the Mughal Empire*, 4 vols., Third ed., Calcutta, 1964.

Sarkar, Jadunath (ed.), *Later Mughals* by Irvine, 2 vols., Calcutta, 1921-22.

Sarkar, Jadunath, *History of Bengal*, 2 vols., Dacca, 1948.

Sarkar, Jadunath, *A Short History of Aurangzeb*, Calcutta, 1930.

Sarkar, Jadunath, *The Mughal Administration*, Orient Longmans, 1972.

Sarkar, Jadunath, *Military History of India*, New Delhi, 1960.

Sen, D.C., *Chaitanya and His Age*, Calcutta, 1922.

Sen, D.C., *History of Bengali Language and Literature*, Calcutta University, Calcutta, 1911.

Sen, Sukumar, *Bangla Sahityer Itihasa*, Calcutta, 1940.

Sender, Henry., *The Kashmiri Pandits: A Study of Cultural Choice*, Oxford University Press, 1988.

Sewell, Robert., *A Forgotten Empire* (Vijayanagar), Publications Division reprint, New Delhi, 1966.

Sharma, Arvind., "The Arab Invasion of Sind, A Study in Divergent Perspectives," Indian History and Culture Society Proceedings, ed. by Devahuti, Books & Books, New Delhi, 1982.

Sharma, Dashrath, Presidential Address, Proceedings of Rajasthan History Congress, Udaipur session, 1969.

Sharma, G.N., *Mewar and the Mughal Emperors*, Agra, 1954.

Sharma, Sri Ram, *The Religious Policy of the Mughal Emperors*, Asia Publishing House, Bombay, 1962.

Sharma, Sri Ram, *Conversion and Re-conversion to Hinduism*, D.A.V. College Historical Series, No. 2, n.d.

Sharma, S.R., *The Crescent in India*, Hind Kitabs Ltd., Bombay, 1954.

Sherwani, H.K. *Mahmud Gawan*, Kitabistan, Allahabad, 1942.

Sherwani, H.K. *The Bahmanis of the Deccan*, Hyderabad, n.d.

Singhal, D.P., *India and World Civilization*, 2 vols., Rupa & Co., Delhi, 1972.

Singhal, D.P., "Battle for the Past" in *Problems of Indian Historiography*, ed. by Devahuti, Indian History and Culture Society, D.K. Publishers, Delhi, 1979.

Smith, V.A., *Akbar the Great Mogul*, Delhi reprint, S. Chand & Co., 1962.

Srivastava, A.L., *The Mughal Empire*, Agra, 1964.

Stephen Carr., *Archaeology and Monumental Remains of Delhi*, Calcutta, 1876.

Strachey, Sir John, *India, Its Administration and Progress*, Third ed.

Sykes, P.M., *A History of Persia*, 2 vols., Macmillan & Co., London, 1915.

Tara Chand, *Influence of Islam on Indian Culture*, Indian Press, Allahabad, 1946.

Thomas, Edward, *Chronicles of the Pathan Kings of Delhi*, London, 1871.

Thornton, Edward, *Gazetteer of the Territories under the Goverment of the East India Co. and of the Native States on the Continent of India, Compiled by the Authority of the Court of Directors and chiefly from the documents in their possession*, 4 vols., Wm. H. Allen & Co., London, 1854.

Titus, Murray, *Islam in India and Pakistan*, Calcutta, 1959.

Tod, James., *Annals and Antiquities of Rajasthan*, Routledge & Kegan Paul, 2 vols., London, 1957.

Tripathi, R.P., *Some Aspects of Muslim Administration*, Allahabad, 1936.

Tripathi, R.P., *Rise and Fall of the Mughal Empire*, Allahabad, 1960.

Tritton, A.S., *Caliphs and their Non-Muslim Subjects*, Oxford, 1930.

Wahed Husain, *Administration of Justice during the Muslim Rule in India*, Calcutta, 1934.

Wahid Mirza, *Life and Works of Amir Khusrau*, Calcutta, 1935.

Wavell, *The Viceroy's Journal*, ed. by Penderal Moon, Oxford University Press.

Weber, Max, *The Theory of Social and Economic Organisation*, Edinburgh, 1947.

Weber, Max, *Essays in Sociology*, trs. and ed. by H.H. Garth and C. Wright, Oxford University Press, New York, 1958.

Westcott, *Kabir and Kabir Panth*, Cawnpore, 1907.

Wink, Andre, *Al-Hind, The Making of the Indo-Islamic World*, Vol.I, *Early Medieval India*, Oxford University Press, Delhi, 1990.

Yugalanand, *Kabir Sahib ki Sakhi*, Lucknow.

Yusuf Husain Khan, *Glimpses of Medieval Indian Culture*, Asia Publishing House, Bombay, 1957.

Zamiruddin Siddiqi, *"Shaikh Abdul Quddus Gangoh and the contemporary rulers"*, Paper read at the Indian History Congress Session, December, 1969.

Index

Abbas, uncle of Prophet Muhammad, 126

Abbasid Caliphate, 126; adopts Persian theories and practices, 135

Abdali, Ahmad Shah, 279; invasions of, 217; invited by Sufi scholar to invade India, 325

Abduction of females, common feature of medieval Muslim period, 283-84

Abdul Haq Muhaddis, criticizes Ulama for corruption, 191

Abdul Majid Khan, on influence of Chaitanya, 243

Abdul Quddus Gangohi, Sufi Shaikh, exhorts Muslim rulers to maintain Shariat, 202, 238; advises Babur to humiliate Hindus, 237-38; Sufi of Chishti silsila, 237

Abdul Rahman, Arab general, levies tribute from Kabul and conquers Zabul, 82

Abdul Wahab, notoriously corrupt Qazi, 184

Abdullah, on prices kept low, 261

Abdullah bin Abbas, obtains Raja Dahir's sister from Caliph, 287

Abdullah Khan Firoz Jung, captures and sells as slaves five lakh Hindu men and women, 287

Abdullah Khan Uzbeg, devastates Kalpi-Kanauj region while extolling excessive cruelty of Muslim rulers, 266

Abdur Razzaq, on Indian people's poor standard of living, 216-17

Abid Husain, 62

Aboriginals in India, mostly caste Hindus who fled into forests to escape Muslim attacks, 275

Abraham, becomes Ibrahim in Islam, 16

Abu Rija, Shamsuddin, story of bribe-taking by, 178-79

Abu Yusuf, disciple of Imam Abu Hanifa, 136

Abul Fazl, Allama, 40, 47, 51, 52, 167; on kingship, 7; mentions fourteen Sufi silsilas, 194; on officers of intermediate grade, 214; on greed of revenue officials, 255; reports ruthless suppression of peasant resistance, 265; on Akbar and Tansen, 305

Abyssinians, slave soldiers, 146; obtain high offices, 163

Achaldas, 154

Acton, Lord, 46, 68

Adil Shah, 308

Adil Shahi Kingdom, foreign Muslims preferred in, 143

Afghanistan, 249; Muslims flock from, 142

Afghans, 103; attract notice of Muslim conquerors, 145-46; ferocious soldiers, 155; dominate army of Lodis and Saiyyads, 155, 232; serve in army of Mahmud of Ghazni, 146; obtain higher offices, 163; alloted most profitable districts, 257

Afif, Shams Siraj, 40, 254; on kingship, 7; on why Muslims joined army, 148; on corruption under Firoz Shah Tughlaq, 176-80; on imposition of jiziyah on Brahmans, 221-22; on plight of Hindu merchants, 224; on people's prosperity in early medieval India, 247, 263; feels jubiliant over low prices, 260; on unwisdom of making peasantry poor, 263; on bribes extracted from beggars, 299-300; on Sultans being chosen by Almighty for destroying temples, 307

African Muslim countries, Muslims arrive from, 141

Agha Khan, 310

Aghnides, N. P., on discriminatory laws of Islam, 121

Agra, 117, 209, 211, 225, 248, 266, 271, 294, 296, 306, 308; becomes Akbarabad, 15; houses of nobles at, 168-69, 188; leading city, 214; Indian crafts-

mies, 83; pre-Revolution and pre-Industrial, 209

France, Anatole, on institution of kingship, 6

Fryer, John, on rate of land revenue, 255

Galileo, 29

Gandhi, Mahatma, acceptable to Muslims only for Khilafat movement, 326; remained more concerned with Muslim minority, 338

Gandhis, practise Nehruvian Congress culture, 344

Gandhism, sounds unmodern in post-independence India, 65

Garibdas, Bhakti saint, 231

Geleynsen, on rate of land revenue in Gujarat, 255

Gesu Daraz, Sufi Shaikh Saiyyad Muhammad, on pilgrimage to Muinuddin's mausoleum, 195

Ghalib, Mirza, commissioned to write history of Timurid (Mughal) dynasty, 132

Ghanchis, remain half-Hindu, 311

Ghauri soldiers, recruited by Balban, 146

Ghaurids, plebians inventing high pedigree, 125; cherish confirmation by Caliph, 127; succeed on strength of slave troops, 149

Ghayaspur, 196

Ghazi Malik, see Tughlaq, Ghiyasuddin

Ghazis, motivated by massive loot, 104-05; rally round Mahmud of Ghazni and Muhammad Ghauri, 105; Muslim mercenaries, 147; enrolled by Sultans in India, 147-48; peculiar to Muslim armies, 158

Ghaznavids, collect valuable merchandise through loot and tribute, 101; militarist and imperialist rule of, 103; impressed by Hindu bravery and spirit of sacrifice, 103; employ Hindu soldiers against rivals and rebels, 103-105; fourteen of them rule over Punjab for 200 years, 105; ousted by Ghaurids,

106-07; plebians inventing high pedigree, 125; cherish confirmation by Caliph, 127; attract hordes of Ghazis, 147; succeed on strength of slave troops, 149

Ghazni, 127; Jama Masjid at, 72; desecration of Hindu idols at, 72-73; sacked by Tughril Beg, 106; burnt by Alauddin Husain of Ghaur, 107; Muhammad Ghauri established at, 107; Hindu slaves of respectable descent bought by shopkeepers of, 279; merchants from Muslim world buy Hindu slaves at, 280

Ghiyasuddin, descendant of extinct Caliphate, visits India from Cairo, 130

Ghiyasuddin bin Sam, Ghaurid Sultan, establishes Muhammad Ghauri at Ghazni, 107

Ghiyasuddin of Bengal, Sultan, 154; receives investiture from Caliph, 128

Ghulam Husain Salim, on worsening plight of peasantry, 259

Ghuris of Malwa, 234

Gianni Palma, Italian translator of Salman Rushdie attacked by Muslim assassin, 44

Gibbon, Edward, 47; on the doings of Islam, 18-19

Gol Gumbaj, 308

Golkunda, 208, 333; becomes Hyderabad, 15

Gopal Krishna, Dr., on shallowness of Nehru's understanding of India, 337-38; on modern state, 340

Gopalgir, garrisoned by Afghan soldiers, 146

Govind Rai, wounds Muhammad Ghauri in the first battle of Tarain, 109; killed in the second battle of Tarain, 111

Great Mughals, see Mughals

Grunebaum, Gustav, E. Von, on consciousness of rank in medieval Muslims, 212

Gujarat, 225, 274, 305, 311; Muhammad Ghauri's expedition to, 108; Solanki Rajputs of, 109; foreign

Muslims preferred in Muslim
Kingdom of, 142; Muslim law prevails in, 144; cavalry of, 152; resistance to destruction of temples in,
227; Hindus destroy mosques in,
228; Bhakti movement spreads in,
231; Muslim Kingdom of, 231, 233;
forcible conversions in, 236, 323;
rate of land revenue in, 255; conversion in lieu of tax arears in, 255;
Muslim atrocities in, 329; Friday
prayers prevented by.Kolis of, 329
Gulbadan Begum, 47
Gulf money, utilized for proselytization, 318
Guttenberg, invention of printing
press by, 5
Gwalior, 305; Indian craftsmen build
at, 246; Hindu slaves captured at,
280
Gyanvapi Masjid at Varanasi, reminds of Mughal vandalism, 74
Gypsies, fall-out from Islamic invasions of India, 112; identify India as
their land of origin, 113; language,
religion, social system, dance and
music of, 114

Habib, Mohammad, 58; pioneers
Marxist interpretation of medieval
Indian history, 63-64; draws
groundless conclusions about Muhammad bin Qasim, 93; regards
Muslim state as non-religious and
secular, 116; on Sufi records being
forgeries, 196; views Chiragh-i-
Delhi as greatest Chishti saint, 197;
on condition of labourers in Rajasthan, 295-96
Hadis, 22, 75, 76, 77, 78, 85, 95, 105,
134, 136, 302; supports disabilities
imposed on Hindus, 121; subject
taught in Madrasas, 189
Haig, Wolseley, on conversions in
Bengal, 234
Hajjaj bin Yusuf Sakfi, 72, 83, 87, 88,
277; sends expeditions to Central
Asia and Sind, 84; has not much
knowledge of Hind and Sind, 84-
85; pays to Caliph double the

amount spent on expedition to
Sind, 90; instructs Muhammad bin
Qasim to kill infidels, 278; forwards
captured Hindus to Caliph, 286
Hakim, see Al-Hakim
Halaku Khan, Buddhist, founds the
Margha observatory, 29
Haldighati, battle of, 276
Hamiduddin Nagauri, Qazi, came
from abroad, 142
Hamiduddin Nagauri, Sufi Shaikh,
disciple of Muinuddin Chishti, 196,
197; becomes pious after leading
voluptuous life, 205
Hanbal, Imam Ahmad bin, 78, 136
Hanifa, Imam Abu, 78, 108, 136; a
converted Jat captured in Sind, 278
Hansi, stormed and sacked by Sultan
Masud, 106; captured with great
slaughter by Muhammad Ghauri,
111
Hardwar, temples destroyed at, 229
Hardy, Peter, on Habib's interpreta-
tion of medieval Indian history, 63-
64
Harihar and Bukka, reconverted to
Hinduism, 231
Harsh Narain, on the myth of Hindu-
Muslim composite culture, 335
Harshavardhan, last great Hindu
Kingdom of, 5
Harun-ur-Rashid, Caliph, 35
Haryana, 281; tablighi of, 316
Hatim, see Al-Hatim
Hawkins, William, on grinding pov-
erty of Indian people, 248; on low
wages of workers, 297
Hidaya, 136; most authentic work on
laws of Islam, 108; supports dis-
abilies imposed on Hindus, 121;
advises impoverishment of infidels,
250
Hindu backlash, misrepresented as
Hindu fundamentalism, 339
Hindu classical music, 306
Hindu converts, high class, frequently
revert to Hinduism, 310
Hindu culture, 337; Marxist, Imperialist, Muslim, and 'secularist' historians converge in hostility to, 66

harems, 169-70; on greed of Muslim kings and nobles, 173; on uncertainty of everything in Mughal Kingdom, 188; on Hindu middle class under Muslim rule, 215; on Hindu exhibition of poverty, 216; on common people's misery, 248, 290-91; on cheapness of servants, 292-93; on hard life of postmen, 295; on Hindu-Muslim tension during Muharram, 329-30

Persia, 249; Mongol Khanates of, 19; Sassanid Empire of, 80; throws off Ghaznavid yoke, 106; Muslim adventurers flock from, 141-42

Persian chronicles and chroniclers, see Muslim chronicles and chroniclers

Persian theories and practices, adopted and developed under Abbasids, 135; brought to India by Turks, 136

Persians, more advanced than Turks, 146; serve in army of Mahmud of Ghazni, 149; in Mughal nobility, 159; obtain high offices, 163; descendants of, 165-66

Peshawar, 308; annexed by Mahmud of Ghazni, 106; annexed by Muhammad Ghauri, 108

Peter the Hermit, inspires the first Crusade, 18

Petro-dollars, fuel Muslim fundamentalism, 319

Piacenza University, 34

Pipa, Bhakti saint, 231

Pirzada sect, remains half-Hindu, 312

Pisa University, 34

Plato, 35

Portuguese, the, 16

Pochhamer, Wilhelm von, on large-scale slaughter of Brahamans by Muslims, 236; on role of Brahmans as saviours of Hindus, 236-37

Pratap, see Rana Pratap

Prices, of commodities kept low to impoverish peasantry, 260; of slaves, 286

Prithviraj Chauhan, 301; ruler of

Ajmer-Delhi, 113; captures and recaptures Bhatinda, 109; defeats Muhammad Ghauri, 109; defeated, captured and killed, 110-11; orders expulsion of Muinuddin Chishti from Ajmer, 199

Proselytization, part of Muslim fundamentalism, 319; has no spiritual sanction, 321; reminds of chasm between two communities, 335

Pulkesin II, 81

Punjab, 109, 328; included in Kingdom of Sind, 82; drained of wealth by Mahmud of Ghazni, 100; loses its prosperity, 105; becomes foothold for Islamic expansionism, 105; conquered by Muhammad Ghauri, 108; Bhakti movement spreads to , 231; large-scale conversions in, 232, 323

Puran Mal, Hindu Raja, offends Islam by keeping Muslim women in his harem, 322; Sher Shah breaks promise with, 323

Purnea district, Muslims of, 312

Pyrard, on poverty of common people, 290

Pyrenees, Islam reaches Gates of, 17

Qabil Khan, amasses wealth through corruption, 184-85

Qadir Billah, see Al-Qadir Billah

Qadiri, prominent Sufi *silsila*, 194

Qalqashindi, see Al-Qalqashindi

Qandhar (Kandhar), 82; bone of contention between Mughals and Persians, 184

Qasais, remain half-Hindu, 312

Qazis, enriched by bribes, 184

Qazvini, Mirza Aminai, on Shahjahan, 324

Qazwini, see Al-Qazwini

Qubacha, destroyed by Iltutmish, 127

Quran, 22, 75, 76, 78, 79, 95, 108, 116, 118, 134, 136, 190, 234, 302, 310, 320, 328; consulted for *fal* by Muslims, 26, 27; historical knowledge indispensable for interpretation of, 46; closer to Judaism of Old Testament

Sijistan, see Seistan

Siri, fort of, given in jagir to Caliph's descendant, 130

Sikandar Butshikan of Kashmir, Sultan, eleven Brahman families survive in reign of, 223; mass conversions forced by, 233; takes captives and converts as a policy, 269; forcible conversions by, 309; destroys Hindu temples, 98, 238, 307

Sikh Kingdoms, adopt many institutions of Muslim administration, 145

Sikhs, fight against Mughals and convert people forcibly, 243; armed peasant contingents of, 265; take Muslim women, 323; demolish mosques in retaliation, 332

Sind, 26, 109, 194, 227, 272, 301; unsuccessful Arab expeditions to, 81, 82; extension of Kingdom of, 82; invaded by Muhammad bin Qasim, 84-85; as seen by Ibn Hauqal, 92; becomes province of Abbasid Caliphate, 127; Islamization of, 232 compulsory conversions in, 233, 309; Arab invasion leads to forcible conversions in, 268; Muhammad bin Qasim's doings in, 277-78; neo-Muslims of, 313

Sindhis, Muslim, remain aboriginals, 311

Singh, V.P., practises Nehruvian Congress culture, 344

Singhal, D.P., on historians in Ancient India, 56

Sirsawa, slaughter at, 102

Sirsuti (Sirsa), captured with great slaughter, 111

Slave Dynasty, see Ilbari Sultans

Slave market, at Delhi and other places, 281

Slave troops, dependable due to lack of roots, 148

Slavery, introduced by Islamic invaders, 112

Slaves, Hindus captured and sold as, 112; prices of, 286

Sirhindi, see Ahmad Sirhindi

Sirhindi, see Yahiya Sirhindi

Smith, V.A., on conversion of musicians, 305-06

Smith, W.C., on Pakistani historians, 63

Solanki Rajputs of Gujarat, defeat Muhammad Ghauri, 109

Soldiers of Allah, 155

Solomon, becomes Sulaiman in Islam, 16

Somaliland, African slaves from, 311

Somnath, Islamic iconoclasm at, 72, 73; idol of, taken to Ghazni and desecrated, 98; sack of, considered a pious act, 98; yields huge plunder, 100; destruction of, 309

Southern India, Muslims of, 313

Spain, Inquistion in, 20; subjected by Muslim armies, 83; no Muslim problem in, 303

Spaniards, conquer a continent for Christianity, 19

Srinagar, Muslims of, 315

Srivastava, A.L., regards medieval age as period of unmitigated suffering for Hindus, 68; on Sultanate and Mughal periods, 69

Stalinist historians, produce manipulated history, 71; treat history as handmaid of politics, 344

Stefano, Santo, 263

Stobden, P., Buddhist scholar from Ladakh, on Muslim efforts to convert Buddhists, 317-18

Straits of Gibraltar, leaped over by Islam, 17

Strict Islamic behaviour, enforced by Sultans, 23

Subuktigin, leads frequent expeditions into Hindustan, 93-94; demolishes temples in Lamghan, 95

Sufi Masaikh, 125, 202; perform miracles, 33-34; counted among upper classes, 163, 189; come with invading armies, 193; forced to migrate by Mongol upheaval, 193; Islamize non-Muslim mystic traditions, 193; stories about miracles of, 195-96; no bridge-builders between Hindus and Muslims, 202; maintain ortho-